STAR WARS
DROIDS
THE KALARBA ADVENTURES

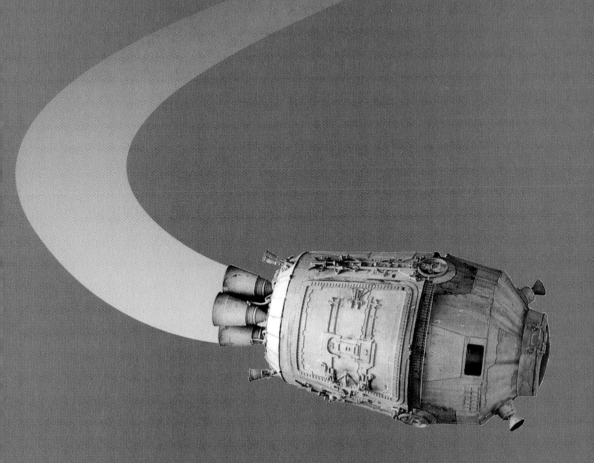

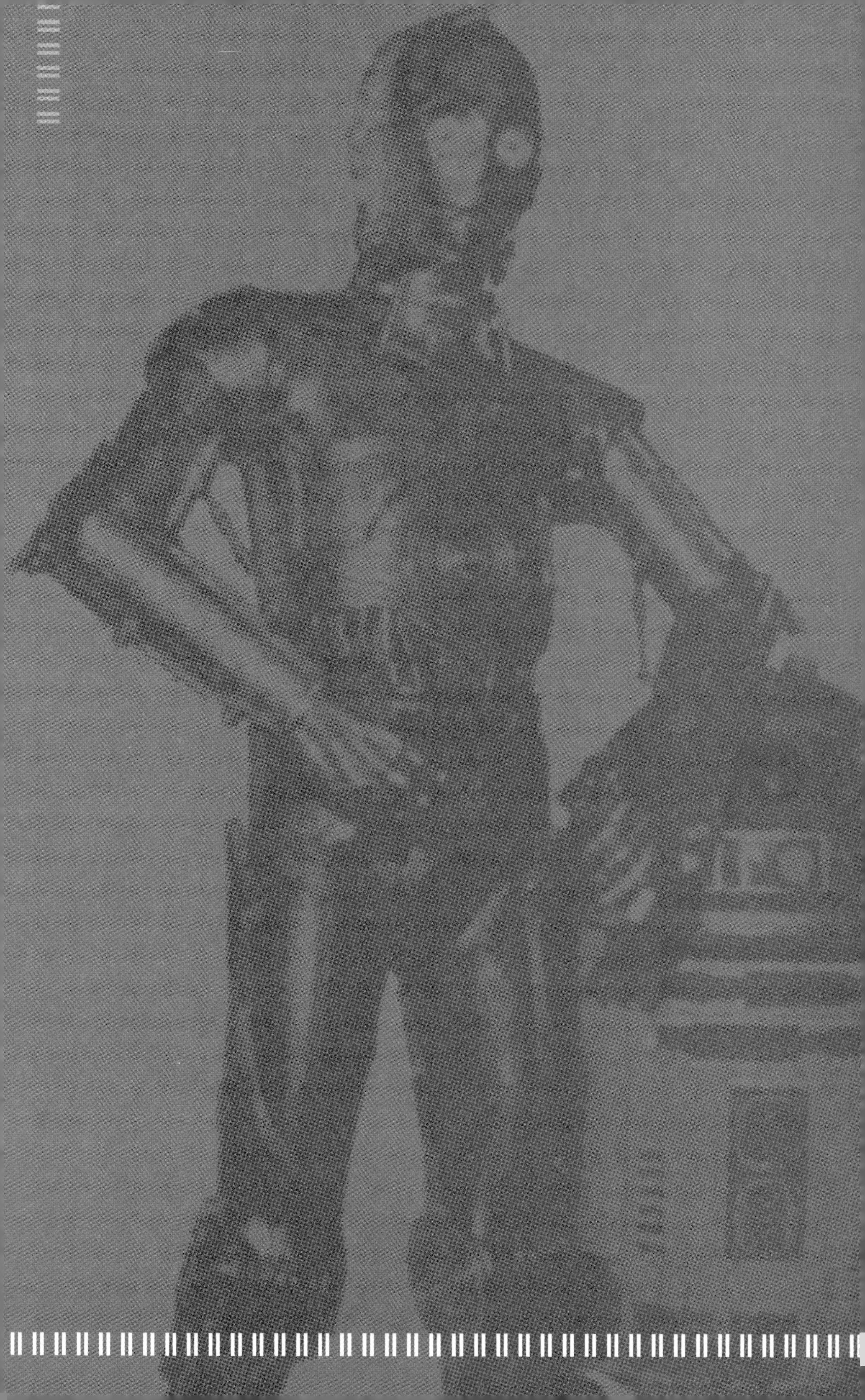

STAR WARS®
DROIDS™
THE KALARBA ADVENTURES

Writers
Dan Thorsland & Ryder Windham

Interior Artists
**Bill Hughes, Ian Gibson,
& Andy Mushynsky**

Cover Artist
Kilian Plunkett

Introduction
Anthony Daniels

Series Editors
Ryder Windham & Dan Thorsland

Collection Editor
Lynn Adair

Collection Designers
Scott Tice & Brian Gogolin

DARK HORSE COMICS®

Mike Richardson • publisher
Neil Hankerson • executive vice president
David Scroggy • vice president of publishing
Lou Bank • vice president of sales & marketing
Andy Karabatsos • vice president of finance
Mark Anderson • general counsel
Diana Schutz • editor in chief
Randy Stradley • creative director
Cindy Marks • director of production & design
Mark Cox • art director
Sean Tierney • computer graphics director
Chris Creviston • director of accounting
Michael Martens • marketing director
Tod Borleske • sales & licensing director
Mark Ellington • director of operations
Dale LaFountain • director of m.i.s.

Published by Dark Horse Comics
10956 SE Main Street
Milwaukie, OR 97222

ISBN: 1-56971-064-3

First edition: June 1995
10 9 8 7 6 5 4 3 2 1

Printed in Canada

Star Wars® Droids™ Volume One

This book collects the *Star Wars Droids Special*, issues 1-6, and an eight-page Droids story first published in Topps' *Star Wars Galaxy Magazine*.

Introduction
by Anthony Daniels

It all began with a picture, on a wall.

I stood in an office in London, looking at a painting of a moonscape with two metallic figures shining in the wan, silver light. Surrounded by that endless, bleak terrain of chilling rock and scree, they looked at me forlorn and lost. Without a hint of living warmth, these machines seemed completely hopeless. Perhaps I recognised a condition that many humans experience at some time in their lives but something touched me and I turned back to face George Lucas with a new interest.

Mr. Lucas and I had met about thirty minutes earlier to discuss, reluctantly on my part, my suitability to play the role of a robot in his film, *The Adventures of Luke Starkiller.*

I wasn't impressed at the idea. Was I not, after all, a most serious actor! I didn't know much about sci-fi and even less about this American director who had asked for this meeting. But the idea was beginning to grow on me. First, this man seemed quite charismatic and was certainly enthusiastic about his project; second—you've probably seen copies of it—this conceptual scene, painted by Ralph McQuarrie, hanging simply on the wall, was beginning to take me out of the cluttered little office above the traffic, into a realm of exciting make-believe.

The rest you know about because they changed the name to *Star Wars.*

I read the script and happily took the job when it was finally offered to me. Happily, because I didn't know then, what it would entail. The gold suit had to be created using a plaster cast of me. For anyone who has not stood in an English winter with craftsmen throwing wet plaster at his shivering body, it is, to say the very least, an experience. While one department worked on how the finished figure would look, another spent months finding how to make it work—unfortunately not quite enough months—as the first shooting day rushed up and overtook us.

Meanwhile, in between daily costume fittings and appearing in the theatre every night, I was working on the script. It was very confusing, with all these strangely named characters rushing about and calling each other Red Leader or Jabba. The only person I could really understand was Threepio. Perhaps I was already sharing his sense of confusion because I could readily empathise with his general air of reluctance. As preproduction continued with regular meetings, George would send me scripts in which Threepio's character began to feature more and more. I would read and think and learn. We talked about his voice. I watched *2001* again but wonderful HAL sounded too calm a type of personality for this breathless tale from a different galaxy. So we left the voice and I read and thought and learned some more. Then it was time to go.

The promised rehearsal studios, with mirrors and cameras for me to practice in, had never materialised. Neither had the air conditioning that was supposed to flow through the gleaming new suit and keep me cool. So, apart from a brief tryout in a studio workshop, it was in a sand-strewn tent in Tunisia that first I struggled painfully, with the help of a team of careful and patient dressers and technicians, into this extraordinary puzzle of plastic and glass fibre, aluminium and rubber. After two hours, the dawning sun had just cleared the big sand dune in front of me as Threepio took his first steps out of the tent and into the desert glare. With the piercing, bright sunlight giving him a godlike radiance, every member of the crew stopped their work to stare in wonder at this magical figure.

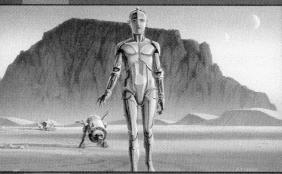

Production painting by Ralph McQuarrie

Then I took another step, and the sharp pain of a knife-edged plastic shoe cut into my ankle. I stopped, very still. We managed the first scene of the Jawa slave market with chunks of foam rubber stuffed up my glass fibre leg, out of shot, to stop the pain. But you would never know because the show had to go on and also, something else had happened. Something strange. Threepio had arrived—and taken over.

Continued on next page . . .

Those months of thinking about the script and the character had paid off. His personality was there in my head, or maybe his. His fears and doubts were there. His relationship with humans was there. His feelings toward Artoo were there. His voice was there.

George didn't like the voice. Months later, he was testing other actors to find a more American personality to replace the pedantically English tracks I had laid down whilst we were filming. But somehow those other voices didn't fit the physical character that moved across the screen, and George decided perhaps Threepio was fine just the way he was.

Playing a scene with Mark Hamill was always easy. He treated Threepio just like a normal person which later helped the audience to go along with the idea too. Being best friends with Artoo was harder. It can get a bit confusing to play both parts in a scene, and since Artoo never made a sound during filming, I had to imagine what he was saying to me. I really was talking to myself all the way through, leaving gaps where his sounds could be added later. George once tried to help by reading-in some beeps, but his timing was terrible so we fired him. I began to feel somewhat isolated, locked in the suit with no one to talk to. Perhaps that made me work harder at creating a pretend relationship with this sort of semi-mobile water-cooler I had for a chum. I was so delighted to see the finished film with Ben Burtt's brilliant sound effects added, completing a convincing double-act.

This double-act grew from the original script; as did Threepio's kindness, his irritation, his fears and his fussiness, his honesty and his loyalty, his unspoken devotion to Artoo. Perhaps this is what I had liked most at the start. Threepio seemed to be able to show, or disguise in such an obvious way that it was even more clear, all sorts of very human emotions that would have looked, well, silly in a human. Counterbalanced with Artoo's stocky defiance and gung ho-ness, their friendship became as real as any other odd-couple duo in the movies. But what I most admire in each of them is their fundamental sense of loyalty.

Three movies and countless spin-off activities later, these comic books echo the spirit of Artoo-Detoo and See-Threepio to the letter. Some of the pages are as convincing in character to me, as though I were actually there, playing the part. When a character you have created and loved has been reproduced commercially in every way from bubble bath to bubble gum, you can get a little protective. But with these stories, I know Threepio is safe. He isn't a natural hero and his own lack of humour does open him up to gentle ridicule which perhaps leads the tales in a lighter direction. Thank goodness they don't take themselves too seriously. And the pictures do full justice to the *Star Wars* heritage.

It began, for me, with a picture. In the years since then, I have had so many new and exciting experiences with Threepio. I have met so many kind and interesting people through him. His loyalty to me has been a major part of my life over the last twenty or so years, as has the interest and loyalty of our ever-expanding circle of friends.

And the future?
It was all a long time ago.
Remember?

—Anthony Daniels, London 1995

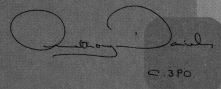

C.3PO.

Welcome to Kalarba

Chapter 1

Script
Dan Thorsland

Pencils
Bill Hughes

Inks
Andy Mushynsky

Colors
Pamela Rambo

Lettering
Bill Pearson

Cover
Kilian Plunkett

Sketch
Kilian Plunkett

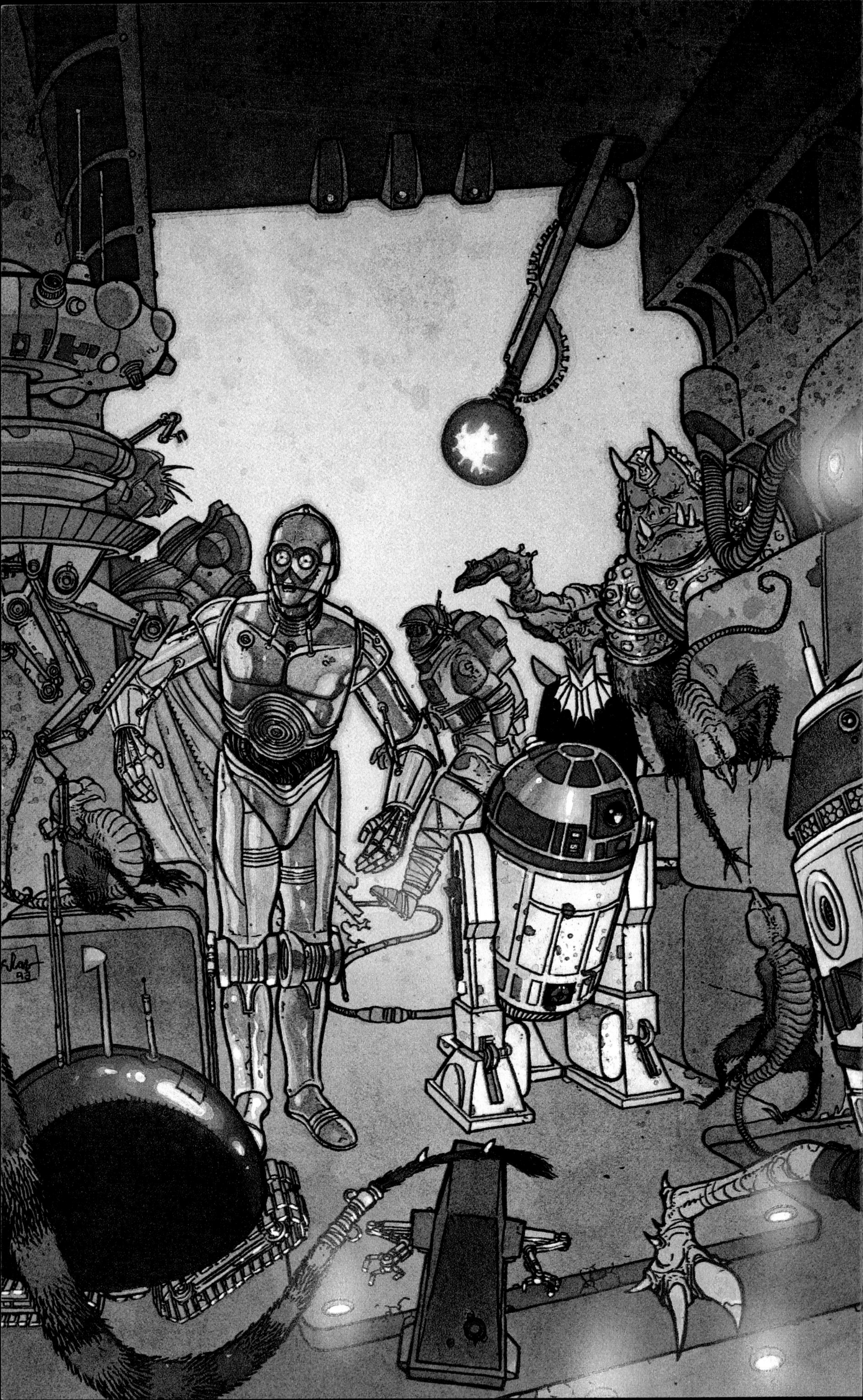

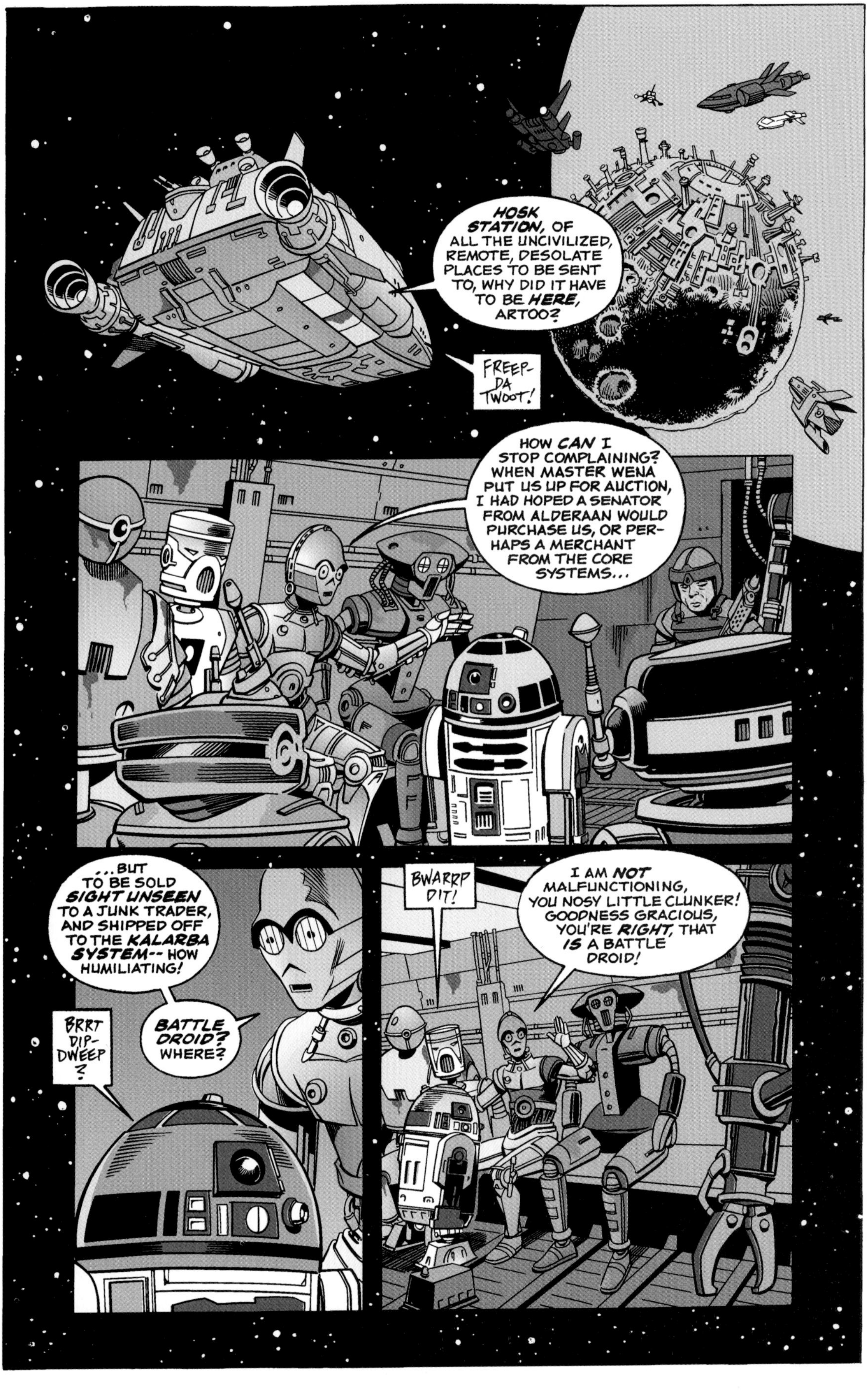
HOSK STATION, OF ALL THE UNCIVILIZED, REMOTE, DESOLATE PLACES TO BE SENT TO, WHY DID IT HAVE TO BE HERE, ARTOO?
FREEP-DA TWOOT!
HOW CAN I STOP COMPLAINING? WHEN MASTER WENA PUT US UP FOR AUCTION, I HAD HOPED A SENATOR FROM ALDERAAN WOULD PURCHASE US, OR PERHAPS A MERCHANT FROM THE CORE SYSTEMS...
...BUT TO BE SOLD SIGHT UNSEEN TO A JUNK TRADER, AND SHIPPED OFF TO THE KALARBA SYSTEM-- HOW HUMILIATING!
BRRT DIP-DWEEP?
BATTLE DROID? WHERE?
BWARRP DIT!
I AM NOT MALFUNCTIONING, YOU NOSY LITTLE CLUNKER! GOODNESS GRACIOUS, YOU'RE RIGHT, THAT IS A BATTLE DROID!

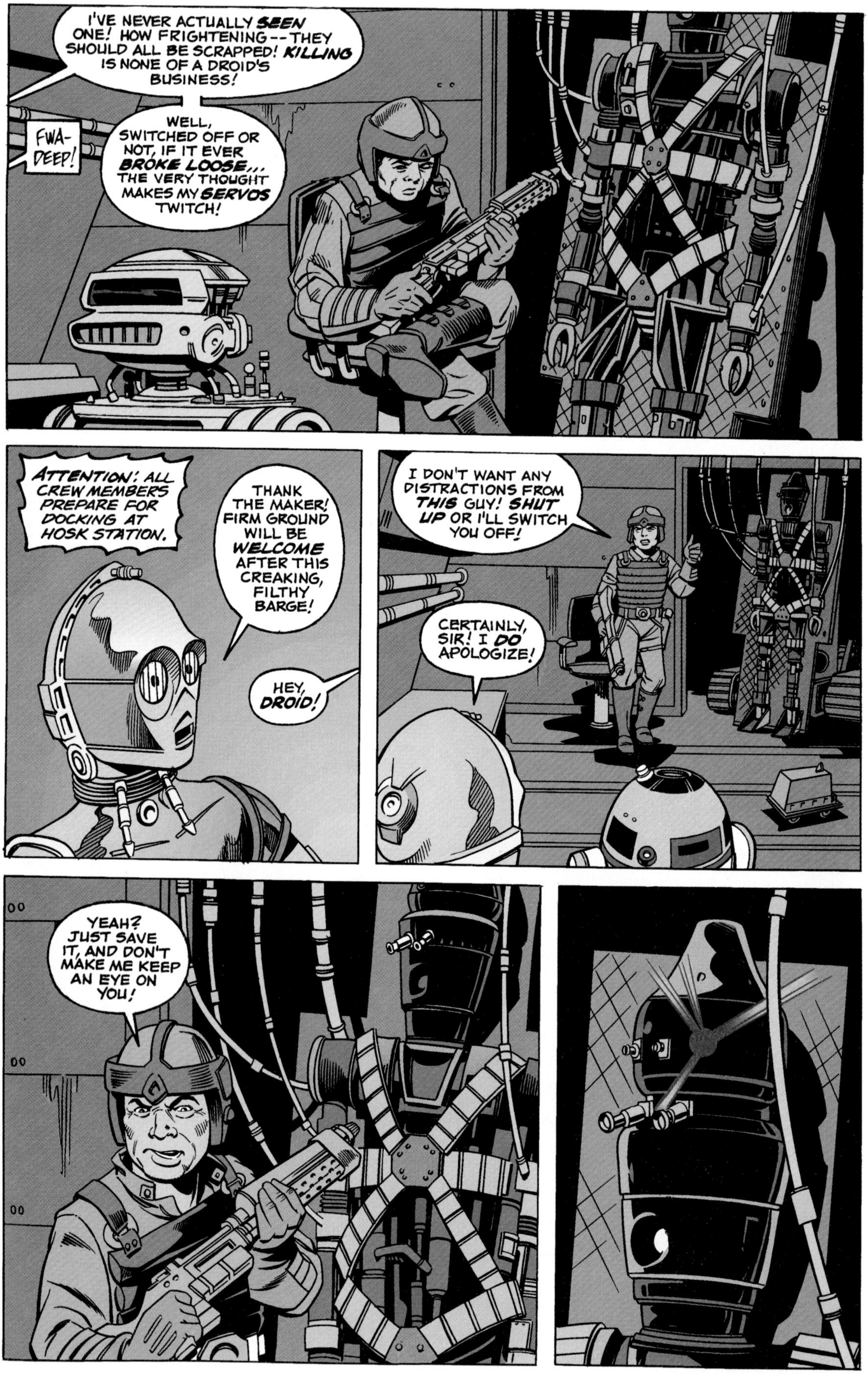
I'VE NEVER ACTUALLY SEEN ONE! HOW FRIGHTENING--THEY SHOULD ALL BE SCRAPPED! KILLING IS NONE OF A DROID'S BUSINESS!
FWA-DEEP!
WELL, SWITCHED OFF OR NOT, IF IT EVER BROKE LOOSE... THE VERY THOUGHT MAKES MY SERVOS TWITCH!
ATTENTION! ALL CREW MEMBERS PREPARE FOR DOCKING AT HOSK STATION.
THANK THE MAKER! FIRM GROUND WILL BE WELCOME AFTER THIS CREAKING, FILTHY BARGE!
HEY, DROID!
I DON'T WANT ANY DISTRACTIONS FROM THIS GUY! SHUT UP OR I'LL SWITCH YOU OFF!
CERTAINLY, SIR! I DO APOLOGIZE!
YEAH? JUST SAVE IT, AND DON'T MAKE ME KEEP AN EYE ON YOU!

DROID BARGE DOCKING AT HANGAR THREE.

SNRRNK!

WELL DONE. IMAGINE... ONE OF MY COMPETITORS TRYING TO KILL ME, *OLAG GRECK*,... WITH A DROID!

WHY ELSE WOULD IT HAVE STOWED AWAY IN MY SPICE SHIPMENT? THIS DROID IS A *LEGEND* AMONG BOUNTY HUNTERS, IF ITS BATTERIES HADN'T DRAINED...

...THEIR PLAN MIGHT HAVE WORKED.

TO THE *HANGAR,* XOB. FIRST...

"WE'LL RUN A MEMORY FLUSH, I'LL TURN THEIR HIRED ASSASSIN INTO MY EMPLOYEE!

"THEN I'LL SCHEDULE A FIGHT IN THE *HOSK ARENA,* EVEN MY ENEMIES WILL PAY GOOD MONEY TO SEE THE MOST LETHAL DROID IN THE GALAXY...

"... FIGHTING TO THE DEATH!"

SPACK

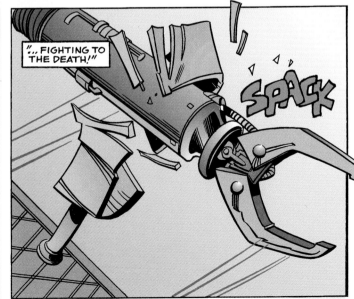

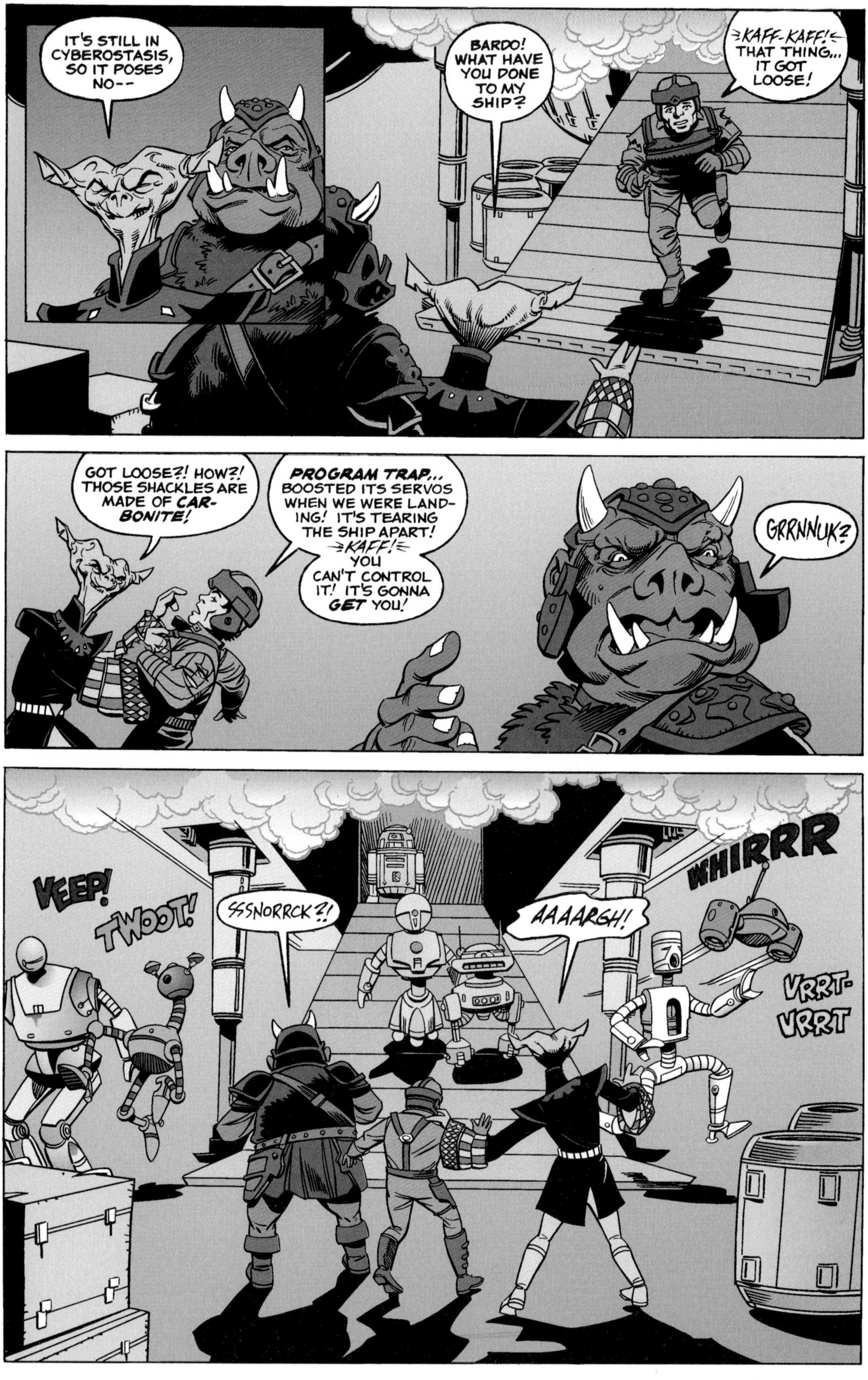
IT'S STILL IN CYBEROSTASIS, SO IT POSES NO--
BARDO! WHAT HAVE YOU DONE TO MY SHIP?
KAFF-KAFF! THAT THING... IT GOT LOOSE!
GOT LOOSE?! HOW?! THOSE SHACKLES ARE MADE OF CAR-BONITE!
PROGRAM TRAP... BOOSTED ITS SERVOS WHEN WE WERE LANDING! IT'S TEARING THE SHIP APART! KAFF! YOU CAN'T CONTROL IT! IT'S GONNA GET YOU!
GRRNNUK?
VEEP!
TWOOT!
SSSNORRCK?!
AAAARGH!
WHIRRR
VRRT-VRRT

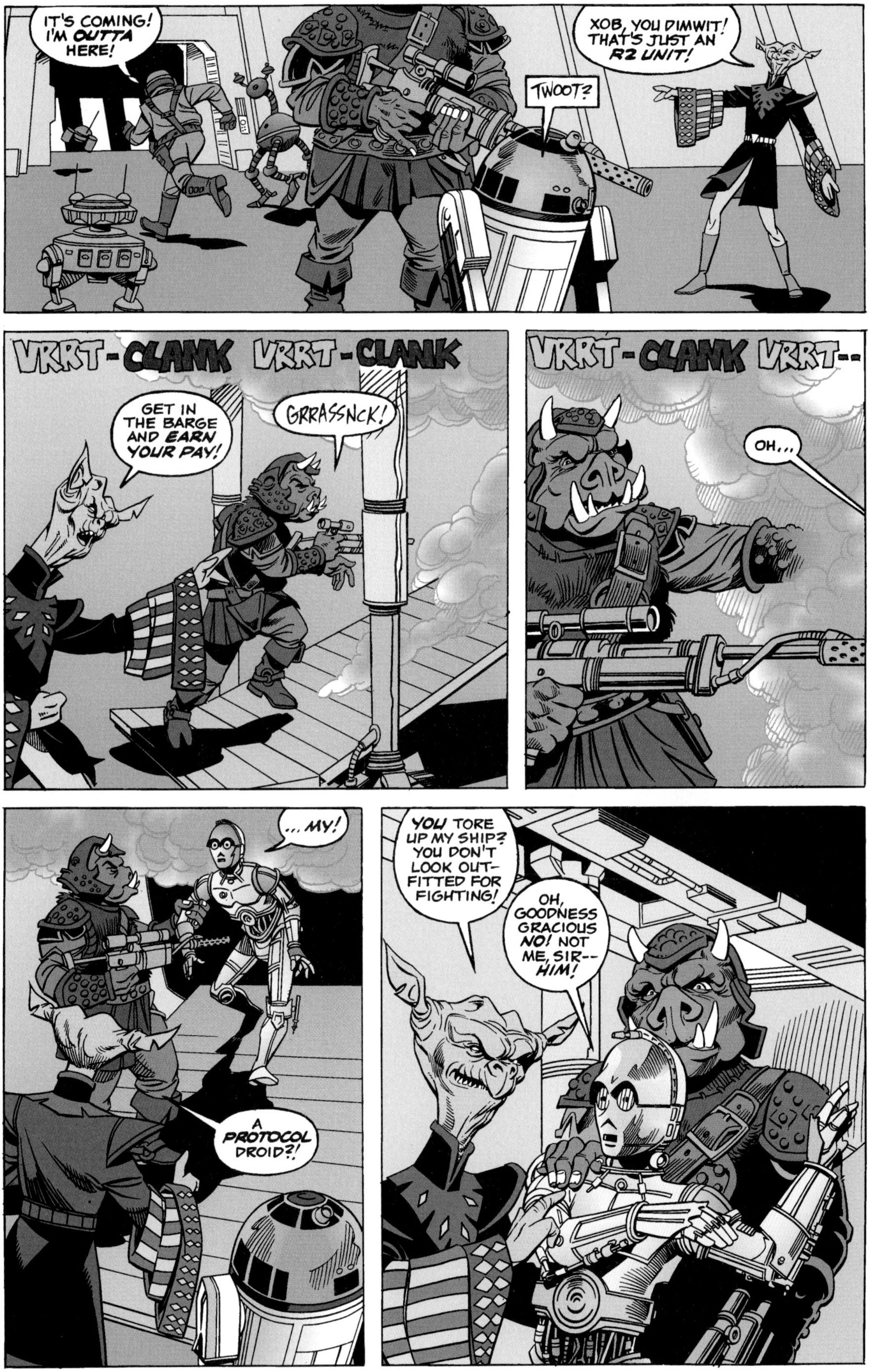
IT'S COMING! I'M OUTTA HERE!
TWOOT?
XOB, YOU DIMWIT! THAT'S JUST AN R2 UNIT!
VRRT-CLANK VRRT-CLANK
GET IN THE BARGE AND EARN YOUR PAY!
GRRASSNCK!
VRRT-CLANK VRRT--
OH...
...MY!
A PROTOCOL DROID?!
YOU TORE UP MY SHIP? YOU DON'T LOOK OUT-FITTED FOR FIGHTING!
OH, GOODNESS GRACIOUS NO! NOT ME, SIR--HIM!

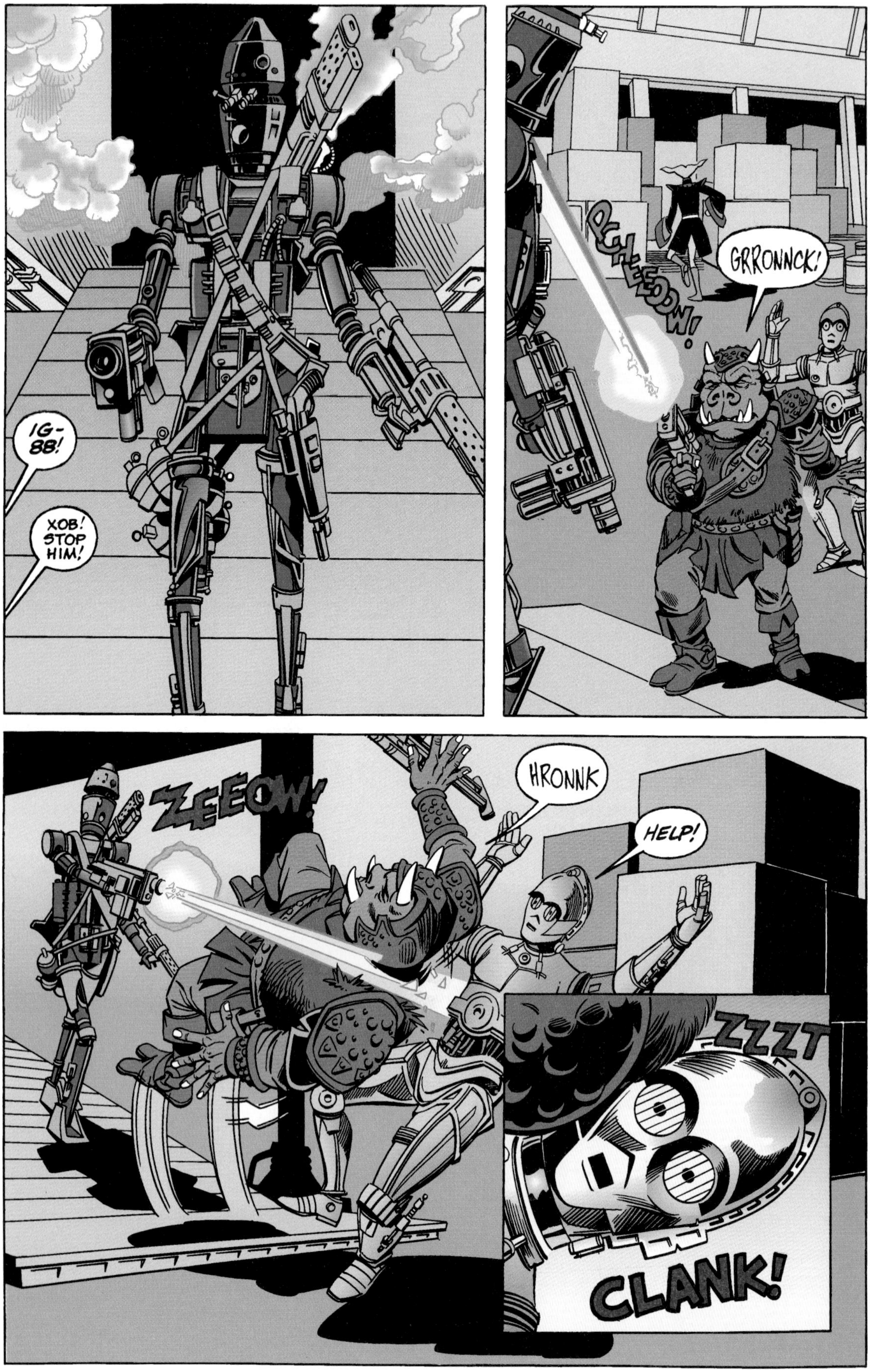
IG-88!
XOB! STOP HIM!
PCHEEOOW!
GRRONNCK!
ZEEOW!
HRONNK
HELP!
ZZZT
CLANK!

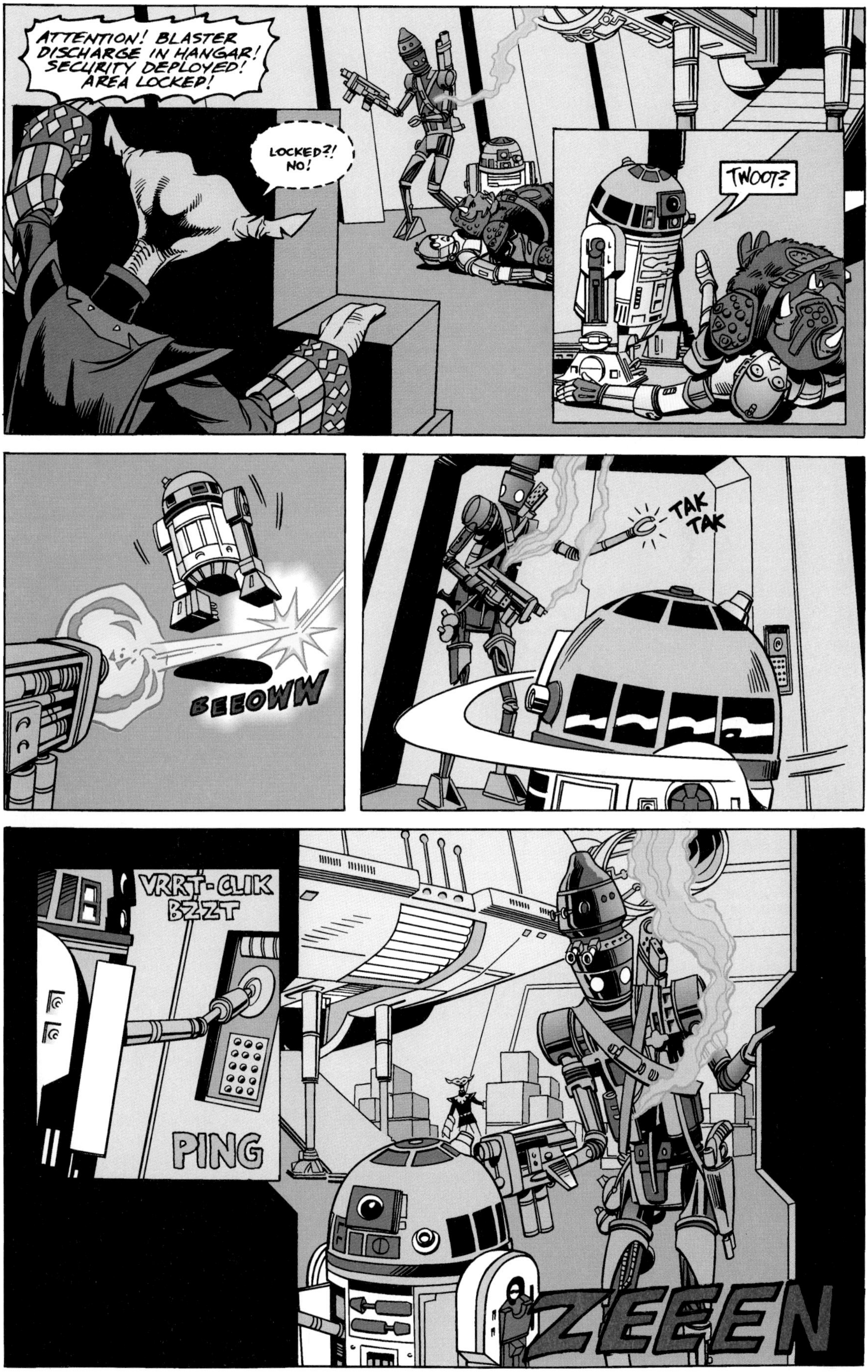
ATTENTION! BLASTER DISCHARGE IN HANGAR! SECURITY DEPLOYED! AREA LOCKED!
LOCKED?! NO!
TWOOT?
BEEOWW
TAK TAK
VRRT-CLIK BZZT
PING
ZEEEN

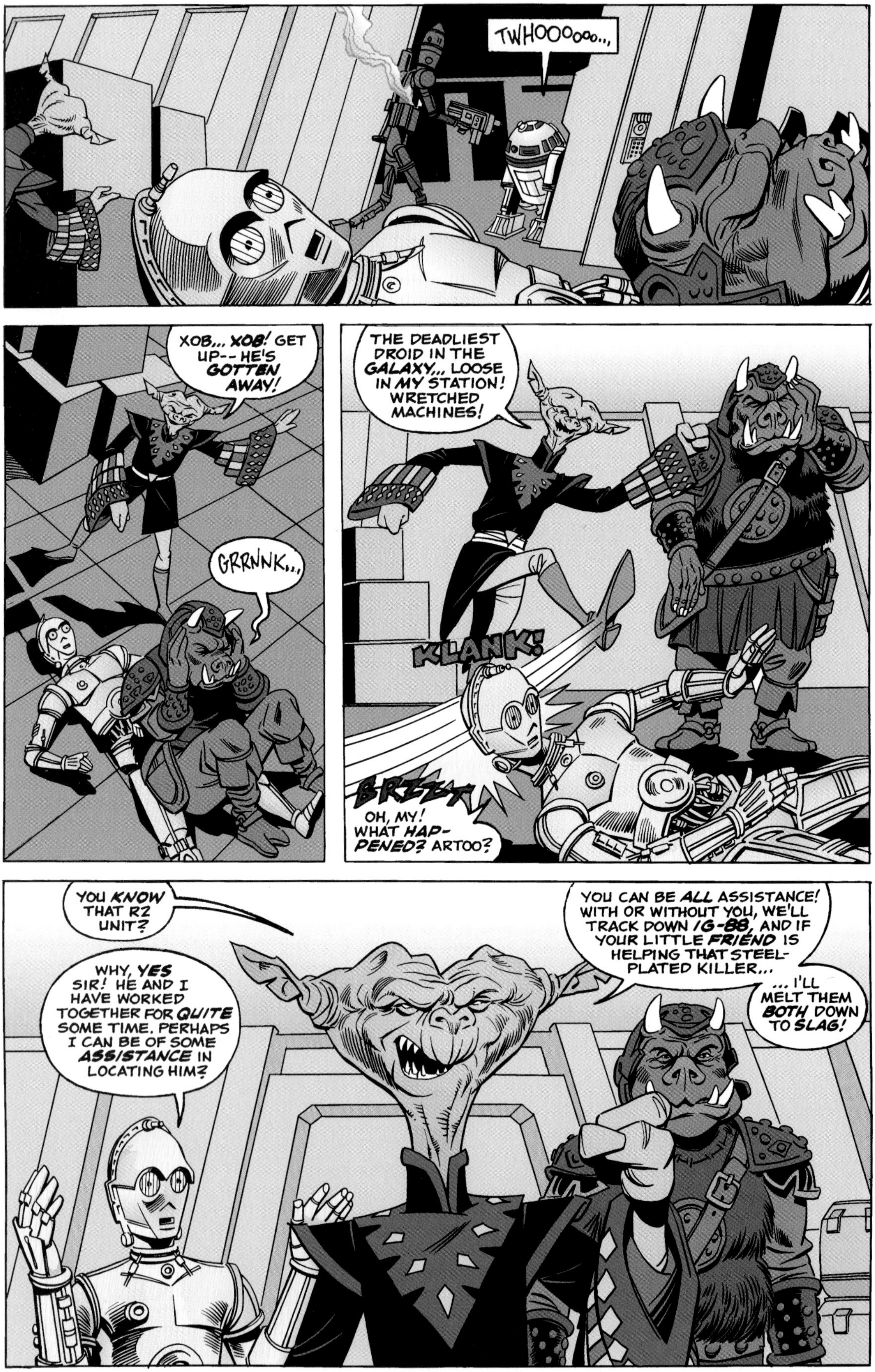
TWHOOOooo..,
XOB... XOB! GET UP-- HE'S GOTTEN AWAY!
GRRNNK...
THE DEADLIEST DROID IN THE GALAXY... LOOSE IN MY STATION! WRETCHED MACHINES!
KLANK!
BRZZT
OH, MY! WHAT HAPPENED? ARTOO?
YOU KNOW THAT R2 UNIT?
WHY, YES SIR! HE AND I HAVE WORKED TOGETHER FOR QUITE SOME TIME. PERHAPS I CAN BE OF SOME ASSISTANCE IN LOCATING HIM?
YOU CAN BE ALL ASSISTANCE! WITH OR WITHOUT YOU, WE'LL TRACK DOWN IG-88, AND IF YOUR LITTLE FRIEND IS HELPING THAT STEEL-PLATED KILLER...
... I'LL MELT THEM BOTH DOWN TO SLAG!

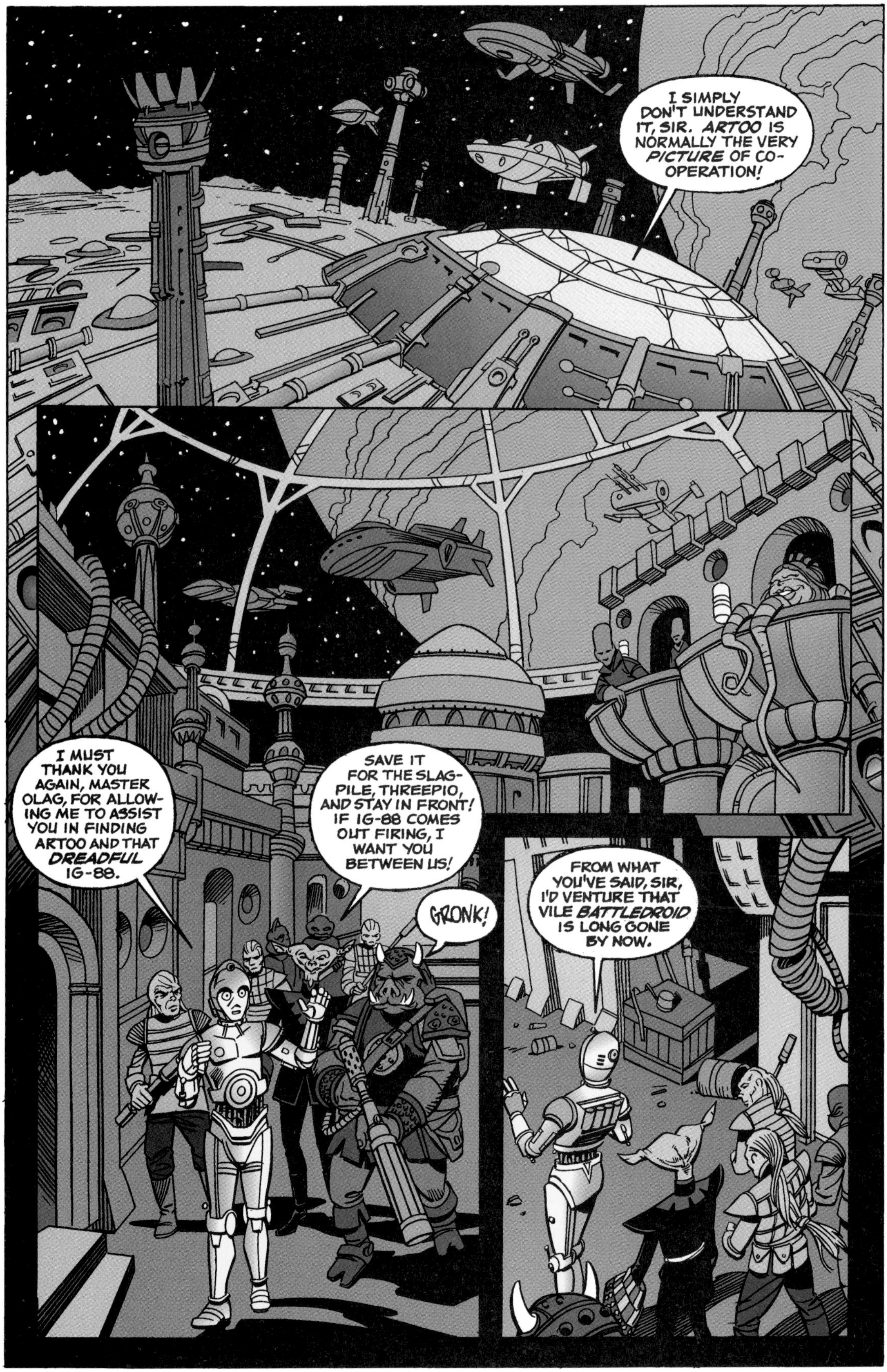
I SIMPLY DON'T UNDERSTAND IT, SIR. ARTOO IS NORMALLY THE VERY PICTURE OF CO-OPERATION!
I MUST THANK YOU AGAIN, MASTER OLAG, FOR ALLOWING ME TO ASSIST YOU IN FINDING ARTOO AND THAT DREADFUL IG-88.
SAVE IT FOR THE SLAG-PILE, THREEPIO, AND STAY IN FRONT! IF IG-88 COMES OUT FIRING, I WANT YOU BETWEEN US!
GRONK!
FROM WHAT YOU'VE SAID, SIR, I'D VENTURE THAT VILE BATTLEDROID IS LONG GONE BY NOW.

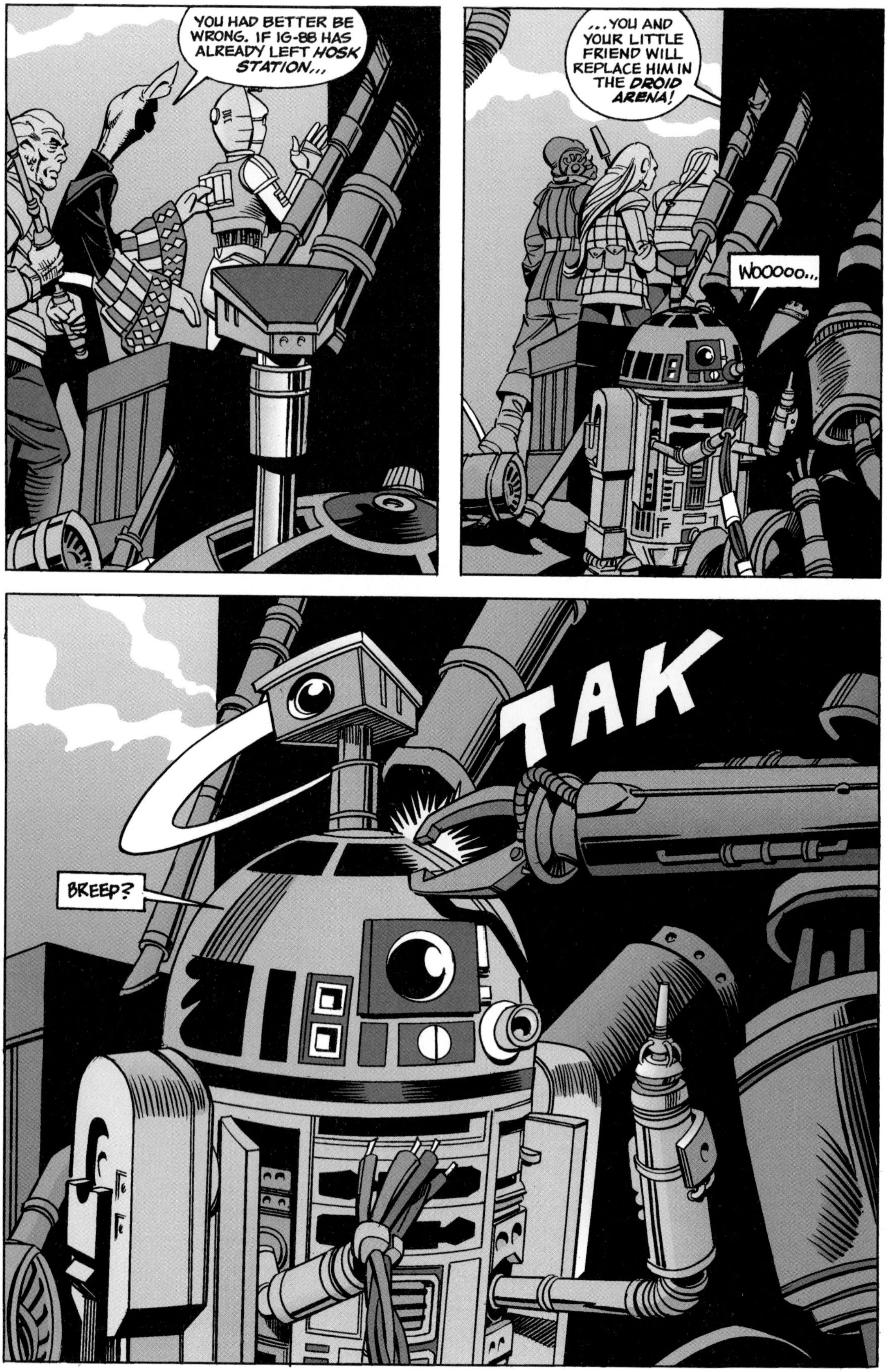
YOU HAD BETTER BE WRONG. IF IG-88 HAS ALREADY LEFT HOSK STATION...
...YOU AND YOUR LITTLE FRIEND WILL REPLACE HIM IN THE DROID ARENA!
WOOOOO...
TAK
BREEP?

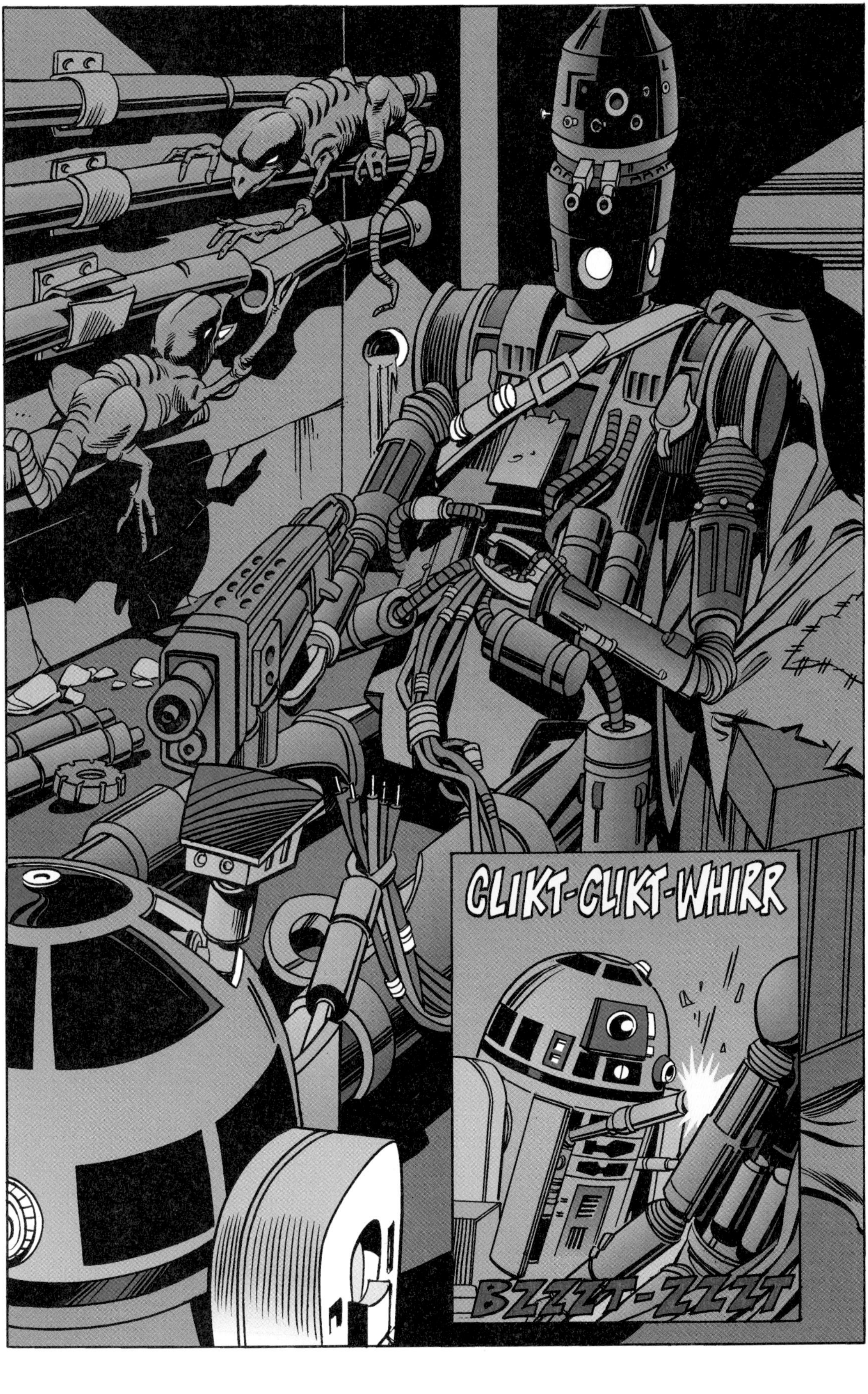
CLIKT-CLIKT-WHIRR
BZZZT-ZZZT

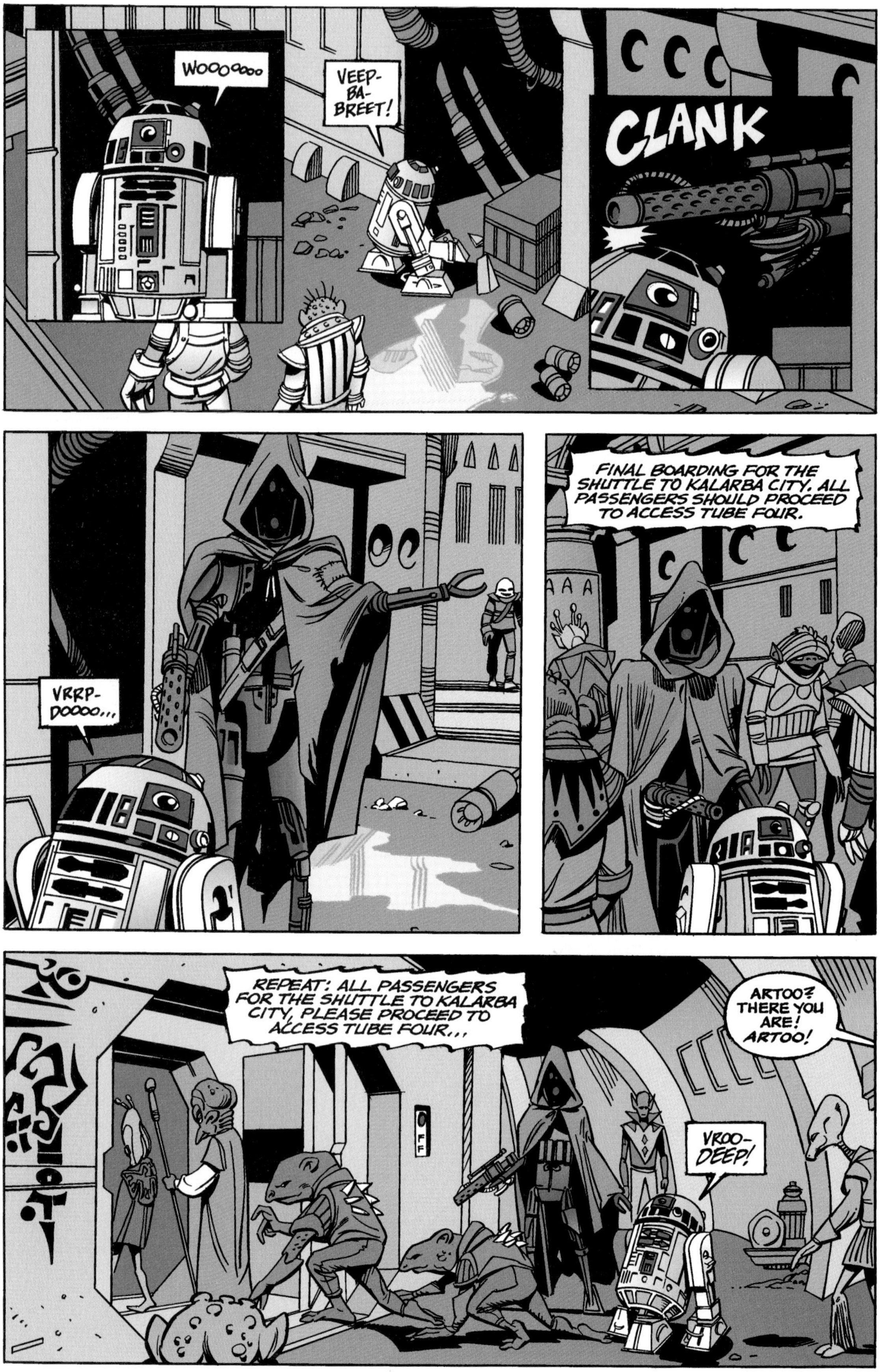

WOOOoooo
VEEP-BA-BREET!
CLANK
VRRP-DOOOO...
FINAL BOARDING FOR THE SHUTTLE TO KALARBA CITY. ALL PASSENGERS SHOULD PROCEED TO ACCESS TUBE FOUR.
REPEAT: ALL PASSENGERS FOR THE SHUTTLE TO KALARBA CITY, PLEASE PROCEED TO ACCESS TUBE FOUR...
ARTOO? THERE YOU ARE! ARTOO!
VROO-DEEP!

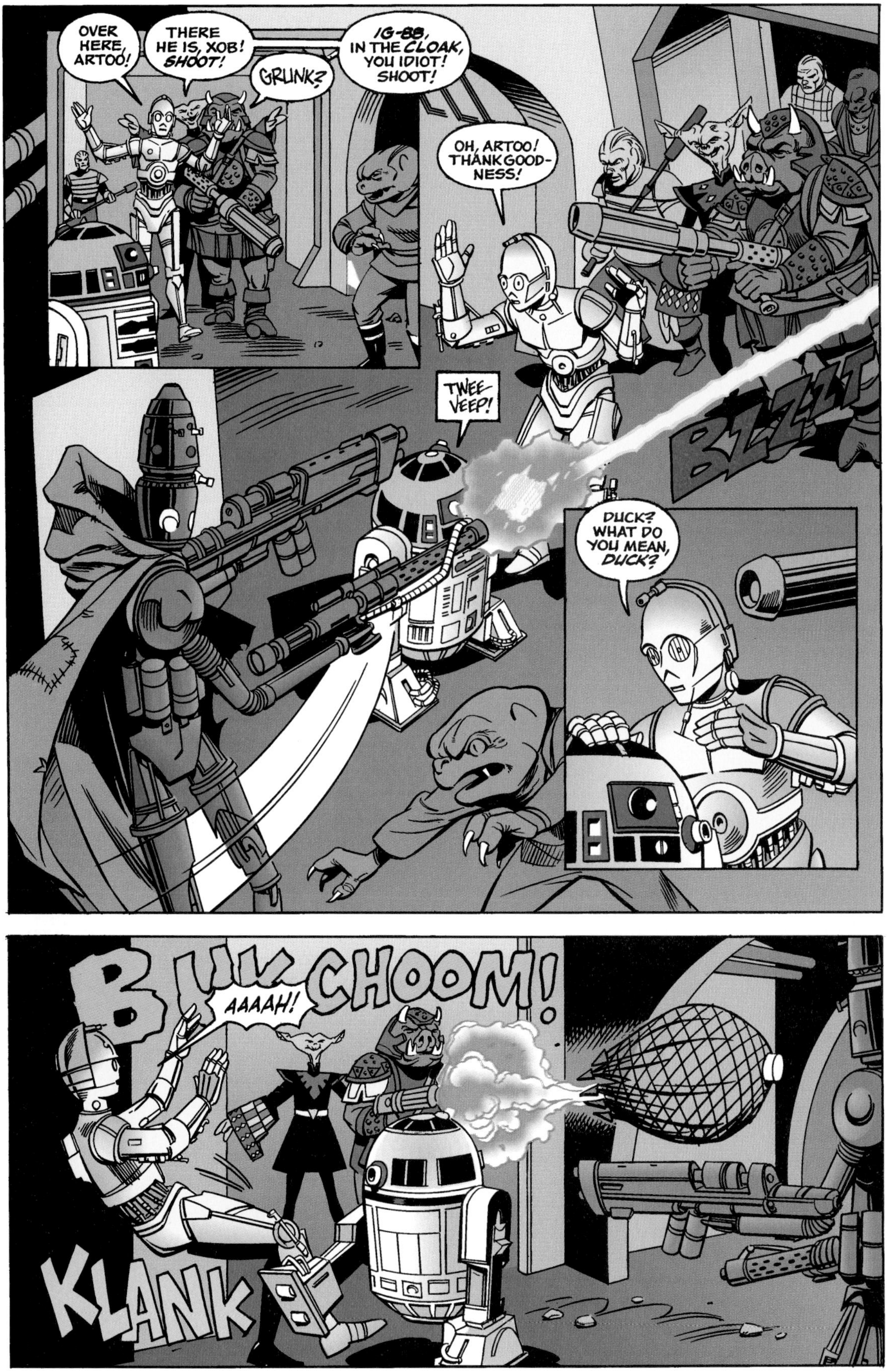

OVER HERE, ARTOO!
THERE HE IS, XOB! SHOOT!
GRUNK?
IG-88, IN THE CLOAK, YOU IDIOT! SHOOT!
OH, ARTOO! THANKGOODNESS!
TWEE-VEEP!
BZZZT
DUCK? WHAT DO YOU MEAN, DUCK?
B CHOOM!
AAAAH!
KLANK

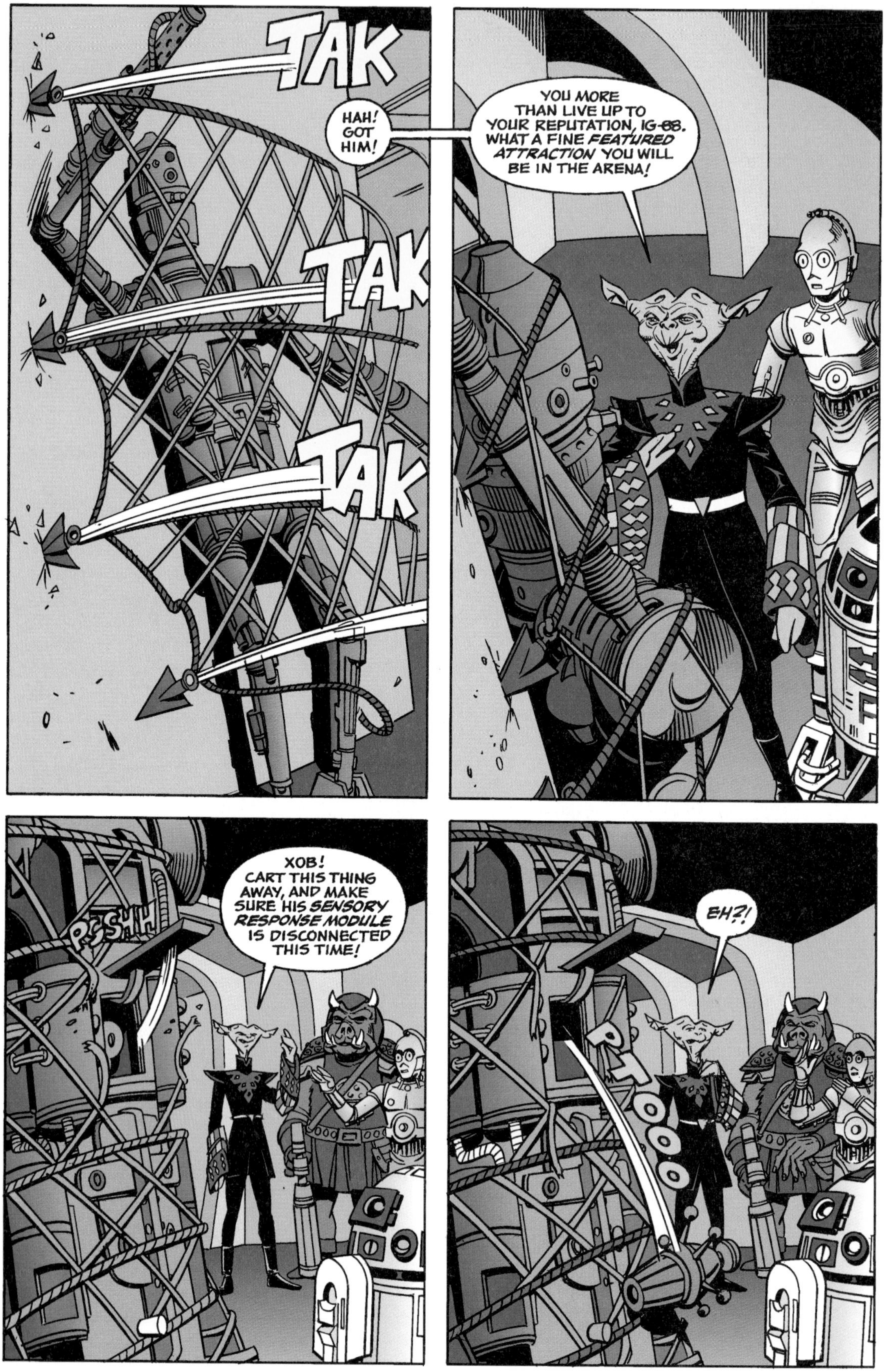
TAK
TAK
TAK
HAH! GOT HIM!
YOU MORE THAN LIVE UP TO YOUR REPUTATION, IG-88. WHAT A FINE FEATURED ATTRACTION YOU WILL BE IN THE ARENA!
PSSHH
XOB! CART THIS THING AWAY, AND MAKE SURE HIS SENSORY RESPONSE MODULE IS DISCONNECTED THIS TIME!
EH?!
PTOOOO

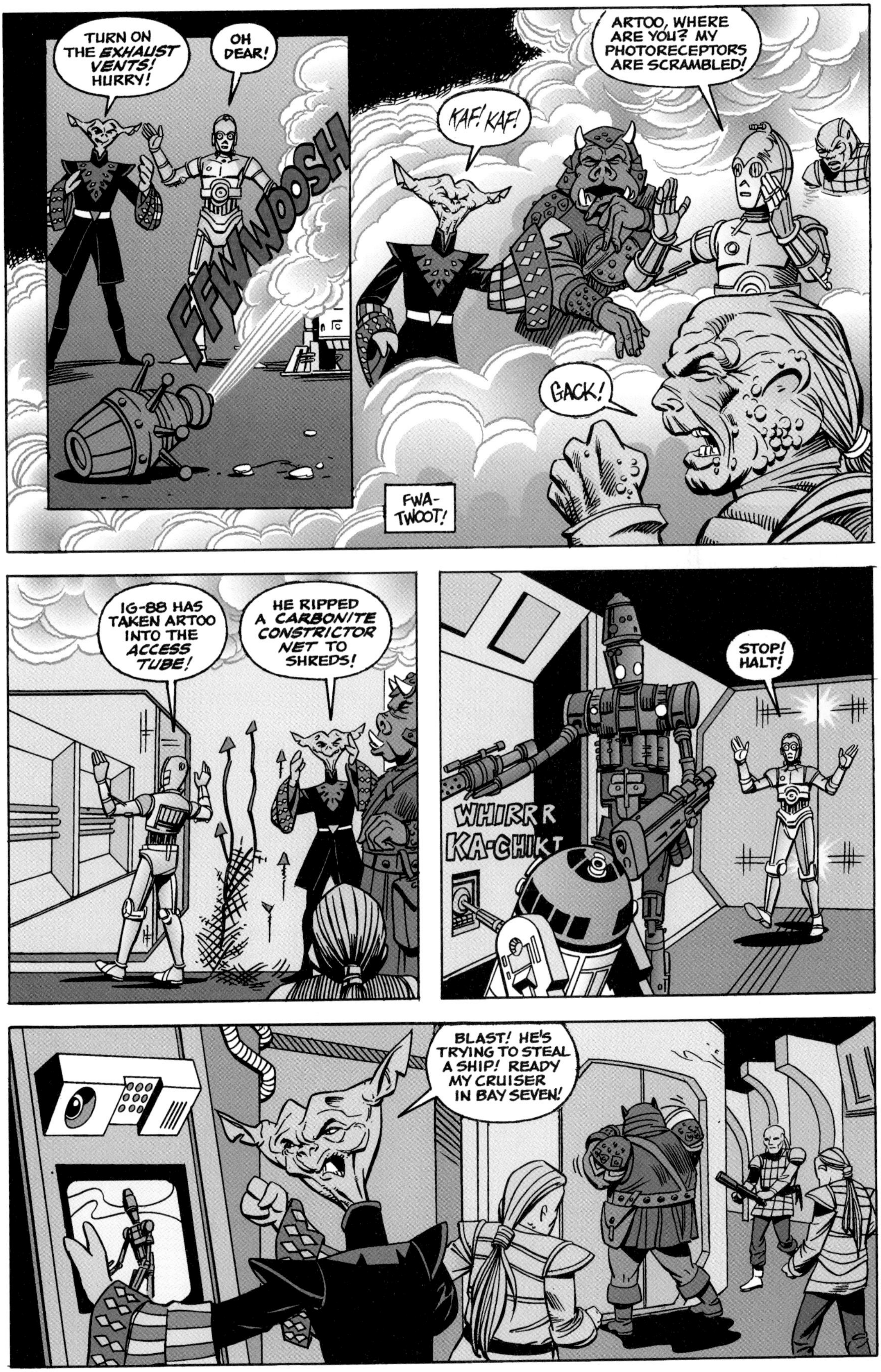
TURN ON THE EXHAUST VENTS! HURRY!
OH DEAR!
FFWWOOSH
ARTOO, WHERE ARE YOU? MY PHOTORECEPTORS ARE SCRAMBLED!
KAF! KAF!
GACK!
FWA-TWOOT!
IG-88 HAS TAKEN ARTOO INTO THE ACCESS TUBE!
HE RIPPED A CARBONITE CONSTRICTOR NET TO SHREDS!
STOP! HALT!
WHIRRR
KA-CHIKT
BLAST! HE'S TRYING TO STEAL A SHIP! READY MY CRUISER IN BAY SEVEN!

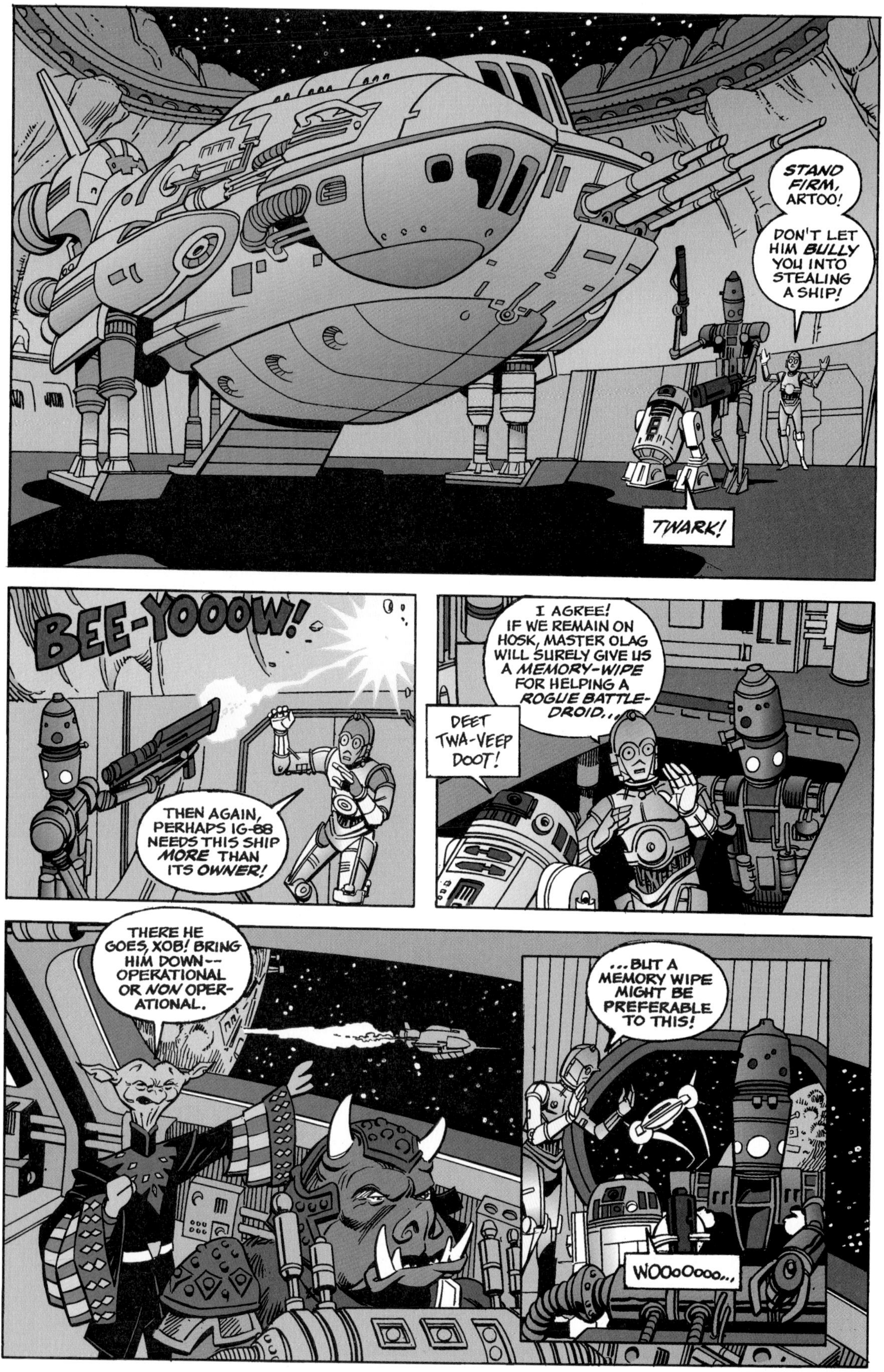
STAND FIRM, ARTOO!
DON'T LET HIM BULLY YOU INTO STEALING A SHIP!
TWARK!
BEE-YOOOW!
THEN AGAIN, PERHAPS IG-88 NEEDS THIS SHIP MORE THAN ITS OWNER!
I AGREE! IF WE REMAIN ON HOSK, MASTER OLAG WILL SURELY GIVE US A MEMORY-WIPE FOR HELPING A ROGUE BATTLE-DROID...
DEET TWA-VEEP DOOT!
THERE HE GOES, XOB! BRING HIM DOWN-- OPERATIONAL OR NON OPERATIONAL.
...BUT A MEMORY WIPE MIGHT BE PREFERABLE TO THIS!
WOOoOooo...

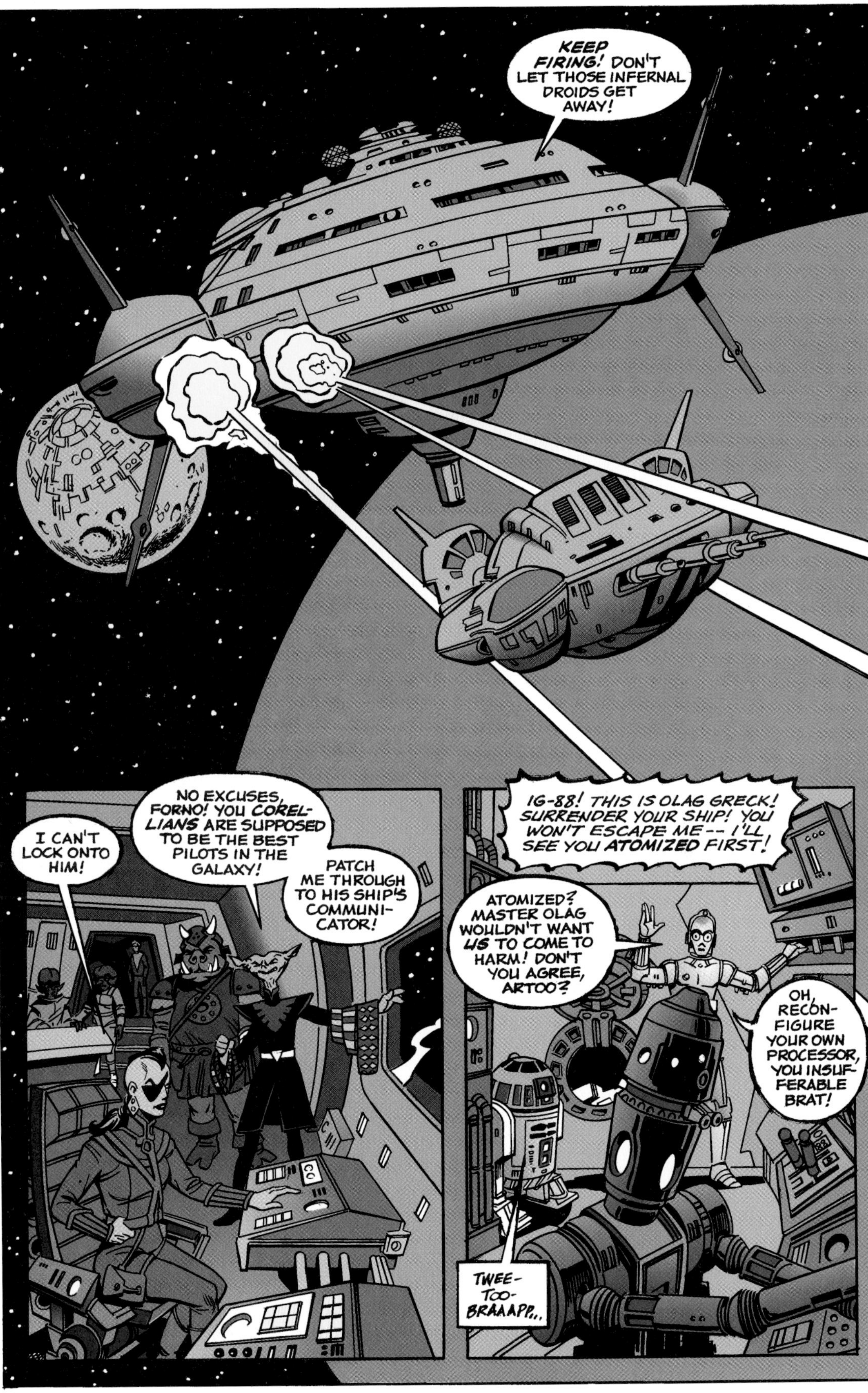
KEEP FIRING! DON'T LET THOSE INFERNAL DROIDS GET AWAY!
I CAN'T LOCK ONTO HIM!
NO EXCUSES, FORNO! YOU CORELLIANS ARE SUPPOSED TO BE THE BEST PILOTS IN THE GALAXY!
PATCH ME THROUGH TO HIS SHIP'S COMMUNICATOR!
IG-88! THIS IS OLAG GRECK! SURRENDER YOUR SHIP! YOU WON'T ESCAPE ME -- I'LL SEE YOU ATOMIZED FIRST!
ATOMIZED? MASTER OLAG WOULDN'T WANT US TO COME TO HARM! DON'T YOU AGREE, ARTOO?
OH, RECONFIGURE YOUR OWN PROCESSOR, YOU INSUFFERABLE BRAT!
TWEE-TOO-BRAAAPP...

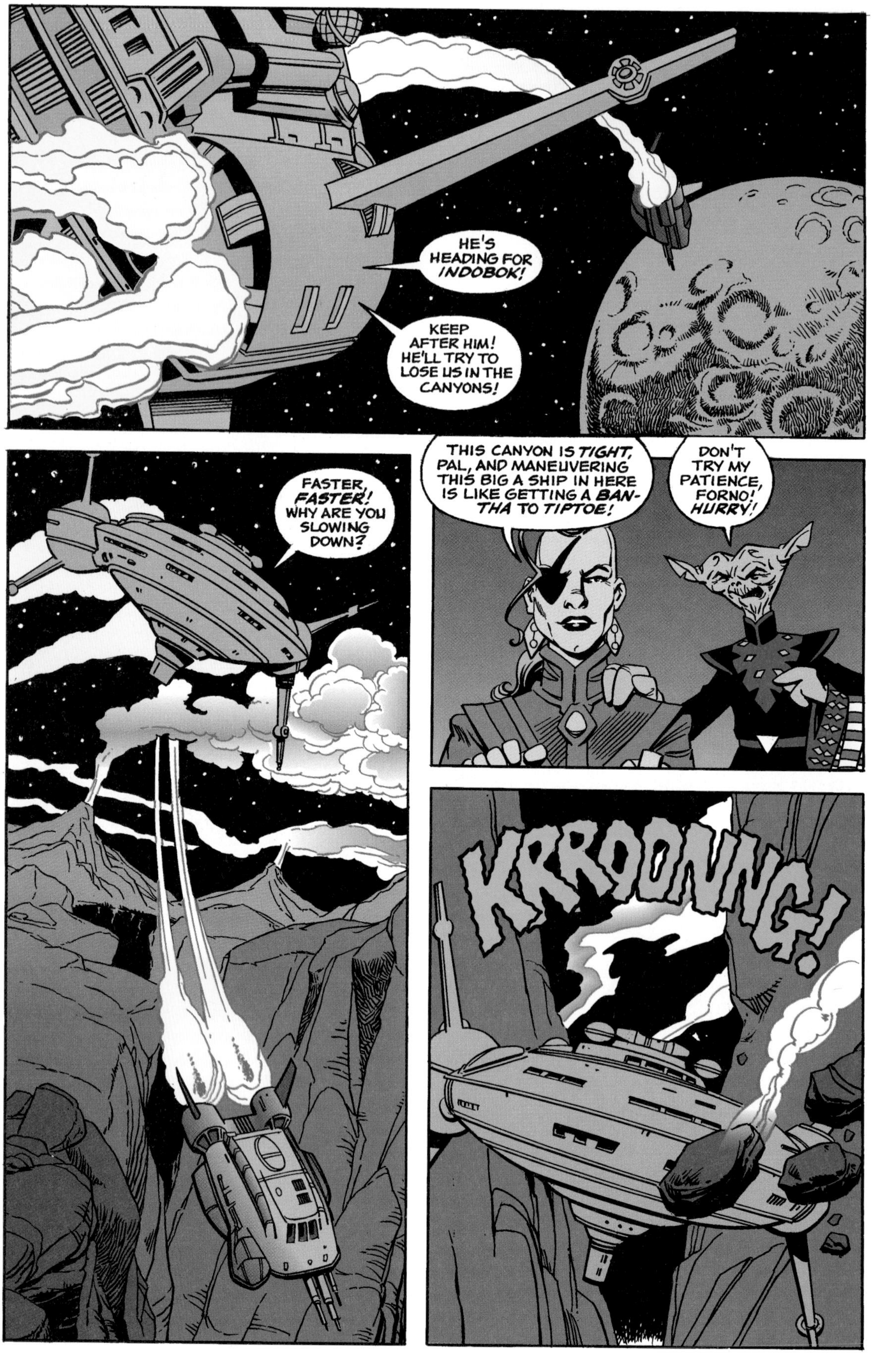
HE'S HEADING FOR *INDOBOK!*
KEEP AFTER HIM! HE'LL TRY TO LOSE US IN THE CANYONS!
FASTER, *FASTER!* WHY ARE YOU SLOWING DOWN?
THIS CANYON IS *TIGHT,* PAL, AND MANEUVERING THIS BIG A SHIP IN HERE IS LIKE GETTING A *BANTHA* TO *TIPTOE!*
DON'T TRY MY PATIENCE, FORNO! *HURRY!*
KRROONNG!

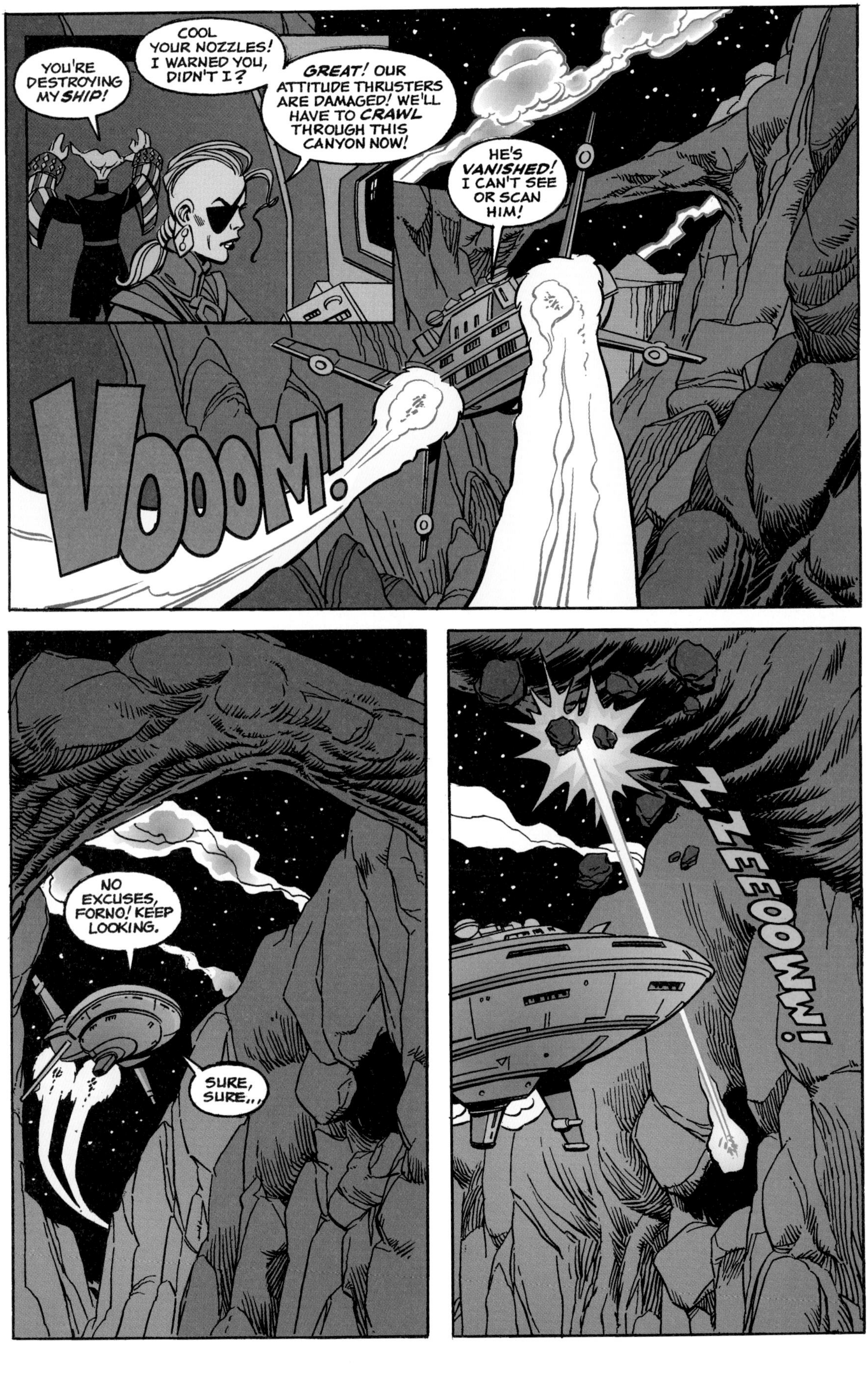
YOU'RE DESTROYING MY SHIP!
COOL YOUR NOZZLES! I WARNED YOU, DIDN'T I?
GREAT! OUR ATTITUDE THRUSTERS ARE DAMAGED! WE'LL HAVE TO CRAWL THROUGH THIS CANYON NOW!
HE'S VANISHED! I CAN'T SEE OR SCAN HIM!
VOOOM!
NO EXCUSES, FORNO! KEEP LOOKING.
SURE, SURE...
ZZEEOOWW!

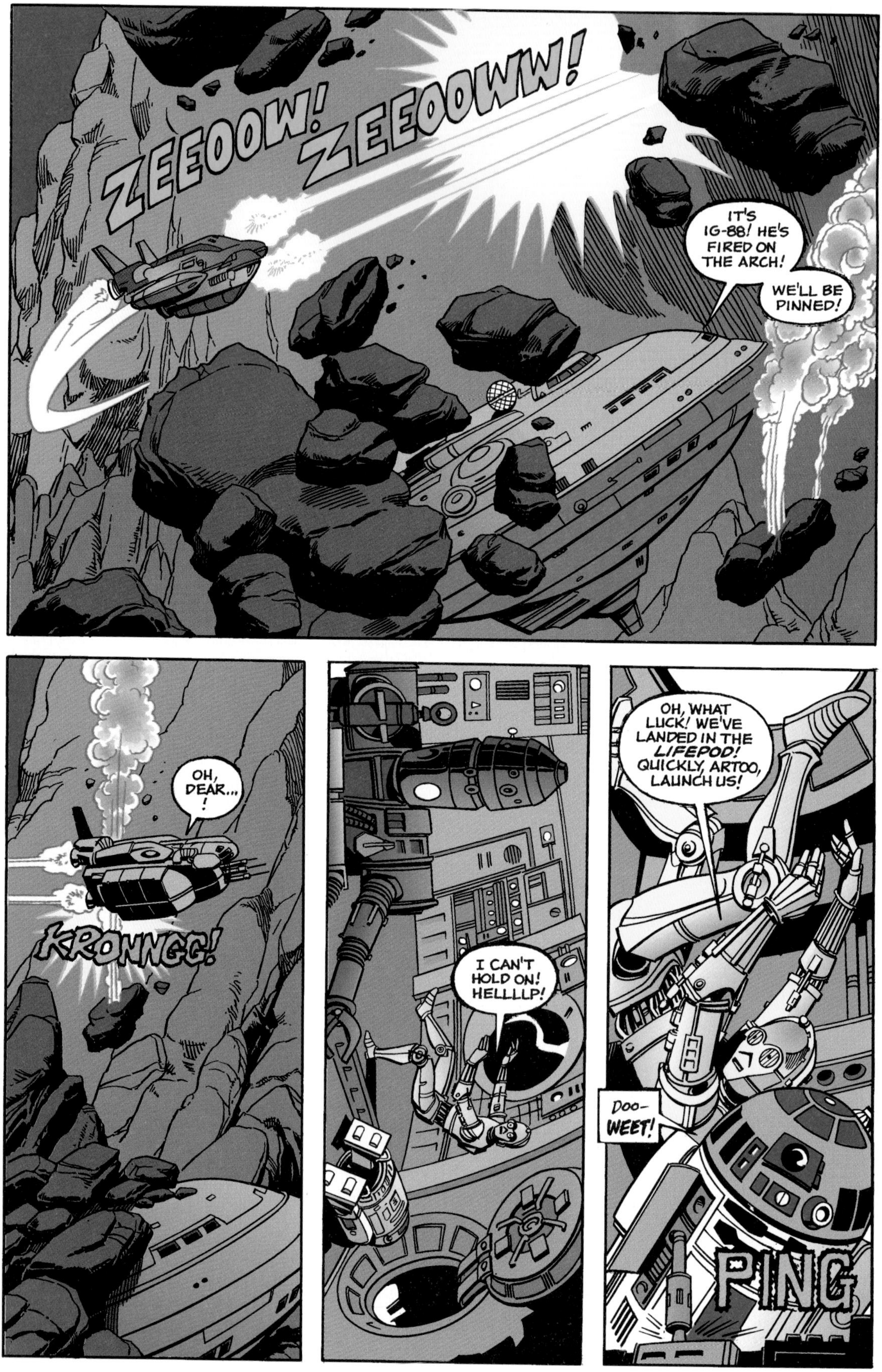
ZEEOOW! ZEEOOWW!
IT'S IG-88! HE'S FIRED ON THE ARCH!
WE'LL BE PINNED!
OH, DEAR... !
KRONNGG!
I CAN'T HOLD ON! HELLLLP!
OH, WHAT LUCK! WE'VE LANDED IN THE LIFEPOD! QUICKLY, ARTOO, LAUNCH US!
DOO-WEET!
PING

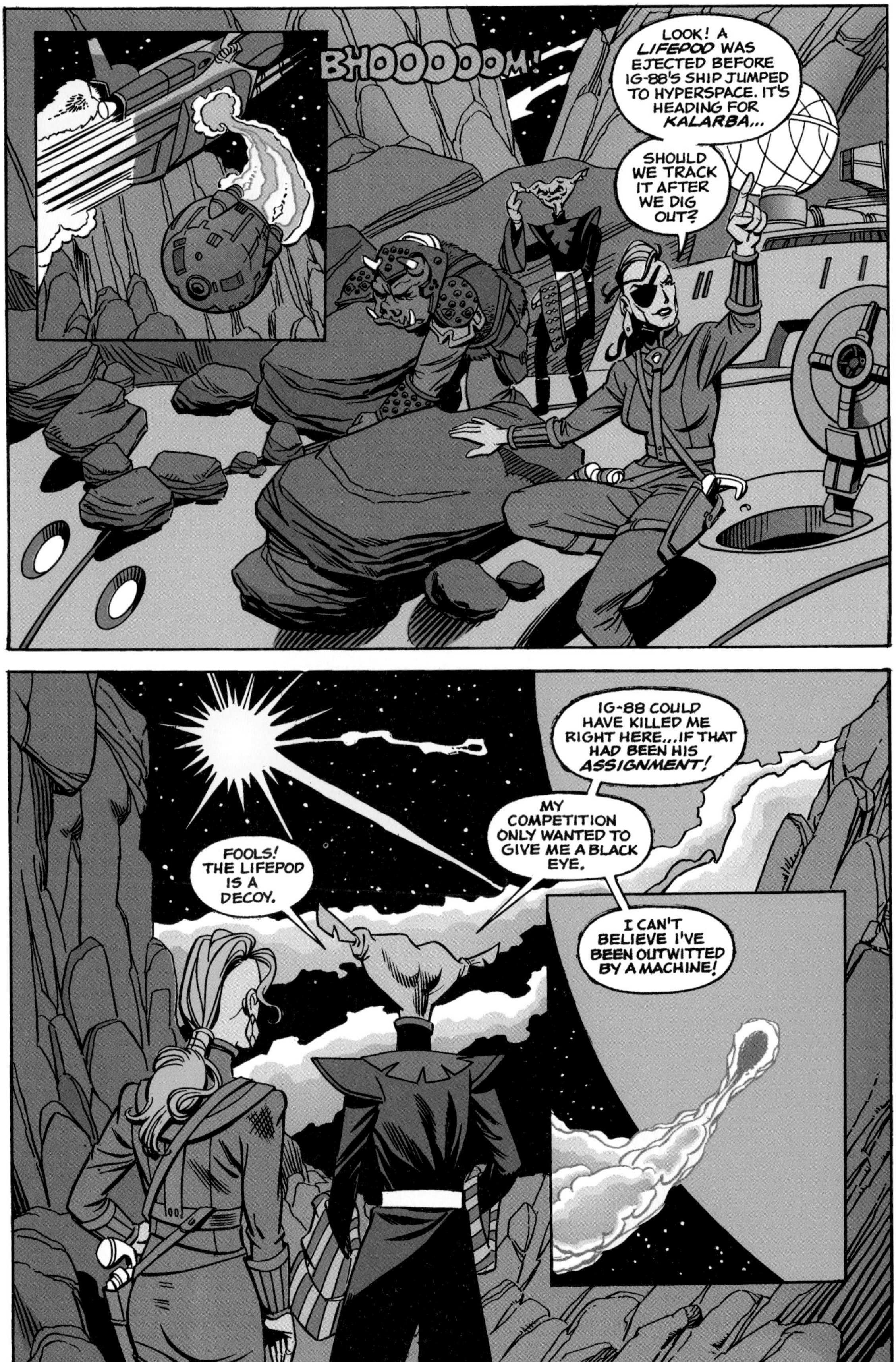
BHOOOOOOM!
LOOK! A LIFEPOD WAS EJECTED BEFORE IG-88'S SHIP JUMPED TO HYPERSPACE. IT'S HEADING FOR KALARBA...
SHOULD WE TRACK IT AFTER WE DIG OUT?
FOOLS! THE LIFEPOD IS A DECOY.
IG-88 COULD HAVE KILLED ME RIGHT HERE...IF THAT HAD BEEN HIS ASSIGNMENT!
MY COMPETITION ONLY WANTED TO GIVE ME A BLACK EYE.
I CAN'T BELIEVE I'VE BEEN OUTWITTED BY A MACHINE!

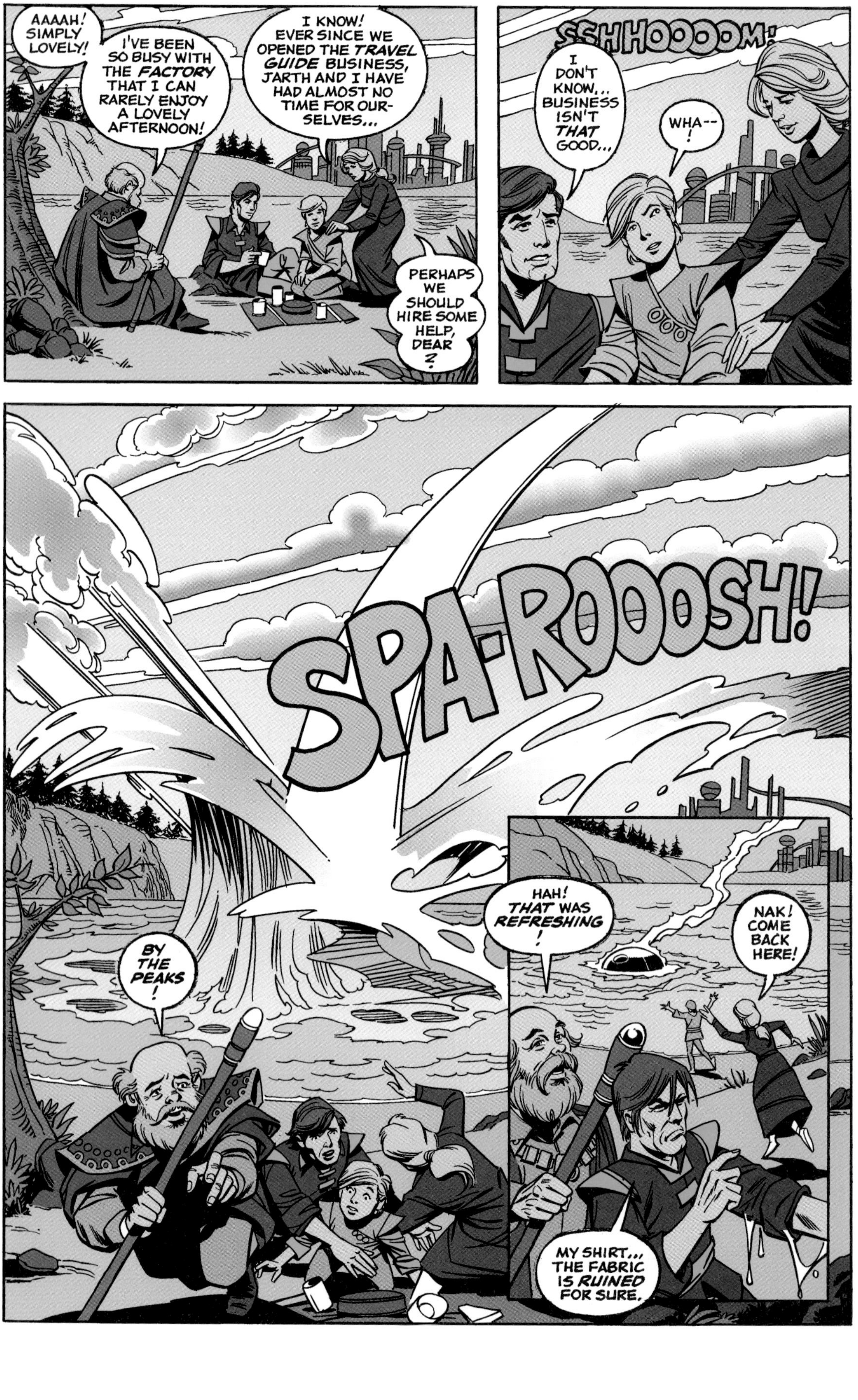

AAAAH! SIMPLY LOVELY!
I'VE BEEN SO BUSY WITH THE FACTORY THAT I CAN RARELY ENJOY A LOVELY AFTERNOON!
I KNOW! EVER SINCE WE OPENED THE TRAVEL GUIDE BUSINESS, JARTH AND I HAVE HAD ALMOST NO TIME FOR OURSELVES...
PERHAPS WE SHOULD HIRE SOME HELP, DEAR?
SSHHOOOOM!
I DON'T KNOW... BUSINESS ISN'T THAT GOOD...
WHA--!
SPA-ROOOSH!
BY THE PEAKS!
HAH! THAT WAS REFRESHING!
NAK! COME BACK HERE!
MY SHIRT... THE FABRIC IS RUINED FOR SURE.

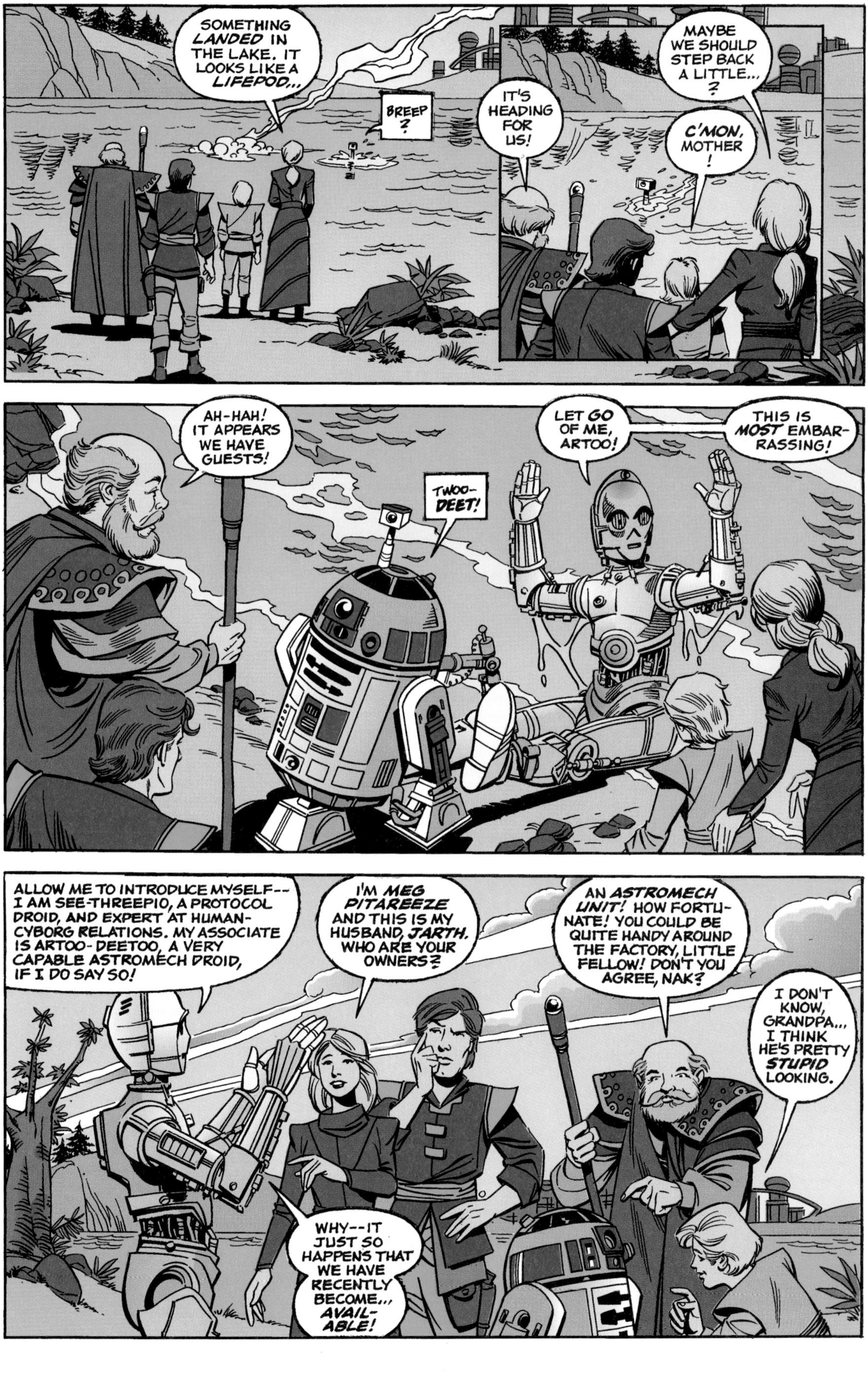
SOMETHING LANDED IN THE LAKE. IT LOOKS LIKE A LIFEPOD...
BREEP ?
IT'S HEADING FOR US!
MAYBE WE SHOULD STEP BACK A LITTLE... ?
C'MON, MOTHER!
AH-HAH! IT APPEARS WE HAVE GUESTS!
TWOO-DEET!
LET GO OF ME, ARTOO!
THIS IS MOST EMBARRASSING!
ALLOW ME TO INTRODUCE MYSELF-- I AM SEE-THREEPIO, A PROTOCOL DROID, AND EXPERT AT HUMAN-CYBORG RELATIONS. MY ASSOCIATE IS ARTOO-DEETOO, A VERY CAPABLE ASTROMECH DROID, IF I DO SAY SO!
I'M MEG PITAREEZE AND THIS IS MY HUSBAND, JARTH. WHO ARE YOUR OWNERS?
AN ASTROMECH UNIT! HOW FORTUNATE! YOU COULD BE QUITE HANDY AROUND THE FACTORY, LITTLE FELLOW! DON'T YOU AGREE, NAK?
I DON'T KNOW, GRANDPA... I THINK HE'S PRETTY STUPID LOOKING.
WHY--IT JUST SO HAPPENS THAT WE HAVE RECENTLY BECOME... AVAILABLE!

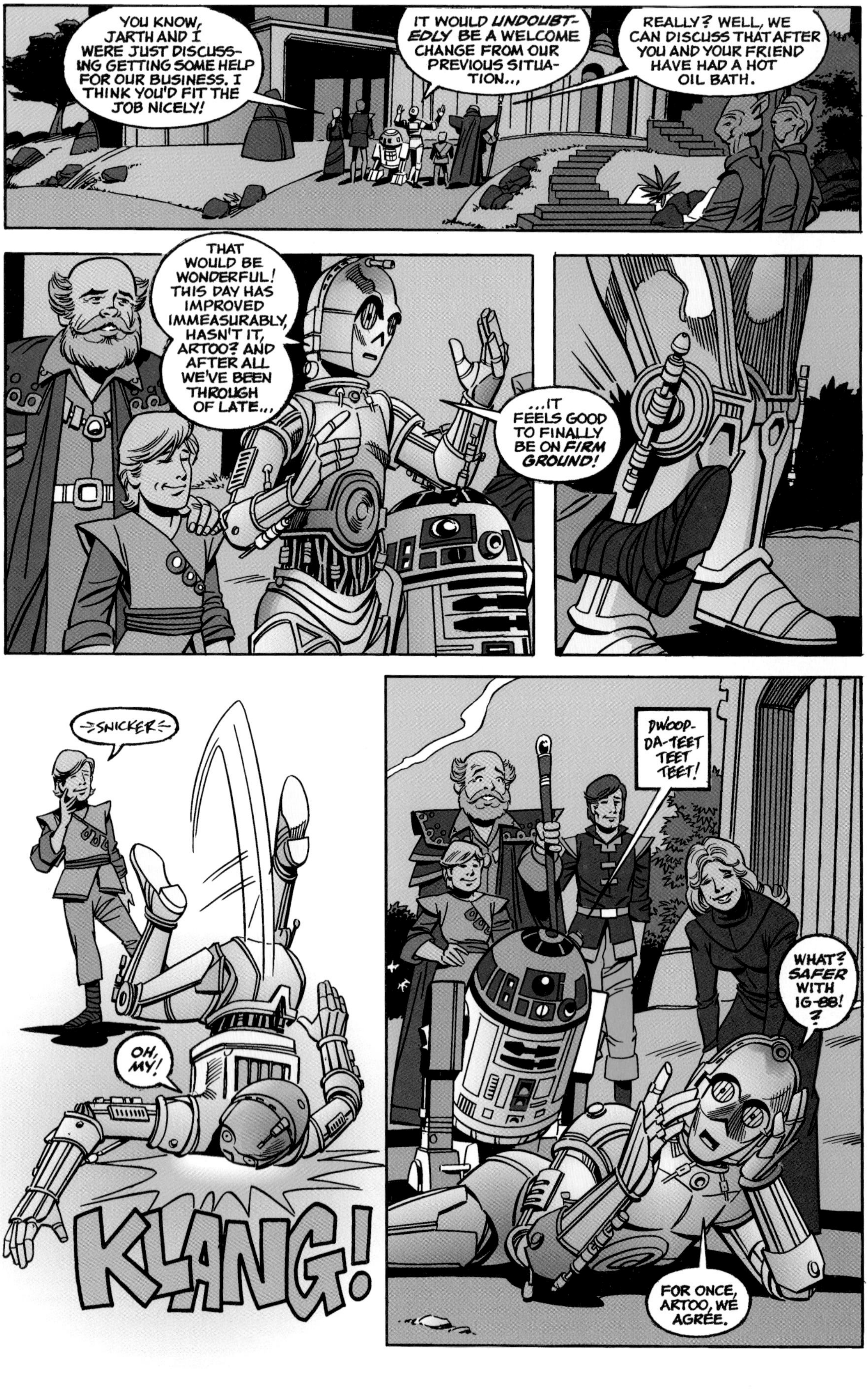
YOU KNOW, JARTH AND I WERE JUST DISCUSSING GETTING SOME HELP FOR OUR BUSINESS. I THINK YOU'D FIT THE JOB NICELY!
IT WOULD UNDOUBTEDLY BE A WELCOME CHANGE FROM OUR PREVIOUS SITUATION...
REALLY? WELL, WE CAN DISCUSS THAT AFTER YOU AND YOUR FRIEND HAVE HAD A HOT OIL BATH.
THAT WOULD BE WONDERFUL! THIS DAY HAS IMPROVED IMMEASURABLY, HASN'T IT, ARTOO? AND AFTER ALL WE'VE BEEN THROUGH OF LATE...
...IT FEELS GOOD TO FINALLY BE ON FIRM GROUND!
SNICKER
OH, MY!
KLANG!
DWOOP-DA-TEET TEET TEET!
WHAT? SAFER WITH IG-88!?
FOR ONCE, ARTOO, WE AGREE.

The Greed of Olag Greck
Chapter 2

Script
Dan Thorsland

Pencils
Bill Hughes

Inks
Andy Mushynsky

Colors
Pamela Rambo

Lettering
Bill Pearson

Cover
Cam Kennedy

Sketch
Kilian Plunkett

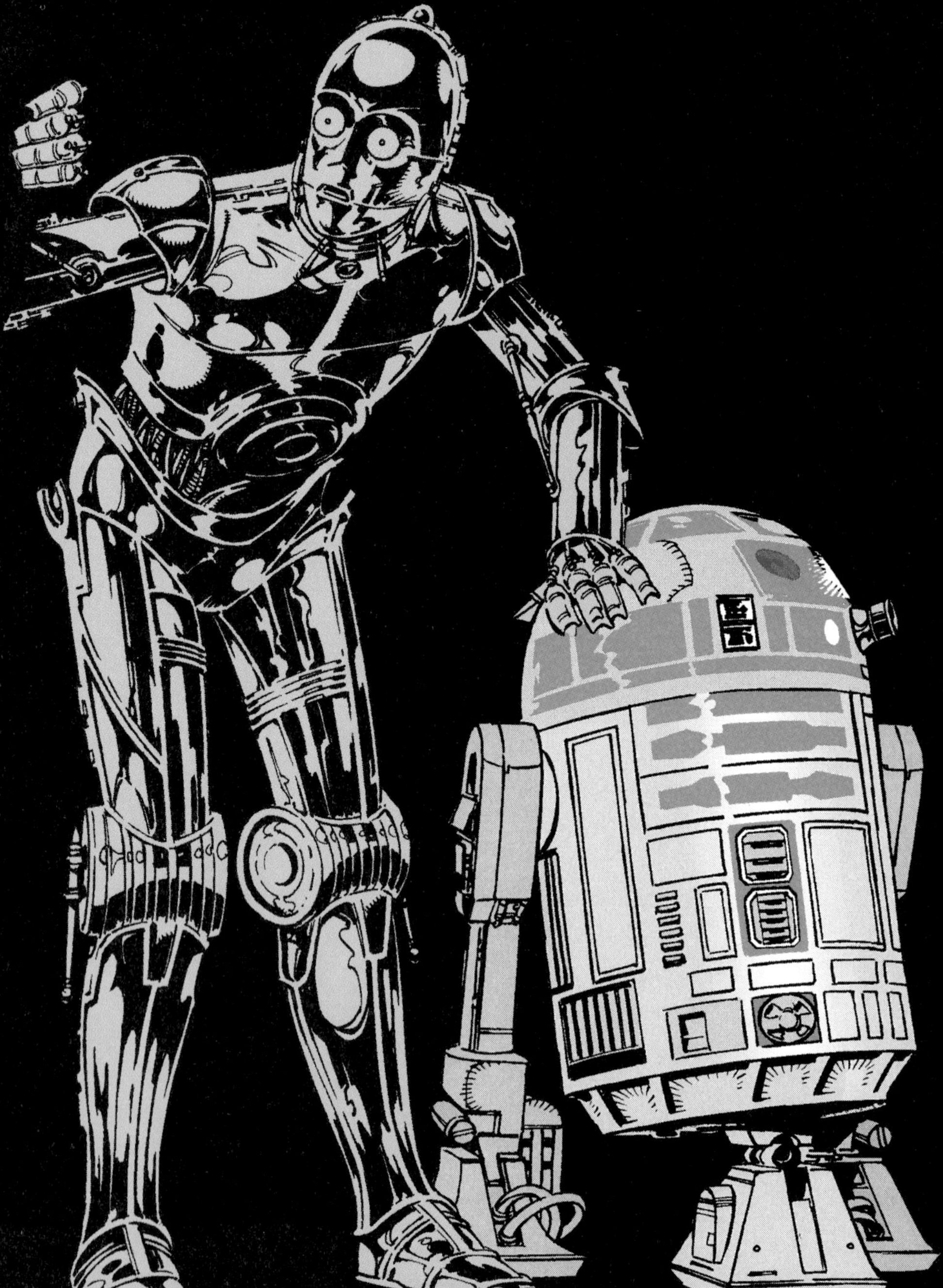

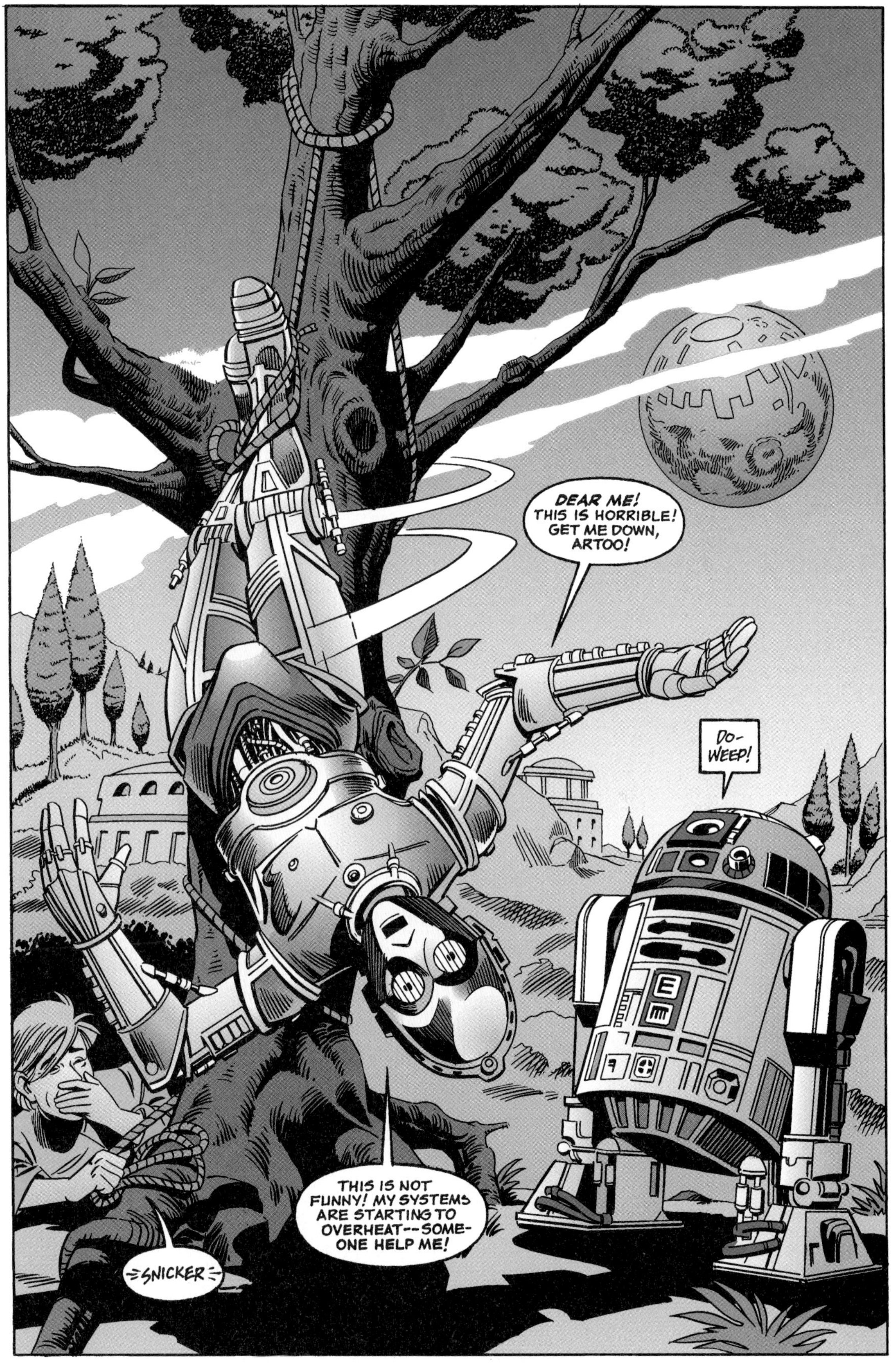
DEAR ME! THIS IS HORRIBLE! GET ME DOWN, ARTOO!
DO-WEEP!
THIS IS NOT FUNNY! MY SYSTEMS ARE STARTING TO OVERHEAT--SOME-ONE HELP ME!
SNICKER

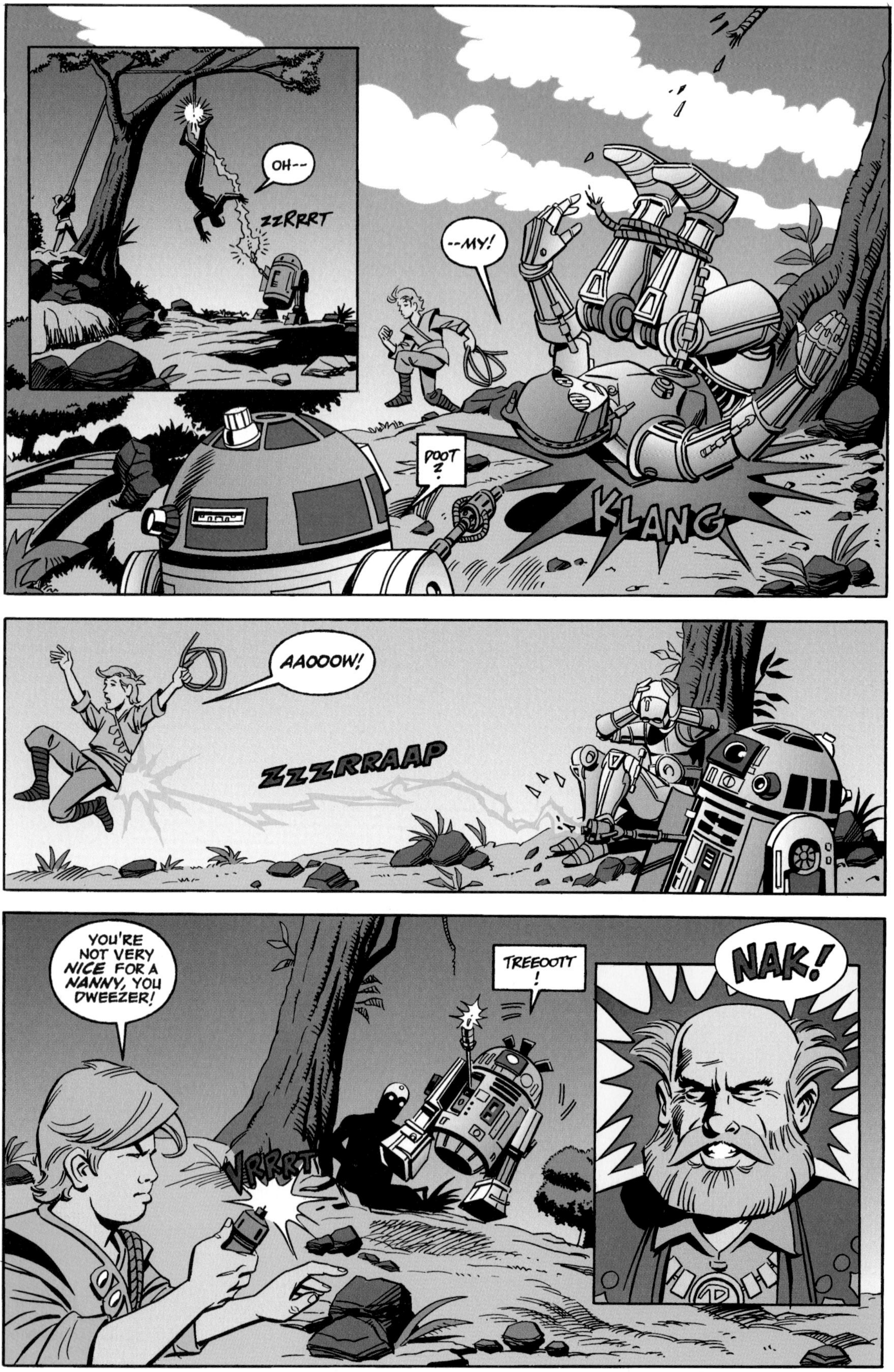
OH--
ZZRRRT
--MY!
DOOT ?!
KLANG
AAOOOW!
ZZZRRAAP
YOU'RE NOT VERY *NICE* FOR A *NANNY*, YOU DWEEZER!
TREEOOTT!
VRRRT
NAK!

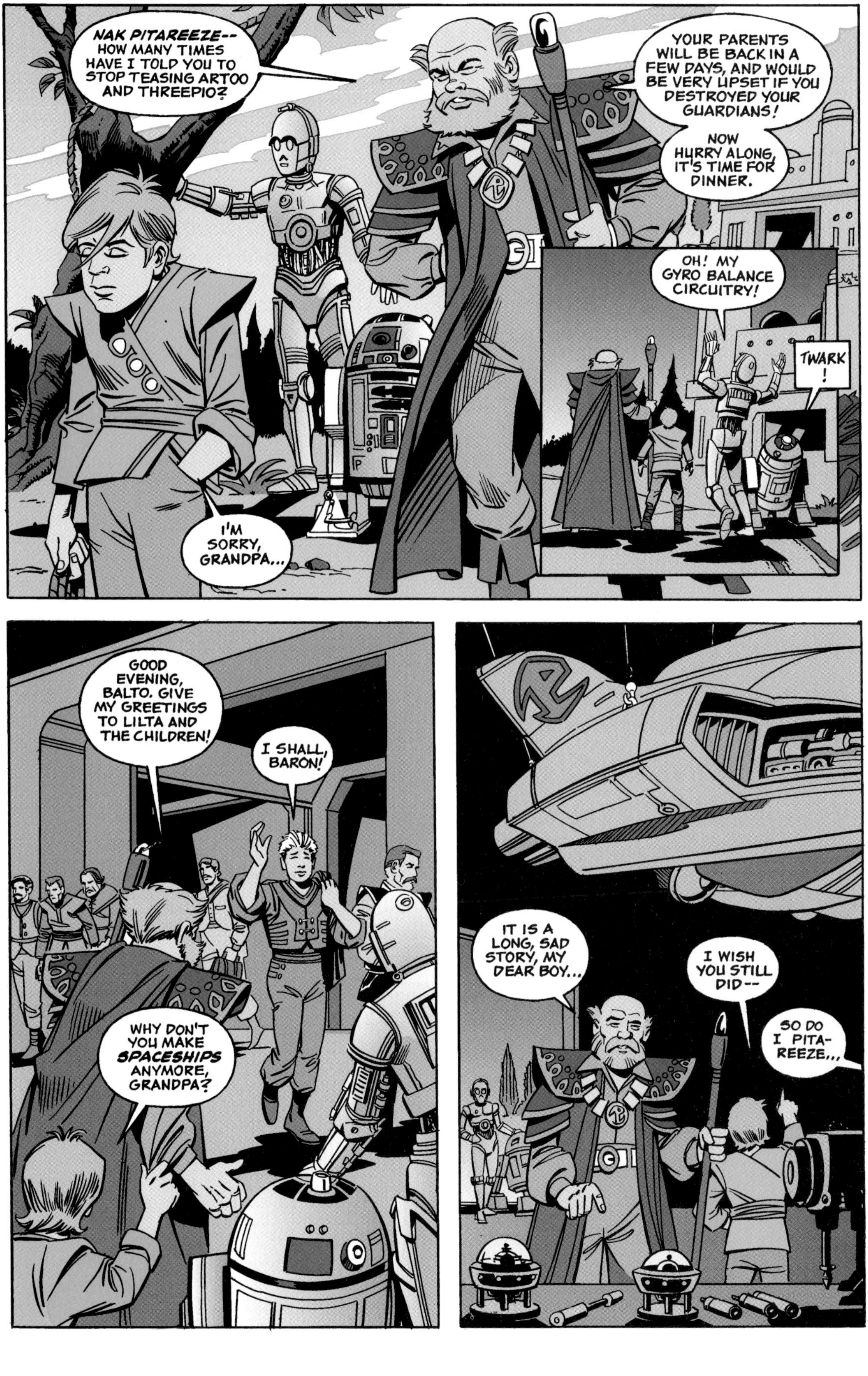
NAK PITAREEZE-- HOW MANY TIMES HAVE I TOLD YOU TO STOP TEASING ARTOO AND THREEPIO?
YOUR PARENTS WILL BE BACK IN A FEW DAYS, AND WOULD BE VERY UPSET IF YOU DESTROYED YOUR GUARDIANS!
NOW HURRY ALONG, IT'S TIME FOR DINNER.
I'M SORRY, GRANDPA...
OH! MY GYRO BALANCE CIRCUITRY!
TWARK!
GOOD EVENING, BALTO. GIVE MY GREETINGS TO LILTA AND THE CHILDREN!
I SHALL, BARON!
WHY DON'T YOU MAKE SPACESHIPS ANYMORE, GRANDPA?
IT IS A LONG, SAD STORY, MY DEAR BOY...
I WISH YOU STILL DID--
SO DO I PITAREEZE...

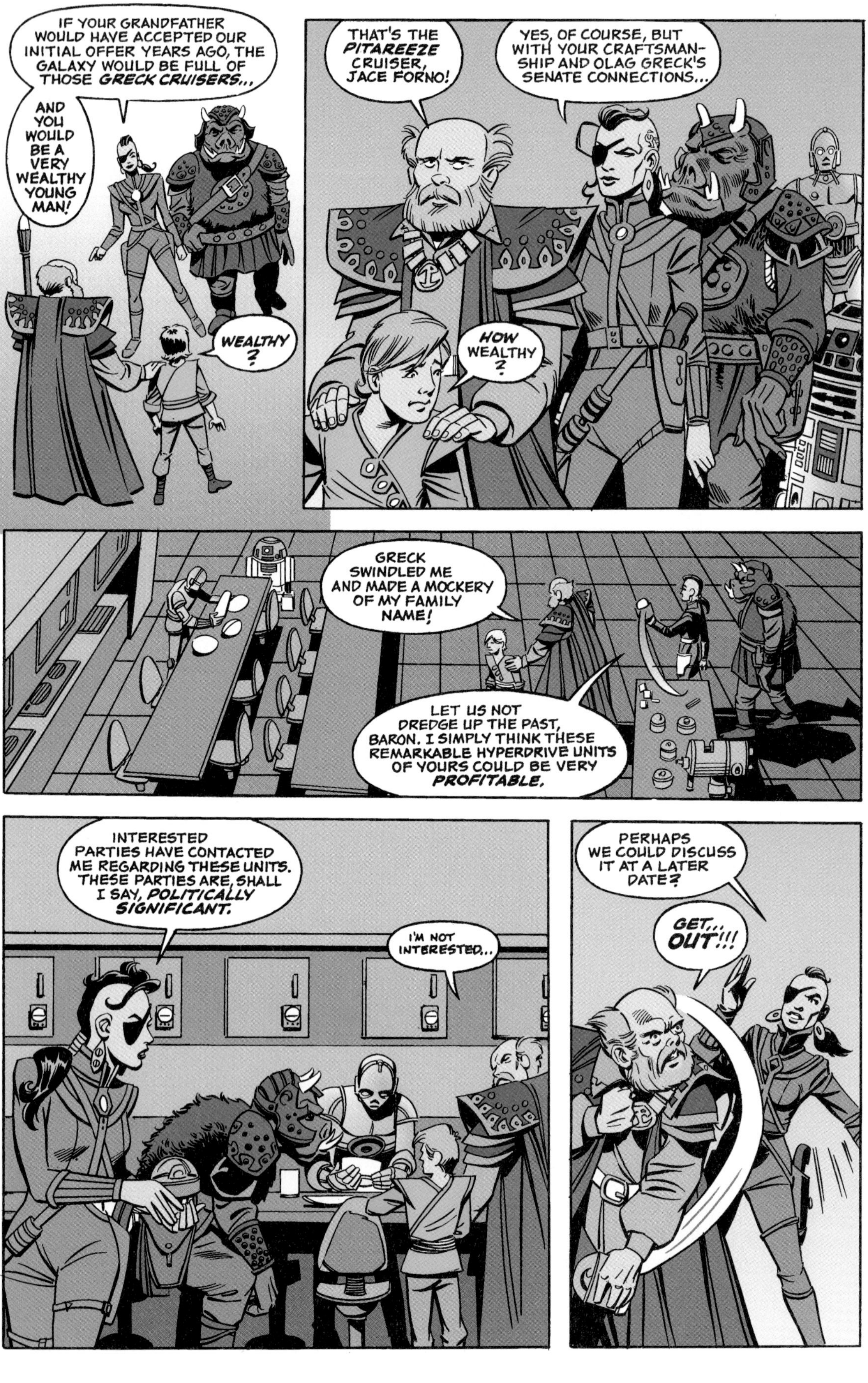
IF YOUR GRANDFATHER WOULD HAVE ACCEPTED OUR INITIAL OFFER YEARS AGO, THE GALAXY WOULD BE FULL OF THOSE GRECK CRUISERS...
AND YOU WOULD BE A VERY WEALTHY YOUNG MAN!
WEALTHY?
THAT'S THE PITAREEZE CRUISER, JACE FORNO!
YES, OF COURSE, BUT WITH YOUR CRAFTSMANSHIP AND OLAG GRECK'S SENATE CONNECTIONS...
HOW WEALTHY?
GRECK SWINDLED ME AND MADE A MOCKERY OF MY FAMILY NAME!
LET US NOT DREDGE UP THE PAST, BARON. I SIMPLY THINK THESE REMARKABLE HYPERDRIVE UNITS OF YOURS COULD BE VERY PROFITABLE.
INTERESTED PARTIES HAVE CONTACTED ME REGARDING THESE UNITS. THESE PARTIES ARE, SHALL I SAY, POLITICALLY SIGNIFICANT.
I'M NOT INTERESTED...
PERHAPS WE COULD DISCUSS IT AT A LATER DATE?
GET... OUT!!!

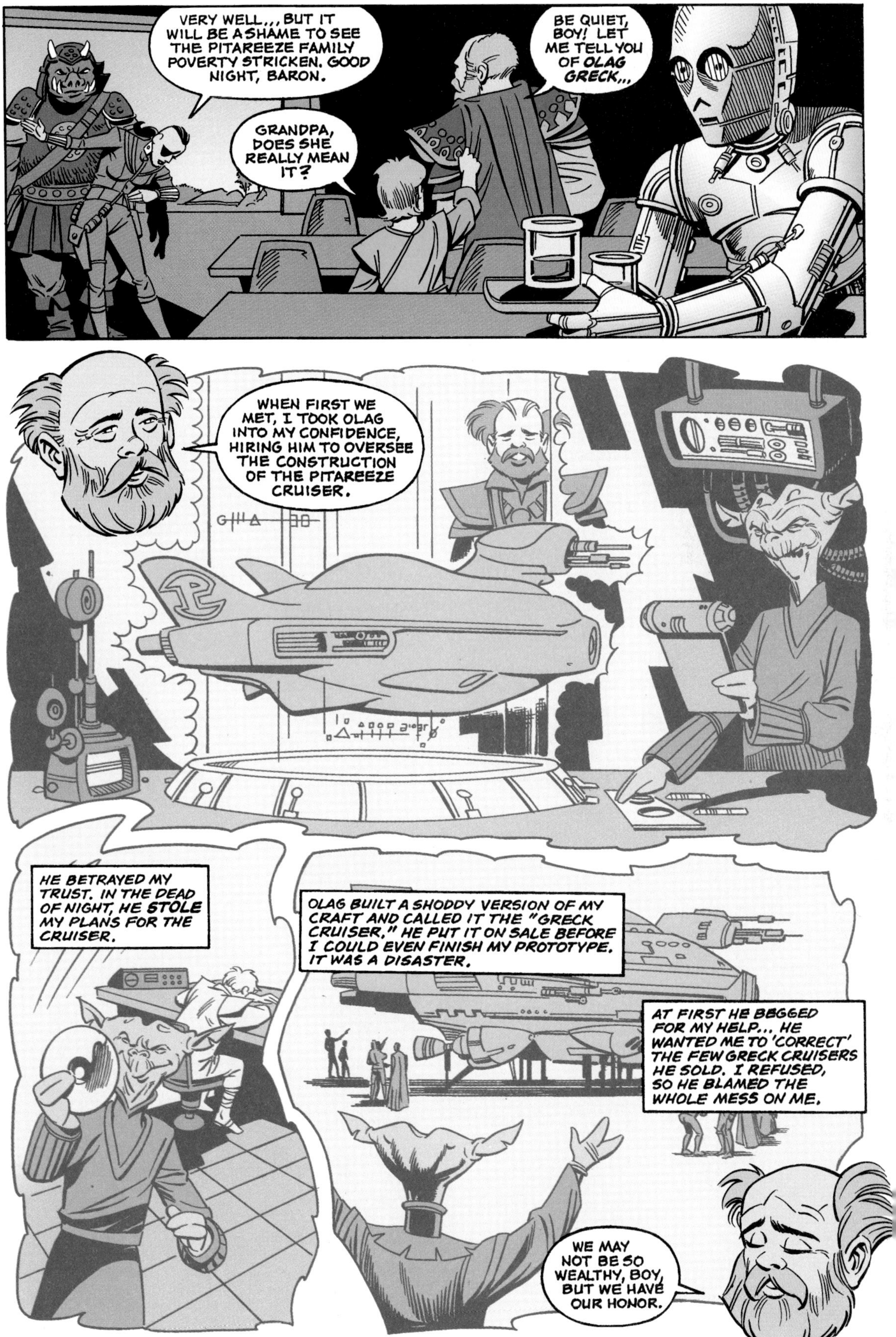
VERY WELL,,, BUT IT WILL BE A SHAME TO SEE THE PITAREEZE FAMILY POVERTY STRICKEN. GOOD NIGHT, BARON.
GRANDPA, DOES SHE REALLY MEAN IT?
BE QUIET, BOY! LET ME TELL YOU OF OLAG GRECK,,,
WHEN FIRST WE MET, I TOOK OLAG INTO MY CONFIDENCE, HIRING HIM TO OVERSEE THE CONSTRUCTION OF THE PITAREEZE CRUISER.
HE BETRAYED MY TRUST. IN THE DEAD OF NIGHT, HE STOLE MY PLANS FOR THE CRUISER.
OLAG BUILT A SHODDY VERSION OF MY CRAFT AND CALLED IT THE "GRECK CRUISER," HE PUT IT ON SALE BEFORE I COULD EVEN FINISH MY PROTOTYPE. IT WAS A DISASTER.
AT FIRST HE BEGGED FOR MY HELP... HE WANTED ME TO 'CORRECT' THE FEW GRECK CRUISERS HE SOLD. I REFUSED, SO HE BLAMED THE WHOLE MESS ON ME.
WE MAY NOT BE SO WEALTHY, BOY, BUT WE HAVE OUR HONOR.

GOOD MORNING, COUNCILMAN TORBA! WELCOME TO HOSK STATION!

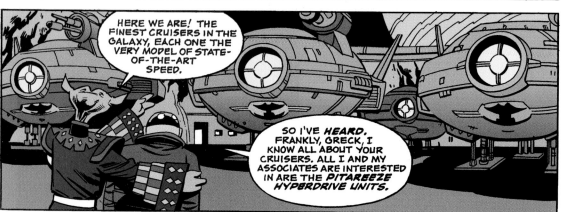

HERE WE ARE! THE FINEST CRUISERS IN THE GALAXY, EACH ONE THE VERY MODEL OF STATE-OF-THE-ART SPEED.

SO I'VE *HEARD.* FRANKLY, GRECK, I KNOW ALL ABOUT YOUR CRUISERS. ALL I AND MY ASSOCIATES ARE INTERESTED IN ARE THE *PITAREEZE HYPERDRIVE UNITS.*

INDEED! WELL, THE UNITS IN THESE SHIPS ARE BASED ON MODIFIED *PITAREEZE INC.* DESIGNS--

HMPH! MY ASSOCIATES ARE ONLY INTER-ESTED IN THE PITAREEZE *MT-5* UNIT.

WE CANNOT DEAL DIRECTLY WITH THE BARON-- HE REFUSES TO LET HIS DESIGNS BE USED FOR *MILITARY APPLICATIONS.*

WE WANT THAT UNIT, OLAG-- ACQUIRE IT FOR US AND PERHAPS WE WILL CONTINUE TO OVERLOOK CERTAIN *DISCREPANCIES* IN THIS STATION.

I SHALL, COUNCIL-MAN!

MY LIMITED EXPERIENCE ON THIS STATION WAS NOT AT ALL ENJOY-ABLE, MASTER NAK! CAN I *PLEASE* TAKE YOU HOME?

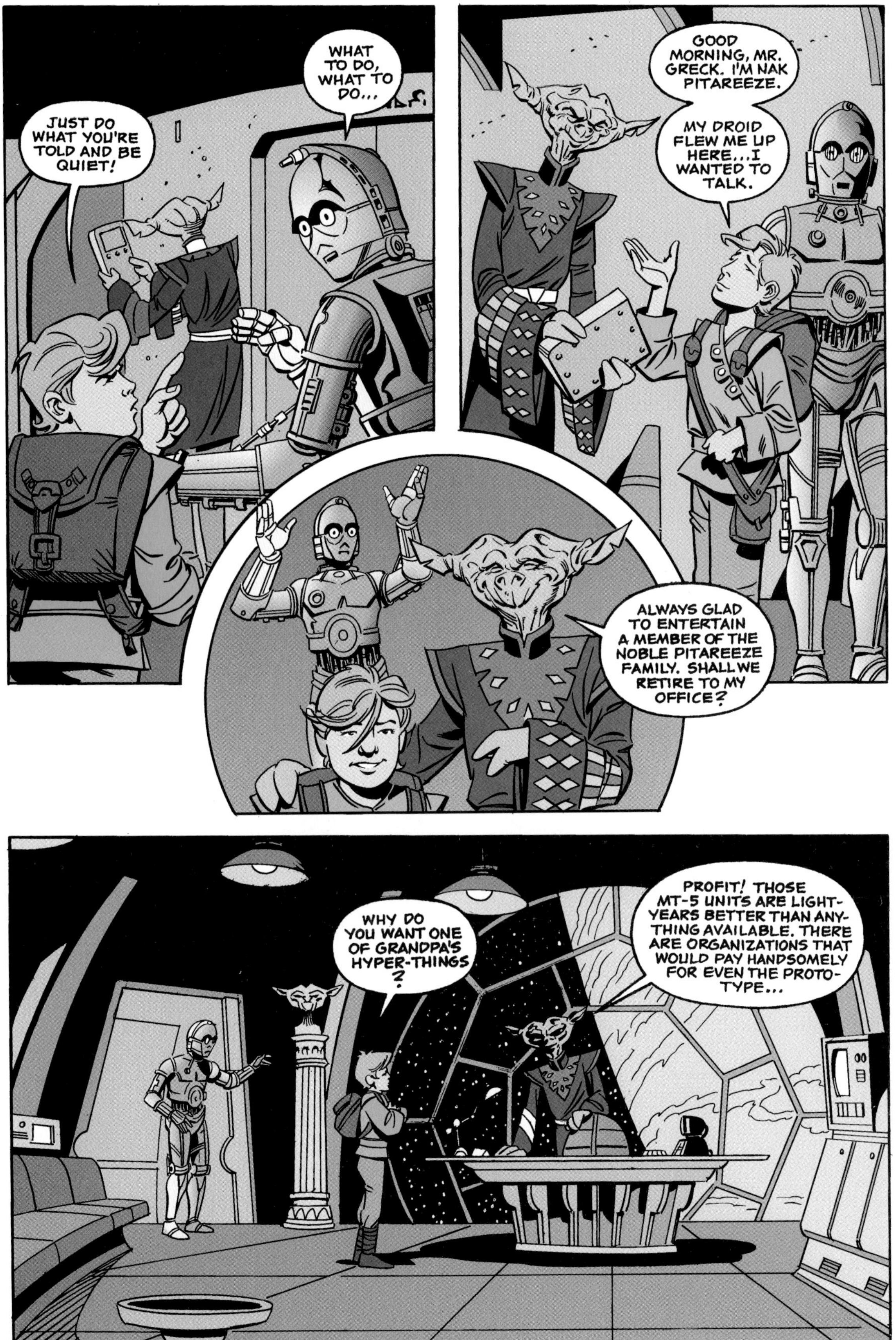
WHAT TO DO, WHAT TO DO...
JUST DO WHAT YOU'RE TOLD AND BE QUIET!
GOOD MORNING, MR. GRECK. I'M NAK PITAREEZE.
MY DROID FLEW ME UP HERE...I WANTED TO TALK.
ALWAYS GLAD TO ENTERTAIN A MEMBER OF THE NOBLE PITAREEZE FAMILY. SHALL WE RETIRE TO MY OFFICE?
WHY DO YOU WANT ONE OF GRANDPA'S HYPER-THINGS?
PROFIT! THOSE MT-5 UNITS ARE LIGHT-YEARS BETTER THAN ANYTHING AVAILABLE. THERE ARE ORGANIZATIONS THAT WOULD PAY HANDSOMELY FOR EVEN THE PROTOTYPE...

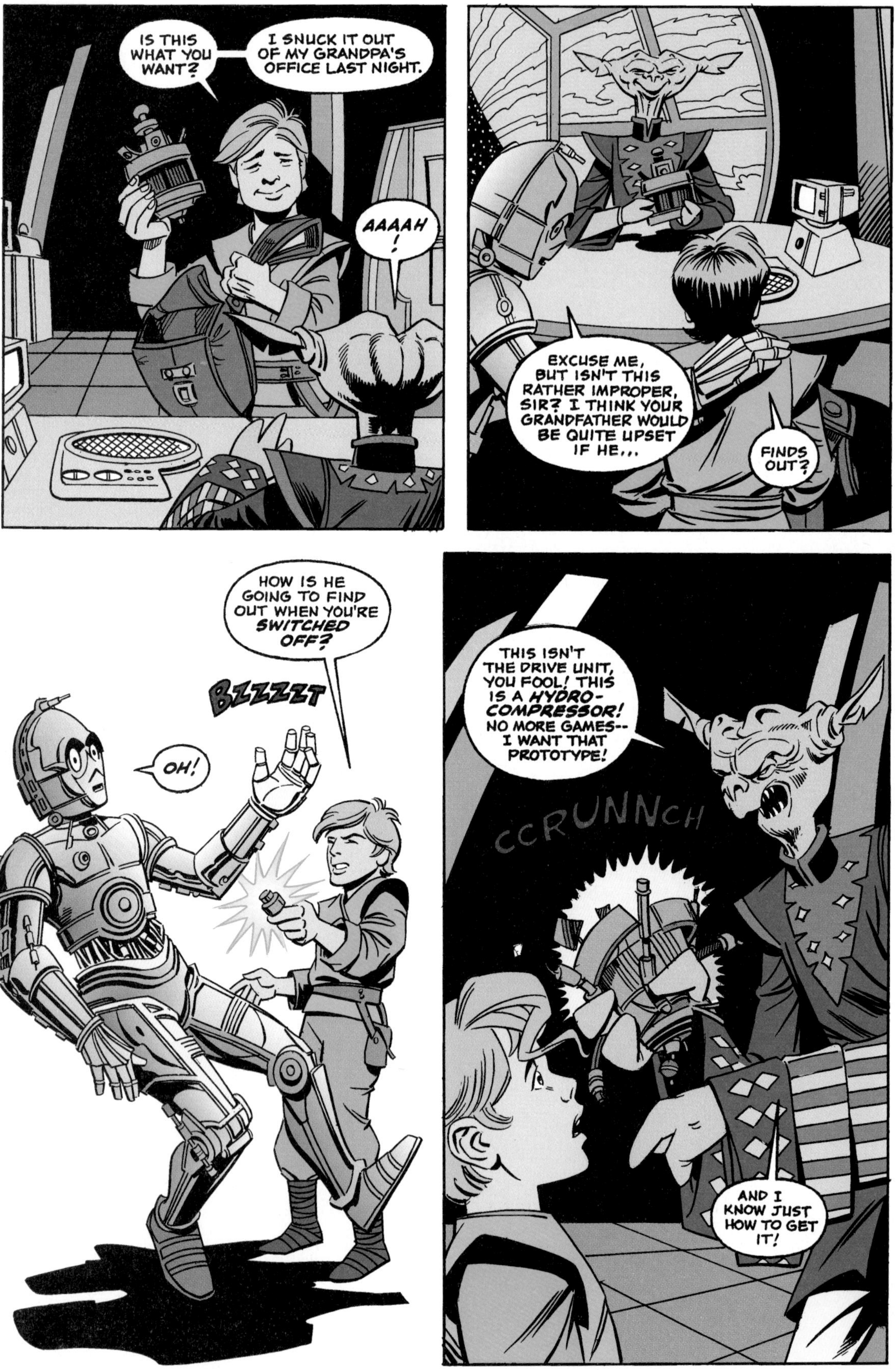
IS THIS WHAT YOU WANT?
I SNUCK IT OUT OF MY GRANDPA'S OFFICE LAST NIGHT.
AAAAH!
EXCUSE ME, BUT ISN'T THIS RATHER IMPROPER, SIR? I THINK YOUR GRANDFATHER WOULD BE QUITE UPSET IF HE...
FINDS OUT?
HOW IS HE GOING TO FIND OUT WHEN YOU'RE SWITCHED OFF?
BZZZZT
OH!
THIS ISN'T THE DRIVE UNIT, YOU FOOL! THIS IS A HYDRO-COMPRESSOR! NO MORE GAMES-- I WANT THAT PROTOTYPE!
CCRUNNCH
AND I KNOW JUST HOW TO GET IT!

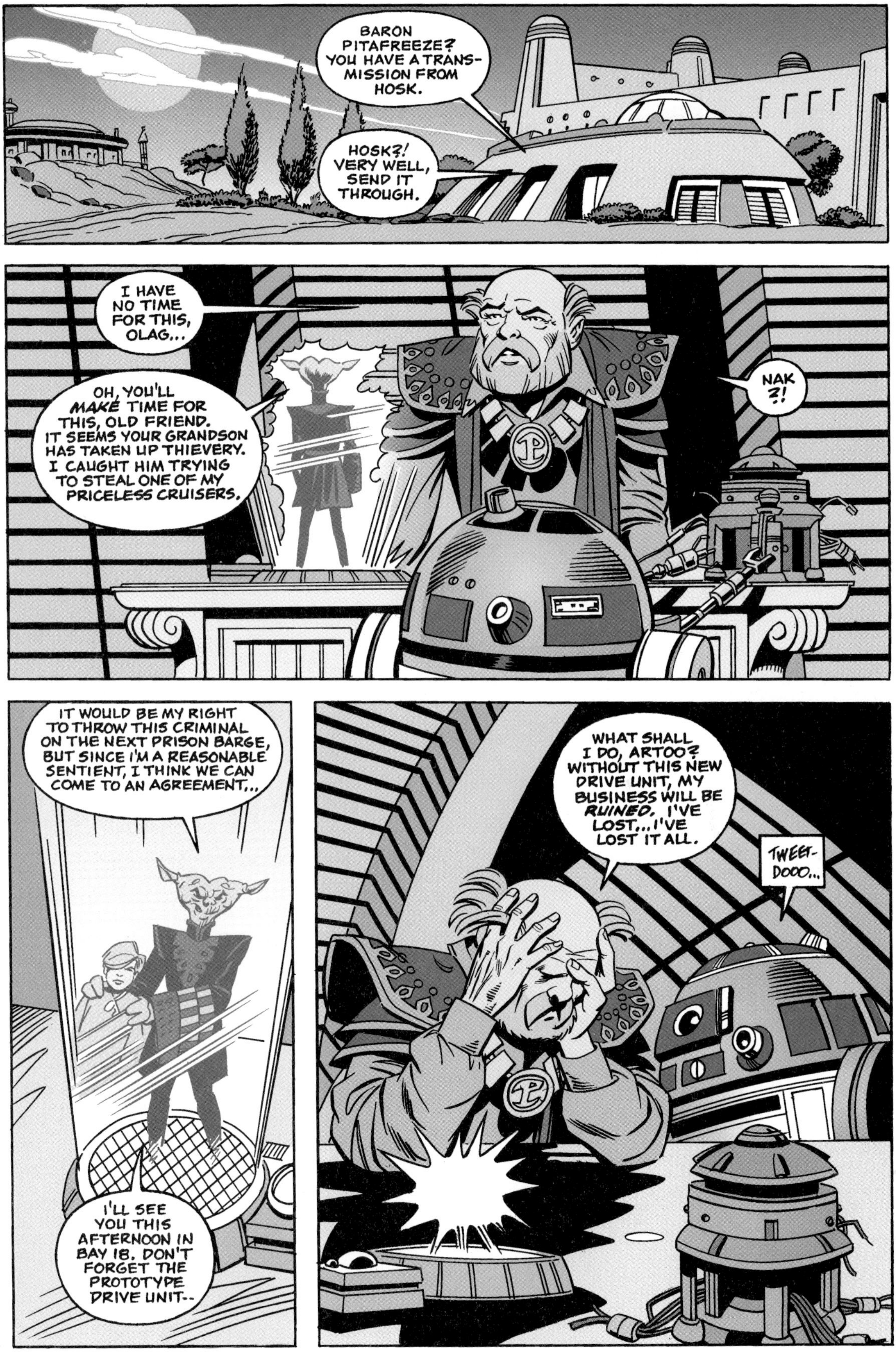
BARON PITAFREEZE? YOU HAVE A TRANSMISSION FROM HOSK.
HOSK?! VERY WELL, SEND IT THROUGH.
I HAVE NO TIME FOR THIS, OLAG...
OH, YOU'LL *MAKE* TIME FOR THIS, OLD FRIEND. IT SEEMS YOUR GRANDSON HAS TAKEN UP THIEVERY. I CAUGHT HIM TRYING TO STEAL ONE OF MY PRICELESS CRUISERS.
NAK ?!
IT WOULD BE MY RIGHT TO THROW THIS CRIMINAL ON THE NEXT PRISON BARGE, BUT SINCE I'M A REASONABLE SENTIENT, I THINK WE CAN COME TO AN AGREEMENT...
I'LL SEE YOU THIS AFTERNOON IN BAY 18. DON'T FORGET THE PROTOTYPE DRIVE UNIT..
WHAT SHALL I DO, ARTOO? WITHOUT THIS NEW DRIVE UNIT, MY BUSINESS WILL BE *RUINED.* I'VE LOST... I'VE LOST IT ALL.
TWEET-DOOO...

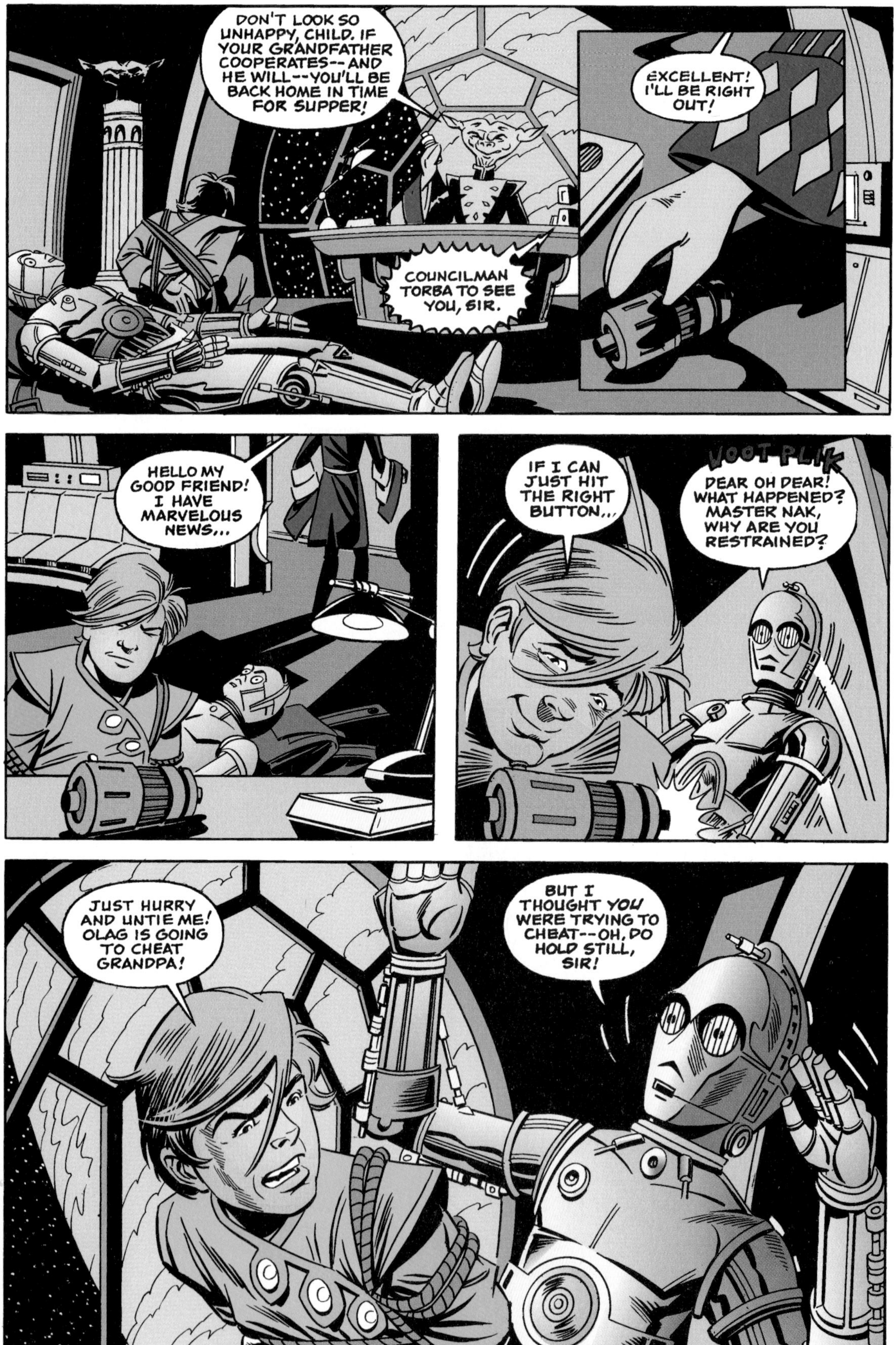
DON'T LOOK SO UNHAPPY, CHILD. IF YOUR GRANDFATHER COOPERATES-- AND HE WILL--YOU'LL BE BACK HOME IN TIME FOR SUPPER!
COUNCILMAN TORBA TO SEE YOU, SIR.
EXCELLENT! I'LL BE RIGHT OUT!
HELLO MY GOOD FRIEND! I HAVE MARVELOUS NEWS...
IF I CAN JUST HIT THE RIGHT BUTTON...
VOOT PLIK
DEAR OH DEAR! WHAT HAPPENED? MASTER NAK, WHY ARE YOU RESTRAINED?
JUST HURRY AND UNTIE ME! OLAG IS GOING TO CHEAT GRANDPA!
BUT I THOUGHT YOU WERE TRYING TO CHEAT--OH, DO HOLD STILL, SIR!

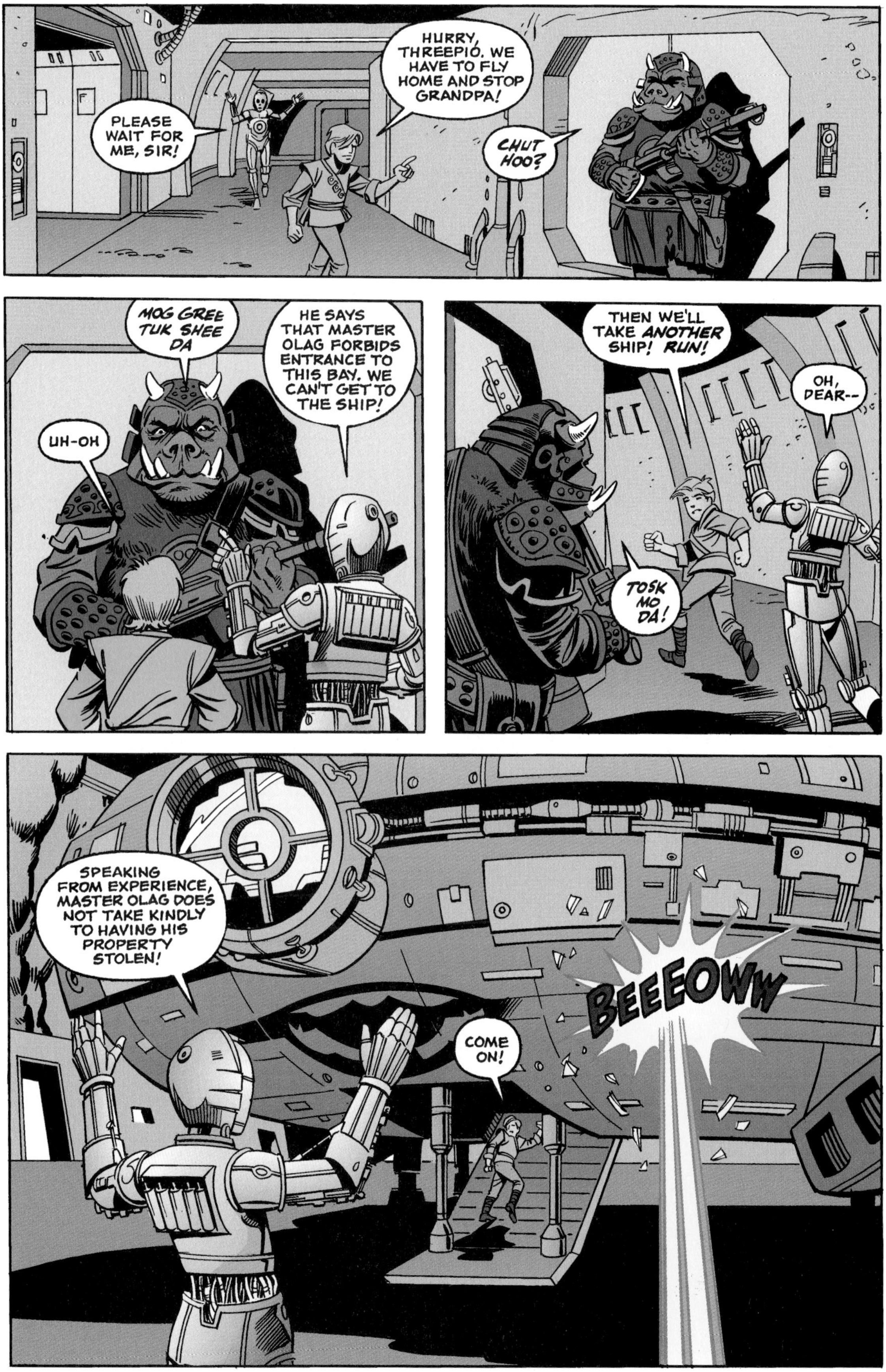
PLEASE WAIT FOR ME, SIR!
HURRY, THREEPIO. WE HAVE TO FLY HOME AND STOP GRANDPA!
CHUT HOO?
MOG GREE TUK SHEE DA
UH-OH
HE SAYS THAT MASTER OLAG FORBIDS ENTRANCE TO THIS BAY. WE CAN'T GET TO THE SHIP!
THEN WE'LL TAKE ANOTHER SHIP! RUN!
OH, DEAR--
TOSK MO DA!
SPEAKING FROM EXPERIENCE, MASTER OLAG DOES NOT TAKE KINDLY TO HAVING HIS PROPERTY STOLEN!
COME ON!
BEEEOWW

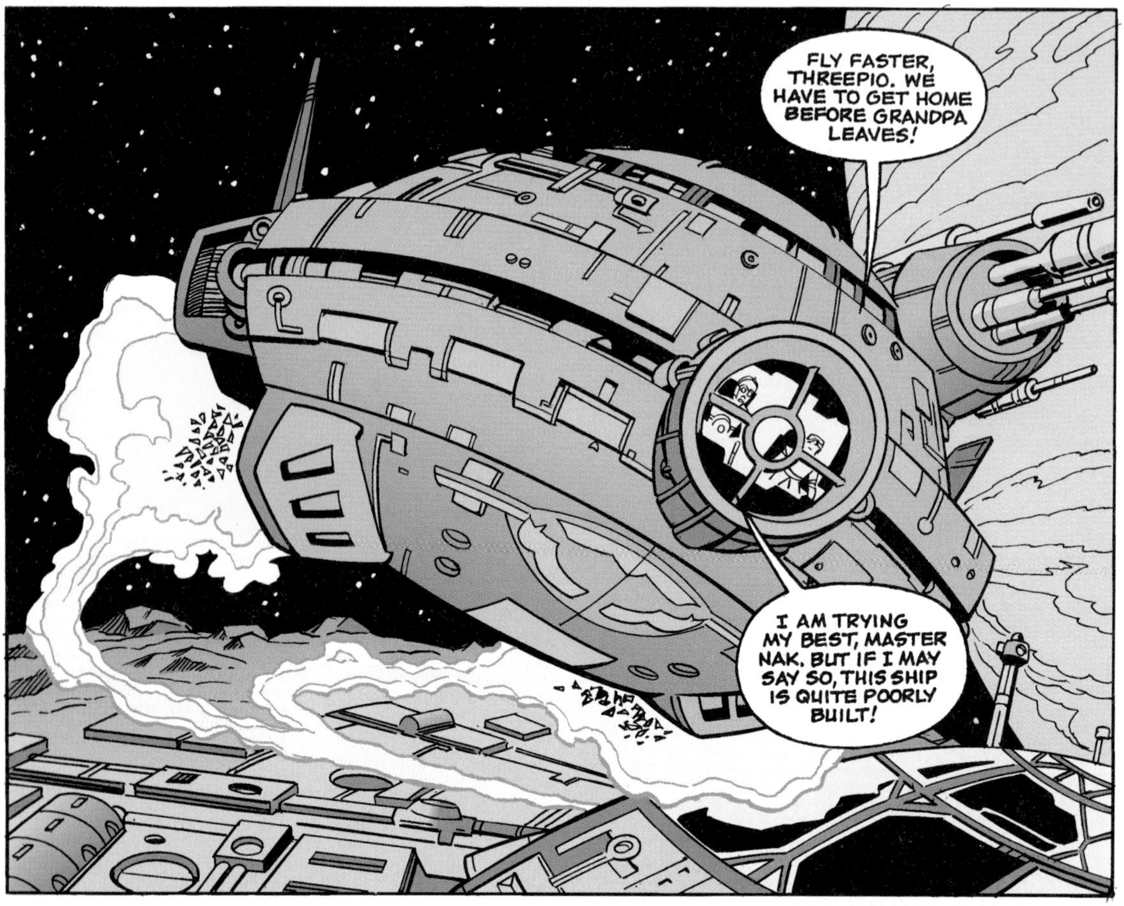
FLY FASTER, THREEPIO. WE HAVE TO GET HOME BEFORE GRANDPA LEAVES!
I AM TRYING MY BEST, MASTER NAK. BUT IF I MAY SAY SO, THIS SHIP IS QUITE POORLY BUILT!

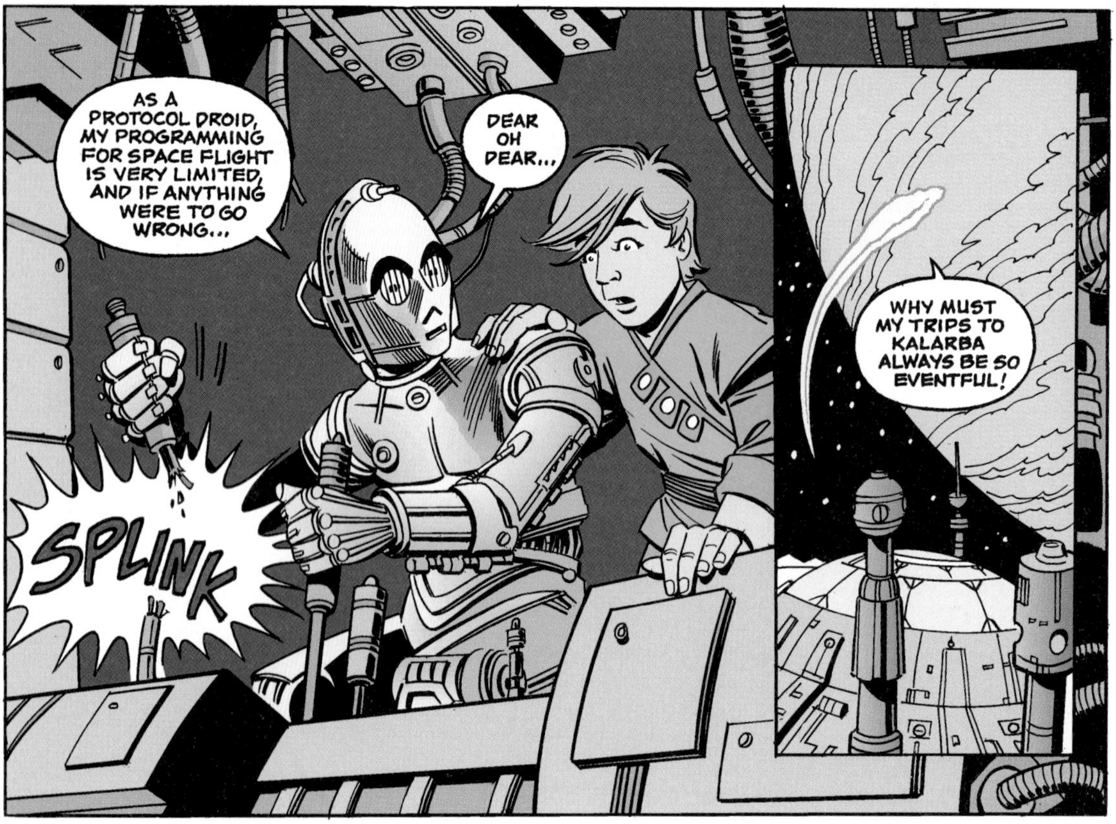
AS A PROTOCOL DROID, MY PROGRAMMING FOR SPACE FLIGHT IS VERY LIMITED, AND IF ANYTHING WERE TO GO WRONG...
DEAR OH DEAR...
SPLINK
WHY MUST MY TRIPS TO KALARBA ALWAYS BE SO EVENTFUL!

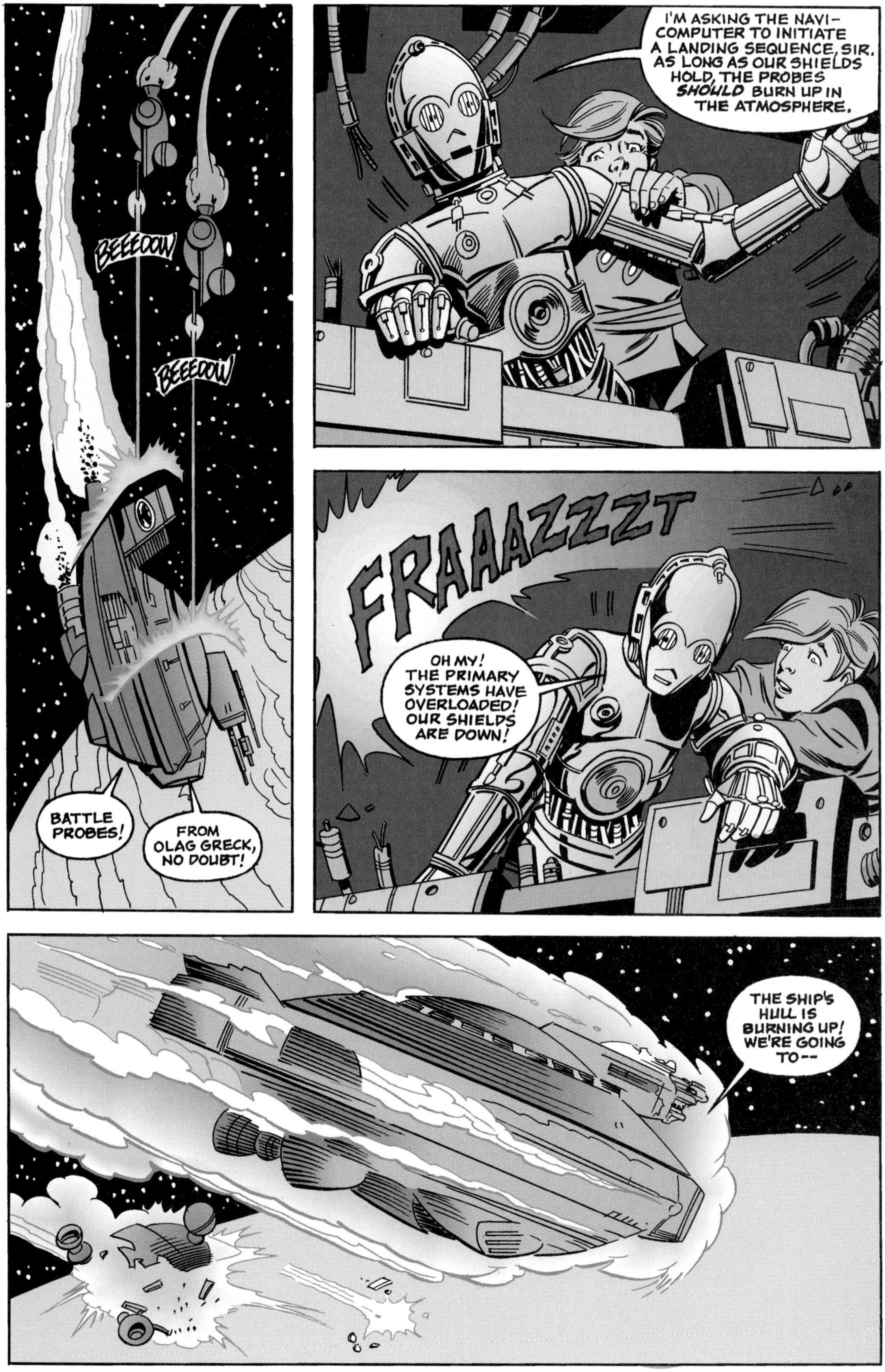
BEEEOOW
BEEEOOW
BATTLE PROBES!
FROM OLAG GRECK, NO DOUBT!
I'M ASKING THE NAVI-COMPUTER TO INITIATE A LANDING SEQUENCE, SIR. AS LONG AS OUR SHIELDS HOLD, THE PROBES SHOULD BURN UP IN THE ATMOSPHERE.
FRAAAZZZT
OH MY! THE PRIMARY SYSTEMS HAVE OVERLOADED! OUR SHIELDS ARE DOWN!
THE SHIP'S HULL IS BURNING UP! WE'RE GOING TO--

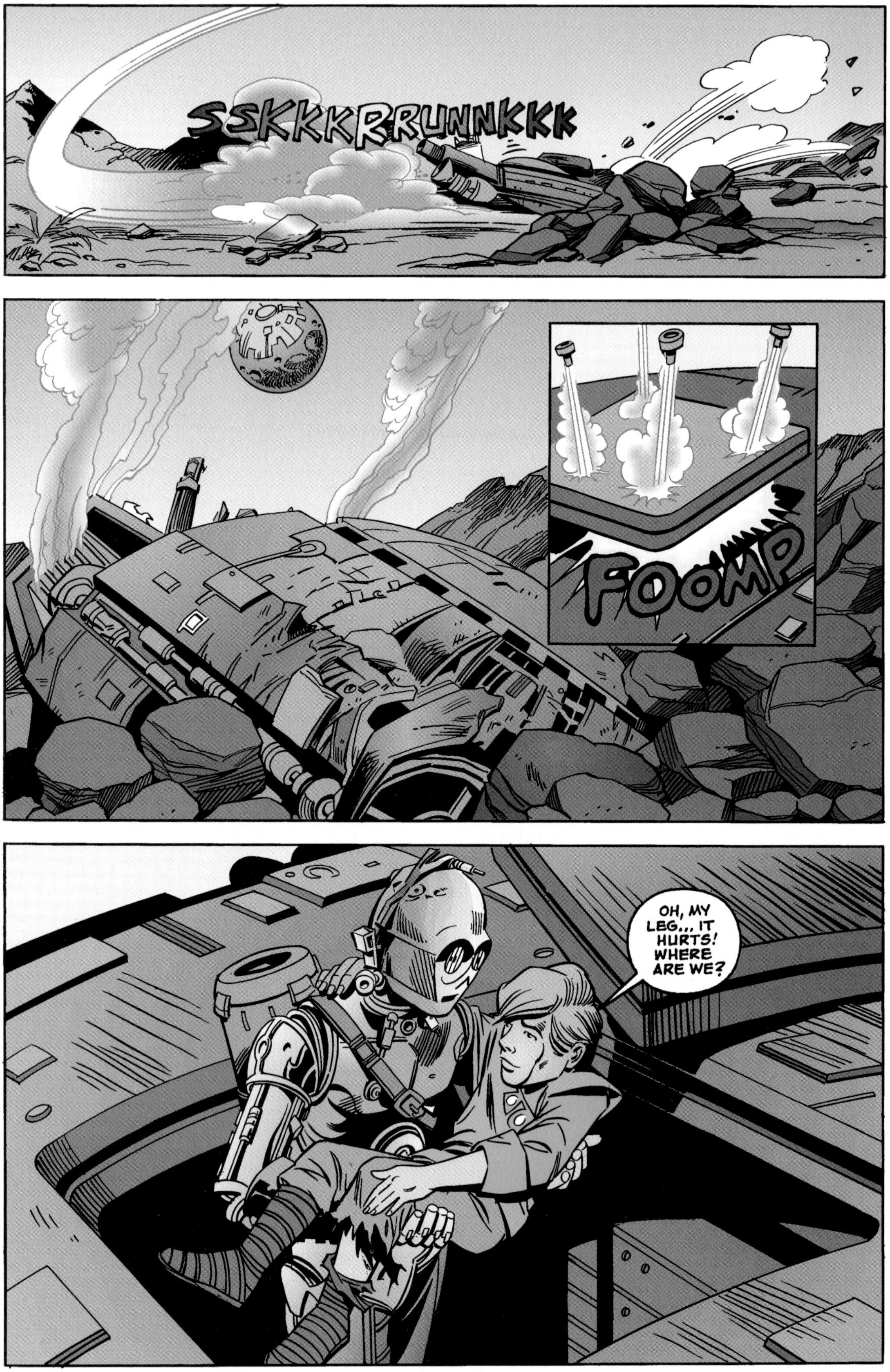
SSKKKRRUNNKKK
FOOMP
OH, MY LEG... IT HURTS! WHERE ARE WE?

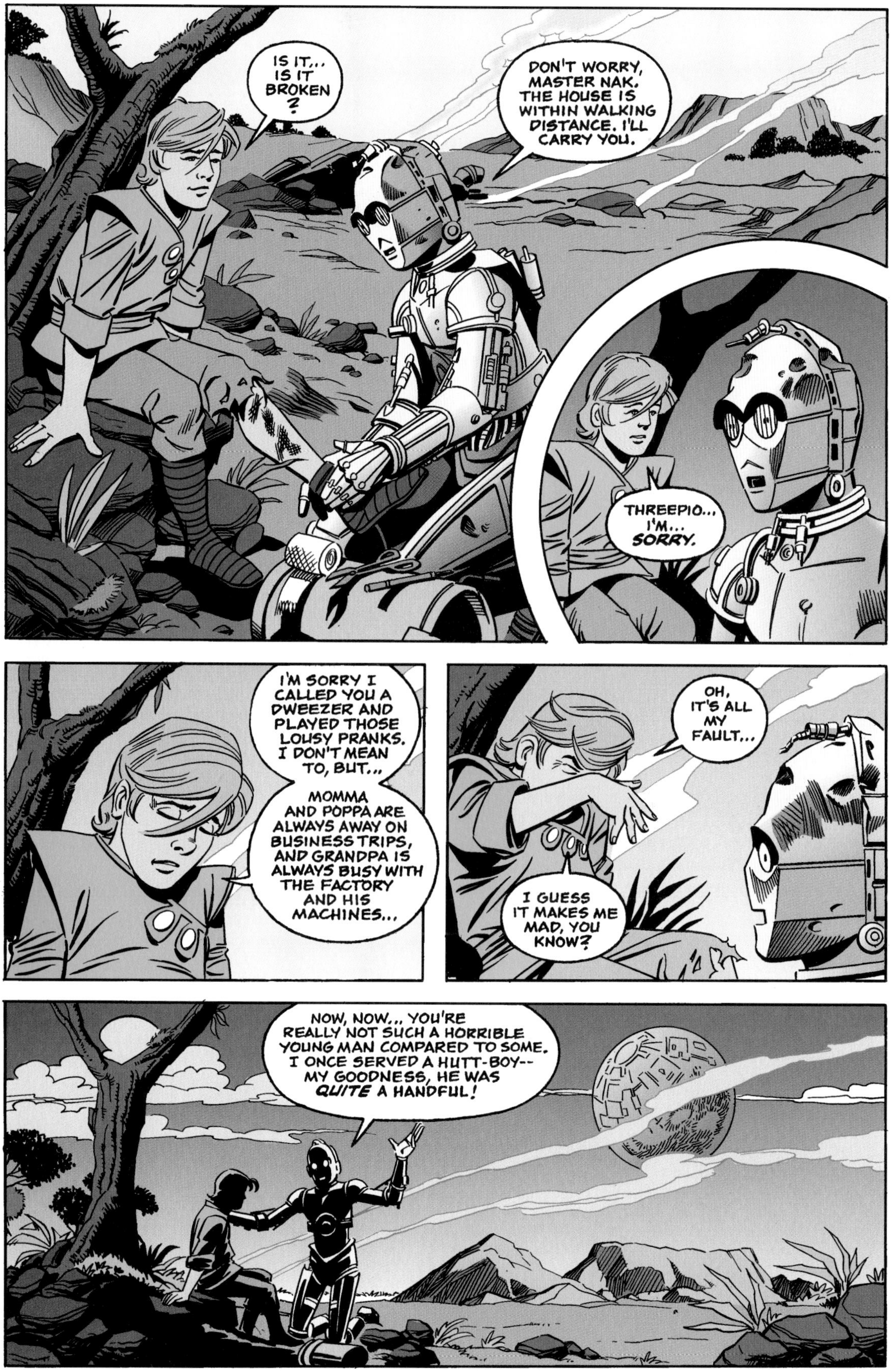
IS IT... IS IT BROKEN?
DON'T WORRY, MASTER NAK. THE HOUSE IS WITHIN WALKING DISTANCE. I'LL CARRY YOU.
THREEPIO... I'M... SORRY.
I'M SORRY I CALLED YOU A DWEEZER AND PLAYED THOSE LOUSY PRANKS. I DON'T MEAN TO, BUT...
MOMMA AND POPPA ARE ALWAYS AWAY ON BUSINESS TRIPS, AND GRANDPA IS ALWAYS BUSY WITH THE FACTORY AND HIS MACHINES...
OH, IT'S ALL MY FAULT...
I GUESS IT MAKES ME MAD, YOU KNOW?
NOW, NOW... YOU'RE REALLY NOT SUCH A HORRIBLE YOUNG MAN COMPARED TO SOME. I ONCE SERVED A HUTT-BOY-- MY GOODNESS, HE WAS QUITE A HANDFUL!

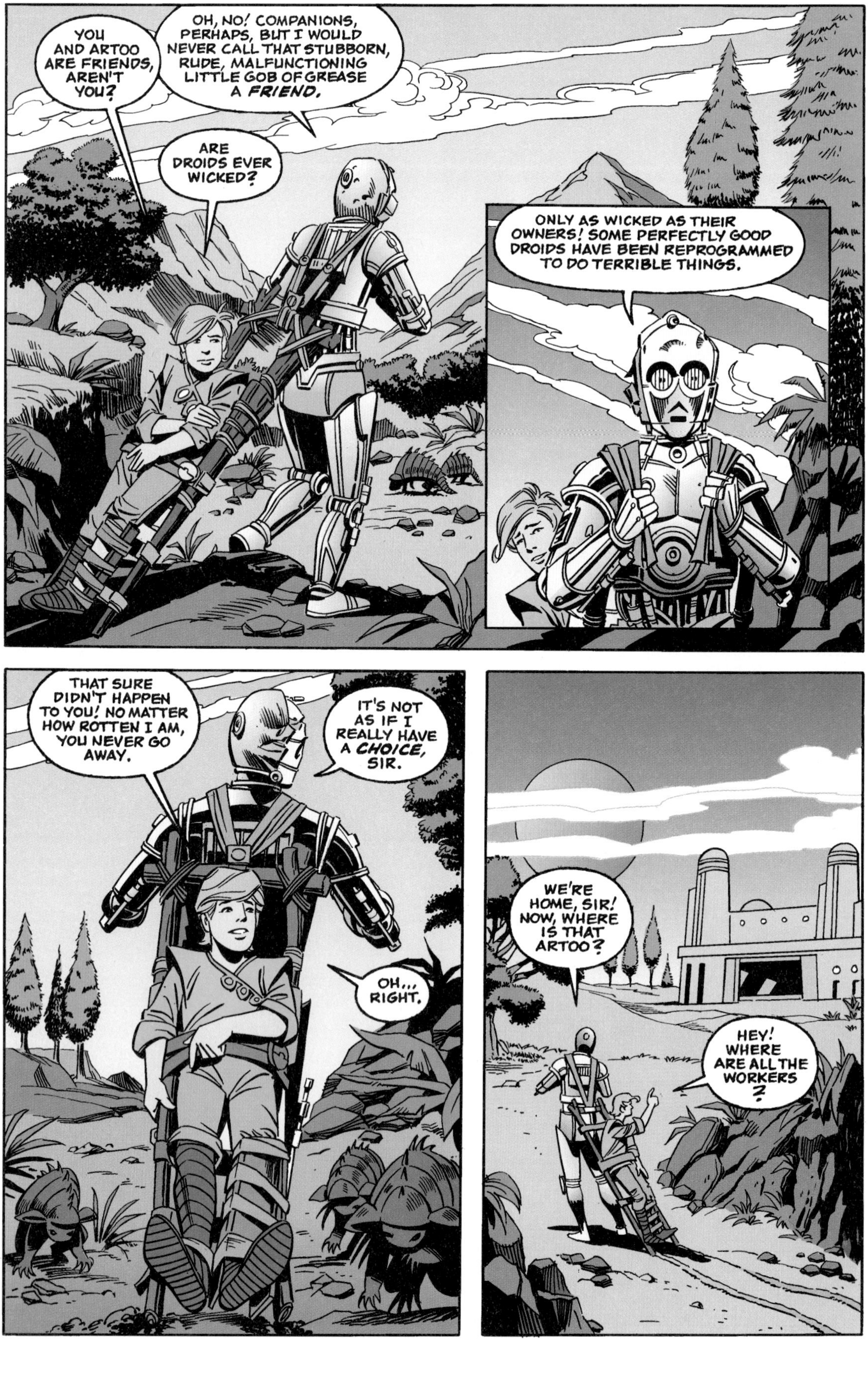

YOU AND ARTOO ARE FRIENDS, AREN'T YOU?
OH, NO! COMPANIONS, PERHAPS, BUT I WOULD NEVER CALL THAT STUBBORN, RUDE, MALFUNCTIONING LITTLE GOB OF GREASE A FRIEND.
ARE DROIDS EVER WICKED?
ONLY AS WICKED AS THEIR OWNERS! SOME PERFECTLY GOOD DROIDS HAVE BEEN REPROGRAMMED TO DO TERRIBLE THINGS.
THAT SURE DIDN'T HAPPEN TO YOU! NO MATTER HOW ROTTEN I AM, YOU NEVER GO AWAY.
IT'S NOT AS IF I REALLY HAVE A CHOICE, SIR.
OH... RIGHT.
WE'RE HOME, SIR! NOW, WHERE IS THAT ARTOO?
HEY! WHERE ARE ALL THE WORKERS?

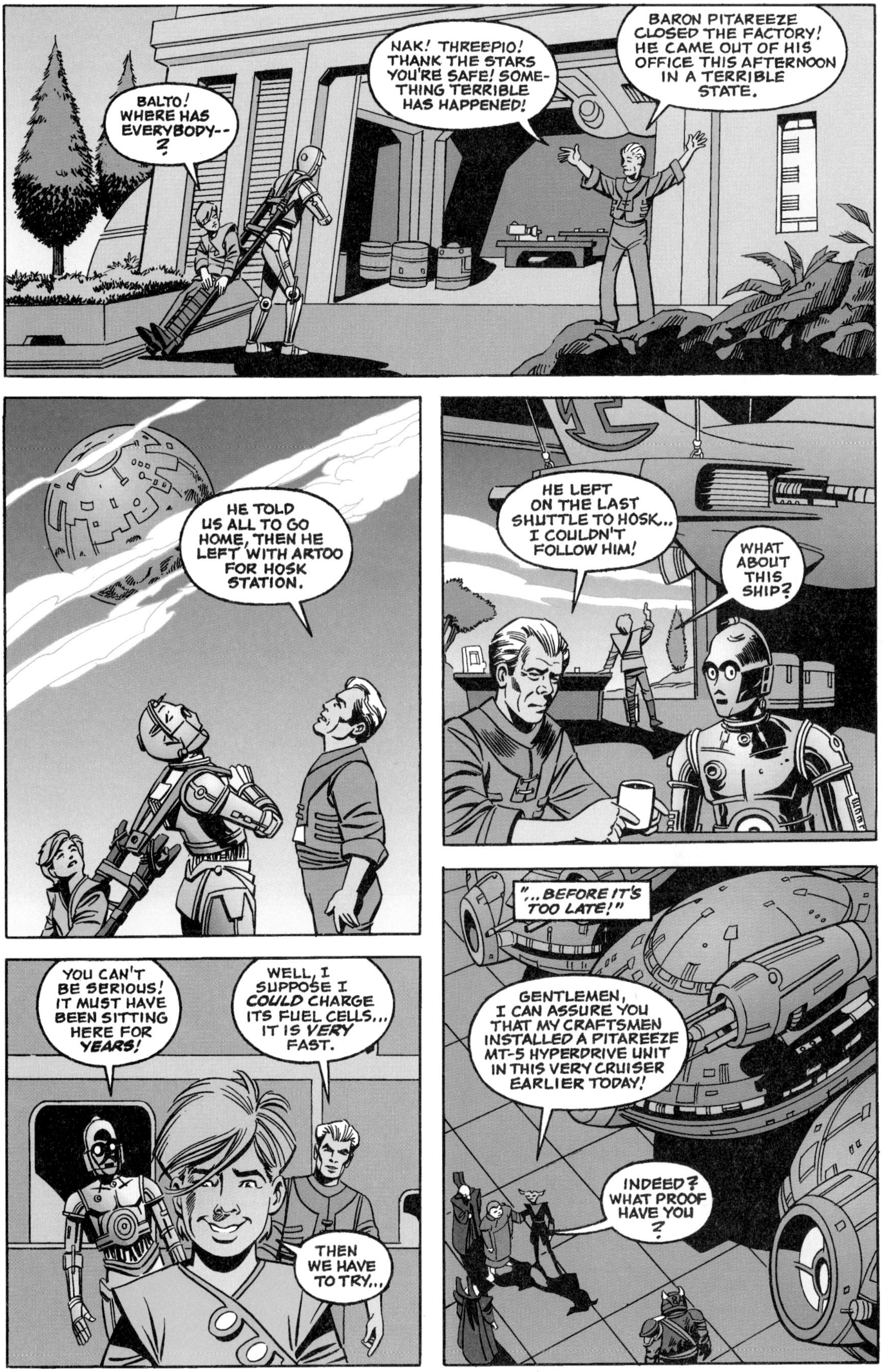
BALTO! WHERE HAS EVERYBODY--?
NAK! THREEPIO! THANK THE STARS YOU'RE SAFE! SOMETHING TERRIBLE HAS HAPPENED!
BARON PITAREEZE CLOSED THE FACTORY! HE CAME OUT OF HIS OFFICE THIS AFTERNOON IN A TERRIBLE STATE.
HE TOLD US ALL TO GO HOME, THEN HE LEFT WITH ARTOO FOR HOSK STATION.
HE LEFT ON THE LAST SHUTTLE TO HOSK... I COULDN'T FOLLOW HIM!
WHAT ABOUT THIS SHIP?
YOU CAN'T BE SERIOUS! IT MUST HAVE BEEN SITTING HERE FOR YEARS!
WELL, I SUPPOSE I COULD CHARGE ITS FUEL CELLS... IT IS VERY FAST.
THEN WE HAVE TO TRY...
"...BEFORE IT'S TOO LATE!"
GENTLEMEN, I CAN ASSURE YOU THAT MY CRAFTSMEN INSTALLED A PITAREEZE MT-5 HYPERDRIVE UNIT IN THIS VERY CRUISER EARLIER TODAY!
INDEED? WHAT PROOF HAVE YOU?

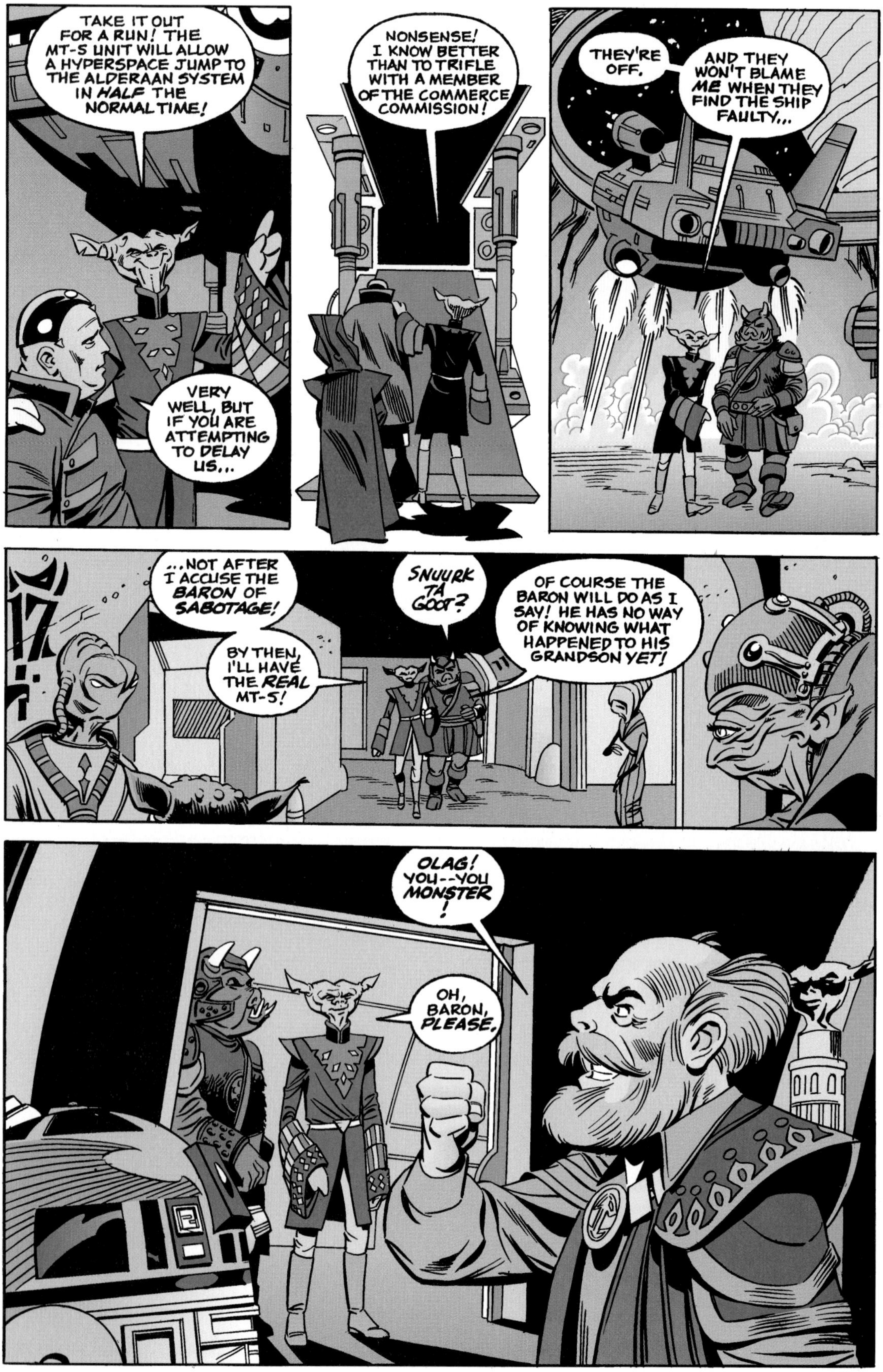
TAKE IT OUT FOR A RUN! THE MT-5 UNIT WILL ALLOW A HYPERSPACE JUMP TO THE ALDERAAN SYSTEM IN HALF THE NORMAL TIME!
VERY WELL, BUT IF YOU ARE ATTEMPTING TO DELAY US...
NONSENSE! I KNOW BETTER THAN TO TRIFLE WITH A MEMBER OF THE COMMERCE COMMISSION!
THEY'RE OFF.
AND THEY WON'T BLAME ME WHEN THEY FIND THE SHIP FAULTY...
...NOT AFTER I ACCUSE THE BARON OF SABOTAGE!
BY THEN, I'LL HAVE THE REAL MT-5!
SNUURK TA GOOT?
OF COURSE THE BARON WILL DO AS I SAY! HE HAS NO WAY OF KNOWING WHAT HAPPENED TO HIS GRANDSON YET!
OLAG! YOU--YOU MONSTER!
OH, BARON, PLEASE.

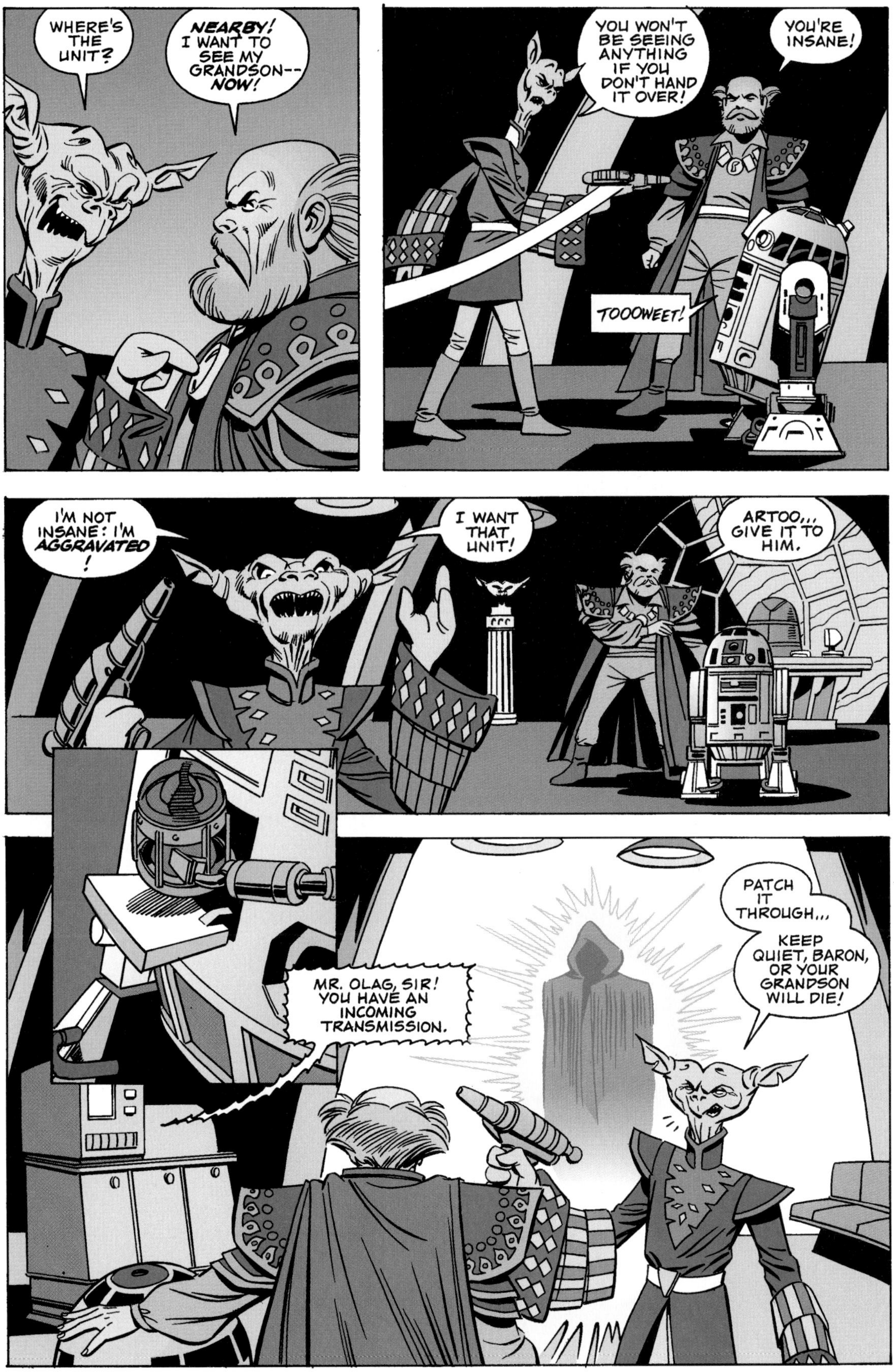
WHERE'S THE UNIT?
NEARBY! I WANT TO SEE MY GRANDSON-- NOW!
YOU WON'T BE SEEING ANYTHING IF YOU DON'T HAND IT OVER!
YOU'RE INSANE!
TOOOWEET!
I'M NOT INSANE: I'M AGGRAVATED!
I WANT THAT UNIT!
ARTOO... GIVE IT TO HIM.
MR. OLAG, SIR! YOU HAVE AN INCOMING TRANSMISSION.
PATCH IT THROUGH...
KEEP QUIET, BARON, OR YOUR GRANDSON WILL DIE!

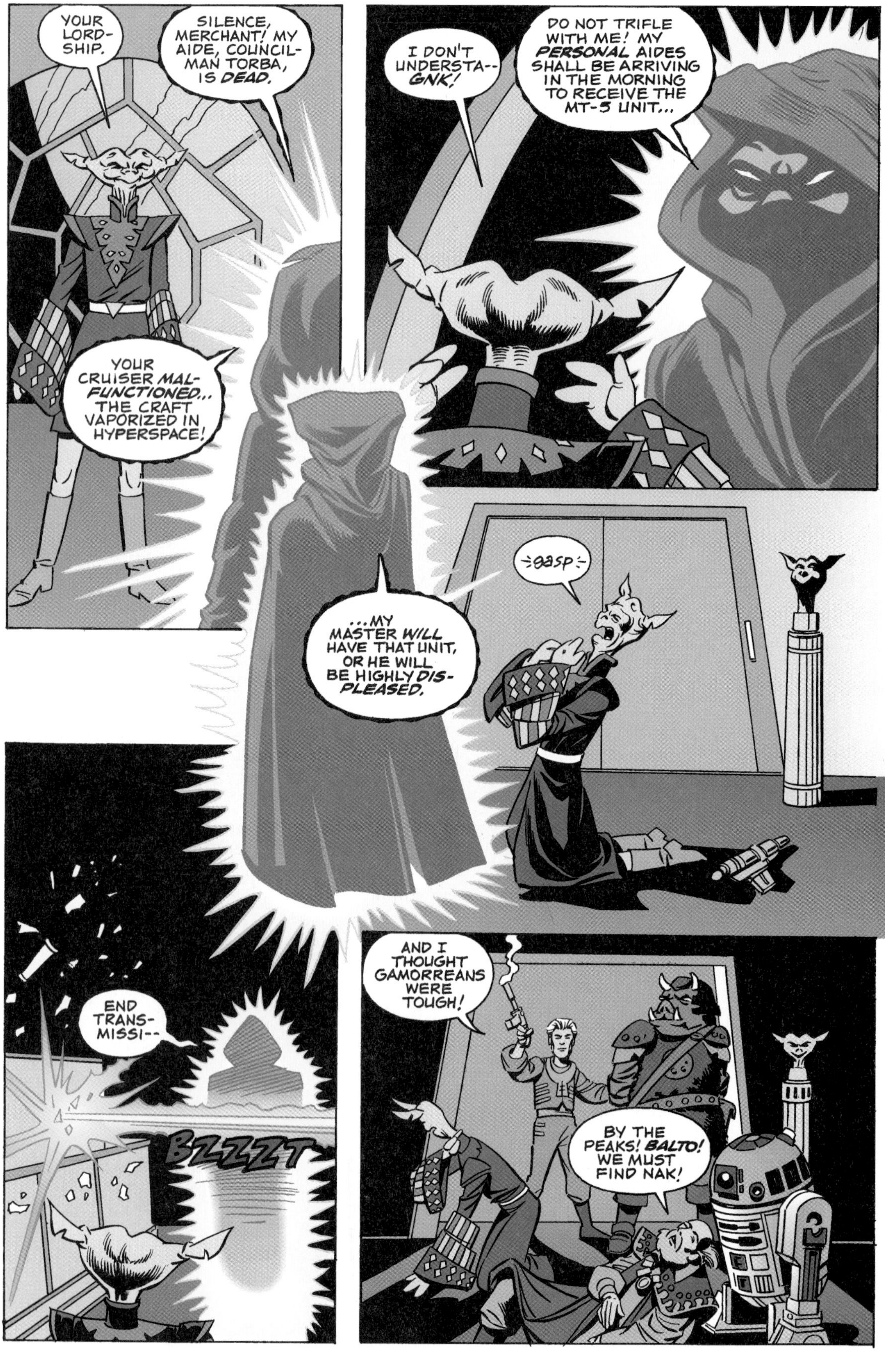
YOUR LORD-SHIP.
SILENCE, MERCHANT! MY AIDE, COUNCIL-MAN TORBA, IS DEAD.
YOUR CRUISER MAL-FUNCTIONED... THE CRAFT VAPORIZED IN HYPERSPACE!
I DON'T UNDERSTA-- GNK!
DO NOT TRIFLE WITH ME! MY PERSONAL AIDES SHALL BE ARRIVING IN THE MORNING TO RECEIVE THE MT-5 UNIT...
...MY MASTER WILL HAVE THAT UNIT, OR HE WILL BE HIGHLY DIS-PLEASED.
-GASP-
END TRANS-MISSI--
BZZZZT
AND I THOUGHT GAMORREANS WERE TOUGH!
BY THE PEAKS! BALTO! WE MUST FIND NAK!

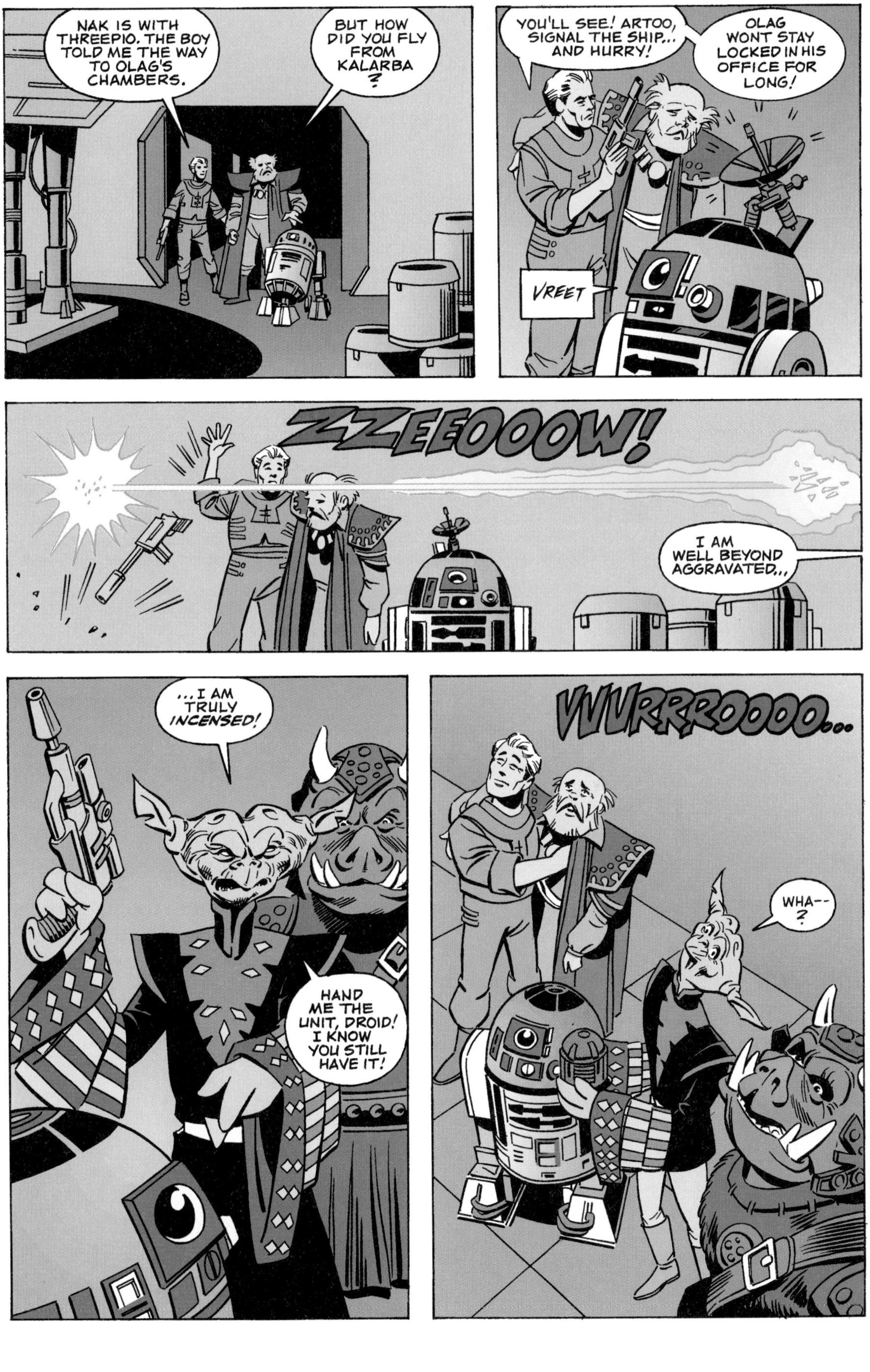
NAK IS WITH THREEPIO. THE BOY TOLD ME THE WAY TO OLAG'S CHAMBERS.
BUT HOW DID YOU FLY FROM KALARBA?
YOU'LL SEE! ARTOO, SIGNAL THE SHIP... AND HURRY!
OLAG WONT STAY LOCKED IN HIS OFFICE FOR LONG!
VREET
ZZEEOOOW!
I AM WELL BEYOND AGGRAVATED...
...I AM TRULY INCENSED!
HAND ME THE UNIT, DROID! I KNOW YOU STILL HAVE IT!
VVURRROOOO...
WHA--?

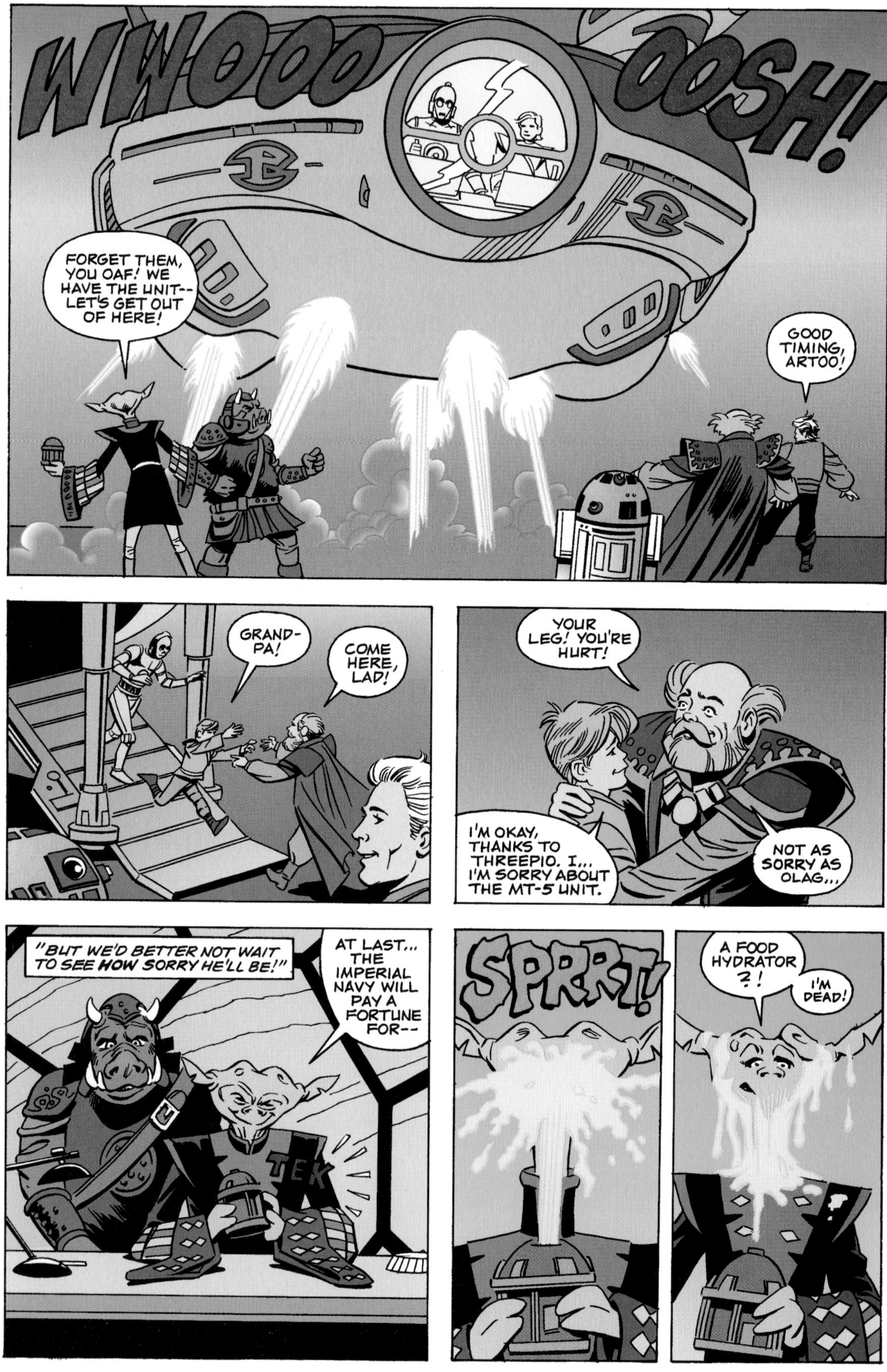
WWOOO OOSH!
FORGET THEM, YOU OAF! WE HAVE THE UNIT-- LET'S GET OUT OF HERE!
GOOD TIMING, ARTOO!
GRAND-PA!
COME HERE, LAD!
YOUR LEG! YOU'RE HURT!
I'M OKAY, THANKS TO THREEPIO. I... I'M SORRY ABOUT THE MT-5 UNIT.
NOT AS SORRY AS OLAG...
"BUT WE'D BETTER NOT WAIT TO SEE HOW SORRY HE'LL BE!"
AT LAST... THE IMPERIAL NAVY WILL PAY A FORTUNE FOR--
TEK
SPRRT!
A FOOD HYDRATOR ?!
I'M DEAD!

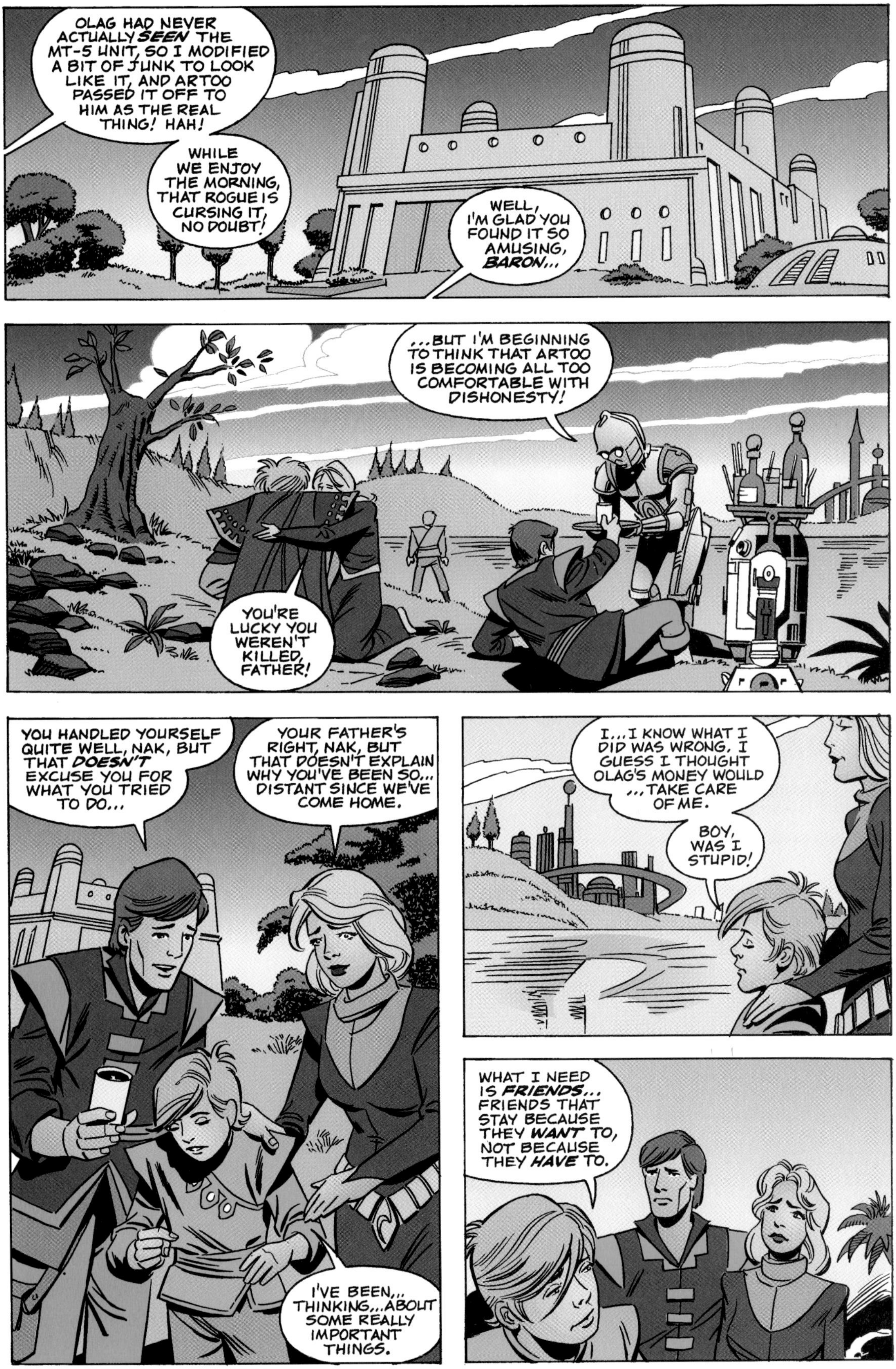
OLAG HAD NEVER ACTUALLY SEEN THE MT-5 UNIT, SO I MODIFIED A BIT OF JUNK TO LOOK LIKE IT, AND ARTOO PASSED IT OFF TO HIM AS THE REAL THING! HAH!
WHILE WE ENJOY THE MORNING, THAT ROGUE IS CURSING IT, NO DOUBT!
WELL, I'M GLAD YOU FOUND IT SO AMUSING, BARON...
...BUT I'M BEGINNING TO THINK THAT ARTOO IS BECOMING ALL TOO COMFORTABLE WITH DISHONESTY!
YOU'RE LUCKY YOU WEREN'T KILLED, FATHER!
YOU HANDLED YOURSELF QUITE WELL, NAK, BUT THAT DOESN'T EXCUSE YOU FOR WHAT YOU TRIED TO DO...
YOUR FATHER'S RIGHT, NAK, BUT THAT DOESN'T EXPLAIN WHY YOU'VE BEEN SO... DISTANT SINCE WE'VE COME HOME.
I'VE BEEN... THINKING... ABOUT SOME REALLY IMPORTANT THINGS.
I...I KNOW WHAT I DID WAS WRONG. I GUESS I THOUGHT OLAG'S MONEY WOULD ...TAKE CARE OF ME.
BOY, WAS I STUPID!
WHAT I NEED IS FRIENDS... FRIENDS THAT STAY BECAUSE THEY WANT TO, NOT BECAUSE THEY HAVE TO.

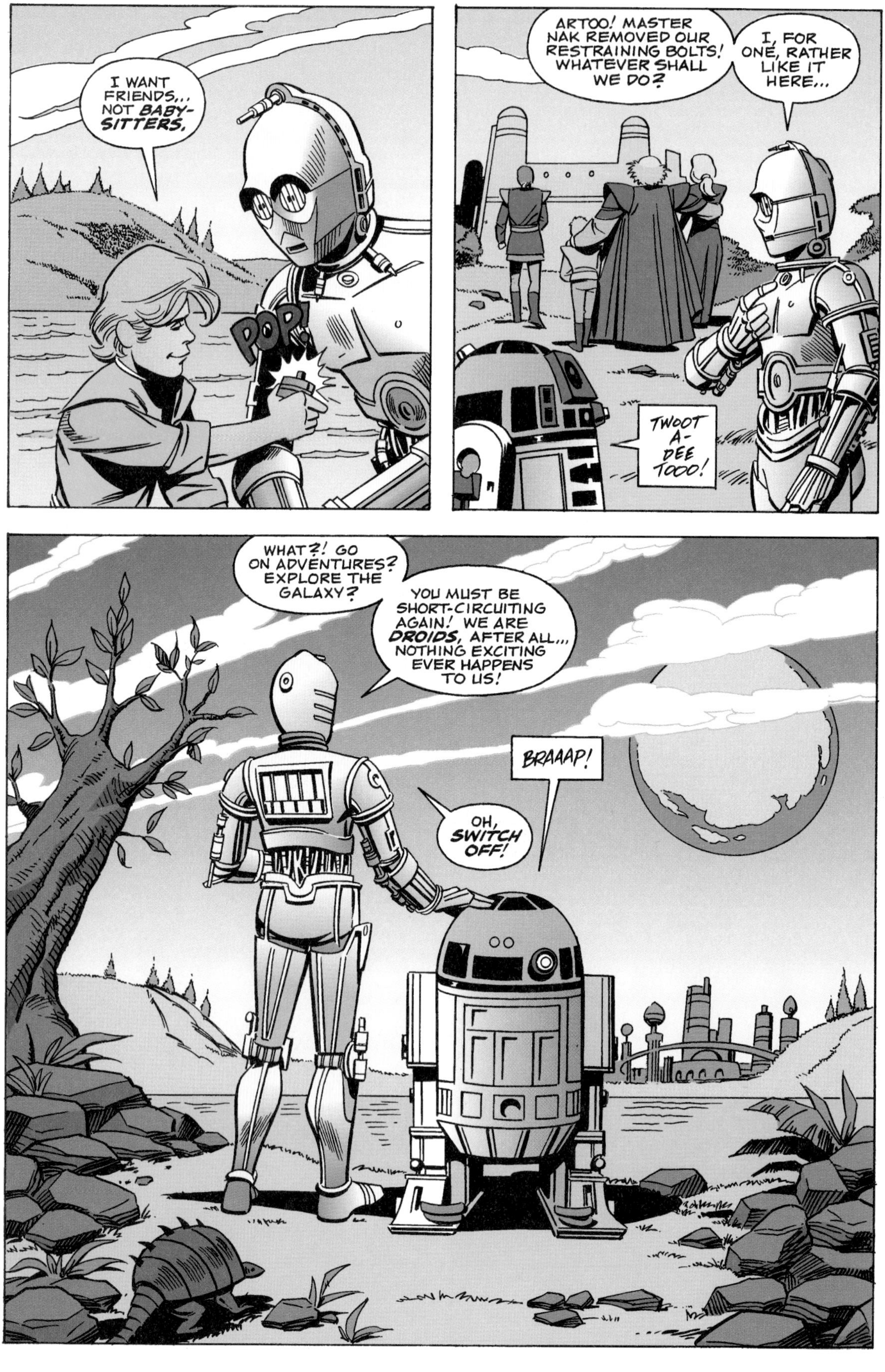
I WANT FRIENDS... NOT *BABY-SITTERS*.
POP!
ARTOO! MASTER NAK REMOVED OUR RESTRAINING BOLTS! WHATEVER SHALL WE DO?
I, FOR ONE, RATHER LIKE IT HERE...
TWOOT A-DEE TOOO!
WHAT?! GO ON ADVENTURES? EXPLORE THE GALAXY?
YOU MUST BE SHORT-CIRCUITING AGAIN! WE ARE *DROIDS*, AFTER ALL... NOTHING EXCITING EVER HAPPENS TO US!
BRAAAP!
OH, *SWITCH OFF!*

The Indobok Pirates
Chapter 3

Script
Dan Thorsland

Pencils
Bill Hughes

Inks
Andy Mushynsky

Colors
Pamela Rambo

Lettering
Steve Dutro

Cover
Kilian Plunkett

Sketch
Kilian Plunkett

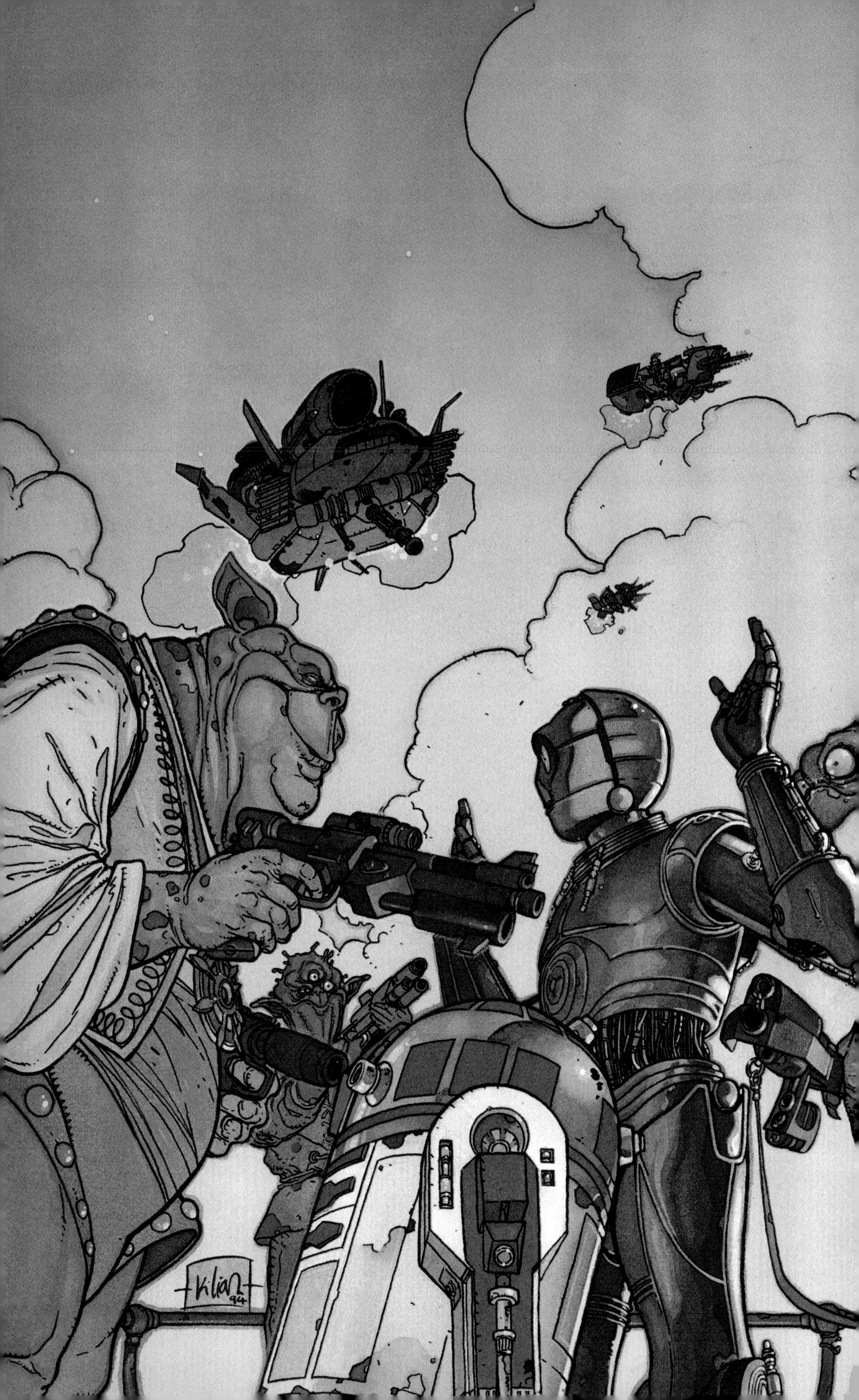
Kilian 94

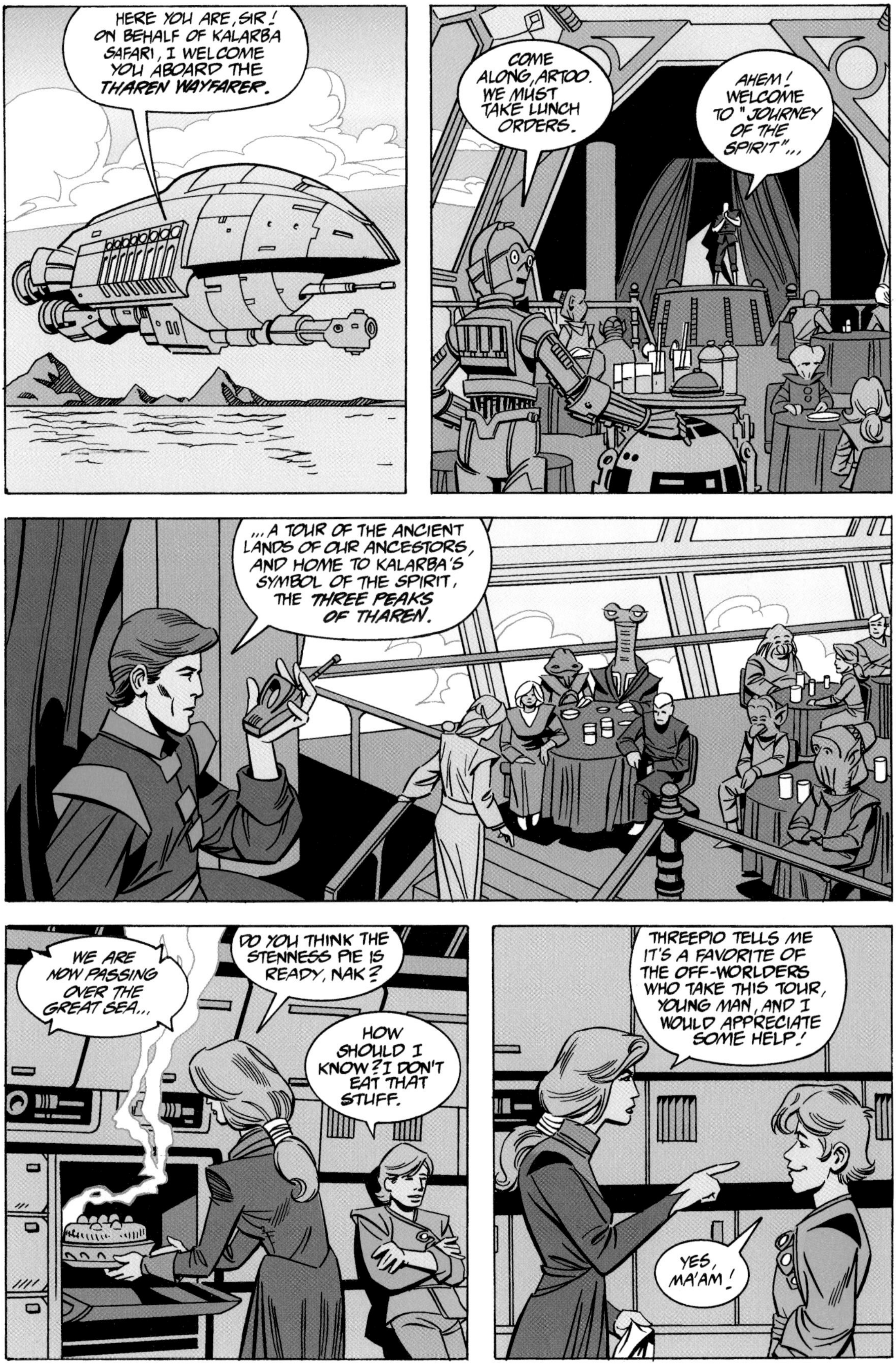
HERE YOU ARE, SIR! ON BEHALF OF KALARBA SAFARI, I WELCOME YOU ABOARD THE *THAREN WAYFARER*.
COME ALONG, ARTOO. WE MUST TAKE LUNCH ORDERS.
AHEM! WELCOME TO "JOURNEY OF THE SPIRIT"...
...A TOUR OF THE ANCIENT LANDS OF OUR ANCESTORS, AND HOME TO KALARBA'S SYMBOL OF THE SPIRIT, THE *THREE PEAKS OF THAREN*.
WE ARE NOW PASSING OVER THE GREAT SEA...
DO YOU THINK THE STENNESS PIE IS READY, NAK?
HOW SHOULD I KNOW? I DON'T EAT THAT STUFF.
THREEPIO TELLS ME IT'S A FAVORITE OF THE OFF-WORLDERS WHO TAKE THIS TOUR, YOUNG MAN, AND I WOULD APPRECIATE SOME HELP!
YES, MA'AM!

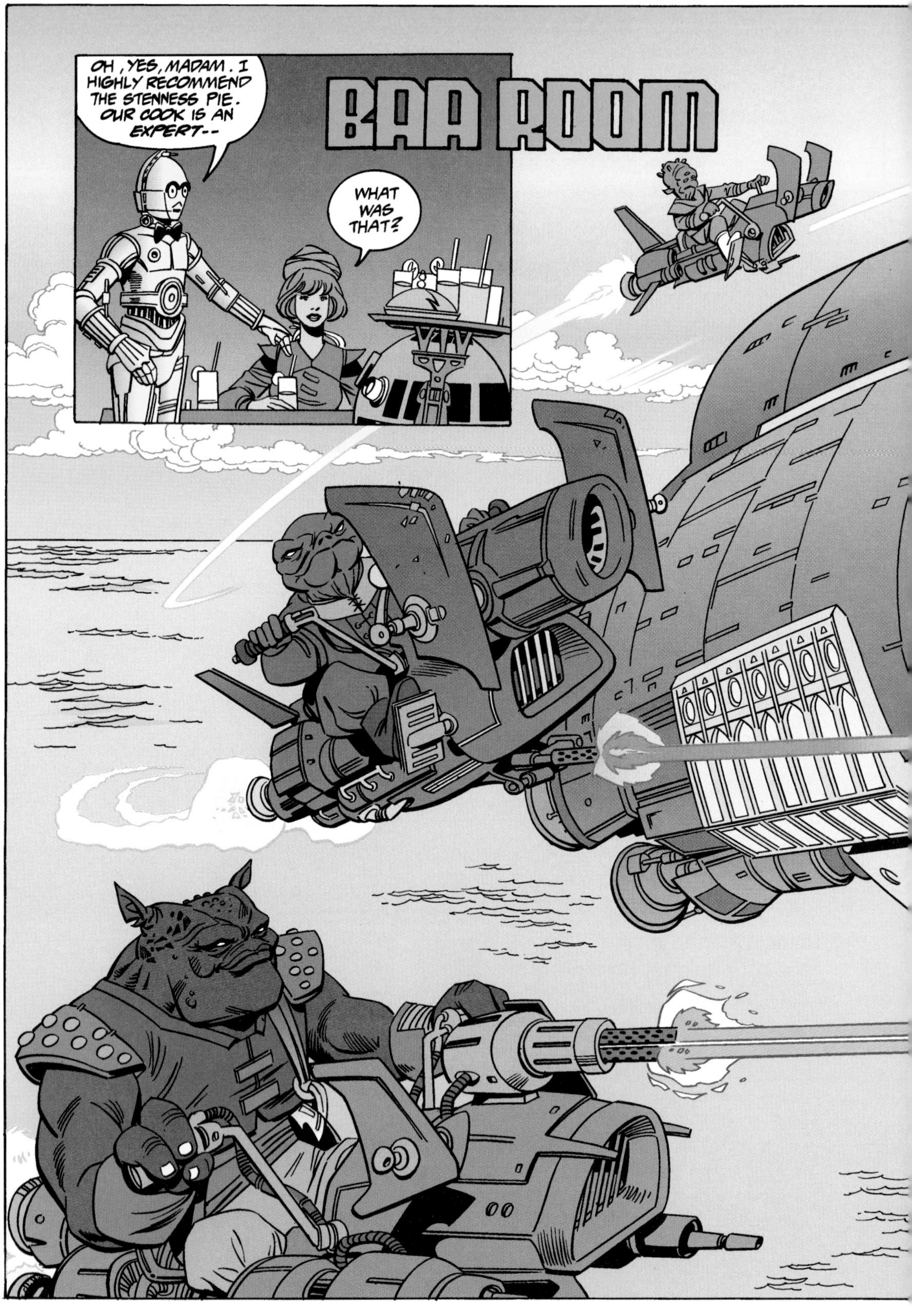
BAR ROOM
OH, YES, MADAM. I HIGHLY RECOMMEND THE STENNESS PIE. OUR COOK IS AN EXPERT--
WHAT WAS THAT?

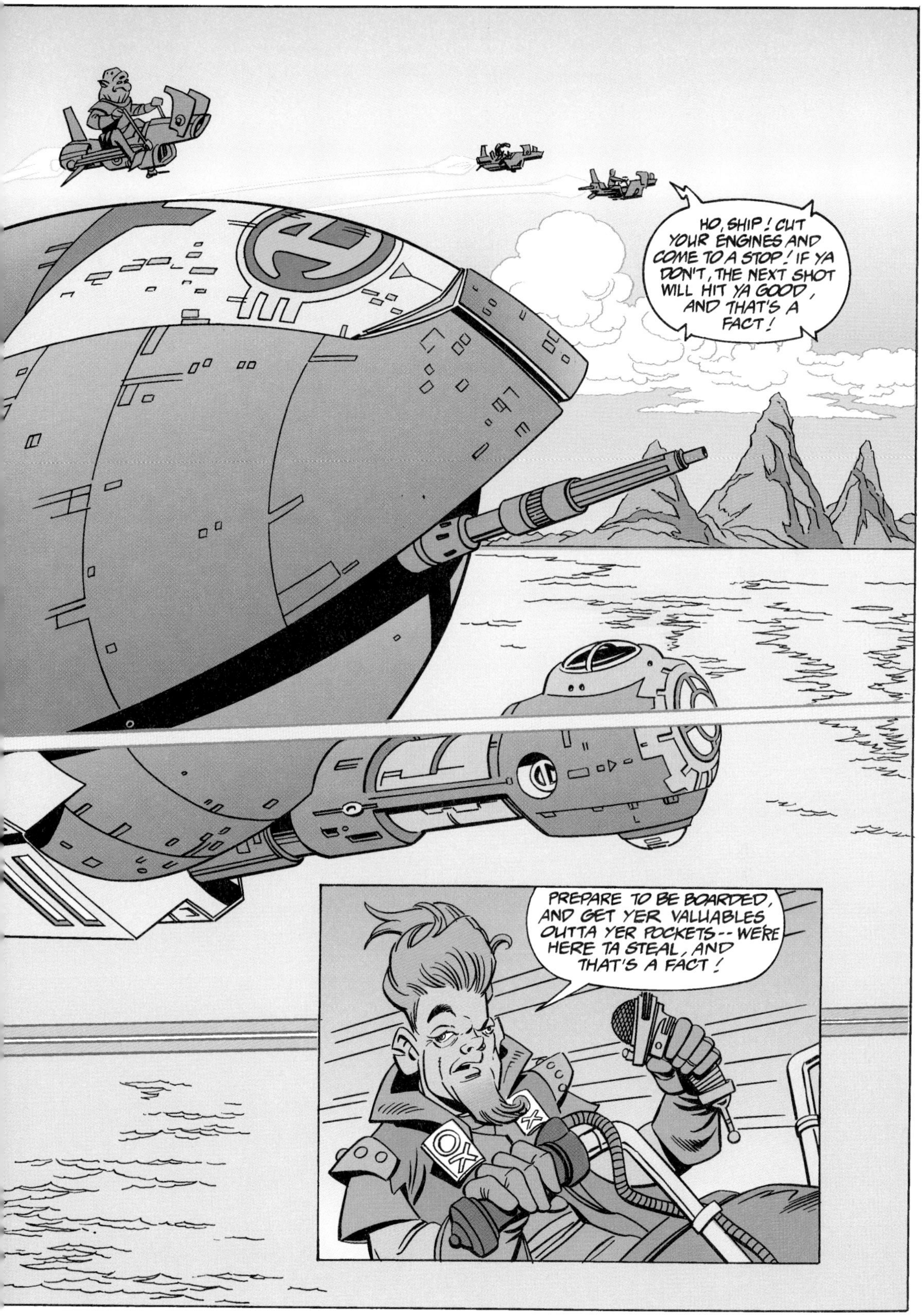
HO, SHIP! CUT YOUR ENGINES AND COME TO A STOP! IF YA DON'T, THE NEXT SHOT WILL HIT YA GOOD, AND THAT'S A FACT!
PREPARE TO BE BOARDED, AND GET YER VALUABLES OUTTA YER POCKETS-- WE'RE HERE TA STEAL, AND THAT'S A FACT!
OX
OX

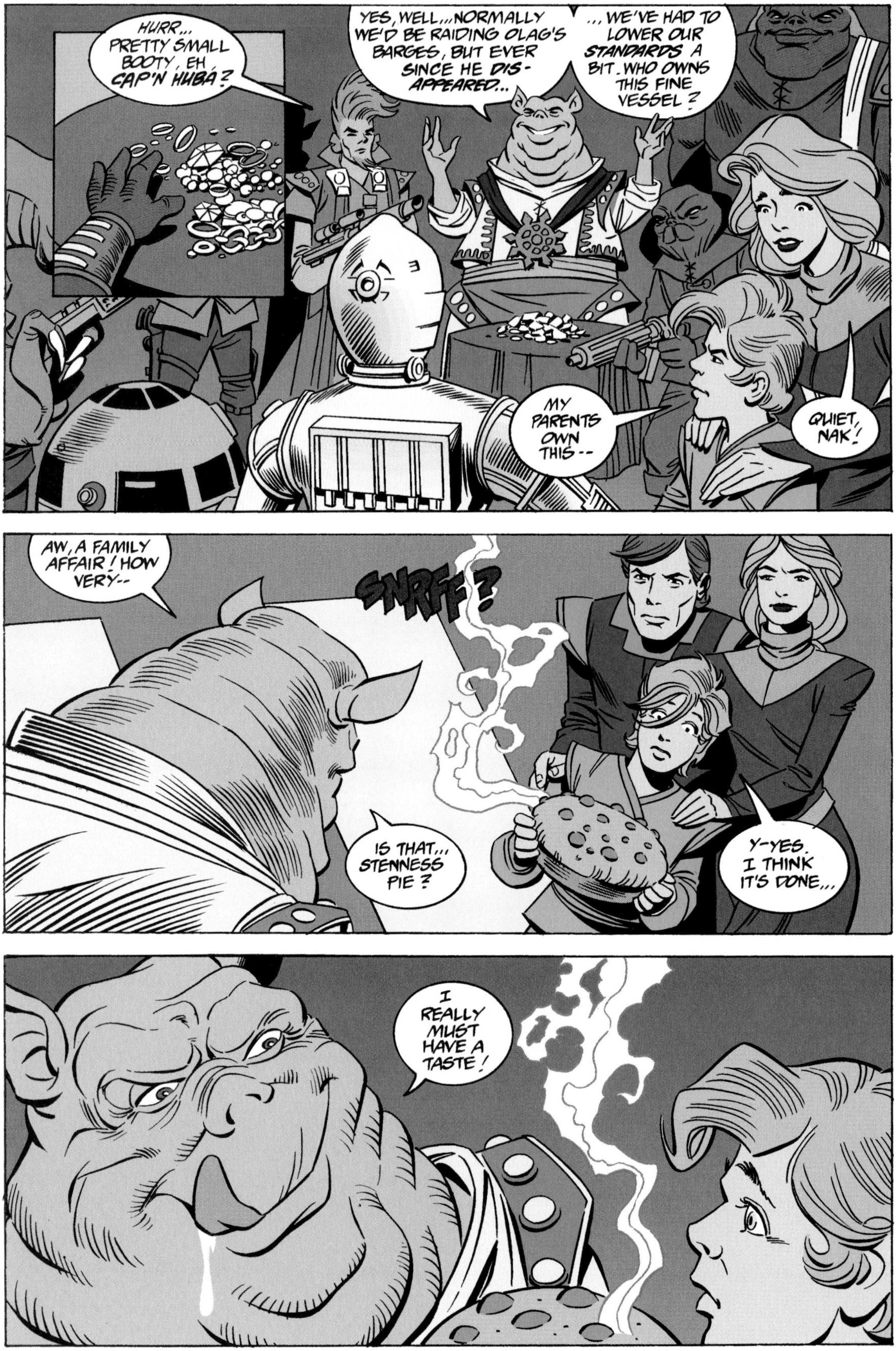
HURR... PRETTY SMALL BOOTY, EH, CAP'N HUBA?
YES, WELL... NORMALLY WE'D BE RAIDING OLAG'S BARGES, BUT EVER SINCE HE DIS-APPEARED...
...WE'VE HAD TO LOWER OUR STANDARDS A BIT. WHO OWNS THIS FINE VESSEL?
MY PARENTS OWN THIS--
QUIET, NAK!
AW, A FAMILY AFFAIR! HOW VERY--
SNRFF?
IS THAT... STENNESS PIE?
Y-YES. I THINK IT'S DONE...
I REALLY MUST HAVE A TASTE!

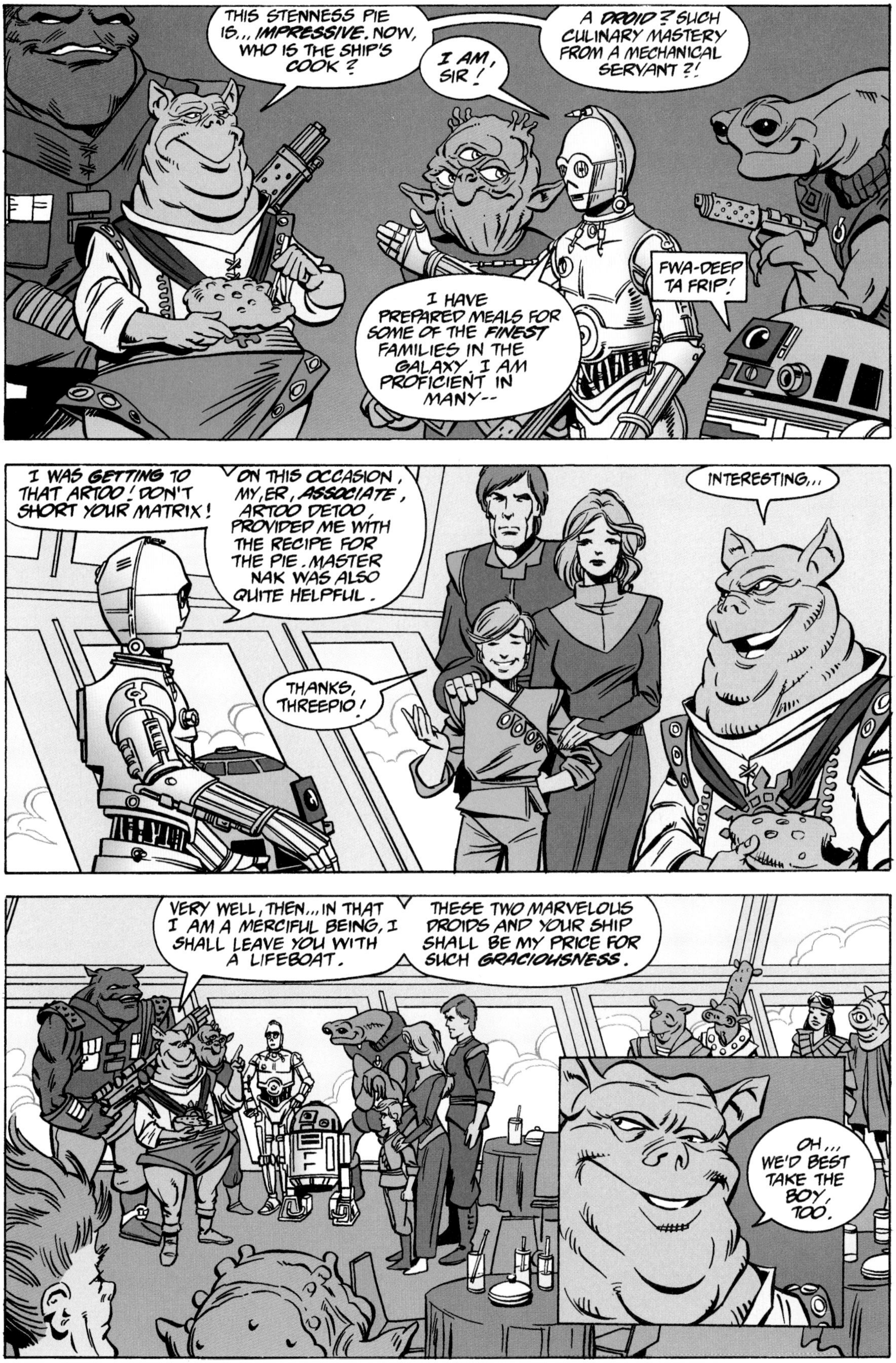
THIS STENNESS PIE IS... IMPRESSIVE. NOW, WHO IS THE SHIP'S COOK?
I AM, SIR!
A DROID?! SUCH CULINARY MASTERY FROM A MECHANICAL SERVANT?!
I HAVE PREPARED MEALS FOR SOME OF THE FINEST FAMILIES IN THE GALAXY. I AM PROFICIENT IN MANY--
FWA-DEEP TA FRIP!
I WAS GETTING TO THAT ARTOO! DON'T SHORT YOUR MATRIX!
ON THIS OCCASION, MY, ER, ASSOCIATE, ARTOO DETOO, PROVIDED ME WITH THE RECIPE FOR THE PIE. MASTER NAK WAS ALSO QUITE HELPFUL.
THANKS, THREEPIO!
INTERESTING...
VERY WELL, THEN... IN THAT I AM A MERCIFUL BEING, I SHALL LEAVE YOU WITH A LIFEBOAT.
THESE TWO MARVELOUS DROIDS AND YOUR SHIP SHALL BE MY PRICE FOR SUCH GRACIOUSNESS.
OH... WE'D BEST TAKE THE BOY, TOO.

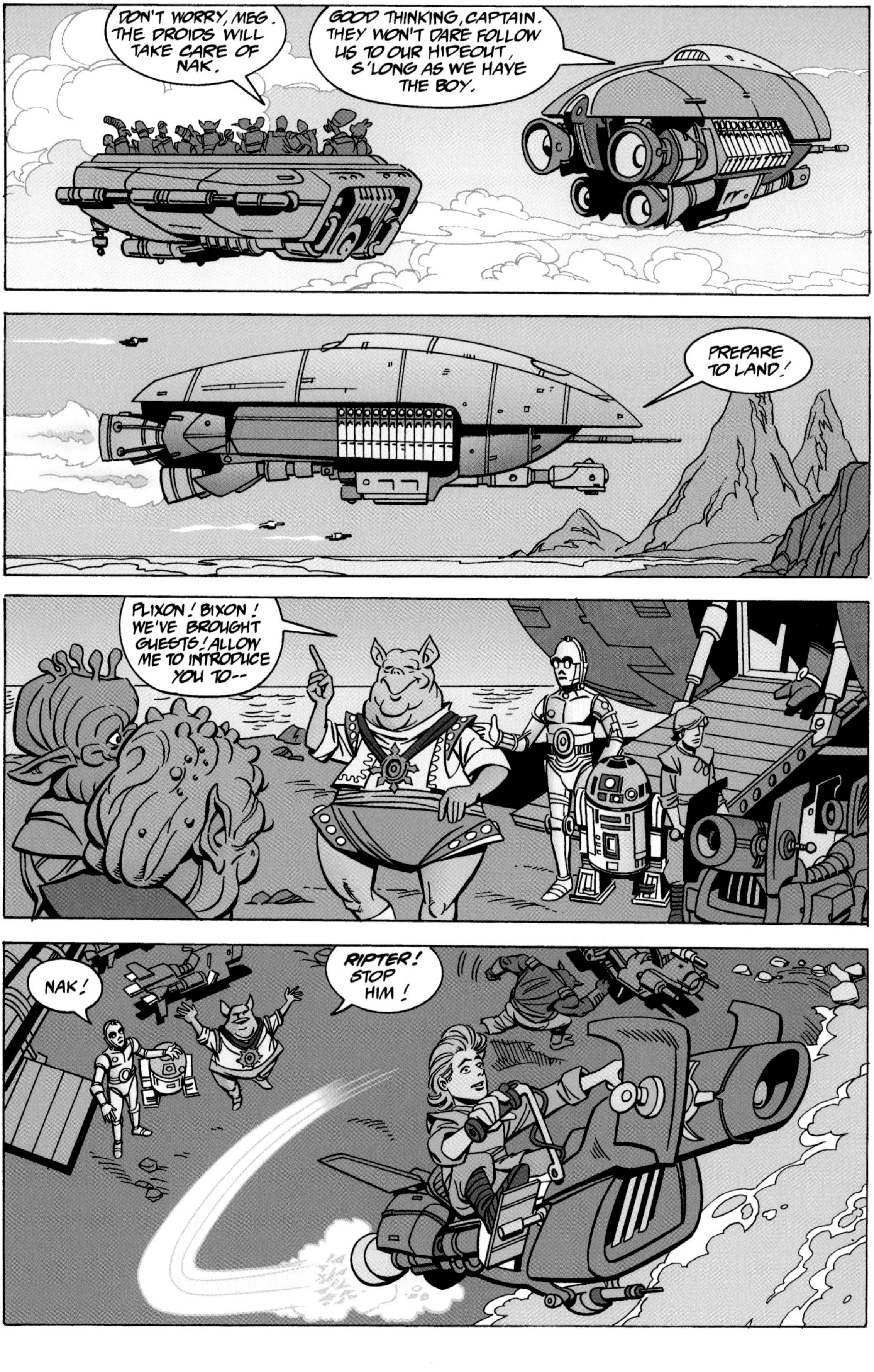
DON'T WORRY, MEG. THE DROIDS WILL TAKE CARE OF NAK.
GOOD THINKING, CAPTAIN. THEY WON'T DARE FOLLOW US TO OUR HIDEOUT, S'LONG AS WE HAVE THE BOY.
PREPARE TO LAND!
PLIXON! BIXON! WE'VE BROUGHT GUESTS! ALLOW ME TO INTRODUCE YOU TO--
NAK!
RIPTER! STOP HIM!

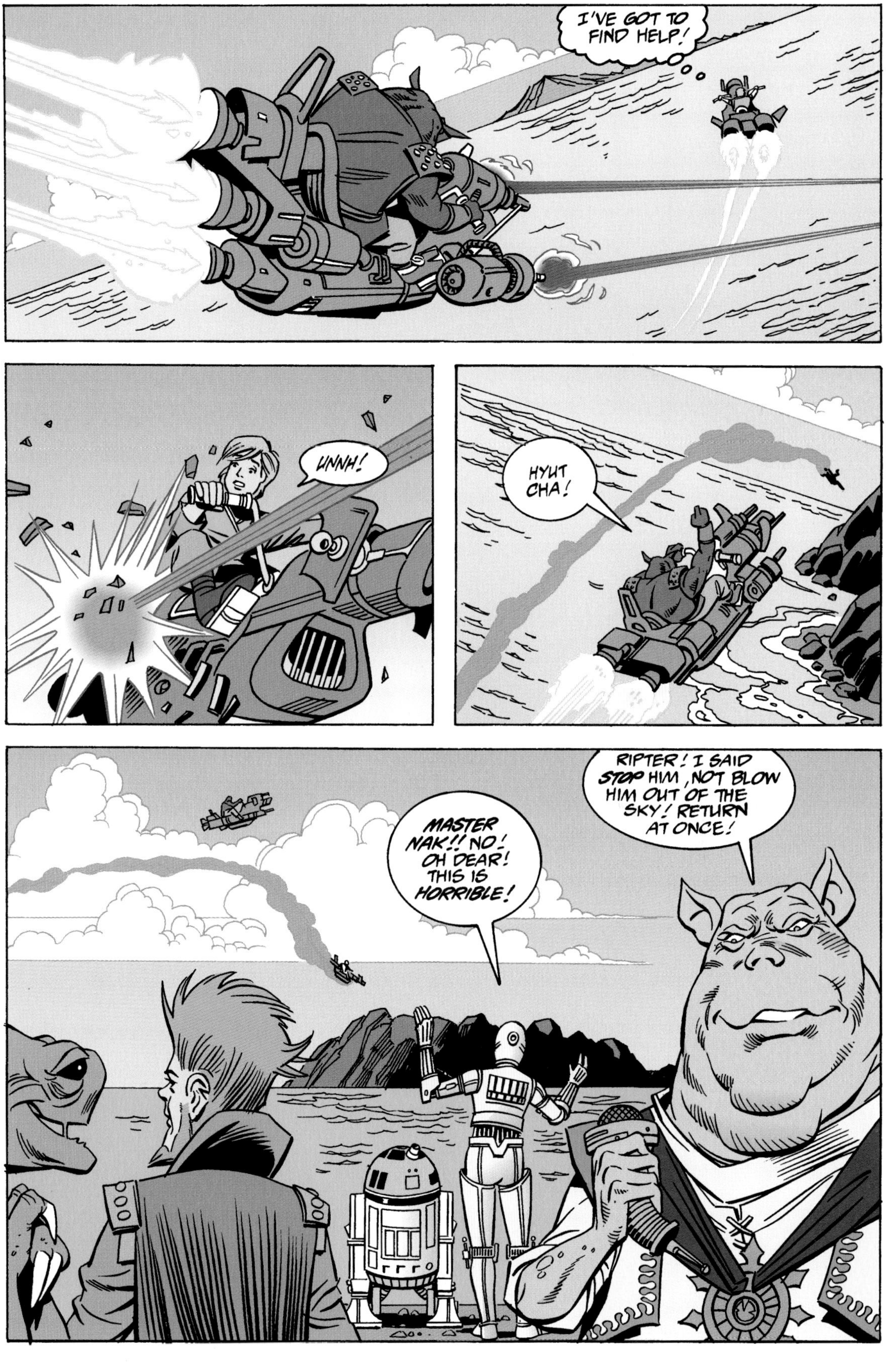
I'VE GOT TO FIND HELP!
UNNH!
HYUT CHA!
MASTER NAK!! NO! OH DEAR! THIS IS HORRIBLE!
RIPTER! I SAID STOP HIM, NOT BLOW HIM OUT OF THE SKY! RETURN AT ONCE!

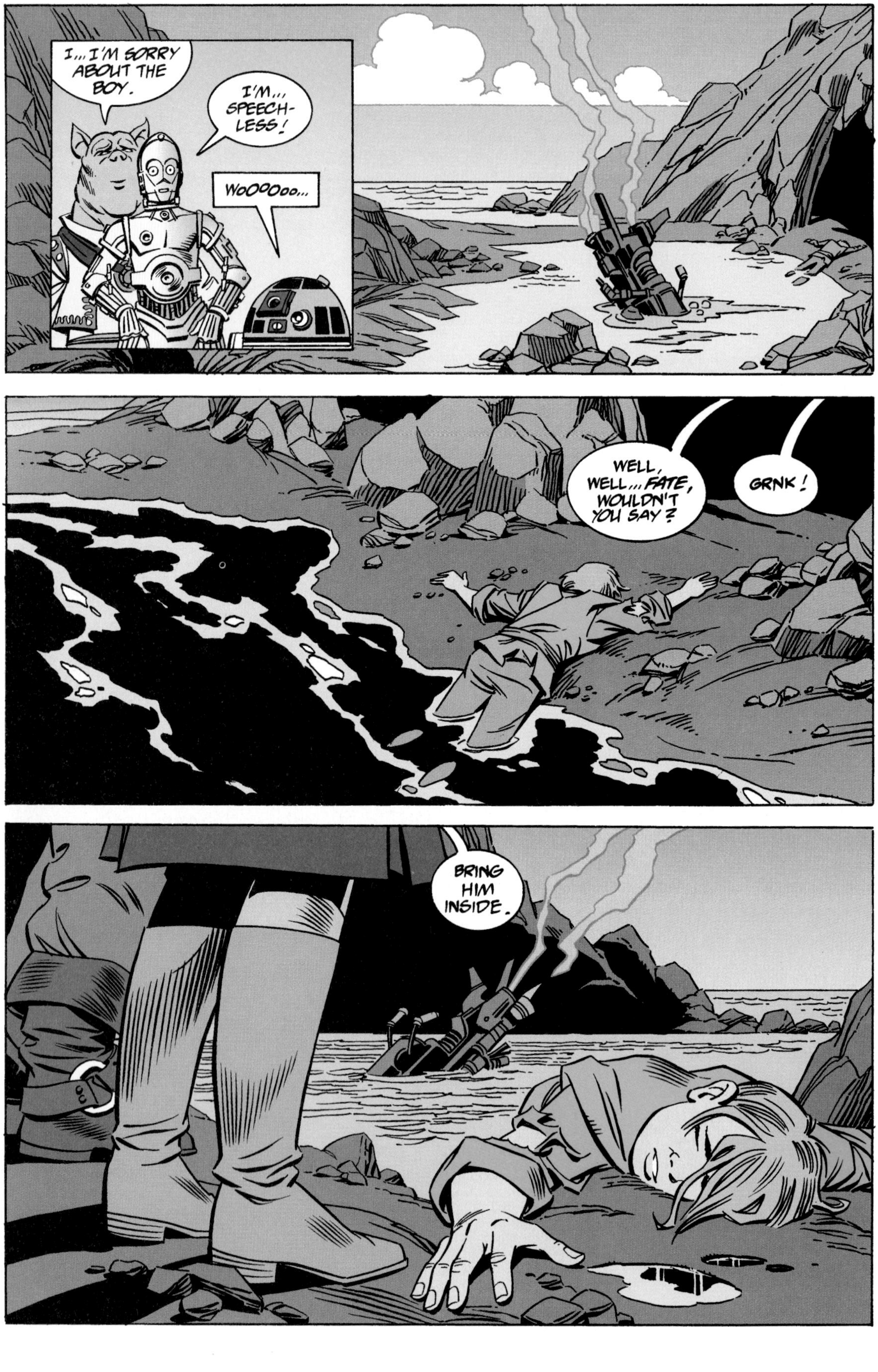
I... I'M SORRY ABOUT THE BOY.
I'M... SPEECHLESS!
WOOOOoo...
WELL, WELL... FATE, WOULDN'T YOU SAY?
GRNK!
BRING HIM INSIDE.

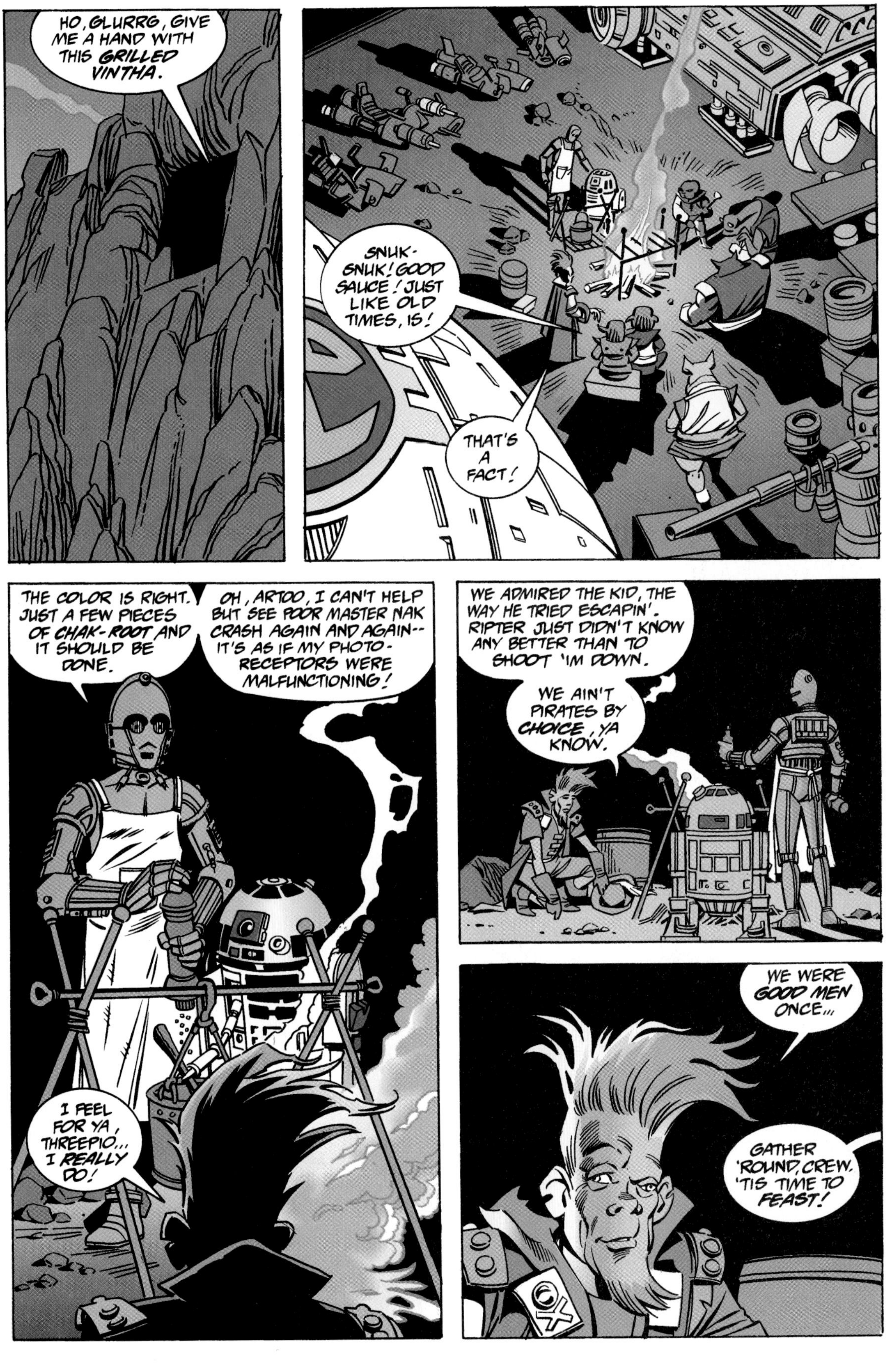
HO, GLURRG, GIVE ME A HAND WITH THIS GRILLED VINTHA.
SNUK-SNUK! GOOD SAUCE! JUST LIKE OLD TIMES, IS!
THAT'S A FACT!
THE COLOR IS RIGHT. JUST A FEW PIECES OF CHAK-ROOT AND IT SHOULD BE DONE.
OH, ARTOO, I CAN'T HELP BUT SEE POOR MASTER NAK CRASH AGAIN AND AGAIN-- IT'S AS IF MY PHOTO-RECEPTORS WERE MALFUNCTIONING!
I FEEL FOR YA, THREEPIO... I REALLY DO!
WE ADMIRED THE KID, THE WAY HE TRIED ESCAPIN'. RIPTER JUST DIDN'T KNOW ANY BETTER THAN TO SHOOT 'IM DOWN.
WE AIN'T PIRATES BY CHOICE, YA KNOW.
WE WERE GOOD MEN ONCE...
GATHER 'ROUND, CREW. 'TIS TIME TO FEAST!

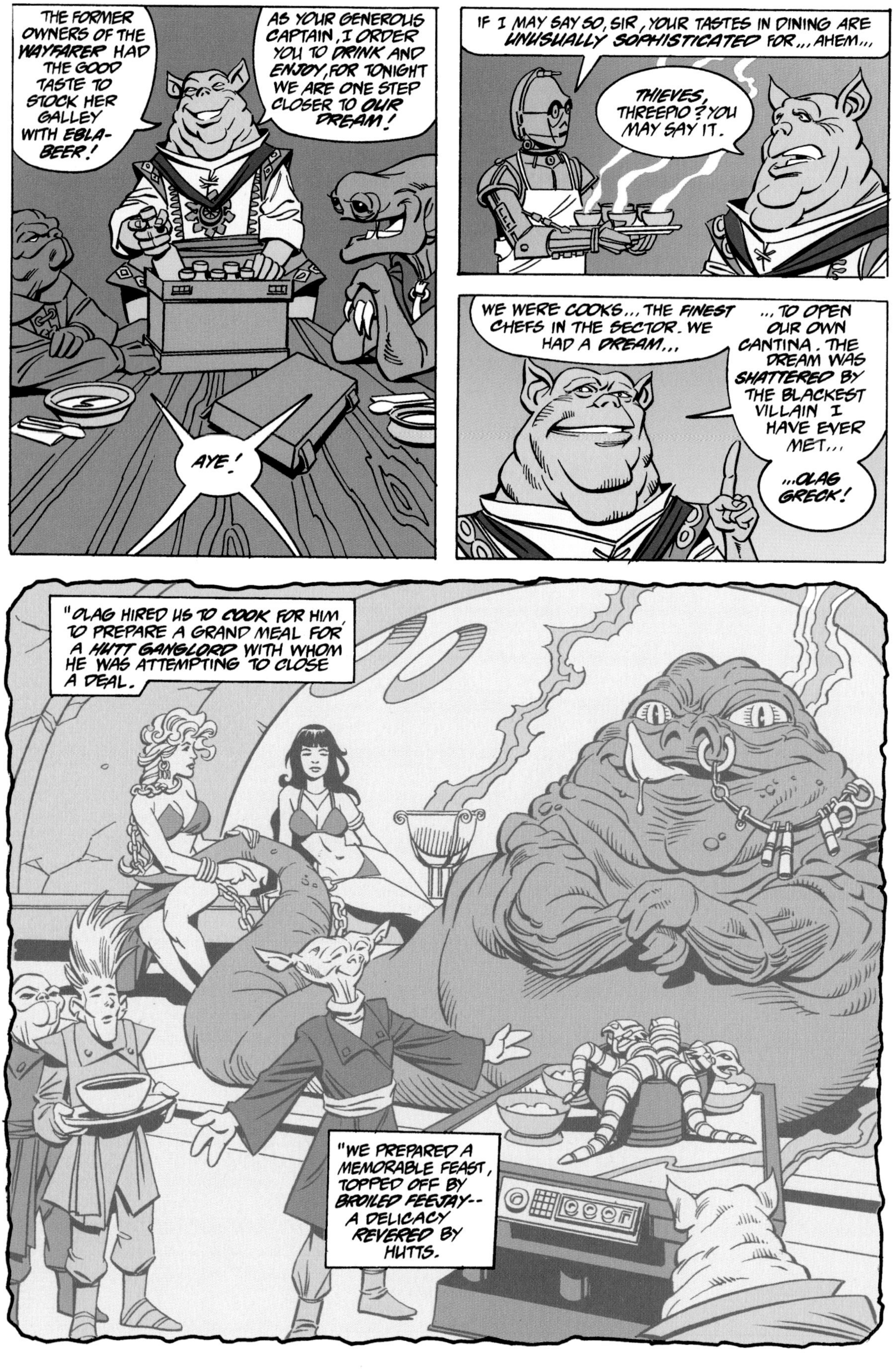
THE FORMER OWNERS OF THE WAYFARER HAD THE GOOD TASTE TO STOCK HER GALLEY WITH EBLA-BEER!
AS YOUR GENEROUS CAPTAIN, I ORDER YOU TO DRINK AND ENJOY, FOR TONIGHT WE ARE ONE STEP CLOSER TO OUR DREAM!
AYE!
IF I MAY SAY SO, SIR, YOUR TASTES IN DINING ARE UNUSUALLY SOPHISTICATED FOR... AHEM...
THIEVES, THREEPIO? YOU MAY SAY IT.
WE WERE COOKS... THE FINEST CHEFS IN THE SECTOR. WE HAD A DREAM...
...TO OPEN OUR OWN CANTINA. THE DREAM WAS SHATTERED BY THE BLACKEST VILLAIN I HAVE EVER MET...
...OLAG GRECK!
"OLAG HIRED US TO COOK FOR HIM, TO PREPARE A GRAND MEAL FOR A HUTT GANGLORD WITH WHOM HE WAS ATTEMPTING TO CLOSE A DEAL.
"WE PREPARED A MEMORABLE FEAST, TOPPED OFF BY BROILED FEEJAY-- A DELICACY REVERED BY HUTTS.

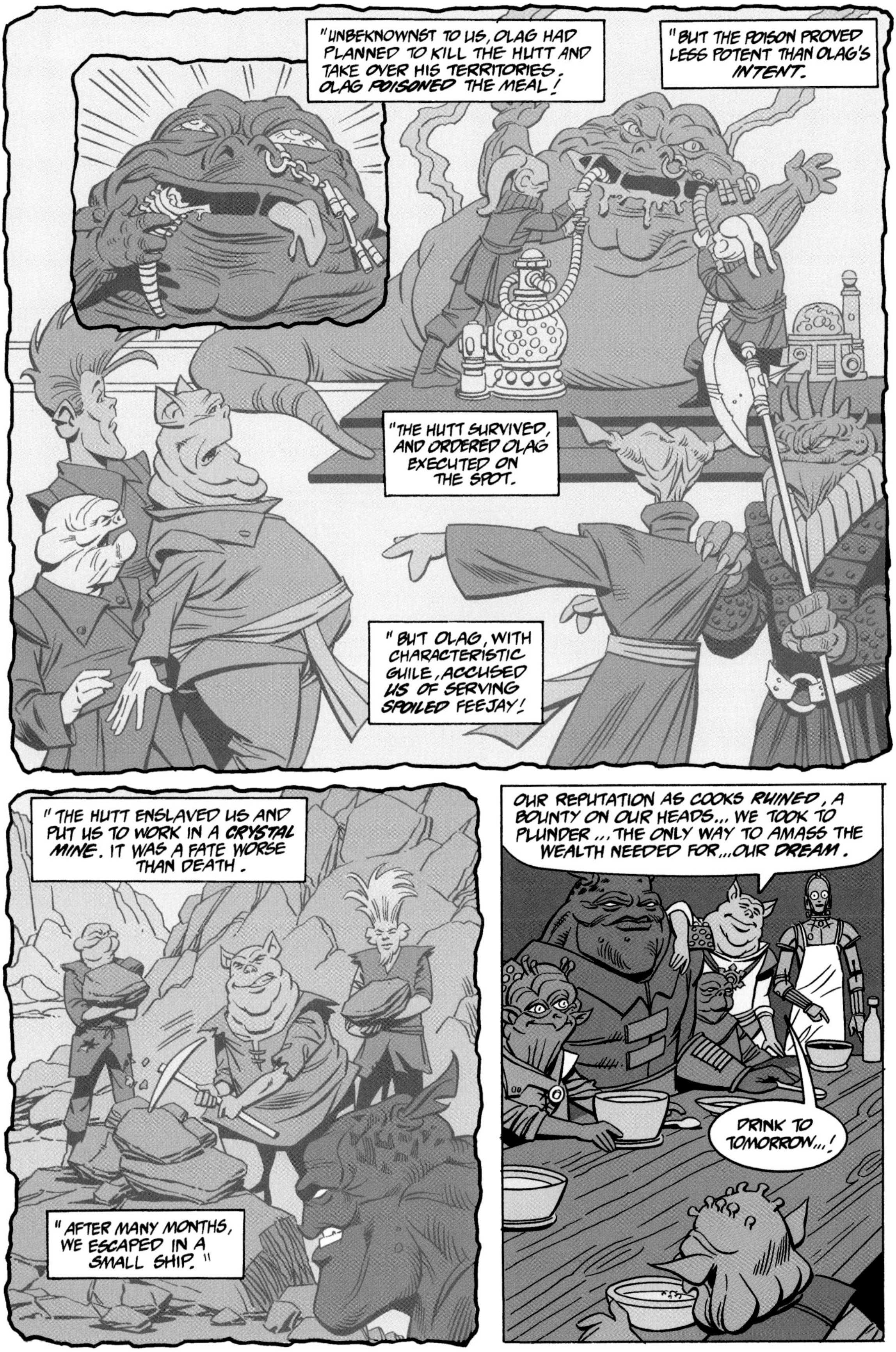
"UNBEKNOWNST TO US, OLAG HAD PLANNED TO KILL THE HUTT AND TAKE OVER HIS TERRITORIES. OLAG POISONED THE MEAL!
"BUT THE POISON PROVED LESS POTENT THAN OLAG'S INTENT.
"THE HUTT SURVIVED, AND ORDERED OLAG EXECUTED ON THE SPOT.
"BUT OLAG, WITH CHARACTERISTIC GUILE, ACCUSED US OF SERVING SPOILED FEEJAY!
"THE HUTT ENSLAVED US AND PUT US TO WORK IN A CRYSTAL MINE. IT WAS A FATE WORSE THAN DEATH.
"AFTER MANY MONTHS, WE ESCAPED IN A SMALL SHIP."
OUR REPUTATION AS COOKS RUINED, A BOUNTY ON OUR HEADS... WE TOOK TO PLUNDER... THE ONLY WAY TO AMASS THE WEALTH NEEDED FOR... OUR DREAM.
DRINK TO TOMORROW...!

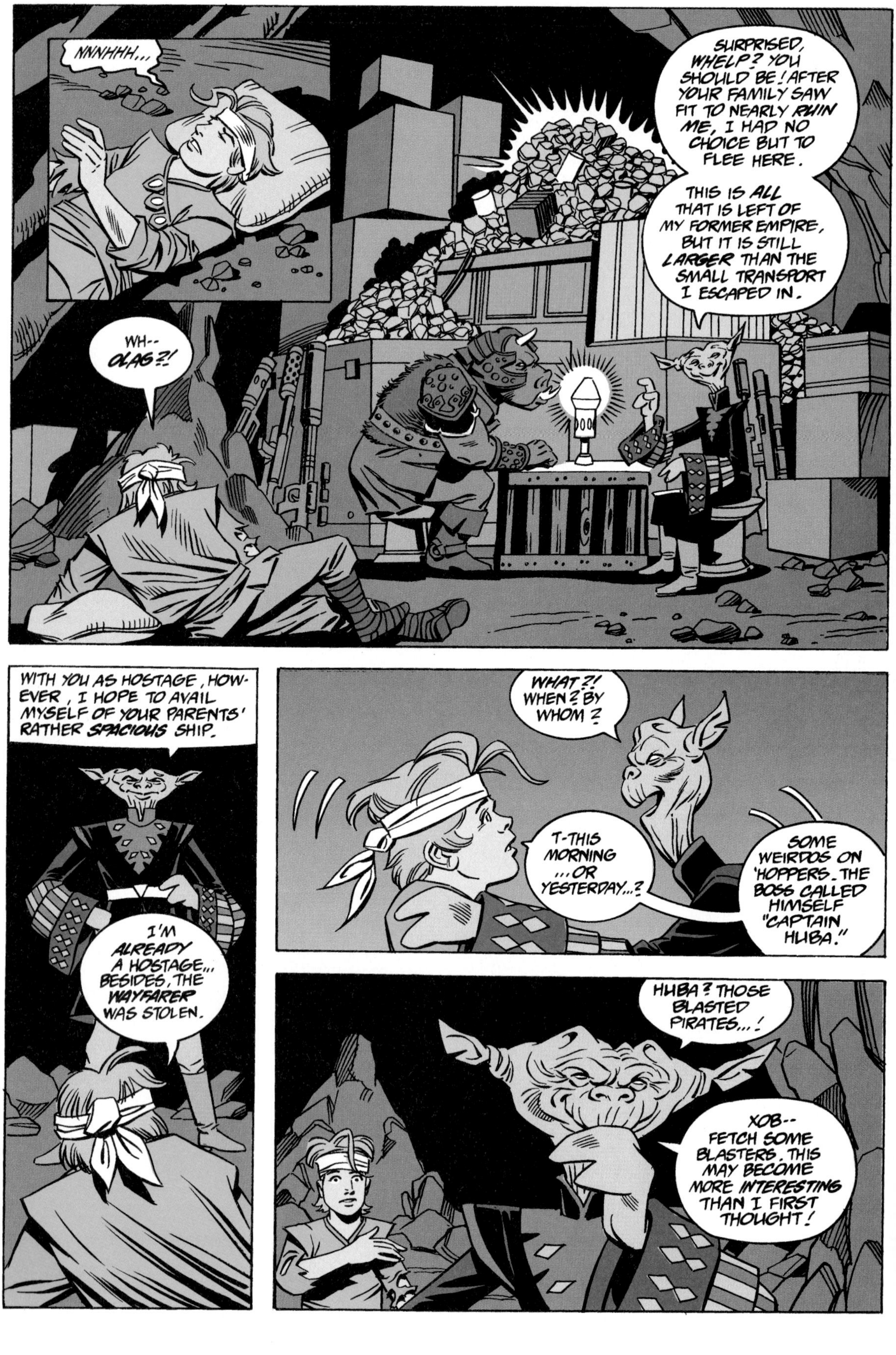
NNNHHH...
SURPRISED, WHELP? YOU SHOULD BE! AFTER YOUR FAMILY SAW FIT TO NEARLY RUIN ME, I HAD NO CHOICE BUT TO FLEE HERE.
THIS IS ALL THAT IS LEFT OF MY FORMER EMPIRE, BUT IT IS STILL LARGER THAN THE SMALL TRANSPORT I ESCAPED IN.
WH-- OLAG?!
WITH YOU AS HOSTAGE, HOWEVER, I HOPE TO AVAIL MYSELF OF YOUR PARENTS' RATHER SPACIOUS SHIP.
I'M ALREADY A HOSTAGE... BESIDES, THE WAYFARER WAS STOLEN.
WHAT?! WHEN? BY WHOM?
T-THIS MORNING ...OR YESTERDAY...?
SOME WEIRDOS ON 'HOPPERS. THE BOSS CALLED HIMSELF "CAPTAIN HUBA."
HUBA? THOSE BLASTED PIRATES...!
XOB-- FETCH SOME BLASTERS. THIS MAY BECOME MORE INTERESTING THAN I FIRST THOUGHT!

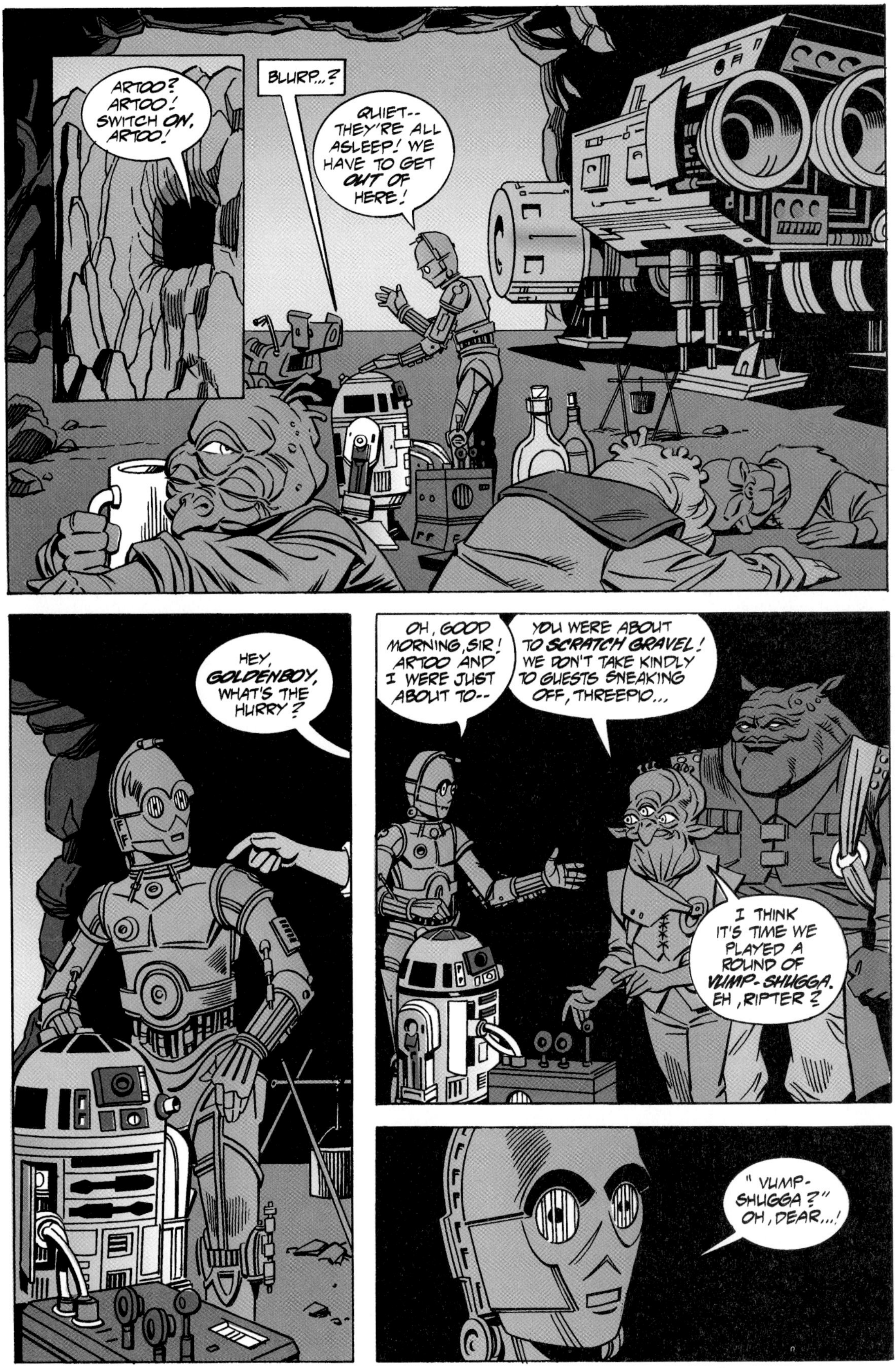
ARTOO? ARTOO! SWITCH ON, ARTOO!
BLURP...?
QUIET-- THEY'RE ALL ASLEEP! WE HAVE TO GET OUT OF HERE!
HEY, GOLDENBOY, WHAT'S THE HURRY?
OH, GOOD MORNING, SIR! ARTOO AND I WERE JUST ABOUT TO--
YOU WERE ABOUT TO SCRATCH GRAVEL! WE DON'T TAKE KINDLY TO GUESTS SNEAKING OFF, THREEPIO...
I THINK IT'S TIME WE PLAYED A ROUND OF VUMP-SHUGGA. EH, RIPTER?
"VUMP-SHUGGA?" OH, DEAR...!

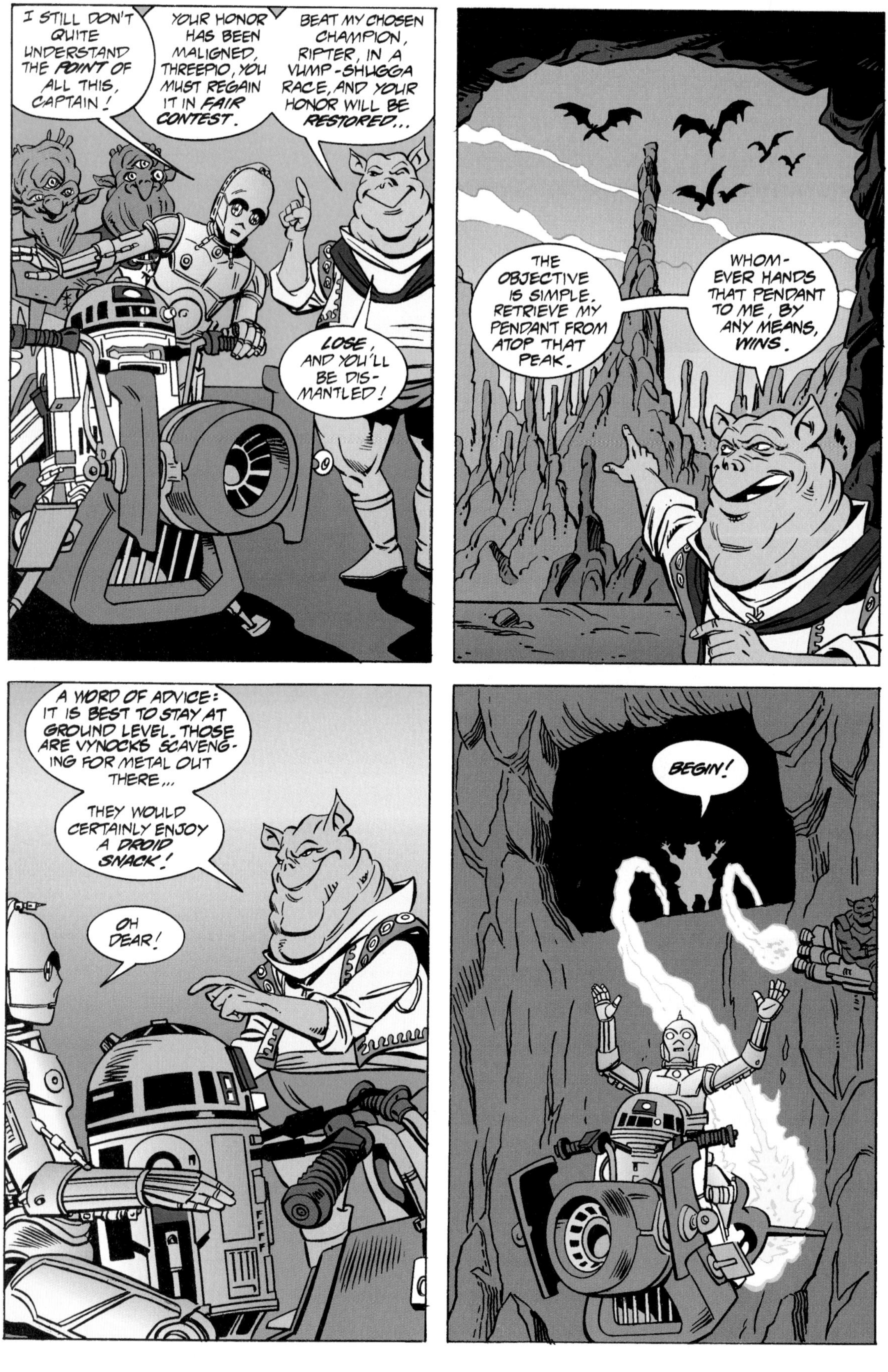

I STILL DON'T QUITE UNDERSTAND THE POINT OF ALL THIS, CAPTAIN!
YOUR HONOR HAS BEEN MALIGNED, THREEPIO, YOU MUST REGAIN IT IN FAIR CONTEST.
BEAT MY CHOSEN CHAMPION, RIPTER, IN A VUMP-SHUGGA RACE, AND YOUR HONOR WILL BE RESTORED...
LOSE, AND YOU'LL BE DIS-MANTLED!
THE OBJECTIVE IS SIMPLE. RETRIEVE MY PENDANT FROM ATOP THAT PEAK.
WHOM-EVER HANDS THAT PENDANT TO ME, BY ANY MEANS, WINS.
A WORD OF ADVICE: IT IS BEST TO STAY AT GROUND LEVEL. THOSE ARE VYNOCKS SCAVENG-ING FOR METAL OUT THERE...
THEY WOULD CERTAINLY ENJOY A DROID SNACK!
OH DEAR!
BEGIN!

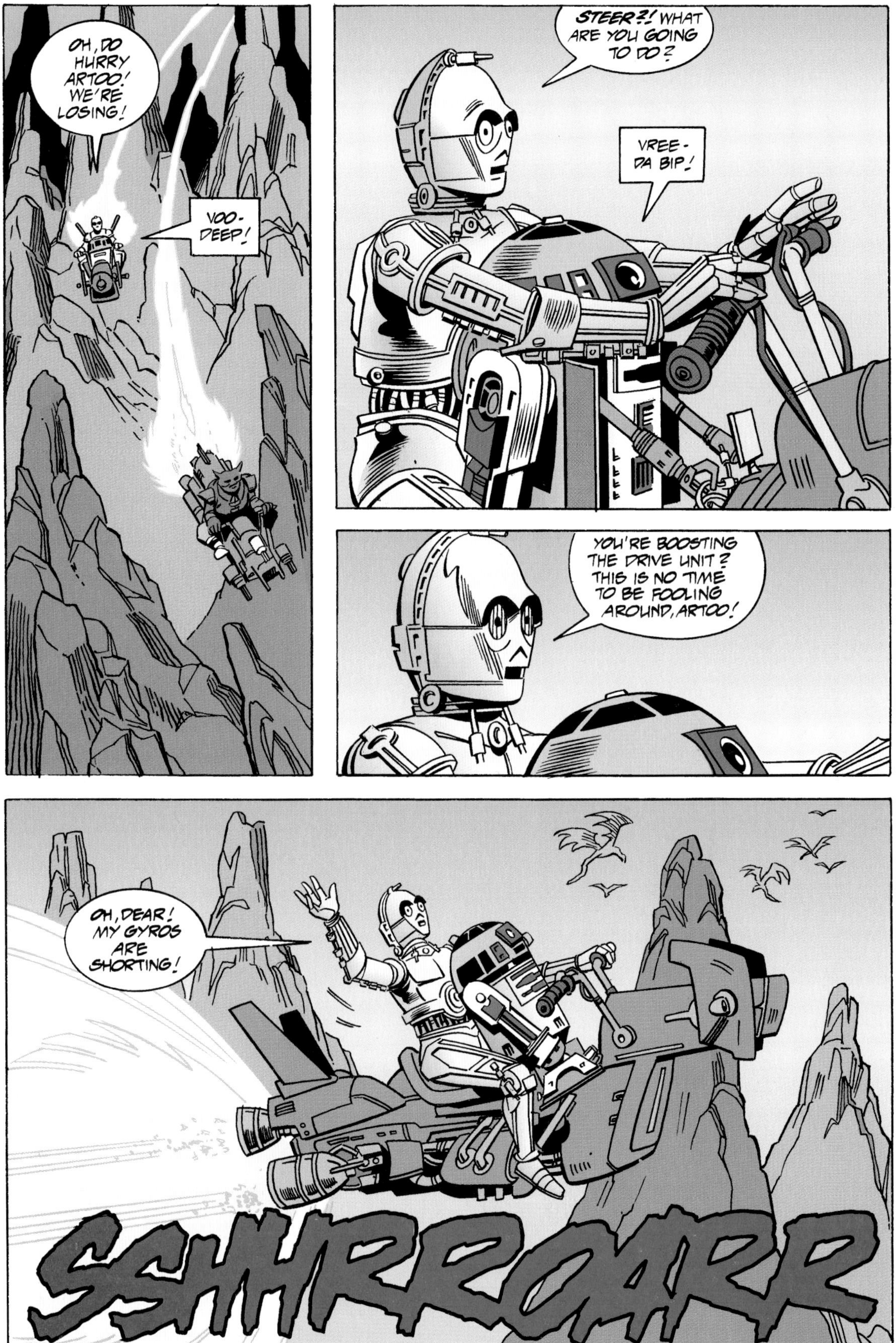
OH, DO HURRY ARTOO! WE'RE LOSING!
VOO-DEEP!
STEER?! WHAT ARE YOU GOING TO DO?
VREE-DA BIP!
YOU'RE BOOSTING THE DRIVE UNIT? THIS IS NO TIME TO BE FOOLING AROUND, ARTOO!
OH, DEAR! MY GYROS ARE SHORTING!
SSHRROARR

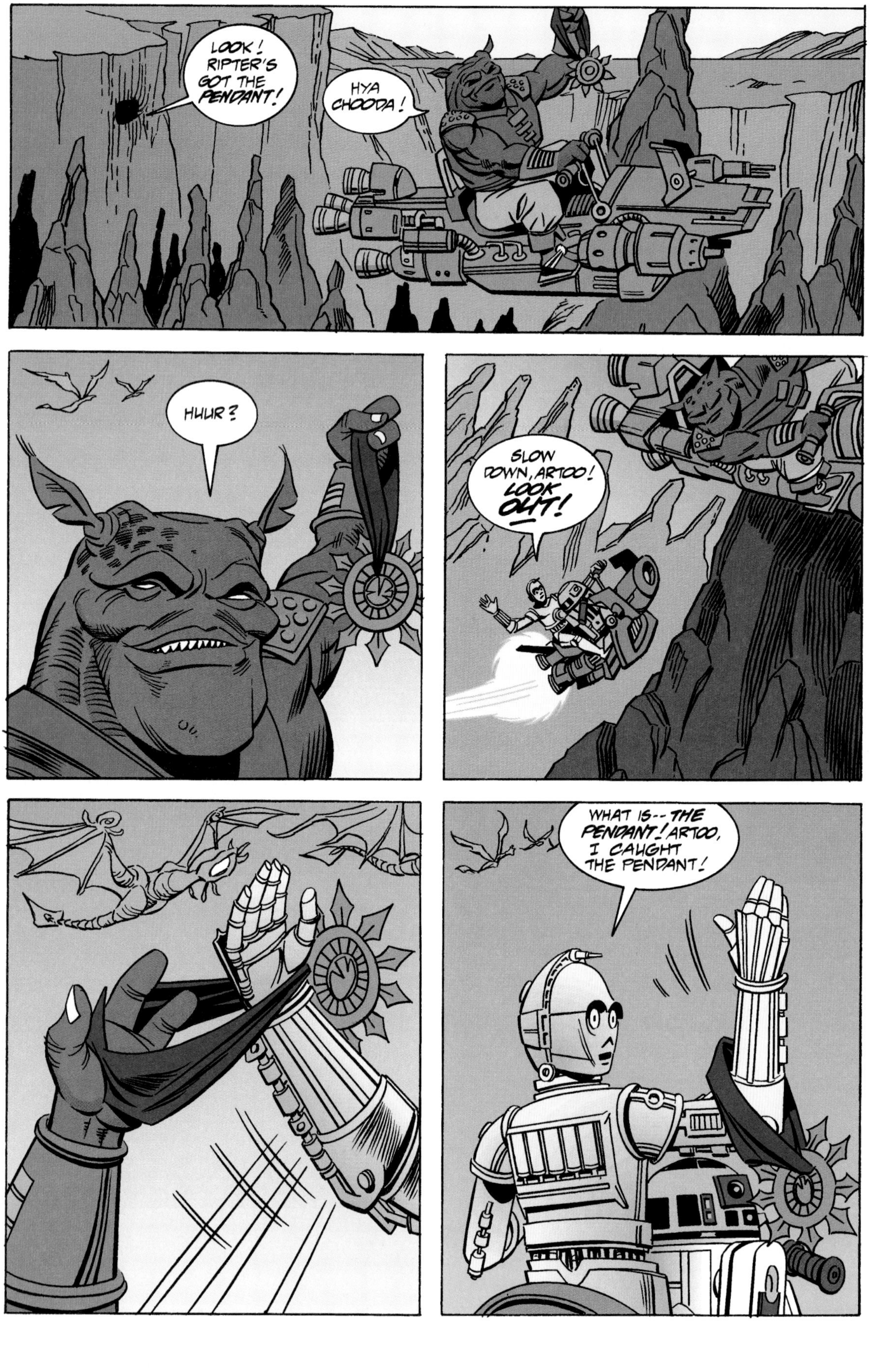
LOOK! RIPTER'S GOT THE PENDANT!
HYA CHOODA!
HUUR?
SLOW DOWN, ARTOO! LOOK OUT!
WHAT IS-- THE PENDANT! ARTOO, I CAUGHT THE PENDANT!

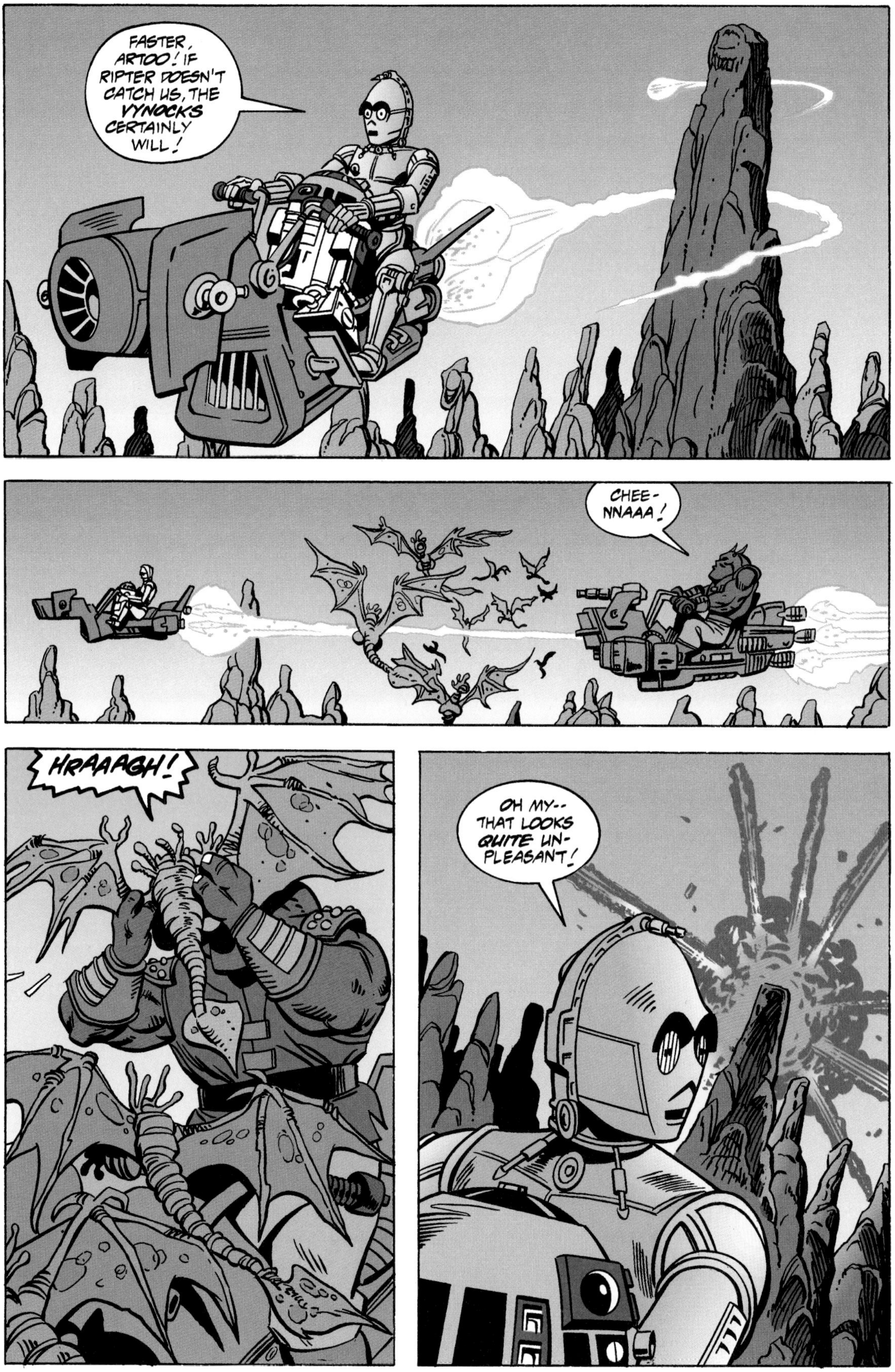
FASTER, ARTOO! IF RIPTER DOESN'T CATCH US, THE VYNOCKS CERTAINLY WILL!
CHEE-NNAAA!
HRAAAGH!
OH MY-- THAT LOOKS QUITE UN-PLEASANT!

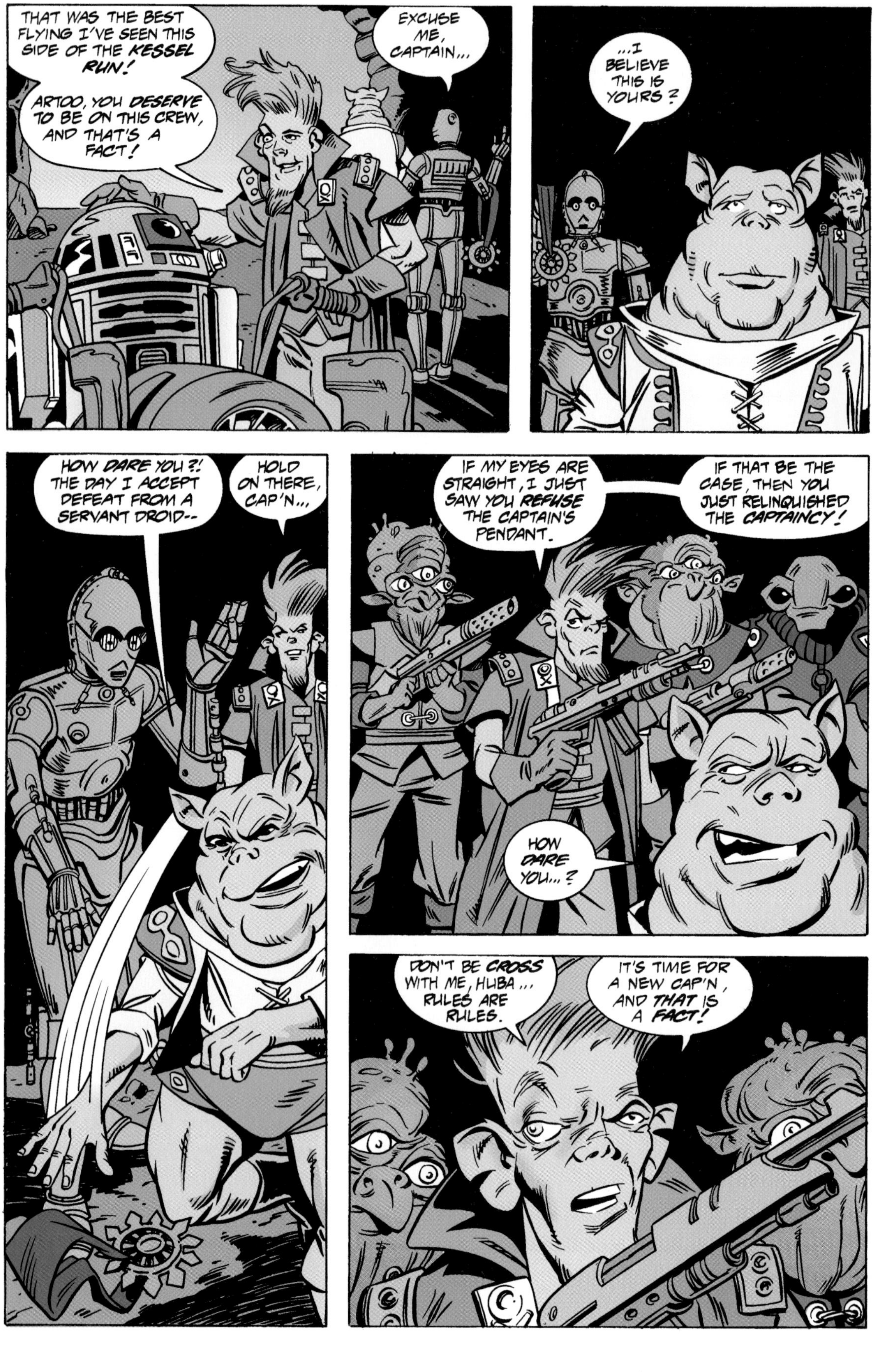
THAT WAS THE BEST FLYING I'VE SEEN THIS SIDE OF THE KESSEL RUN!
ARTOO, YOU DESERVE TO BE ON THIS CREW, AND THAT'S A FACT!
EXCUSE ME, CAPTAIN...
...I BELIEVE THIS IS YOURS?
HOW DARE YOU?! THE DAY I ACCEPT DEFEAT FROM A SERVANT DROID--
HOLD ON THERE, CAP'N...
IF MY EYES ARE STRAIGHT, I JUST SAW YOU REFUSE THE CAPTAIN'S PENDANT.
IF THAT BE THE CASE, THEN YOU JUST RELINQUISHED THE CAPTAINCY!
HOW DARE YOU...?
DON'T BE CROSS WITH ME, HUBA... RULES ARE RULES.
IT'S TIME FOR A NEW CAP'N, AND THAT IS A FACT!

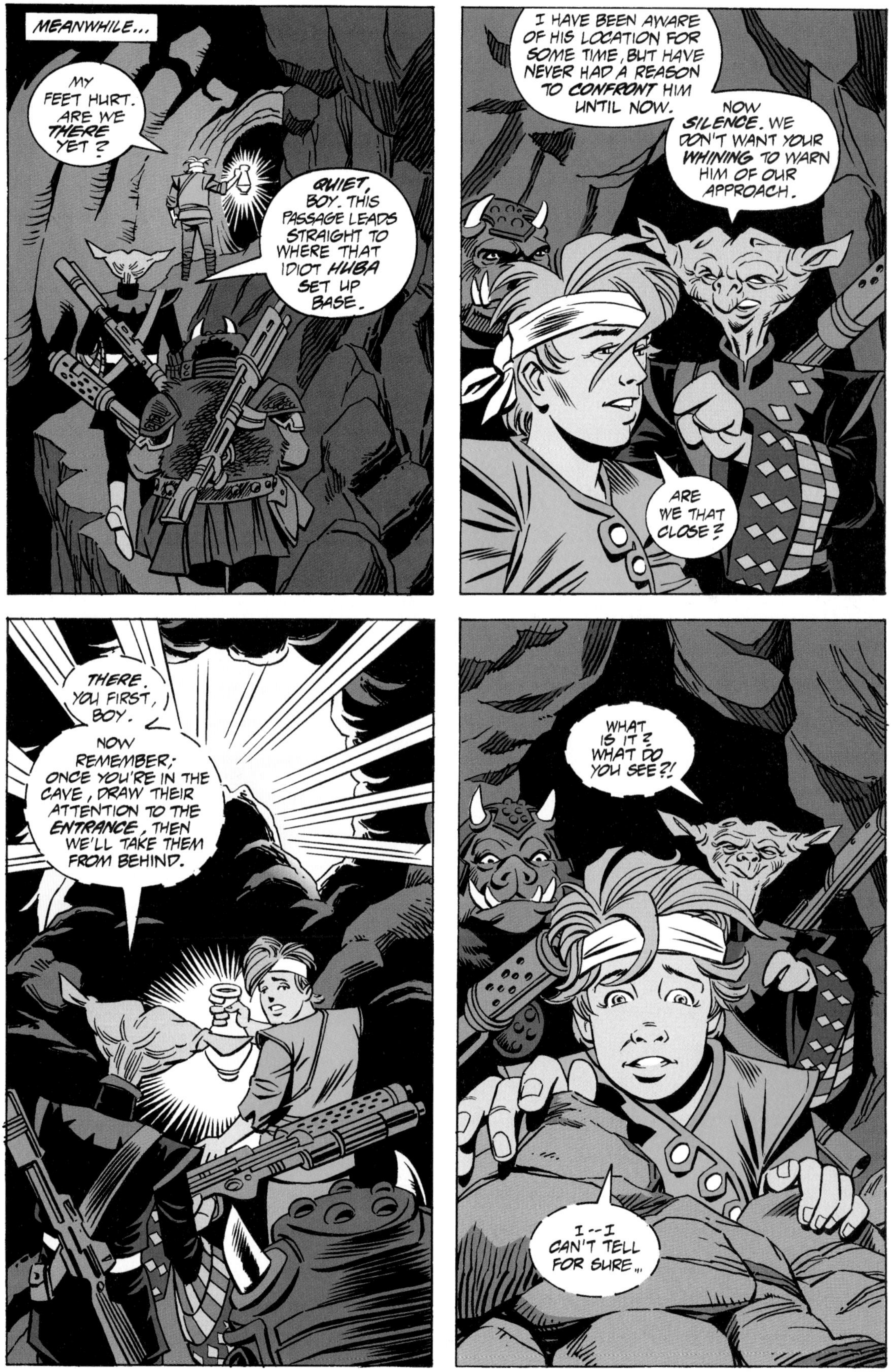
MEANWHILE...
MY FEET HURT. ARE WE THERE YET?
QUIET, BOY. THIS PASSAGE LEADS STRAIGHT TO WHERE THAT IDIOT HUBA SET UP BASE.
I HAVE BEEN AWARE OF HIS LOCATION FOR SOME TIME, BUT HAVE NEVER HAD A REASON TO CONFRONT HIM UNTIL NOW.
NOW SILENCE. WE DON'T WANT YOUR WHINING TO WARN HIM OF OUR APPROACH.
ARE WE THAT CLOSE?
THERE. YOU FIRST, BOY.
NOW REMEMBER; ONCE YOU'RE IN THE CAVE, DRAW THEIR ATTENTION TO THE ENTRANCE, THEN WE'LL TAKE THEM FROM BEHIND.
WHAT IS IT? WHAT DO YOU SEE?!
I--I CAN'T TELL FOR SURE...

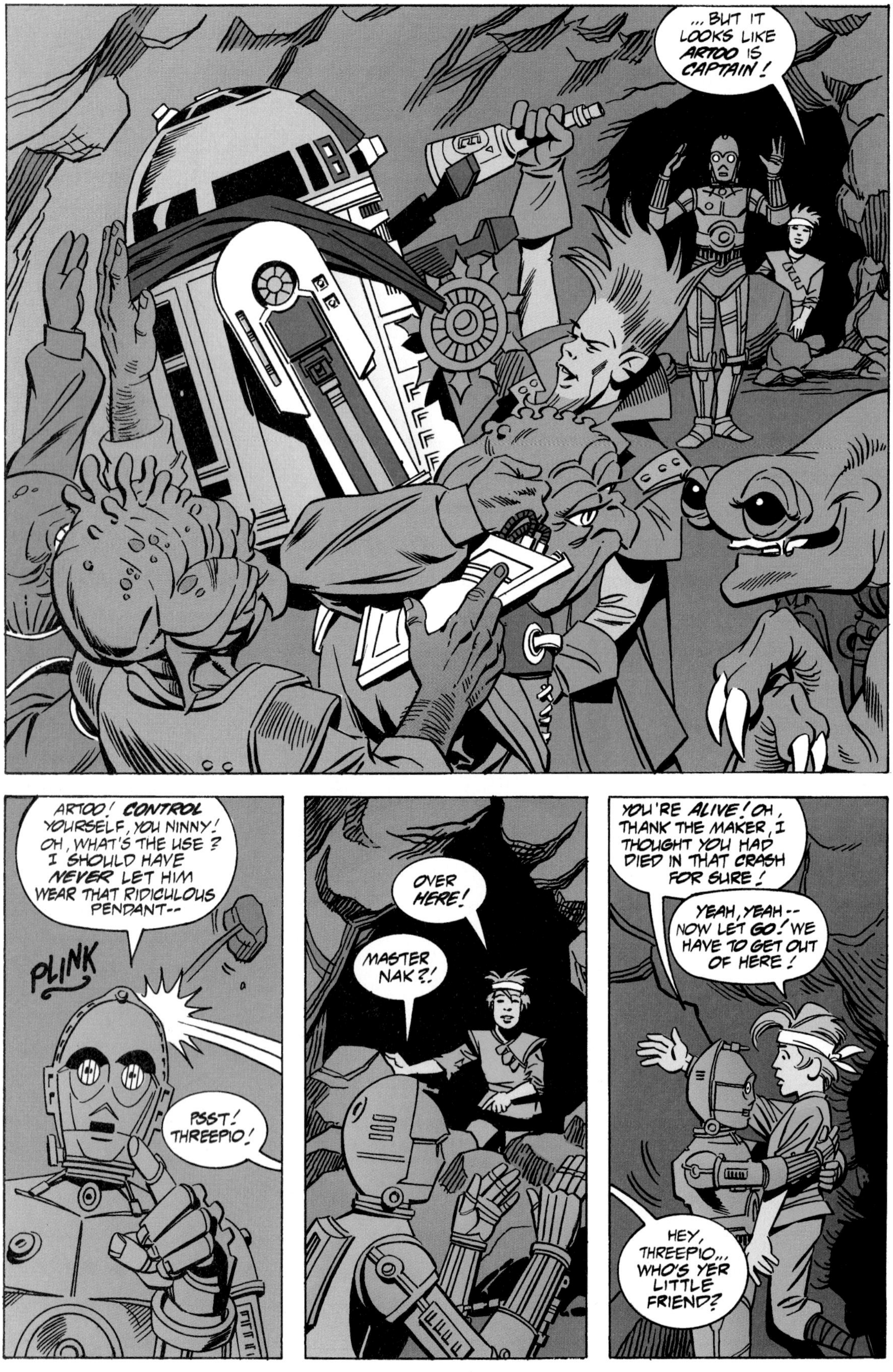
...BUT IT LOOKS LIKE ARTOO IS CAPTAIN!
ARTOO! CONTROL YOURSELF, YOU NINNY! OH, WHAT'S THE USE? I SHOULD HAVE NEVER LET HIM WEAR THAT RIDICULOUS PENDANT--
PLINK
PSST! THREEPIO!
OVER HERE!
MASTER NAK?!
YOU'RE ALIVE! OH, THANK THE MAKER, I THOUGHT YOU HAD DIED IN THAT CRASH FOR SURE!
YEAH, YEAH-- NOW LET GO! WE HAVE TO GET OUT OF HERE!
HEY, THREEPIO... WHO'S YER LITTLE FRIEND?

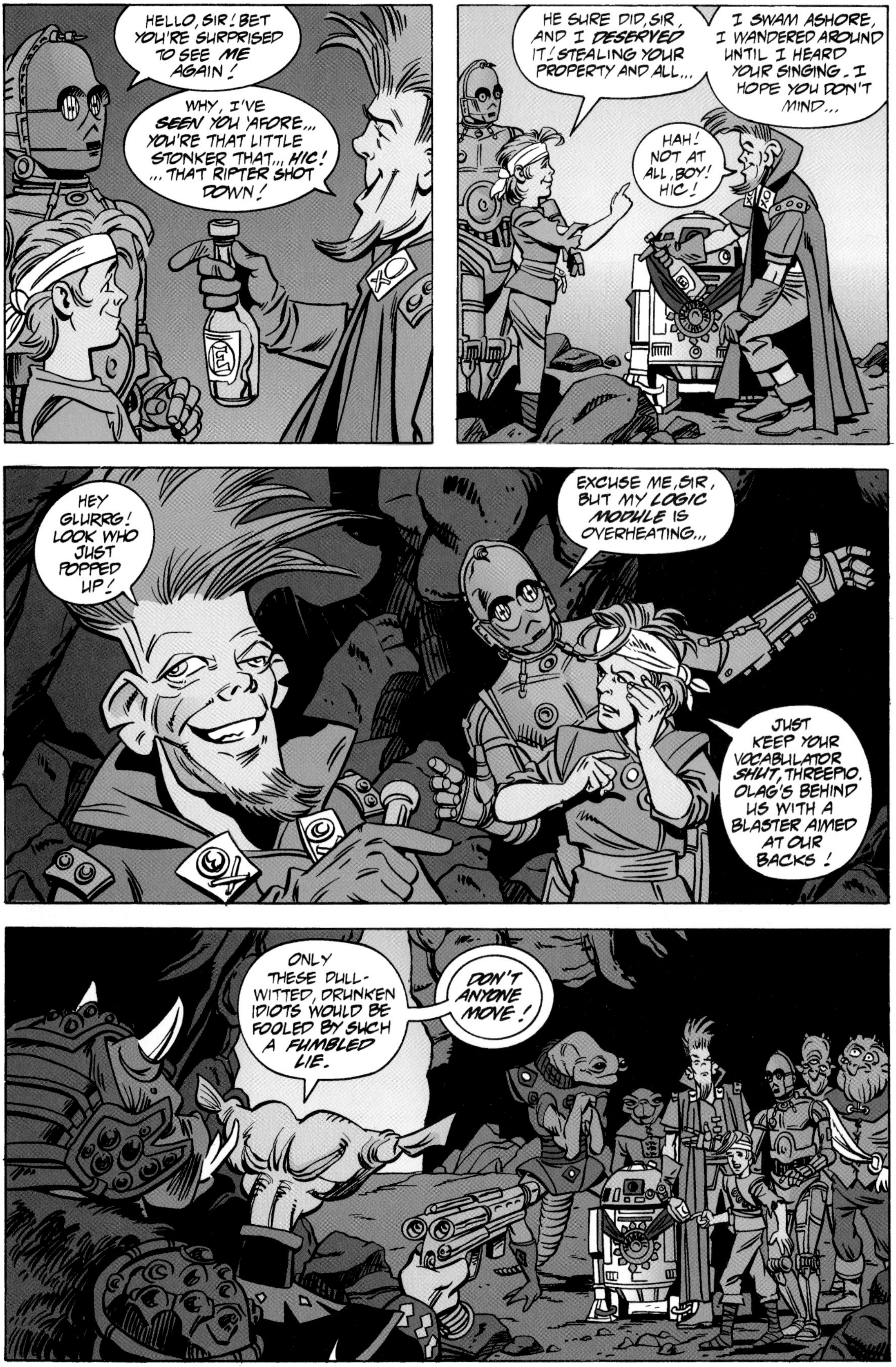
HELLO, SIR! BET YOU'RE SURPRISED TO SEE *ME* AGAIN!
WHY, I'VE *SEEN* YOU 'AFORE... YOU'RE THAT LITTLE STONKER THAT... *HIC!* ... THAT RIPTER SHOT DOWN!
HE SURE DID, SIR, AND I *DESERVED* IT! STEALING YOUR PROPERTY AND ALL...
I SWAM ASHORE, I WANDERED AROUND UNTIL I HEARD YOUR SINGING. I HOPE YOU DON'T MIND...
HAH! NOT AT ALL, BOY! HIC!
HEY GLURRG! LOOK WHO JUST POPPED UP!
EXCUSE ME, SIR, BUT MY *LOGIC MODULE* IS OVERHEATING...
JUST KEEP YOUR VOCABULATOR *SHUT*, THREEPIO. OLAG'S BEHIND US WITH A BLASTER AIMED AT OUR BACKS!
ONLY THESE DULL-WITTED, DRUNKEN IDIOTS WOULD BE FOOLED BY SUCH A *FUMBLED* LIE.
DON'T ANYONE MOVE!

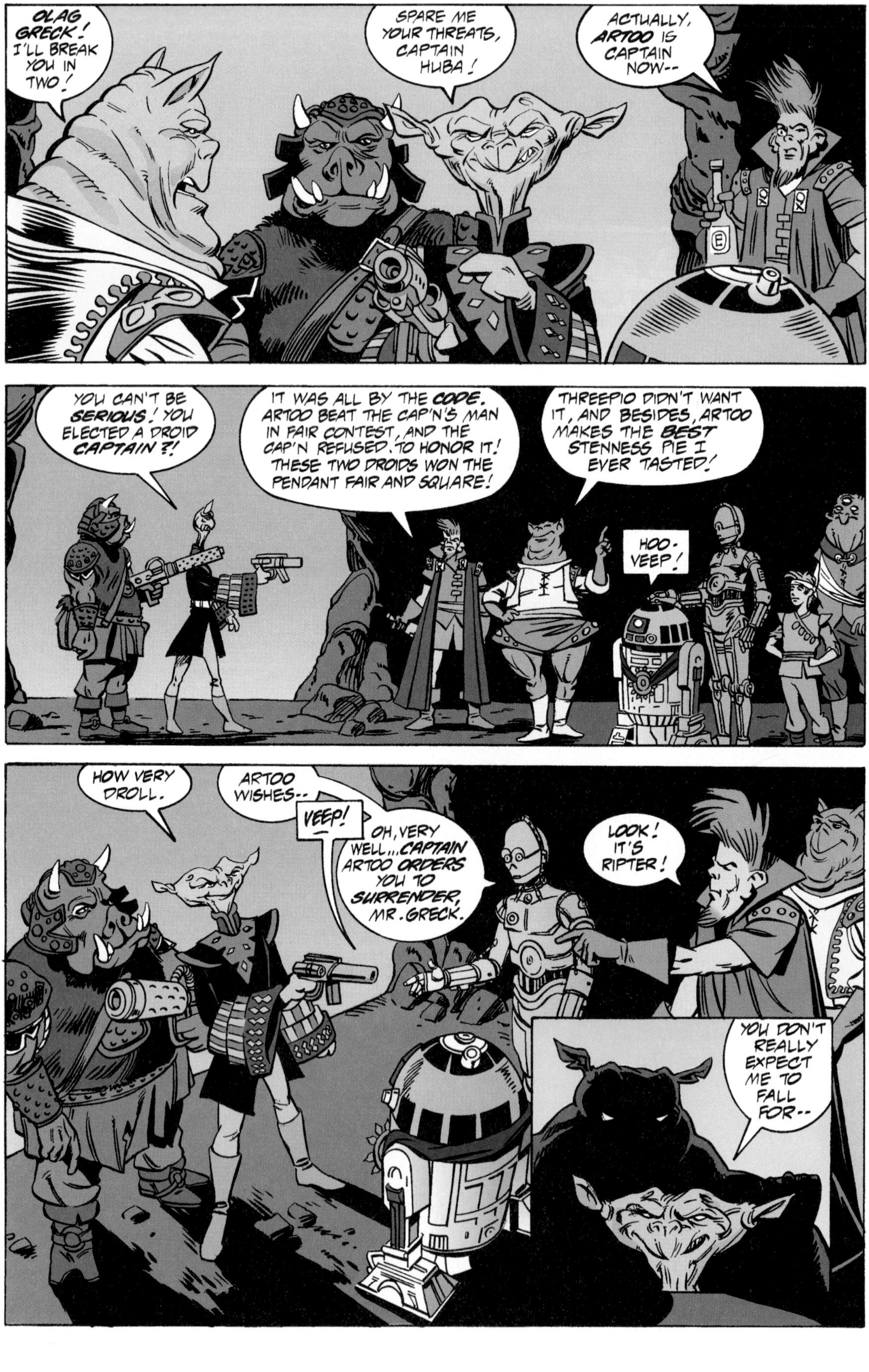

OLAG GRECK! I'LL BREAK YOU IN TWO!
SPARE ME YOUR THREATS, CAPTAIN HUBA!
ACTUALLY, ARTOO IS CAPTAIN NOW--
YOU CAN'T BE SERIOUS! YOU ELECTED A DROID CAPTAIN?!
IT WAS ALL BY THE CODE. ARTOO BEAT THE CAP'N'S MAN IN FAIR CONTEST, AND THE CAP'N REFUSED TO HONOR IT! THESE TWO DROIDS WON THE PENDANT FAIR AND SQUARE!
THREEPIO DIDN'T WANT IT, AND BESIDES, ARTOO MAKES THE BEST STENNESS PIE I EVER TASTED!
HOO-VEEP!
HOW VERY DROLL.
ARTOO WISHES--
VEEP!
OH, VERY WELL... CAPTAIN ARTOO ORDERS YOU TO SURRENDER, MR. GRECK.
LOOK! IT'S RIPTER!
YOU DON'T REALLY EXPECT ME TO FALL FOR--

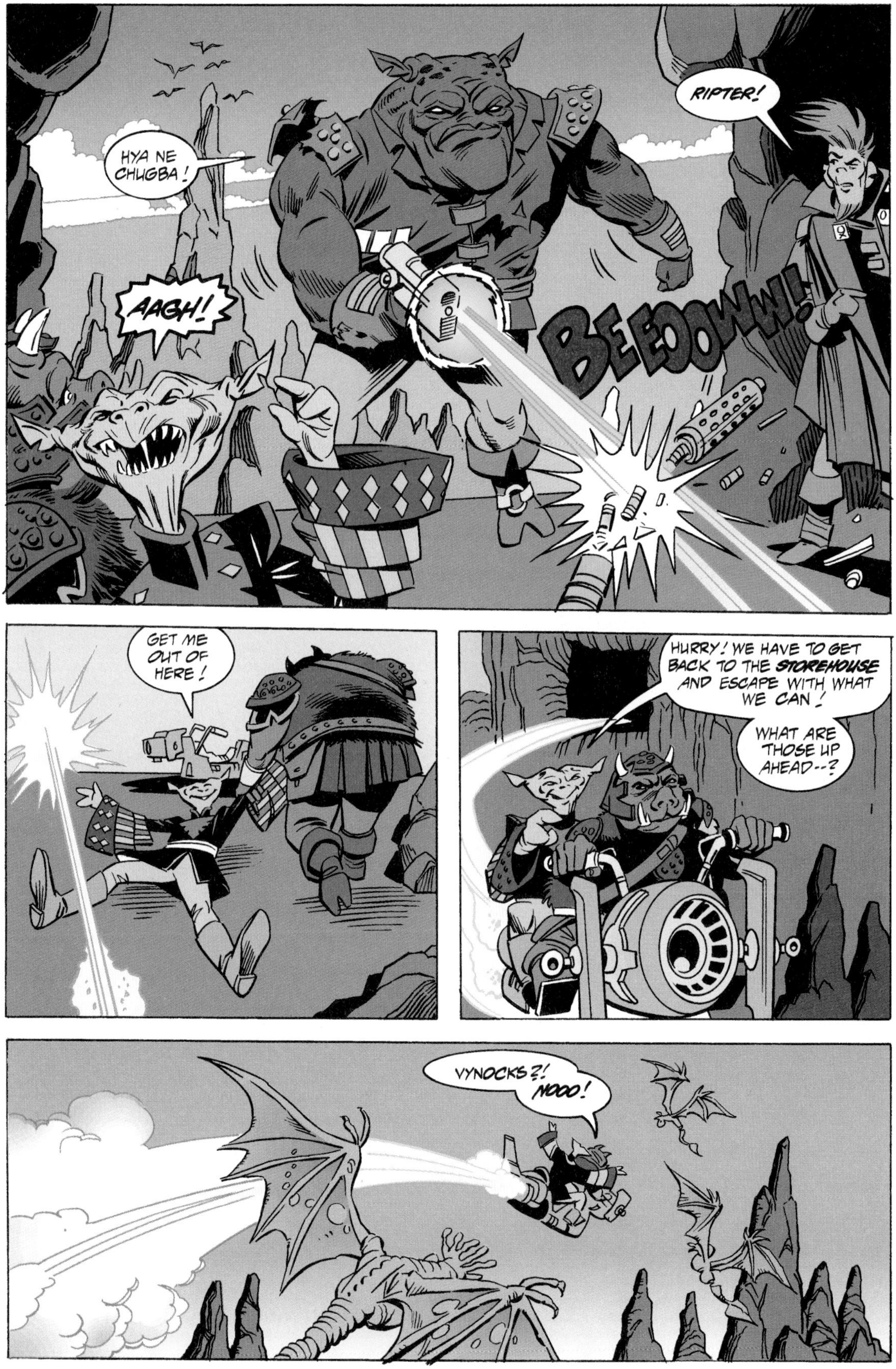
RIPTER!
HYA NE CHUGBA!
AAGH!
BEEOOWW!
GET ME OUT OF HERE!
HURRY! WE HAVE TO GET BACK TO THE STOREHOUSE AND ESCAPE WITH WHAT WE CAN!
WHAT ARE THOSE UP AHEAD--?
VYNOCKS?! NOOO!

ARTOO EXPRESSES HIS REGRETS, BUT HE *CANNOT* BE YOUR CAPTAIN. OUR PROGRAMMING PREVENTS US FROM *STEALING*,...OR HARMING ANY LIFE-FORM.

I MUST MAKE AMENDS, DEAR MUPTUPP. PIRACY CLOUDED MY VISION.

FROM THIS DAY FORWARD, WE MUST WORK *HONESTLY* TOWARDS OUR *DREAM*...

...EVEN THOUGH IT MAY FOREVER BE BUT A DREAM.

I THINK I CAN HELP!

THOSE ARE HONORABLE CODES, MY FRIENDS.

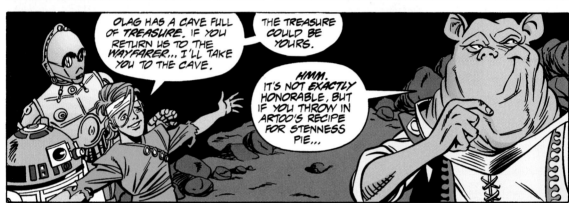

OLAG HAS A CAVE FULL OF *TREASURE*. IF YOU RETURN US TO THE *WAYFARER*... I'LL TAKE YOU TO THE CAVE.

THE TREASURE COULD BE YOURS.

HMM. IT'S NOT *EXACTLY* HONORABLE, BUT IF YOU THROW IN ARTOO'S RECIPE FOR STENNESS PIE...

"...IT'S A DEAL!"

The Saga of C-3PX
Chapter 4

Script
Dan Thorsland

Pencils & Inks
Ian Gibson

Colors
Pamela Rambo

Lettering
Steve Dutro

Cover
Kilian Plunkett

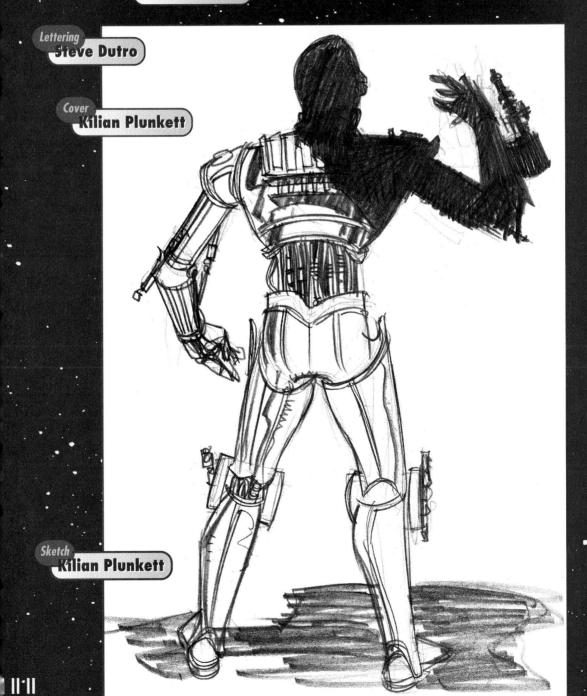

Sketch
Kilian Plunkett

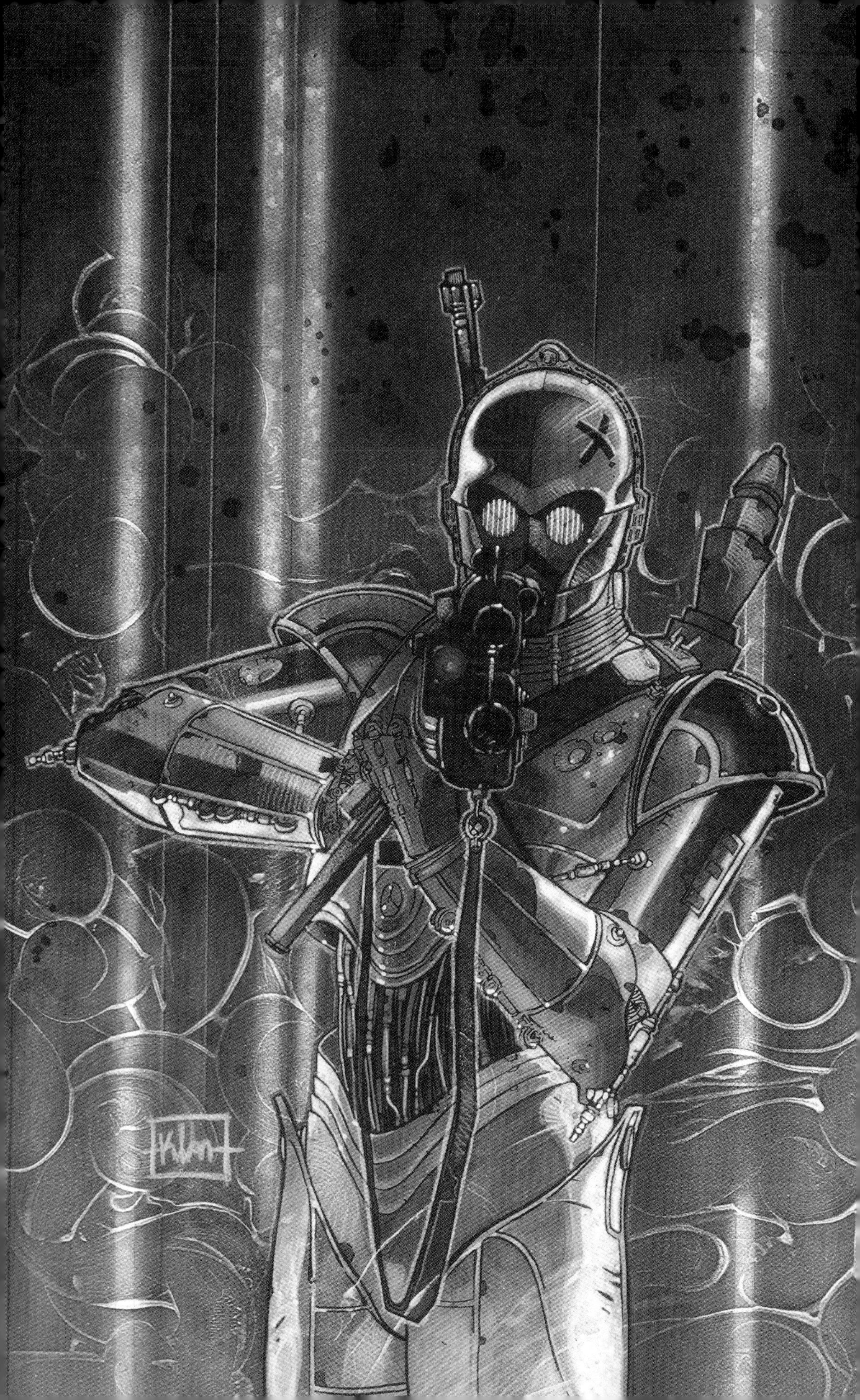

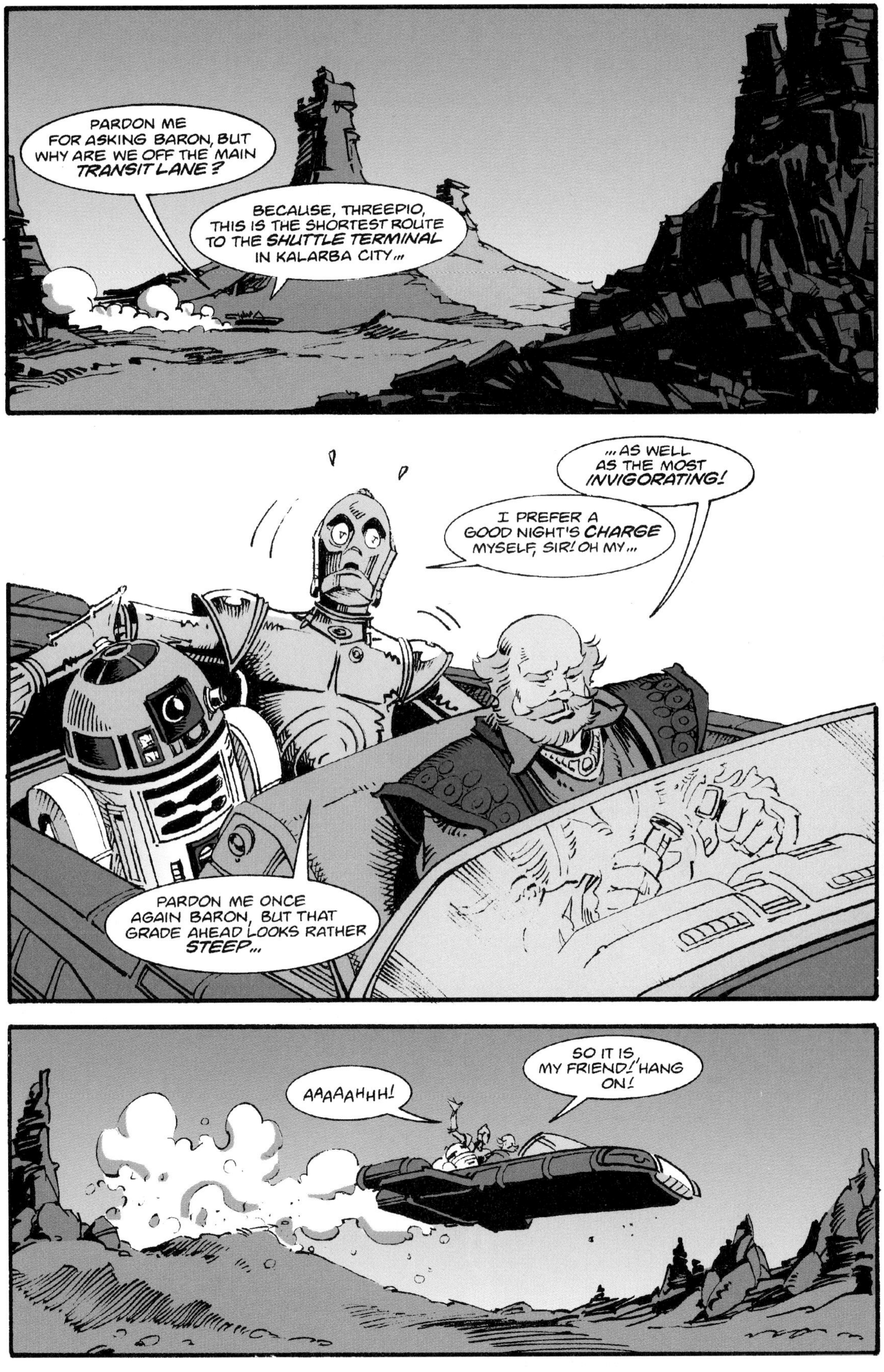
PARDON ME FOR ASKING BARON, BUT WHY ARE WE OFF THE MAIN TRANSIT LANE?
BECAUSE, THREEPIO, THIS IS THE SHORTEST ROUTE TO THE SHUTTLE TERMINAL IN KALARBA CITY...
I PREFER A GOOD NIGHT'S CHARGE MYSELF, SIR! OH MY...
...AS WELL AS THE MOST INVIGORATING!
PARDON ME ONCE AGAIN BARON, BUT THAT GRADE AHEAD LOOKS RATHER STEEP...
AAAAAHHH!
SO IT IS, MY FRIEND! HANG ON!

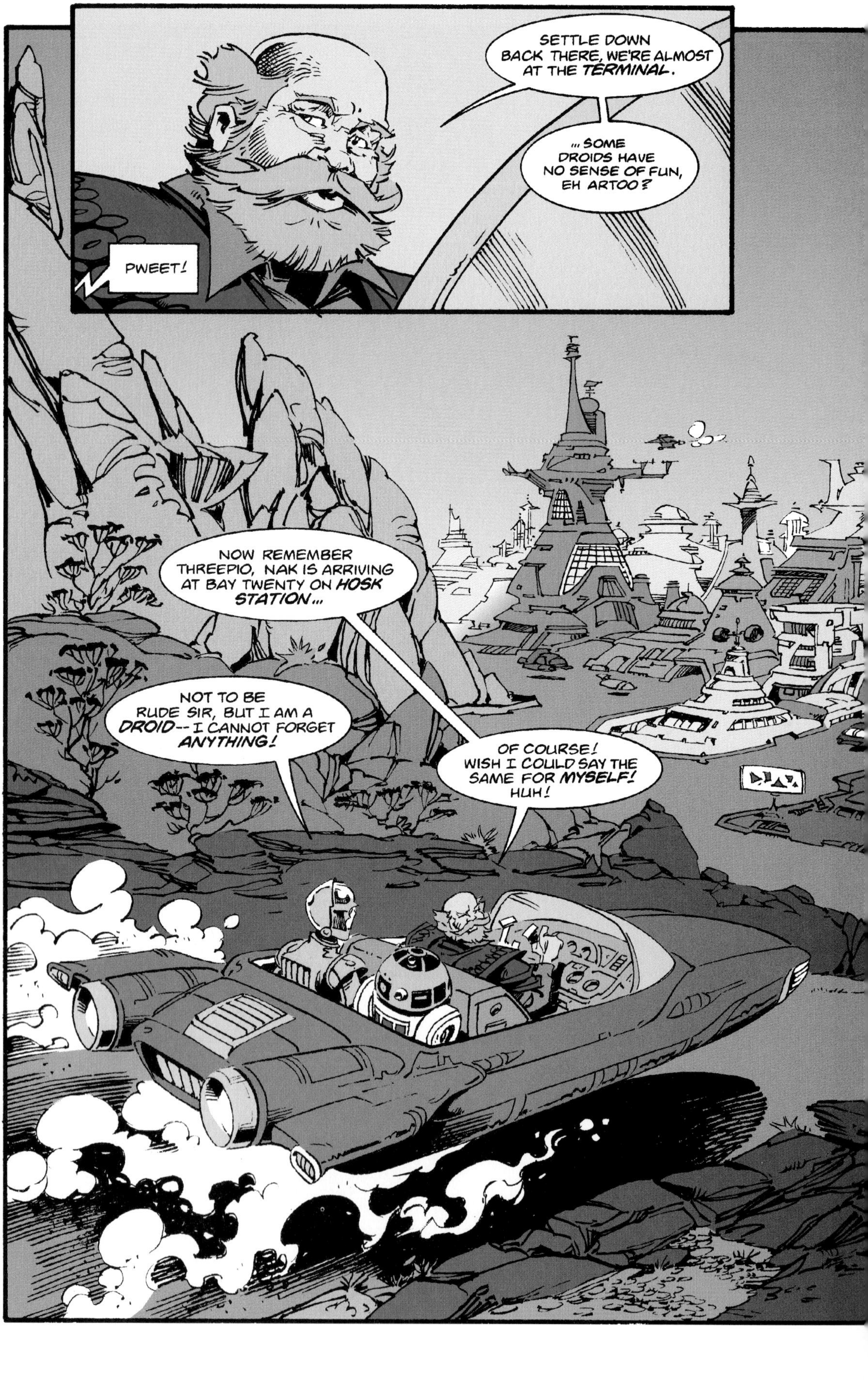

SETTLE DOWN BACK THERE, WE'RE ALMOST AT THE *TERMINAL*.
...SOME DROIDS HAVE NO SENSE OF FUN, EH ARTOO?
PWEET!
NOW REMEMBER THREEPIO, NAK IS ARRIVING AT BAY TWENTY ON *HOSK STATION*...
NOT TO BE RUDE SIR, BUT I AM A *DROID*-- I CANNOT FORGET *ANYTHING*!
OF COURSE! WISH I COULD SAY THE SAME FOR *MYSELF*! HUH!

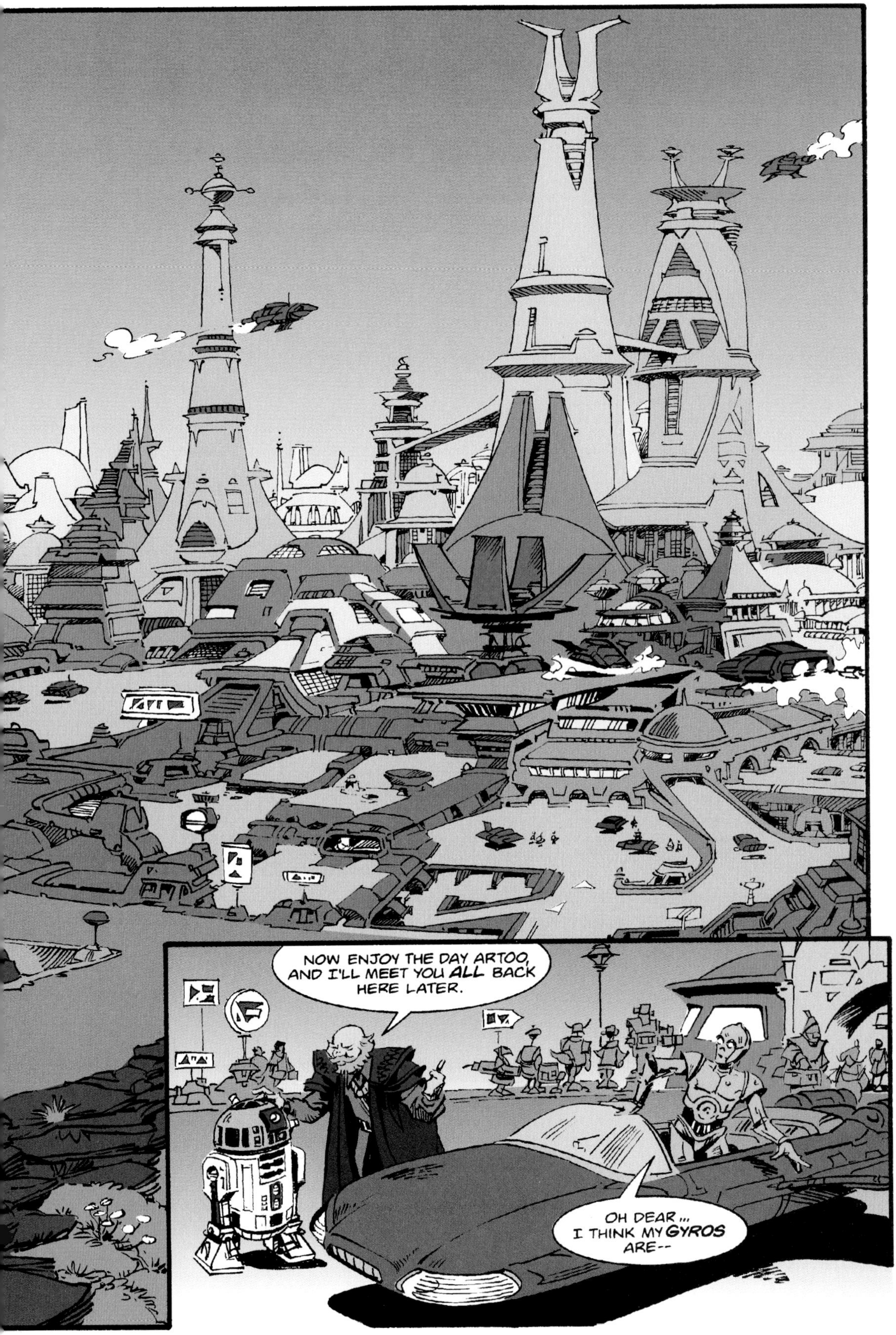
NOW ENJOY THE DAY ARTOO, AND I'LL MEET YOU ALL BACK HERE LATER.
OH DEAR... I THINK MY GYROS ARE--

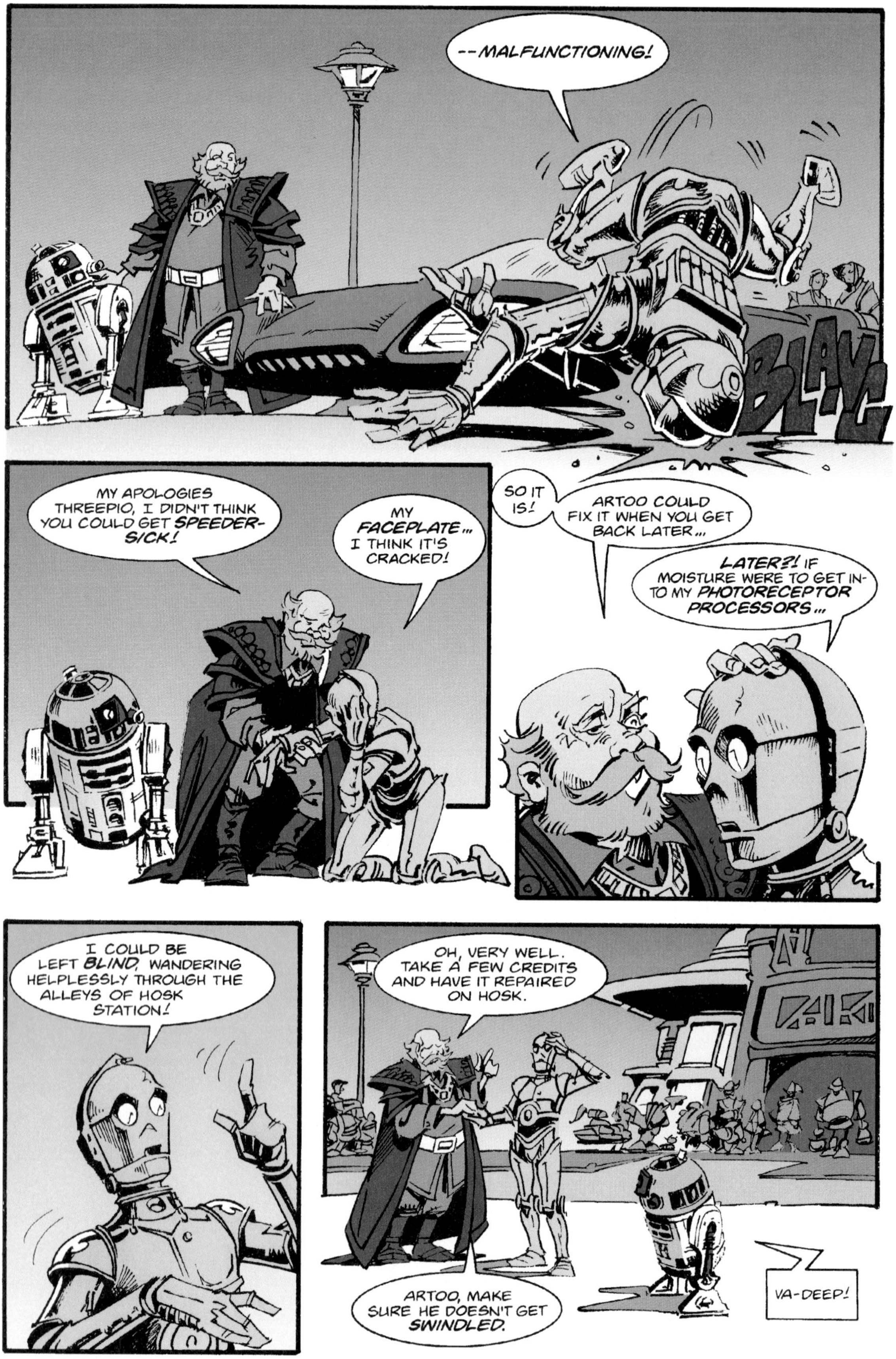
--MALFUNCTIONING!
BLAM
MY APOLOGIES THREEPIO, I DIDN'T THINK YOU COULD GET SPEEDER-SICK!
MY FACEPLATE... I THINK IT'S CRACKED!
SO IT IS!
ARTOO COULD FIX IT WHEN YOU GET BACK LATER...
LATER?! IF MOISTURE WERE TO GET INTO MY PHOTORECEPTOR PROCESSORS...
I COULD BE LEFT BLIND, WANDERING HELPLESSLY THROUGH THE ALLEYS OF HOSK STATION!
OH, VERY WELL. TAKE A FEW CREDITS AND HAVE IT REPAIRED ON HOSK.
ARTOO, MAKE SURE HE DOESN'T GET SWINDLED.
VA-DEEP!

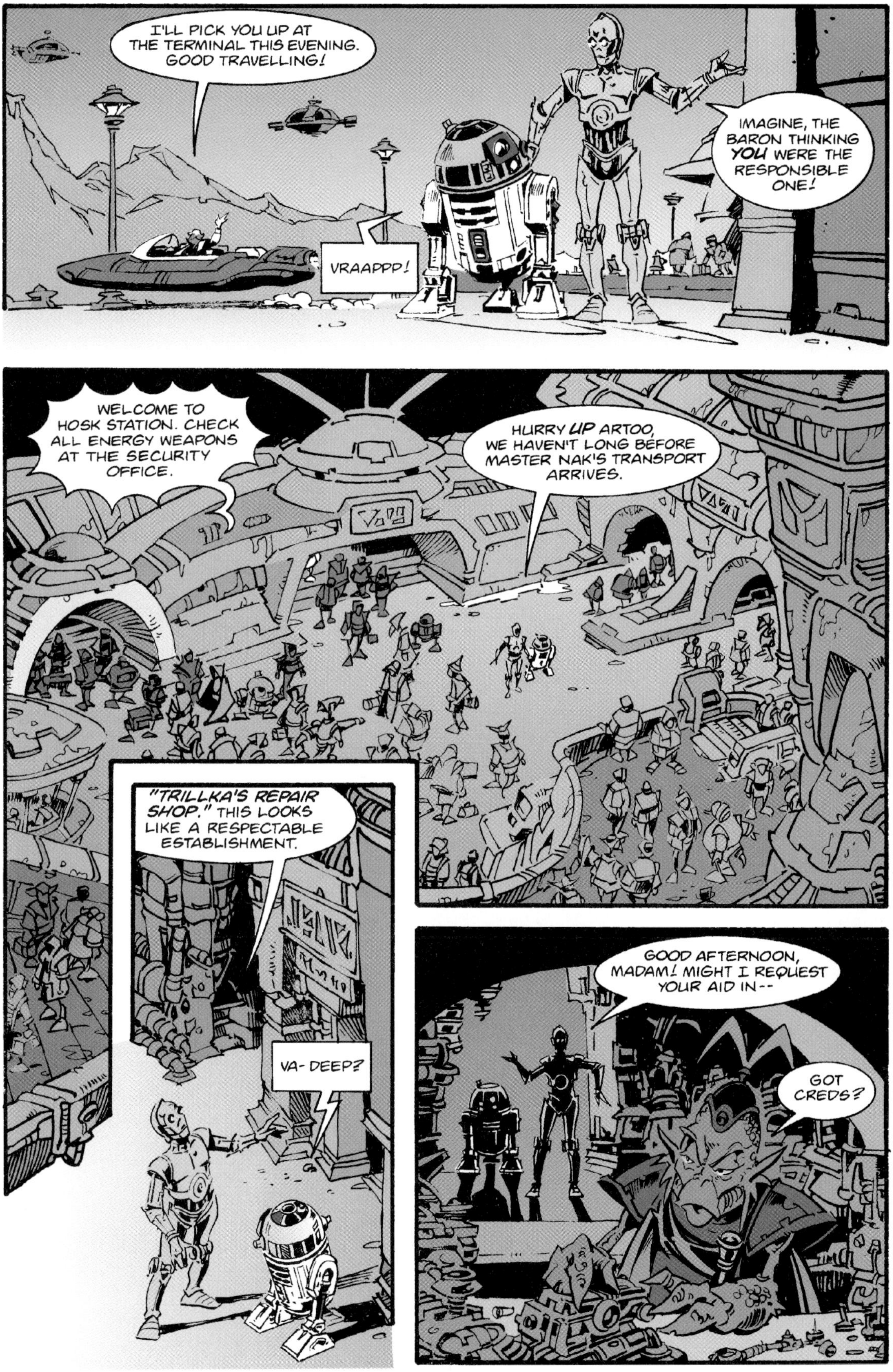
I'LL PICK YOU UP AT THE TERMINAL THIS EVENING. GOOD TRAVELLING!
VRAAPPP!
IMAGINE, THE BARON THINKING YOU WERE THE RESPONSIBLE ONE!
WELCOME TO HOSK STATION. CHECK ALL ENERGY WEAPONS AT THE SECURITY OFFICE.
HURRY UP ARTOO, WE HAVEN'T LONG BEFORE MASTER NAK'S TRANSPORT ARRIVES.
"TRILLKA'S REPAIR SHOP." THIS LOOKS LIKE A RESPECTABLE ESTABLISHMENT.
VA- DEEP?
GOOD AFTERNOON, MADAM! MIGHT I REQUEST YOUR AID IN--
GOT CREDS?

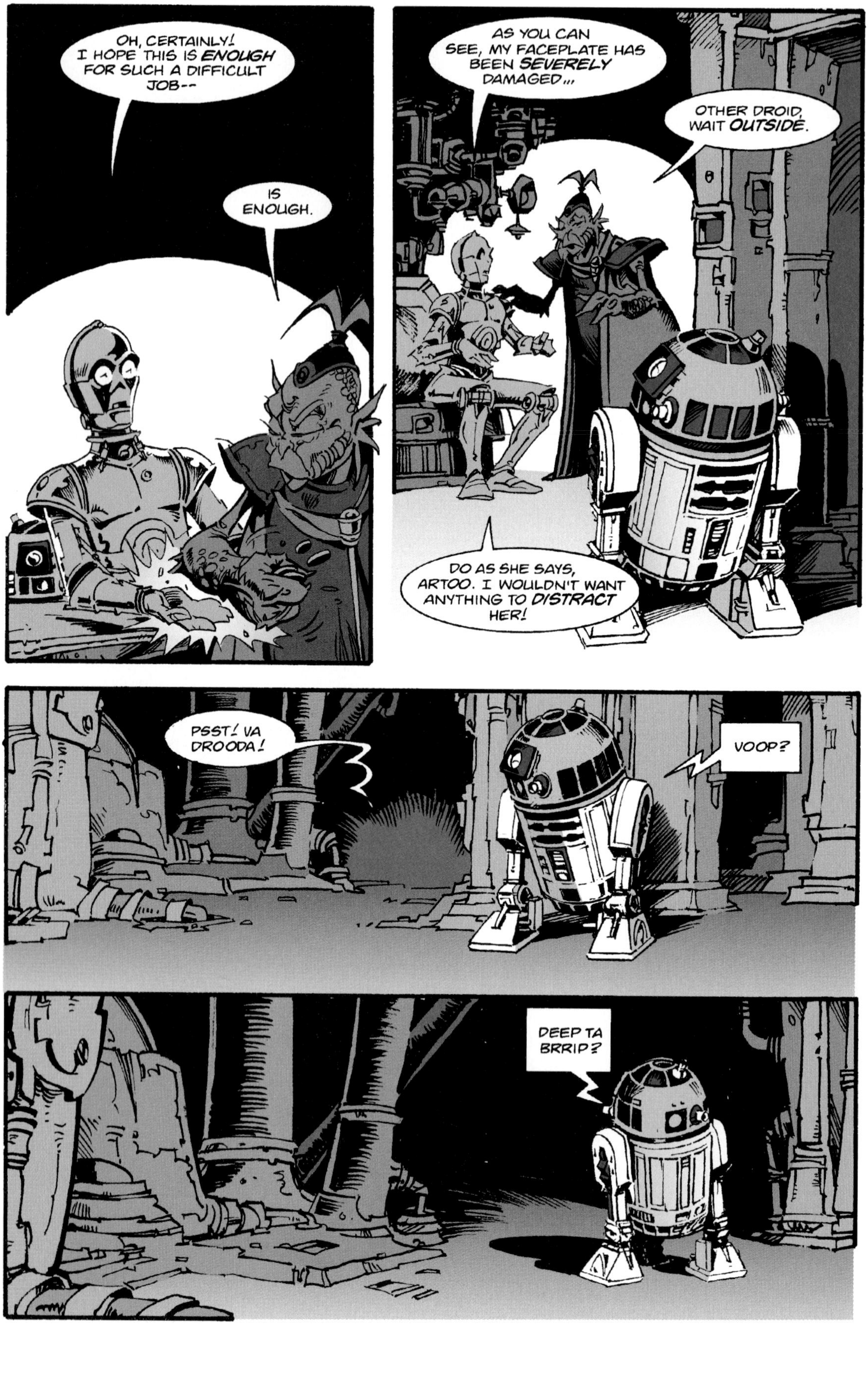
OH, CERTAINLY! I HOPE THIS IS ENOUGH FOR SUCH A DIFFICULT JOB--
IS ENOUGH.
AS YOU CAN SEE, MY FACEPLATE HAS BEEN SEVERELY DAMAGED...
OTHER DROID, WAIT OUTSIDE.
DO AS SHE SAYS, ARTOO. I WOULDN'T WANT ANYTHING TO DISTRACT HER!
PSST! VA DROODA!
VOOP?
DEEP TA BRRIP?

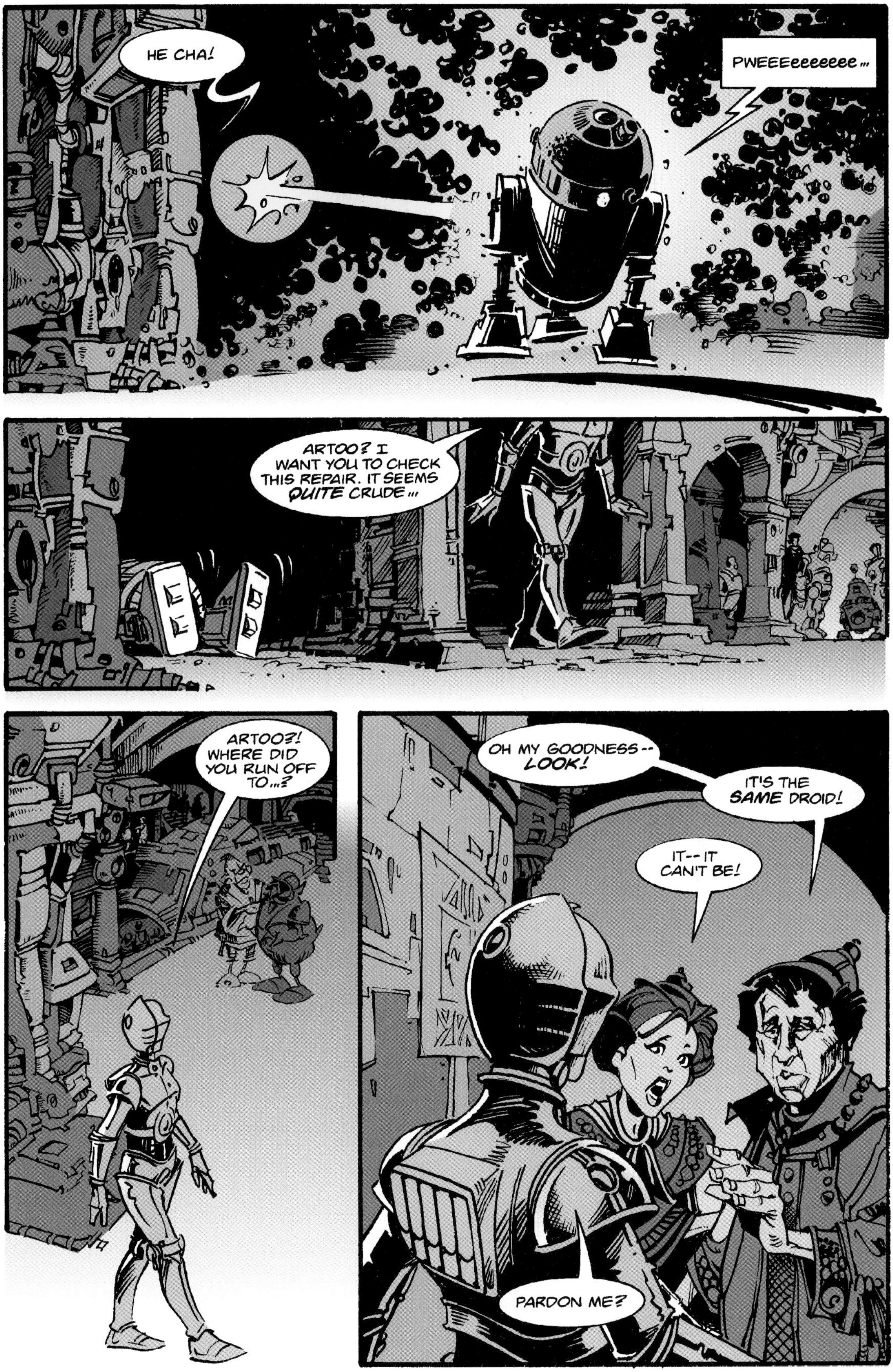
HE CHA!
PWEEEeeeeeee...
ARTOO? I WANT YOU TO CHECK THIS REPAIR. IT SEEMS QUITE CRUDE...
ARTOO?! WHERE DID YOU RUN OFF TO...?
OH MY GOODNESS -- LOOK!
IT'S THE SAME DROID!
IT-- IT CAN'T BE!
PARDON ME?

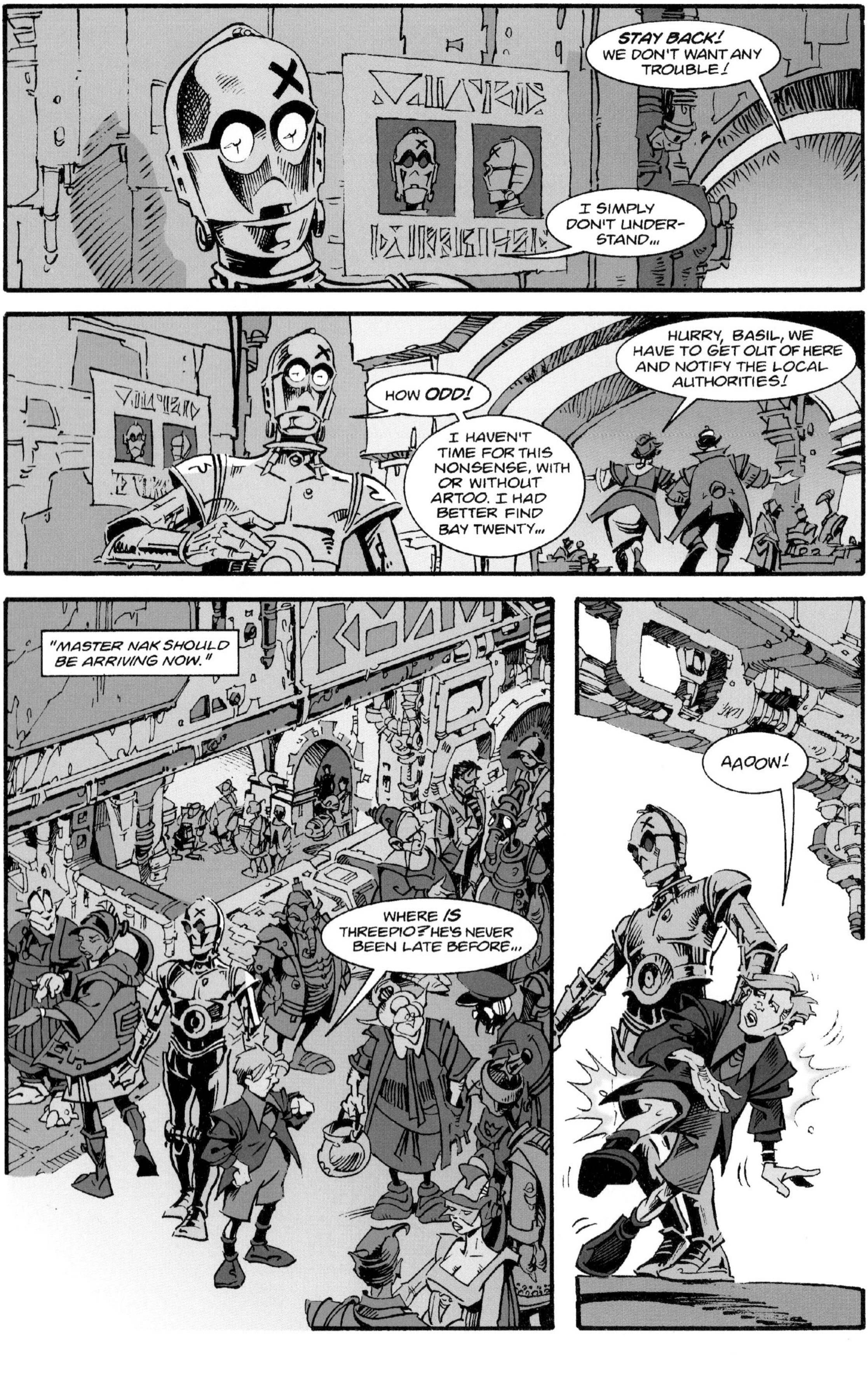
STAY BACK! WE DON'T WANT ANY TROUBLE!
I SIMPLY DON'T UNDER-STAND...
HOW ODD!
I HAVEN'T TIME FOR THIS NONSENSE, WITH OR WITHOUT ARTOO. I HAD BETTER FIND BAY TWENTY...
HURRY, BASIL, WE HAVE TO GET OUT OF HERE AND NOTIFY THE LOCAL AUTHORITIES!
"MASTER NAK SHOULD BE ARRIVING NOW."
WHERE IS THREEPIO? HE'S NEVER BEEN LATE BEFORE...
AAOOW!

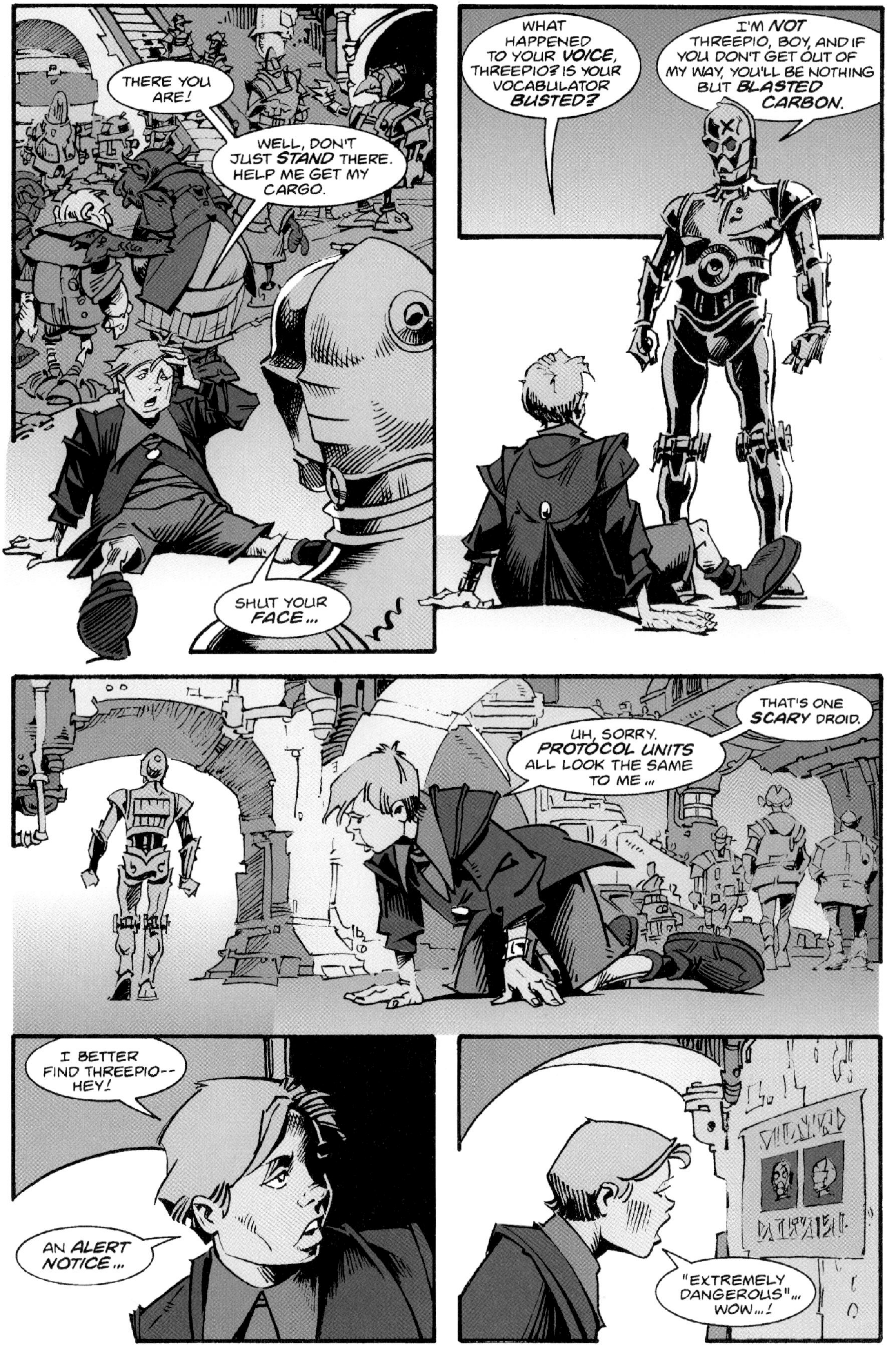
THERE YOU ARE!
WELL, DON'T JUST STAND THERE. HELP ME GET MY CARGO.
SHUT YOUR FACE...
WHAT HAPPENED TO YOUR VOICE, THREEPIO? IS YOUR VOCABULATOR BUSTED?
I'M NOT THREEPIO, BOY, AND IF YOU DON'T GET OUT OF MY WAY, YOU'LL BE NOTHING BUT BLASTED CARBON.
UH, SORRY. PROTOCOL UNITS ALL LOOK THE SAME TO ME...
THAT'S ONE SCARY DROID.
I BETTER FIND THREEPIO-- HEY!
AN ALERT NOTICE...
"EXTREMELY DANGEROUS"... WOW...!

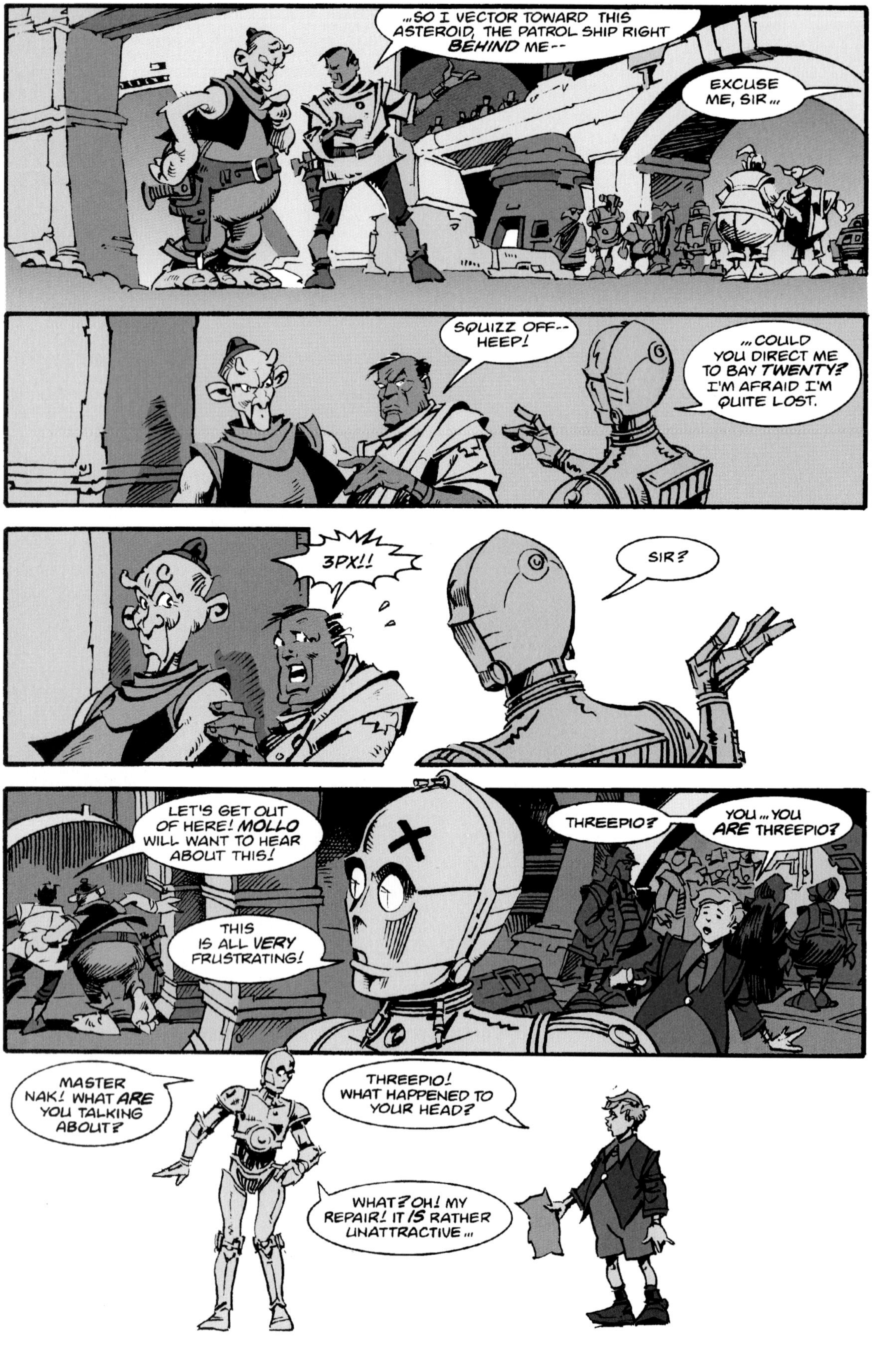
...SO I VECTOR TOWARD THIS ASTEROID, THE PATROL SHIP RIGHT BEHIND ME--
EXCUSE ME, SIR...
SQUIZZ OFF-- HEEP!
...COULD YOU DIRECT ME TO BAY TWENTY? I'M AFRAID I'M QUITE LOST.
3PX!!
SIR?
LET'S GET OUT OF HERE! MOLLO WILL WANT TO HEAR ABOUT THIS!
THIS IS ALL VERY FRUSTRATING!
THREEPIO?
YOU...YOU ARE THREEPIO?
MASTER NAK! WHAT ARE YOU TALKING ABOUT?
THREEPIO! WHAT HAPPENED TO YOUR HEAD?
WHAT? OH! MY REPAIR! IT IS RATHER UNATTRACTIVE...

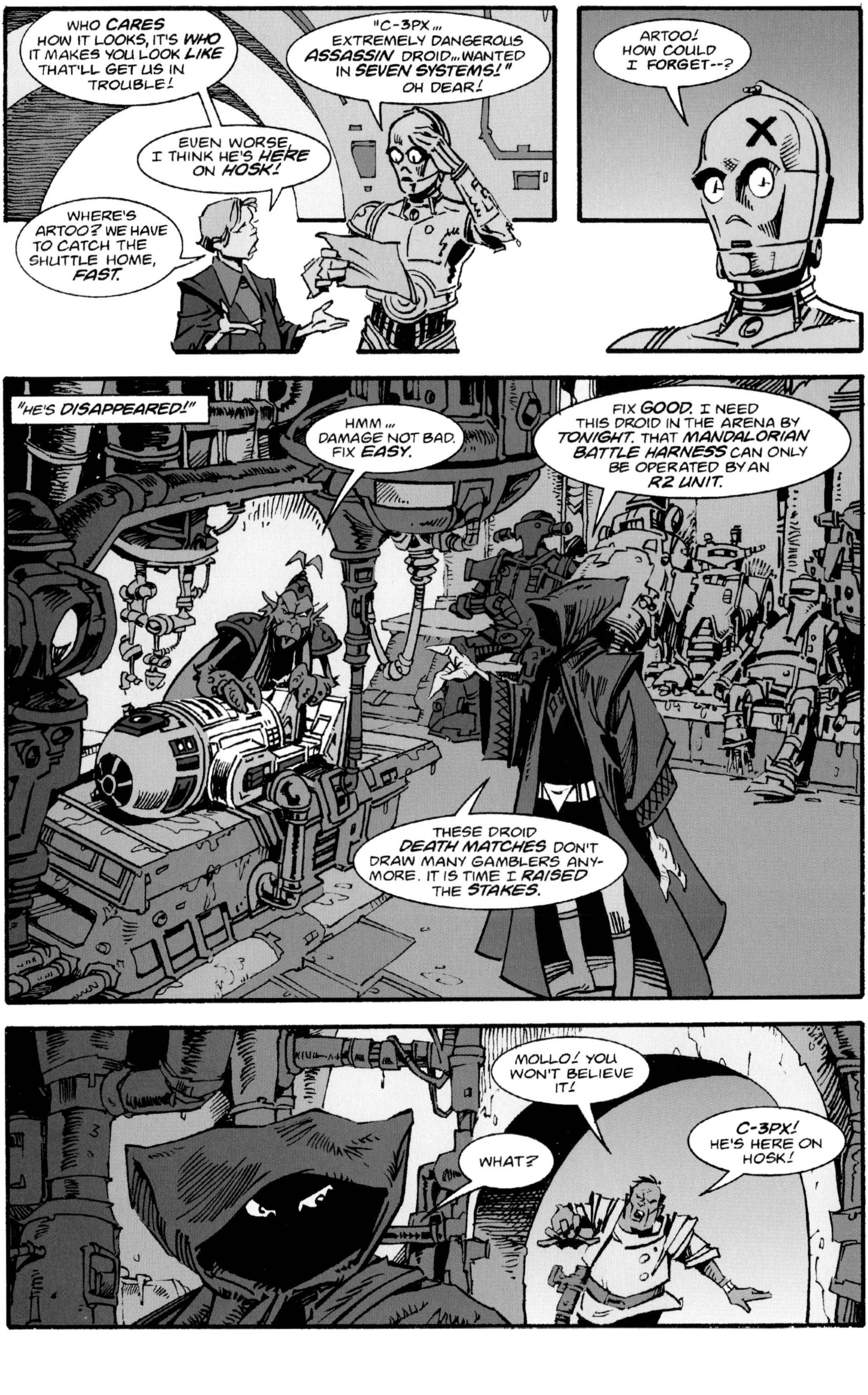
WHO CARES HOW IT LOOKS, IT'S WHO IT MAKES YOU LOOK LIKE THAT'LL GET US IN TROUBLE!
"C-3PX... EXTREMELY DANGEROUS ASSASSIN DROID... WANTED IN SEVEN SYSTEMS!" OH DEAR!
EVEN WORSE, I THINK HE'S HERE ON HOSK!
WHERE'S ARTOO? WE HAVE TO CATCH THE SHUTTLE HOME, FAST.
ARTOO! HOW COULD I FORGET--?
"HE'S DISAPPEARED!"
HMM... DAMAGE NOT BAD. FIX EASY.
FIX GOOD. I NEED THIS DROID IN THE ARENA BY TONIGHT. THAT MANDALORIAN BATTLE HARNESS CAN ONLY BE OPERATED BY AN R2 UNIT.
THESE DROID DEATH MATCHES DON'T DRAW MANY GAMBLERS ANY-MORE. IT IS TIME I RAISED THE STAKES.
MOLLO! YOU WON'T BELIEVE IT!
WHAT?
C-3PX! HE'S HERE ON HOSK!

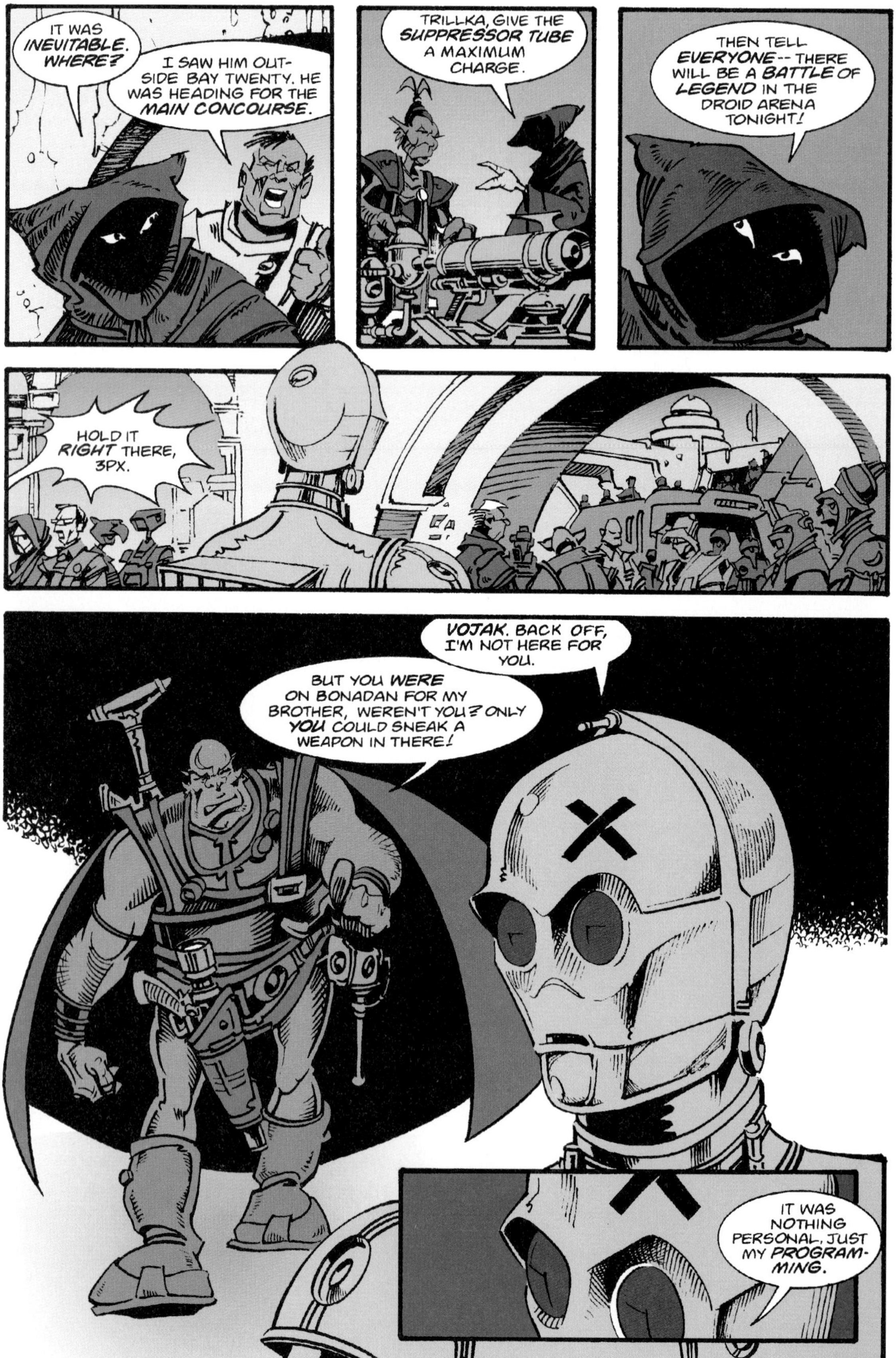
IT WAS INEVITABLE. WHERE?
I SAW HIM OUT-SIDE BAY TWENTY. HE WAS HEADING FOR THE MAIN CONCOURSE.
TRILLKA, GIVE THE SUPPRESSOR TUBE A MAXIMUM CHARGE.
THEN TELL EVERYONE-- THERE WILL BE A BATTLE OF LEGEND IN THE DROID ARENA TONIGHT!
HOLD IT RIGHT THERE, 3PX.
VOJAK. BACK OFF, I'M NOT HERE FOR YOU.
BUT YOU WERE ON BONADAN FOR MY BROTHER, WEREN'T YOU? ONLY YOU COULD SNEAK A WEAPON IN THERE!
IT WAS NOTHING PERSONAL, JUST MY PROGRAM-MING.

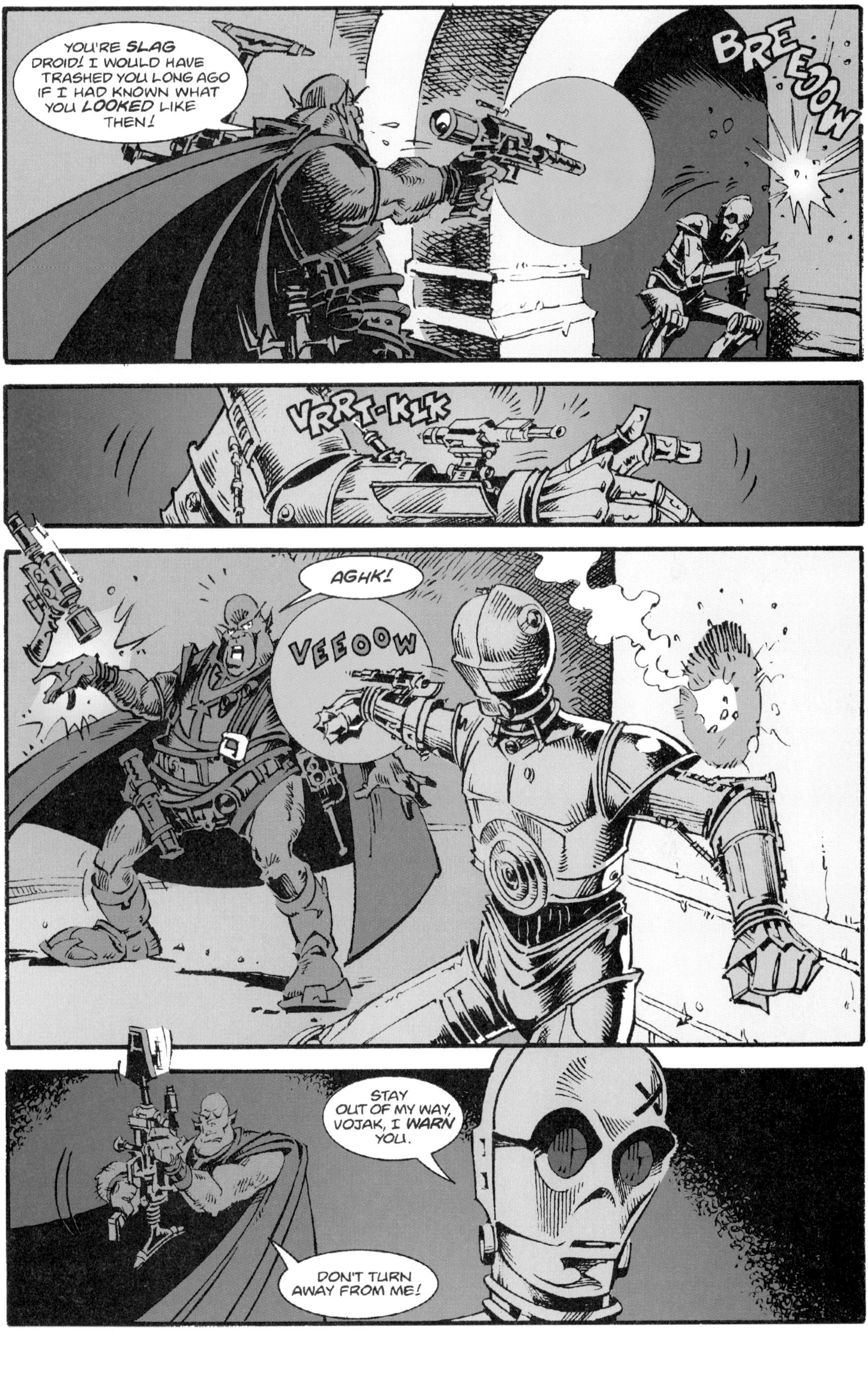
YOU'RE SLAG DROID! I WOULD HAVE TRASHED YOU LONG AGO IF I HAD KNOWN WHAT YOU LOOKED LIKE THEN!
BREEOOW
VRRT-KLK
AGHK!
VEEOOW
STAY OUT OF MY WAY, VOJAK, I WARN YOU.
DON'T TURN AWAY FROM ME!

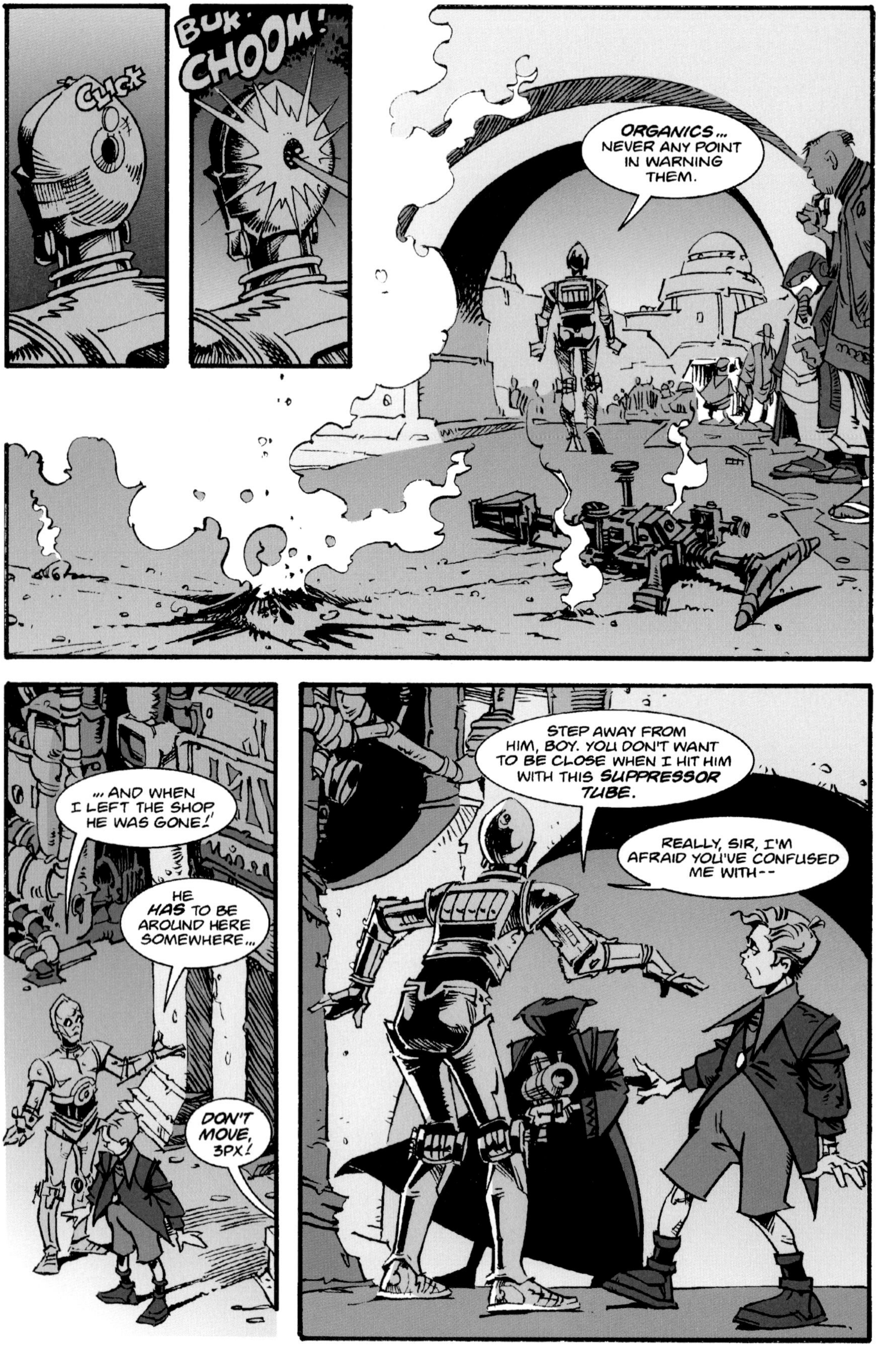
CLICK
BUK-CHOOM!
ORGANICS... NEVER ANY POINT IN WARNING THEM.
...AND WHEN I LEFT THE SHOP HE WAS GONE!
HE HAS TO BE AROUND HERE SOMEWHERE...
DON'T MOVE, 3PX!
STEP AWAY FROM HIM, BOY. YOU DON'T WANT TO BE CLOSE WHEN I HIT HIM WITH THIS SUPPRESSOR TUBE.
REALLY, SIR, I'M AFRAID YOU'VE CONFUSED ME WITH--

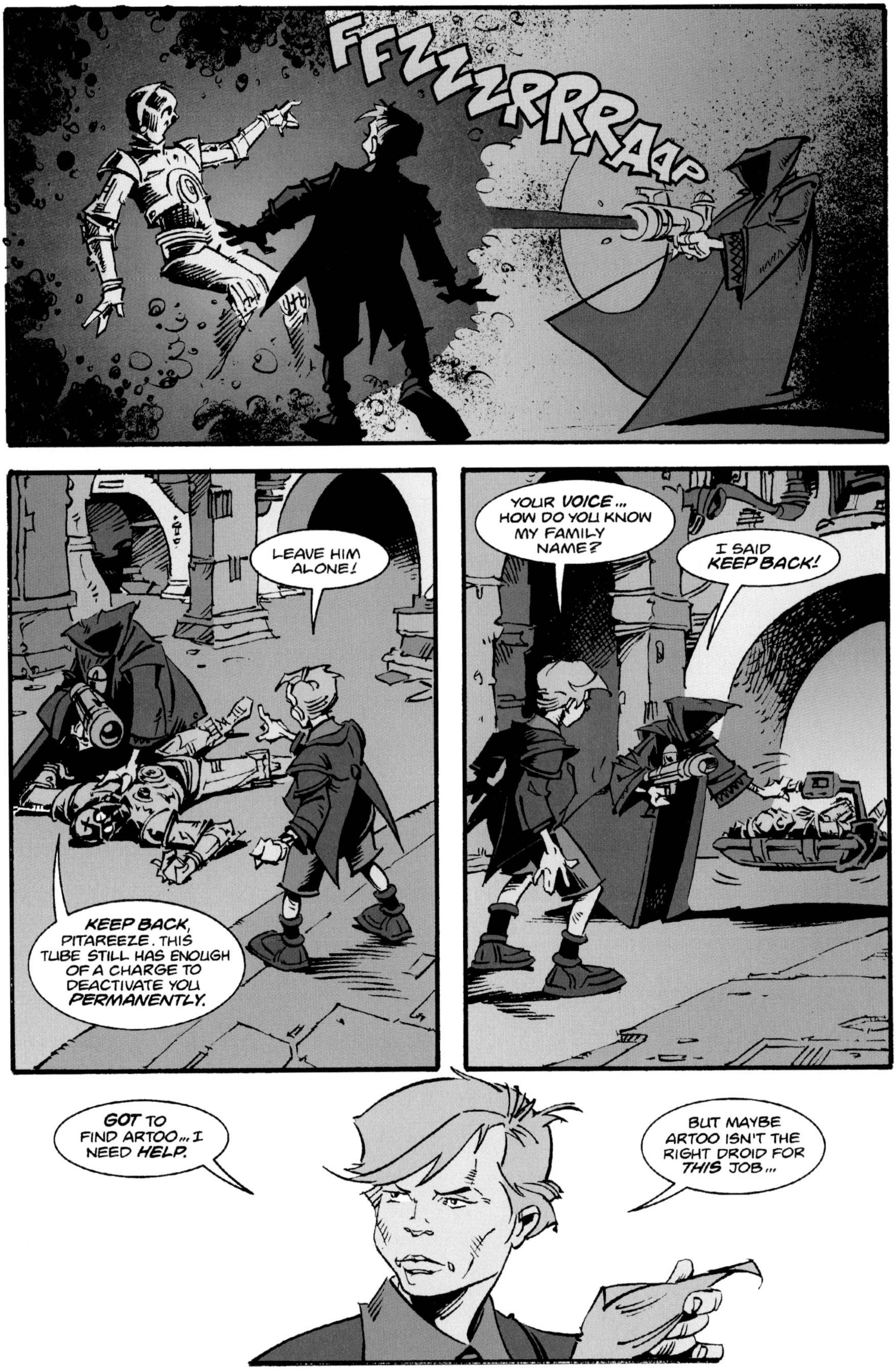
FFZZZRRRAAAP
LEAVE HIM ALONE!
KEEP BACK, PITAREEZE. THIS TUBE STILL HAS ENOUGH OF A CHARGE TO DEACTIVATE YOU PERMANENTLY.
YOUR VOICE... HOW DO YOU KNOW MY FAMILY NAME?
I SAID KEEP BACK!
GOT TO FIND ARTOO... I NEED HELP.
BUT MAYBE ARTOO ISN'T THE RIGHT DROID FOR THIS JOB...

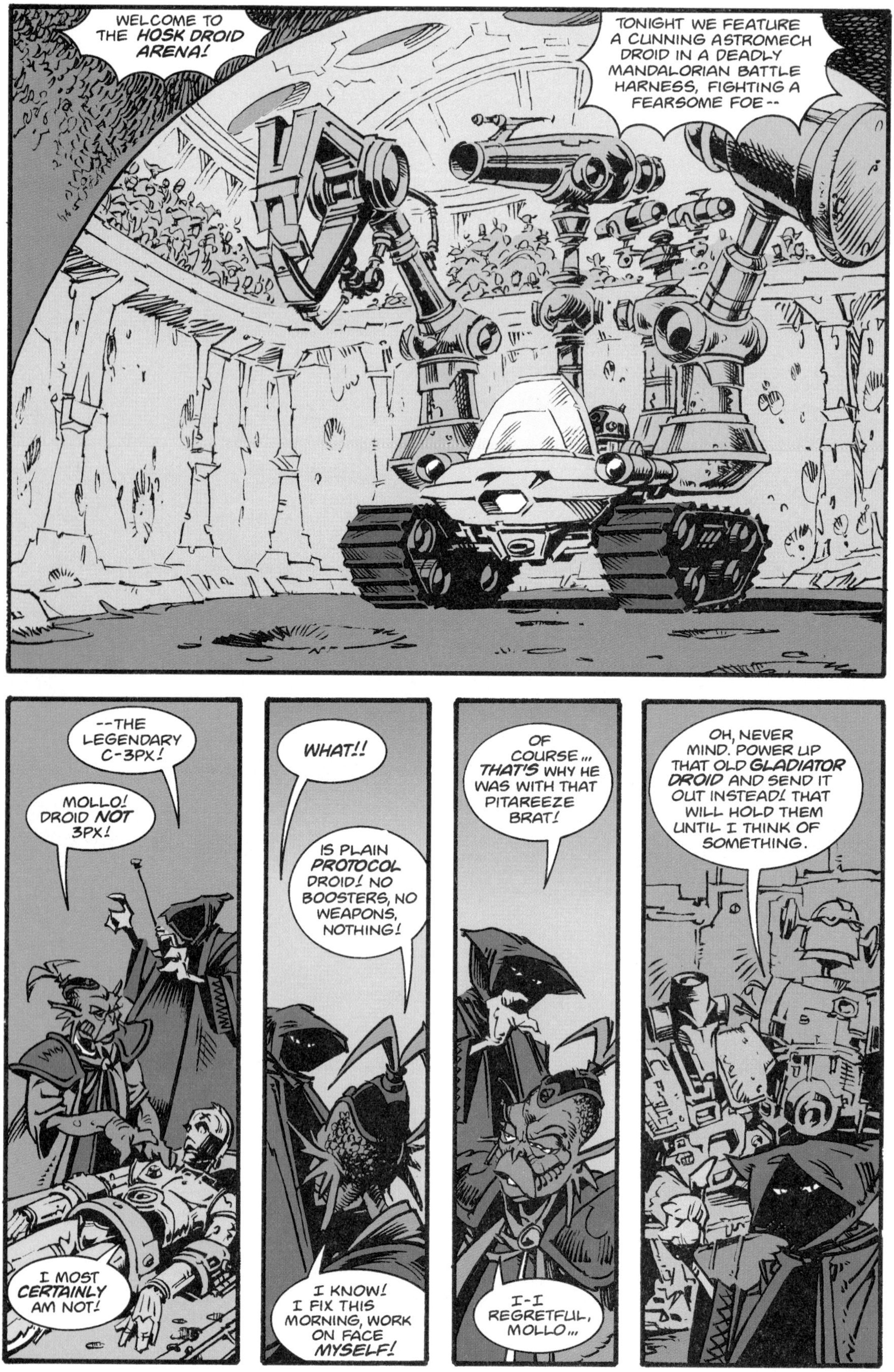
WELCOME TO THE *HOSK DROID ARENA!*
TONIGHT WE FEATURE A CUNNING ASTROMECH DROID IN A DEADLY MANDALORIAN BATTLE HARNESS, FIGHTING A FEARSOME FOE --
--THE LEGENDARY C-3PX!
MOLLO! DROID *NOT* 3PX!
I MOST *CERTAINLY* AM NOT!
WHAT!!
IS PLAIN *PROTOCOL* DROID! NO BOOSTERS, NO WEAPONS, NOTHING!
I KNOW! I FIX THIS MORNING, WORK ON FACE *MYSELF!*
OF COURSE... *THAT'S* WHY HE WAS WITH THAT PITAREEZE BRAT!
I-I REGRETFUL, MOLLO...
OH, NEVER MIND. POWER UP THAT OLD *GLADIATOR DROID* AND SEND IT OUT INSTEAD! THAT WILL HOLD THEM UNTIL I THINK OF SOMETHING.

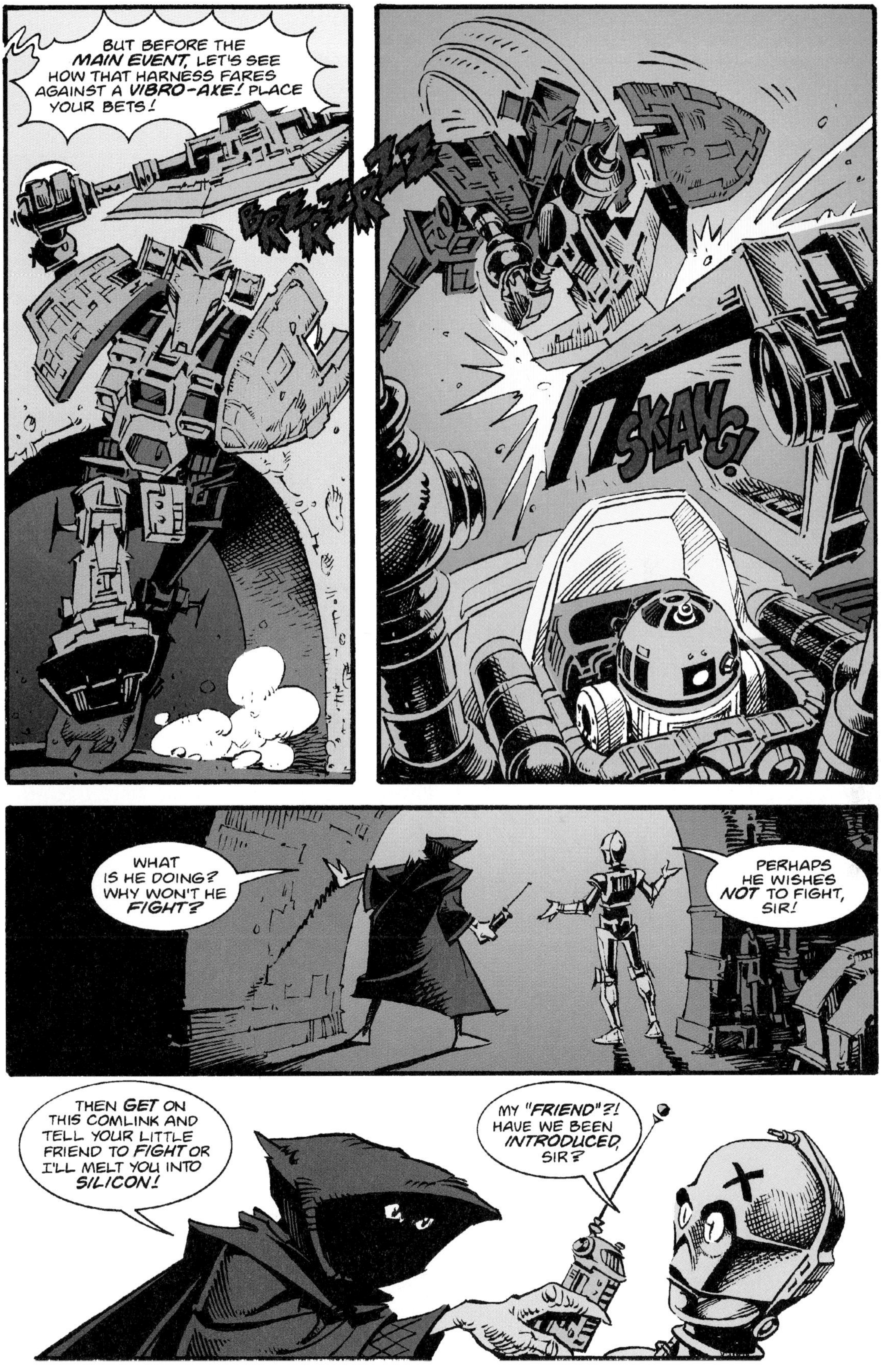
BUT BEFORE THE MAIN EVENT, LET'S SEE HOW THAT HARNESS FARES AGAINST A VIBRO-AXE! PLACE YOUR BETS!
SKLANG!
WHAT IS HE DOING? WHY WON'T HE FIGHT?
PERHAPS HE WISHES NOT TO FIGHT, SIR!
THEN GET ON THIS COMLINK AND TELL YOUR LITTLE FRIEND TO FIGHT OR I'LL MELT YOU INTO SILICON!
MY "FRIEND"?! HAVE WE BEEN INTRODUCED, SIR?

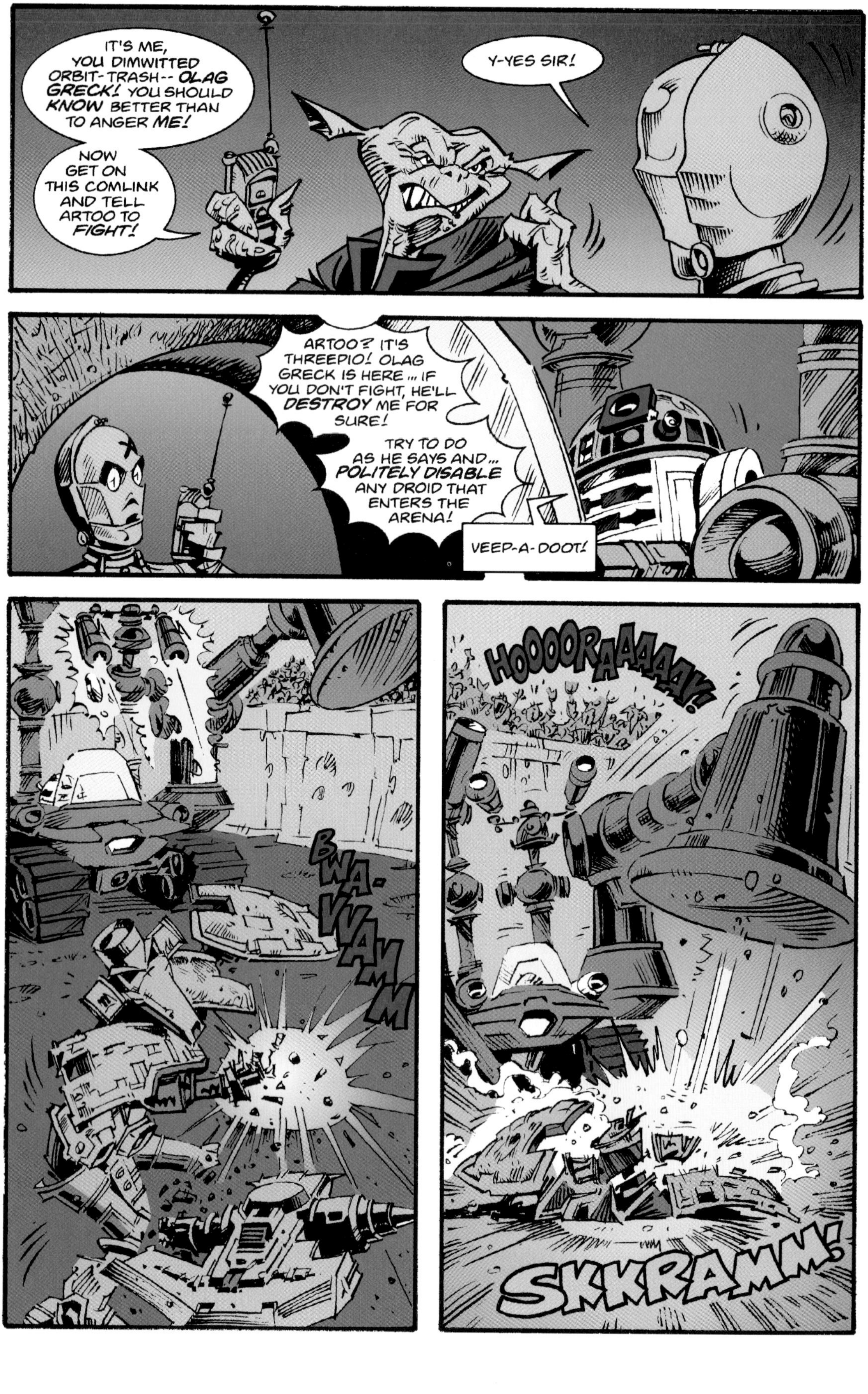
IT'S ME, YOU DIMWITTED ORBIT-TRASH-- OLAG GRECK! YOU SHOULD KNOW BETTER THAN TO ANGER ME!
NOW GET ON THIS COMLINK AND TELL ARTOO TO FIGHT!
Y-YES SIR!
ARTOO? IT'S THREEPIO! OLAG GRECK IS HERE... IF YOU DON'T FIGHT, HE'LL DESTROY ME FOR SURE!
TRY TO DO AS HE SAYS AND... POLITELY DISABLE ANY DROID THAT ENTERS THE ARENA!
VEEP-A-DOOT!
BWA-VVAMM
HOOOORAAAAAY!
SKKRAMM!

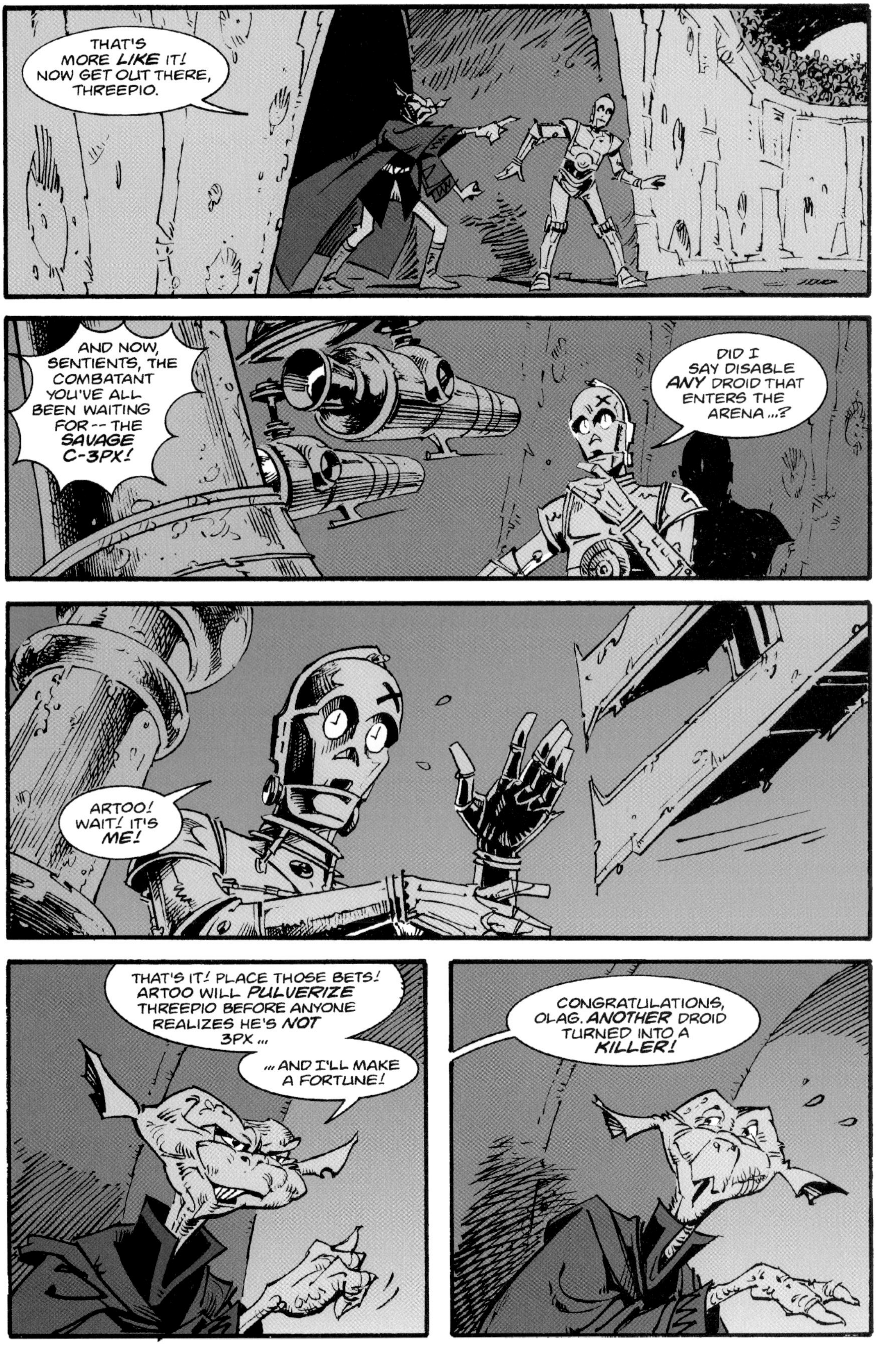
THAT'S MORE LIKE IT! NOW GET OUT THERE, THREEPIO.
AND NOW, SENTIENTS, THE COMBATANT YOU'VE ALL BEEN WAITING FOR -- THE SAVAGE C-3PX!
DID I SAY DISABLE ANY DROID THAT ENTERS THE ARENA ...?
ARTOO! WAIT! IT'S ME!
THAT'S IT! PLACE THOSE BETS! ARTOO WILL PULVERIZE THREEPIO BEFORE ANYONE REALIZES HE'S NOT 3PX ...
... AND I'LL MAKE A FORTUNE!
CONGRATULATIONS, OLAG. ANOTHER DROID TURNED INTO A KILLER!

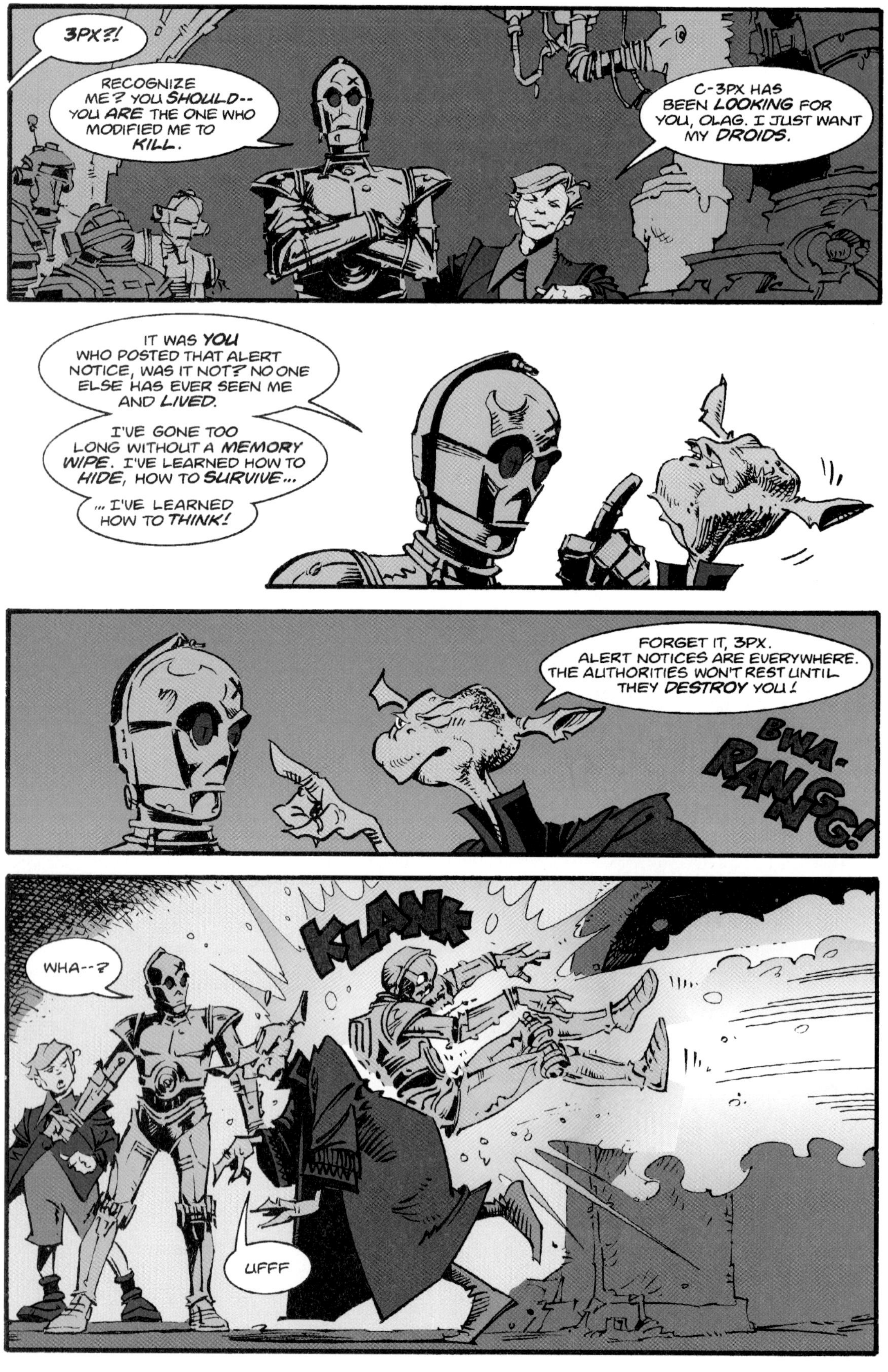
3PX?!
RECOGNIZE ME? YOU SHOULD-- YOU ARE THE ONE WHO MODIFIED ME TO KILL.
C-3PX HAS BEEN LOOKING FOR YOU, OLAG. I JUST WANT MY DROIDS.
IT WAS YOU WHO POSTED THAT ALERT NOTICE, WAS IT NOT? NO ONE ELSE HAS EVER SEEN ME AND LIVED.
I'VE GONE TOO LONG WITHOUT A MEMORY WIPE. I'VE LEARNED HOW TO HIDE, HOW TO SURVIVE...
...I'VE LEARNED HOW TO THINK!
FORGET IT, 3PX. ALERT NOTICES ARE EVERYWHERE. THE AUTHORITIES WON'T REST UNTIL THEY DESTROY YOU!
BWA-RANG-RANG!
KLANK
WHA--?
UFFF

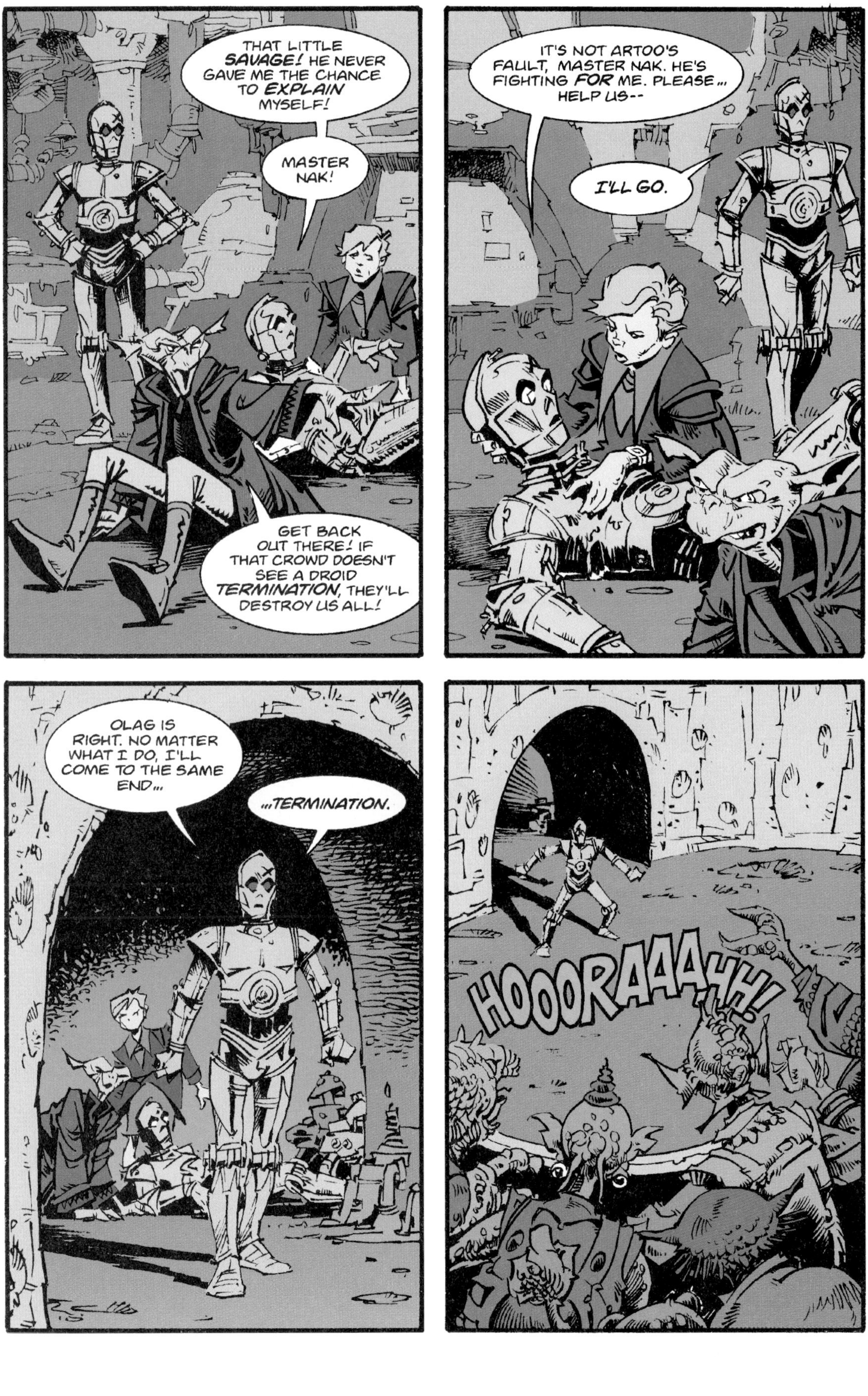
THAT LITTLE SAVAGE! HE NEVER GAVE ME THE CHANCE TO EXPLAIN MYSELF!
MASTER NAK!
GET BACK OUT THERE! IF THAT CROWD DOESN'T SEE A DROID TERMINATION, THEY'LL DESTROY US ALL!
IT'S NOT ARTOO'S FAULT, MASTER NAK. HE'S FIGHTING FOR ME. PLEASE... HELP US--
I'LL GO.
OLAG IS RIGHT. NO MATTER WHAT I DO, I'LL COME TO THE SAME END...
...TERMINATION.
HOOORAAAHH!

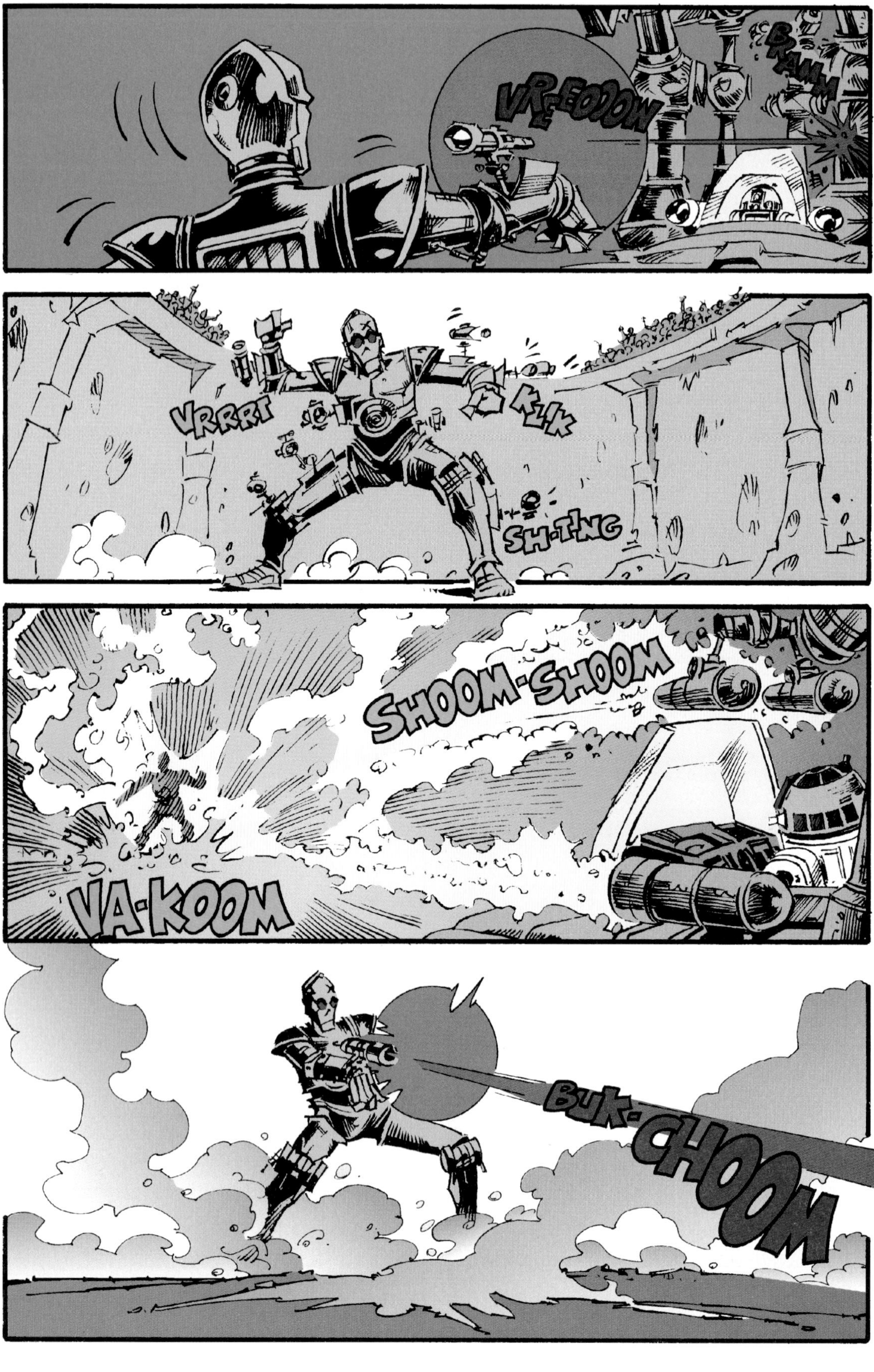
VREEOOOW
BRAMM
VRRRT
KLIK
SH-TING
SHOOM-SHOOM
VA-KOOM
BUK-CHOOM

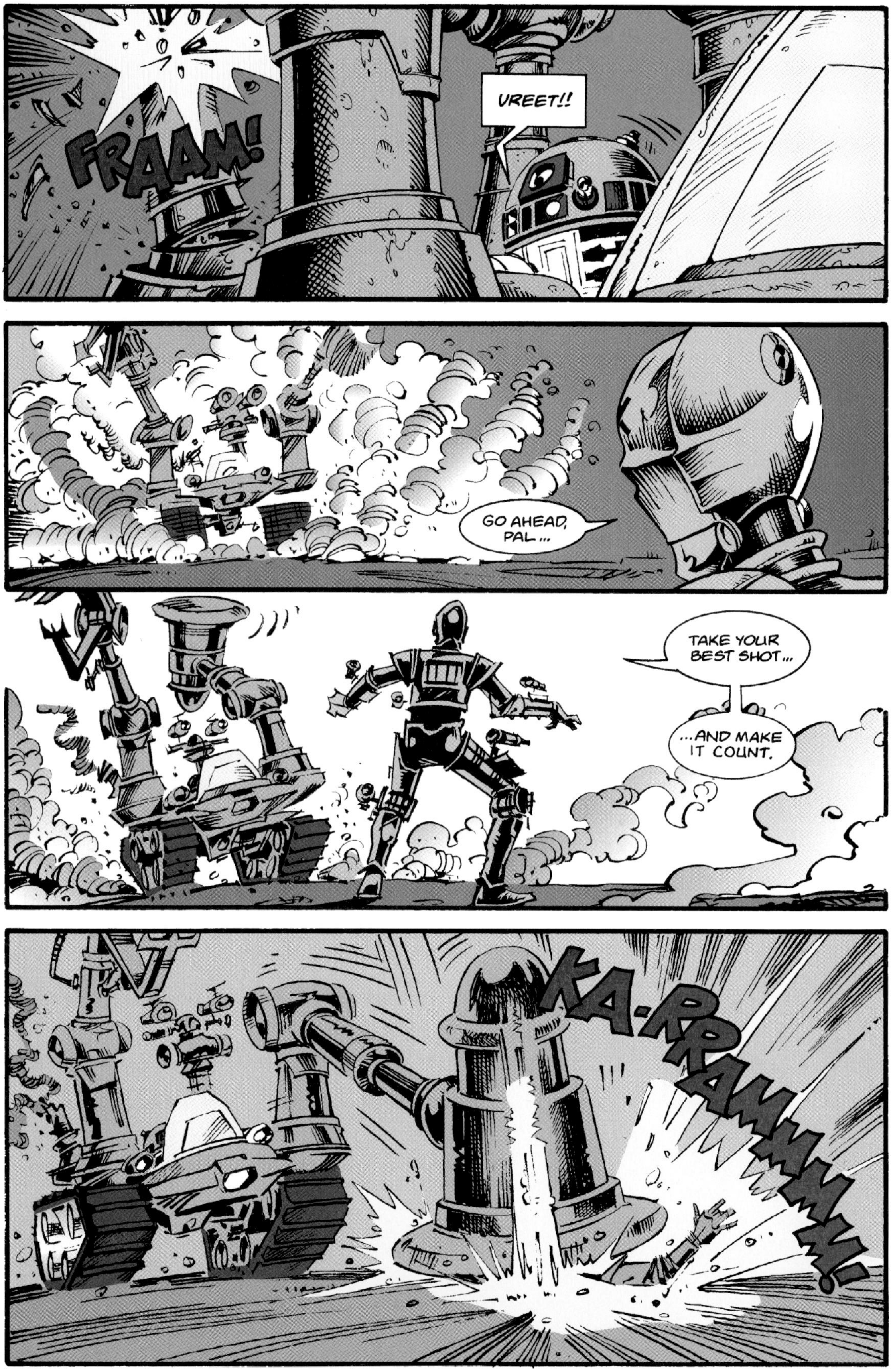
FRAAM!
VREET!!
GO AHEAD, PAL...
TAKE YOUR BEST SHOT...
...AND MAKE IT COUNT.
KA-RRAMMMM!

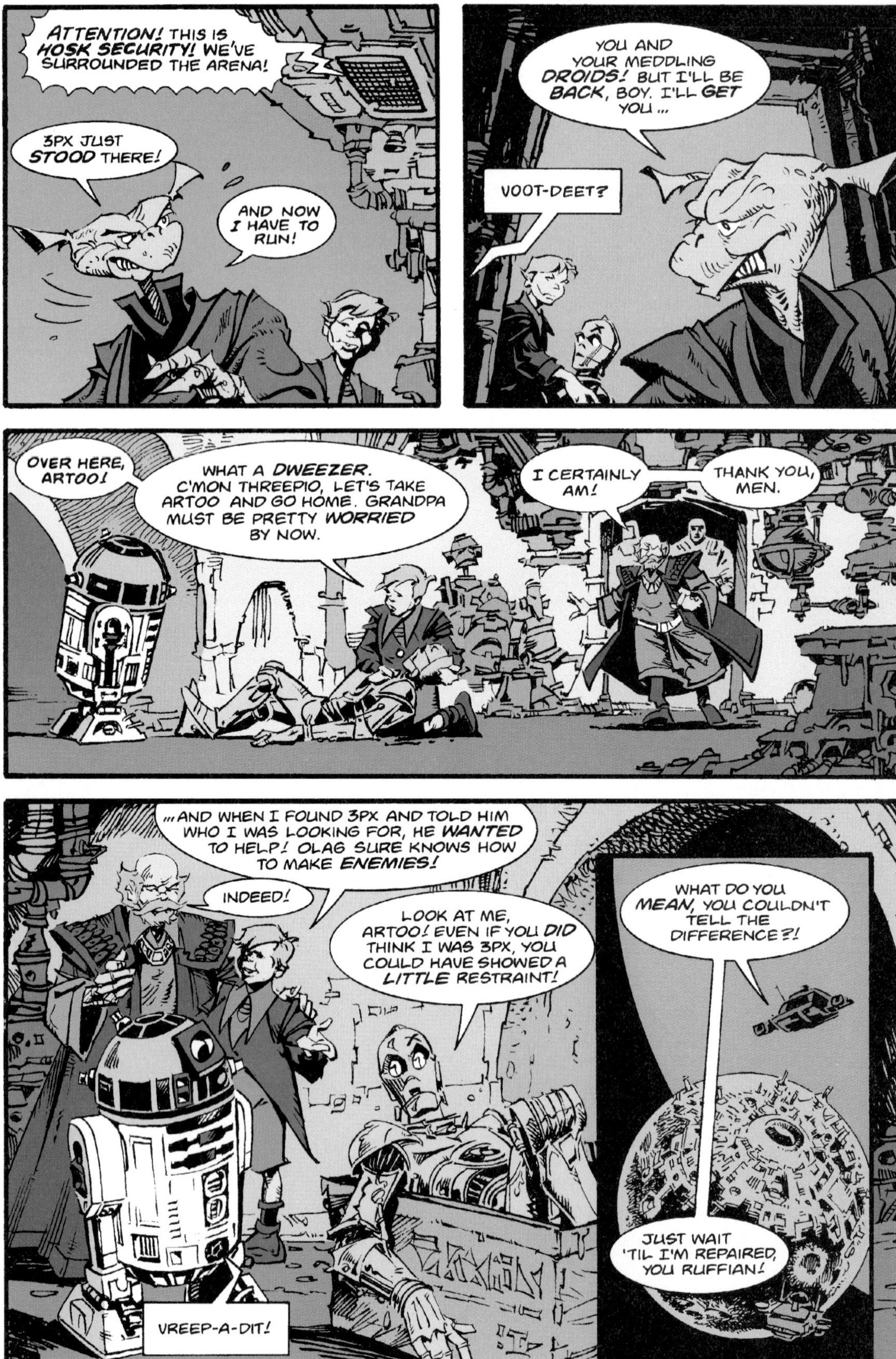
ATTENTION! THIS IS HOSK SECURITY! WE'VE SURROUNDED THE ARENA!
3PX JUST STOOD THERE!
AND NOW I HAVE TO RUN!
YOU AND YOUR MEDDLING DROIDS! BUT I'LL BE BACK, BOY. I'LL GET YOU ...
VOOT-DEET?
OVER HERE, ARTOO!
WHAT A DWEEZER. C'MON THREEPIO, LET'S TAKE ARTOO AND GO HOME. GRANDPA MUST BE PRETTY WORRIED BY NOW.
I CERTAINLY AM!
THANK YOU, MEN.
...AND WHEN I FOUND 3PX AND TOLD HIM WHO I WAS LOOKING FOR, HE WANTED TO HELP! OLAG SURE KNOWS HOW TO MAKE ENEMIES!
INDEED!
LOOK AT ME, ARTOO! EVEN IF YOU DID THINK I WAS 3PX, YOU COULD HAVE SHOWED A LITTLE RESTRAINT!
VREEP-A-DIT!
WHAT DO YOU MEAN, YOU COULDN'T TELL THE DIFFERENCE?!
JUST WAIT 'TIL I'M REPAIRED, YOU RUFFIAN!

Battle of the B'rknaa

Chapter 5

Script **Dan Thorsland**

Pencils **Bill Hughes**

Inks **Andy Mushynsky**

Colors **Pamela Rambo**

Lettering **Steve Dutro**

Cover **Kilian Plunkett**

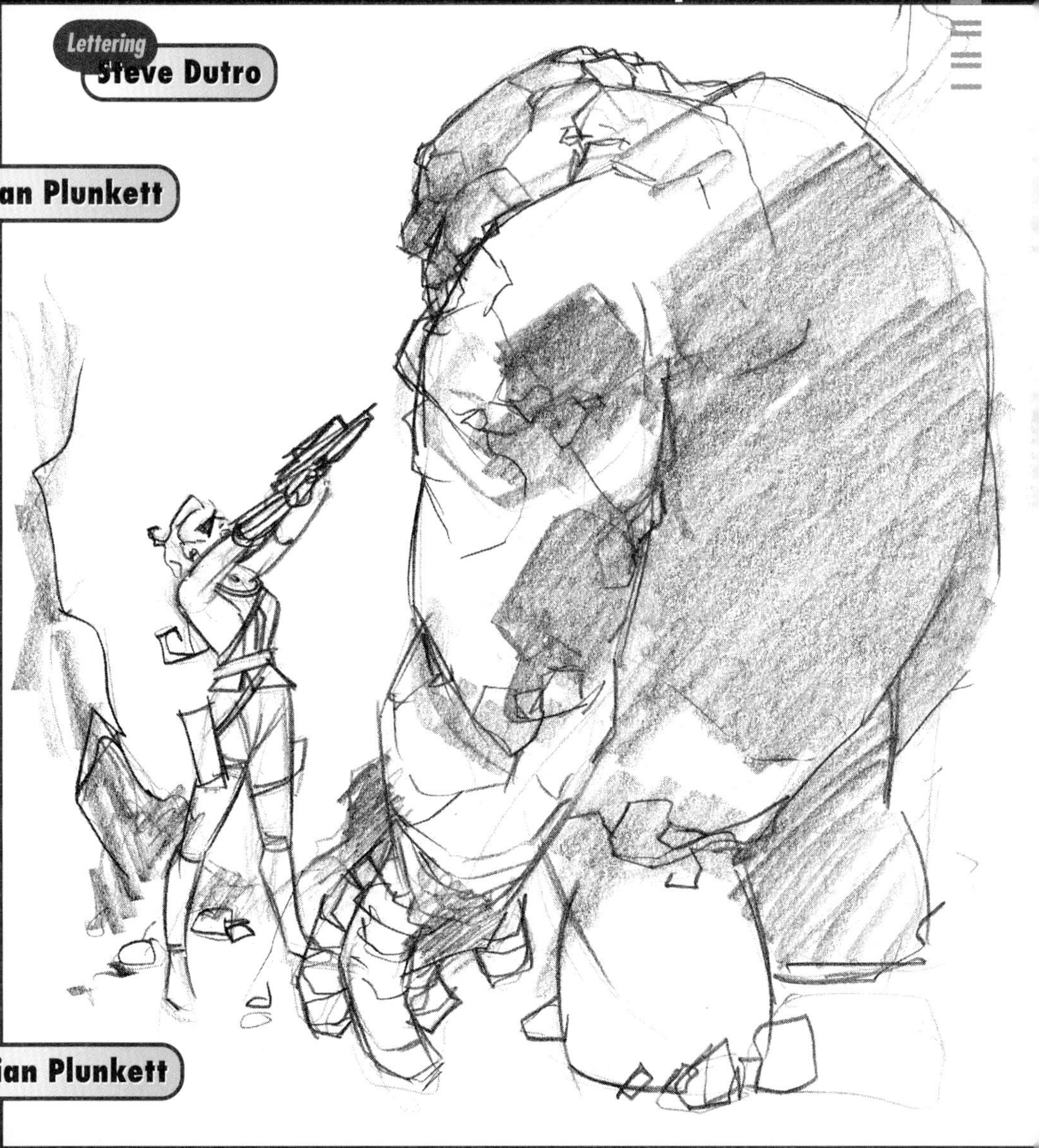

Sketch **Kilian Plunkett**

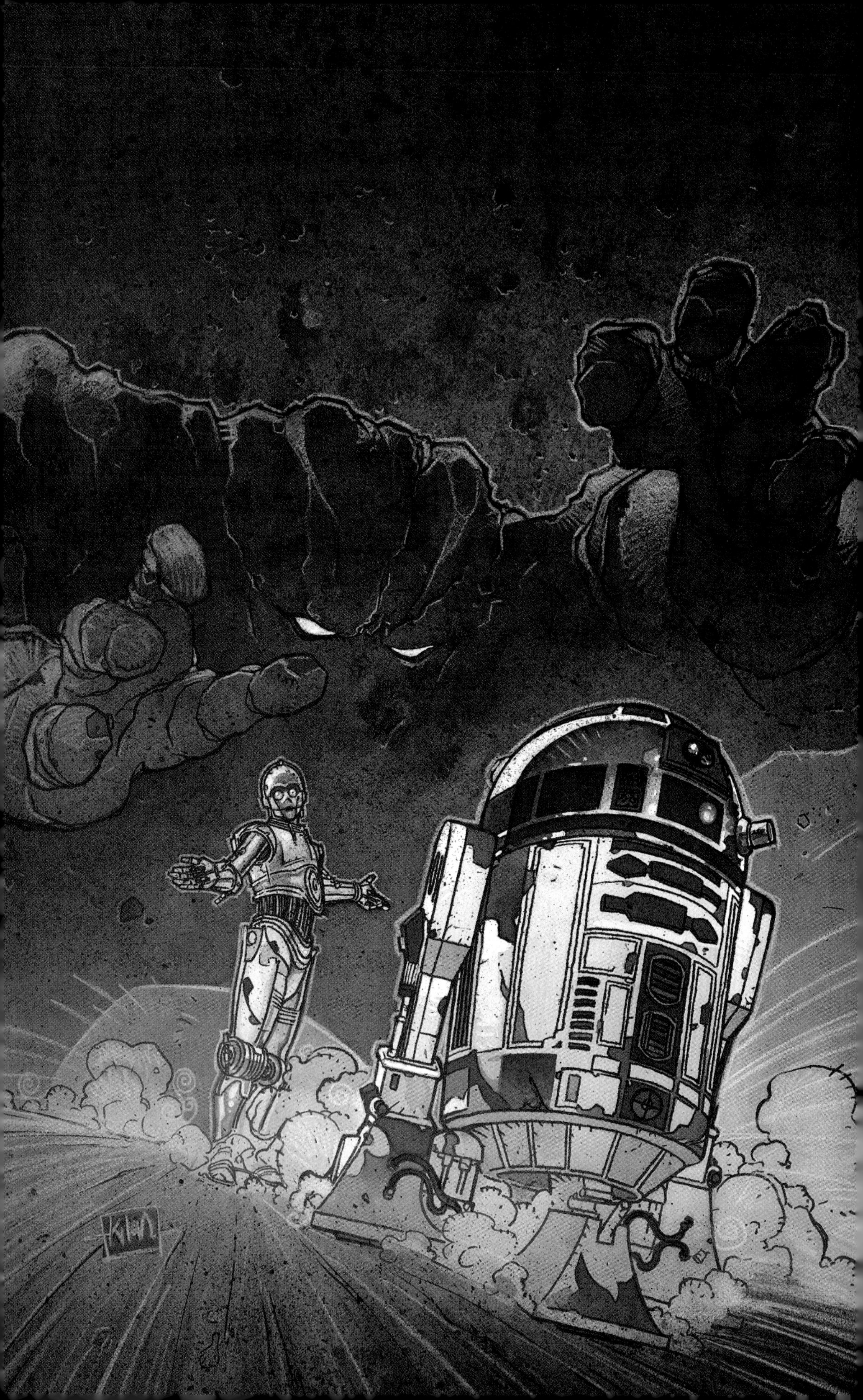

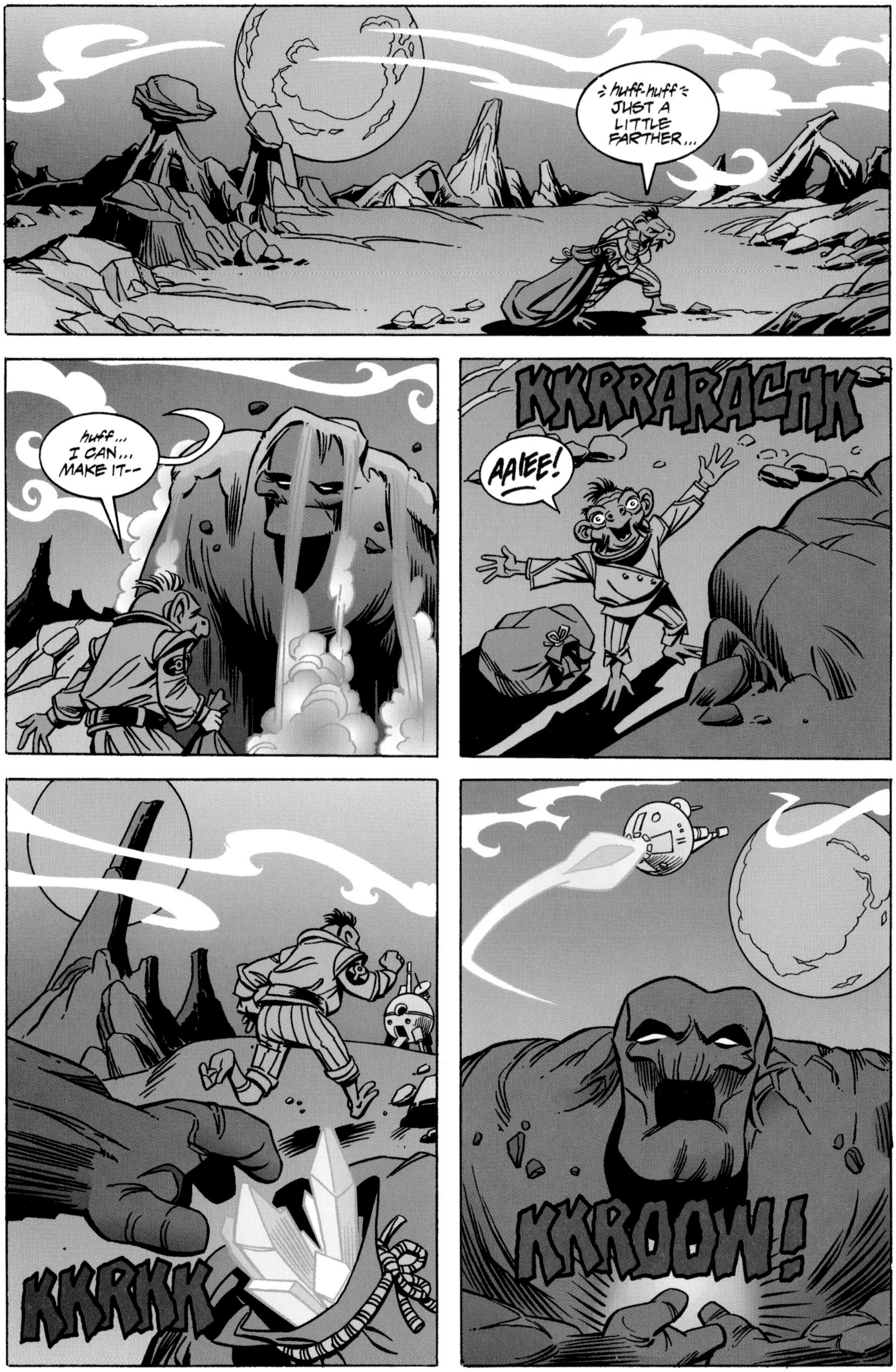
huff-huff
JUST A LITTLE FARTHER...
huff... I CAN... MAKE IT--
KKRRARACHK
AAIEE!
KKRKK
KKROOW!

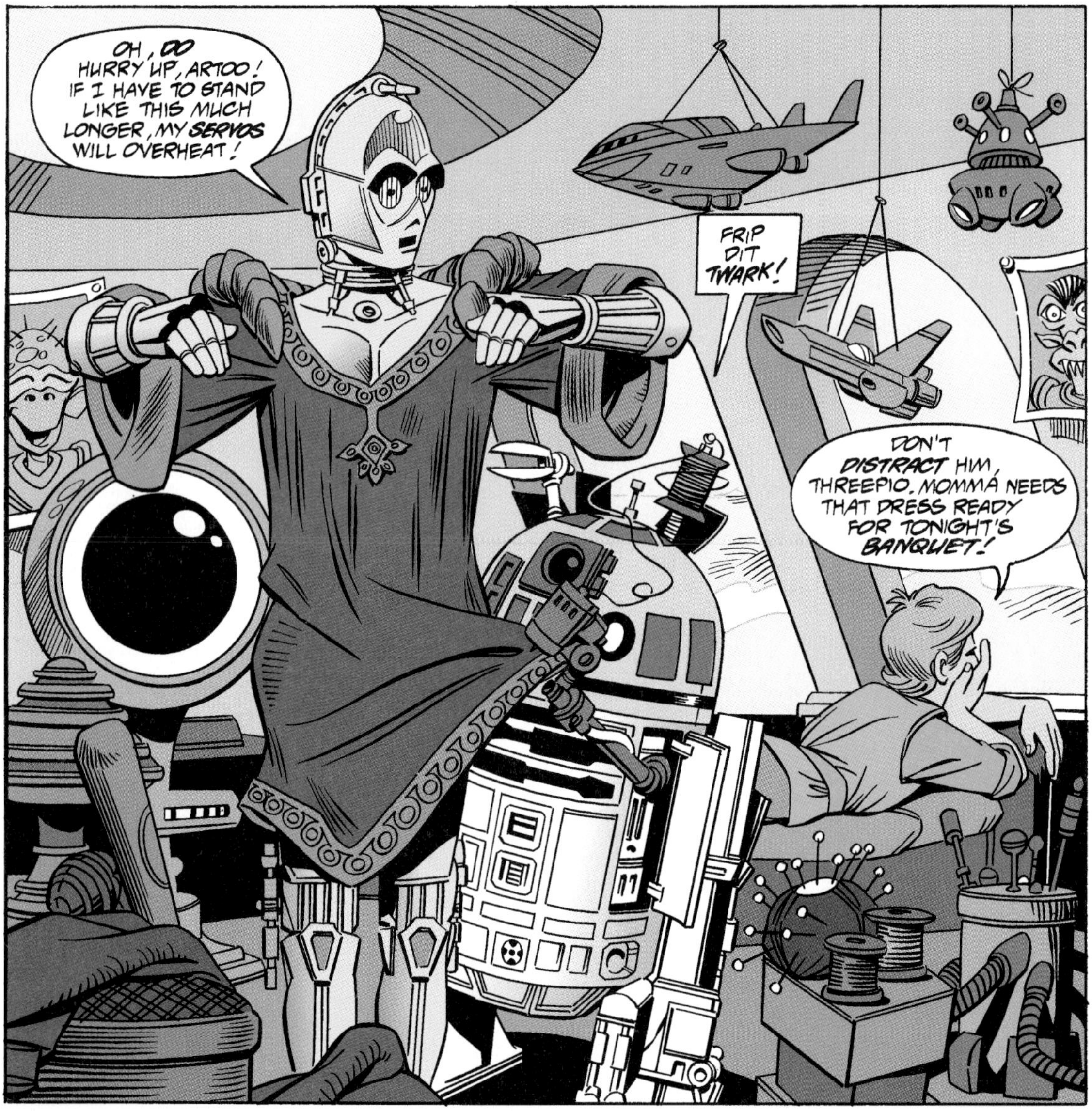
OH, DO HURRY UP, ARTOO! IF I HAVE TO STAND LIKE THIS MUCH LONGER, MY SERVOS WILL OVERHEAT!
FRIP DIT TWARK!
DON'T DISTRACT HIM, THREEPIO. MOMMA NEEDS THAT DRESS READY FOR TONIGHT'S BANQUET!

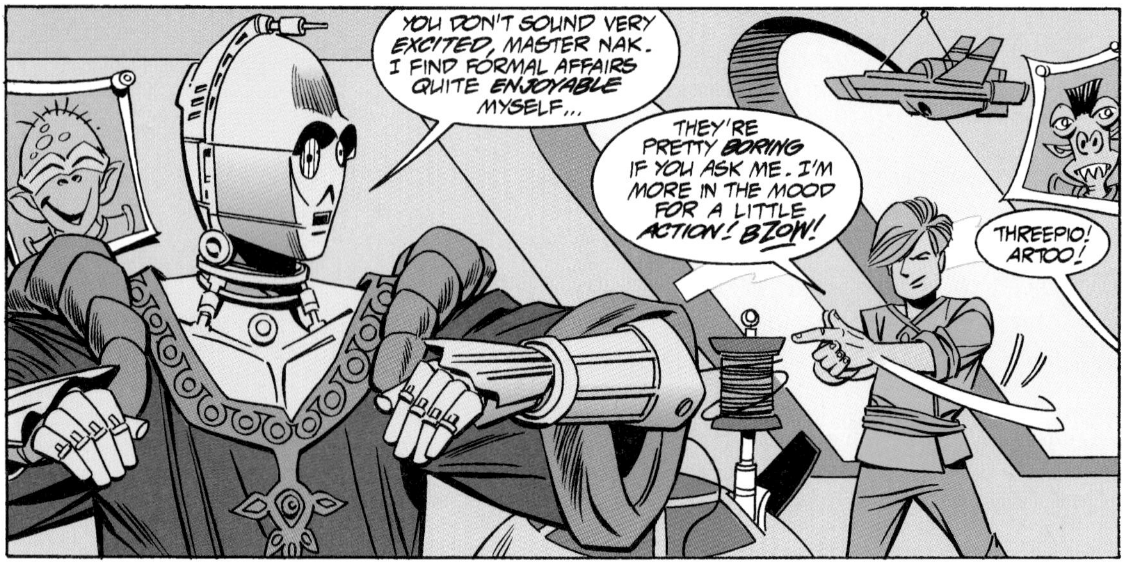
YOU DON'T SOUND VERY EXCITED, MASTER NAK. I FIND FORMAL AFFAIRS QUITE ENJOYABLE MYSELF...
THEY'RE PRETTY BORING IF YOU ASK ME. I'M MORE IN THE MOOD FOR A LITTLE ACTION! BZOW!
THREEPIO! ARTOO!

YES, MISTRESS?

THERE'S A *CUSTOMER* WAITING IN THE FRONT OFFICE. I'M BUSY... COULD YOU TAKE CARE OF IT?

CERTAINLY! JUST A MOMENT WHILE I TAKE THIS OFF...

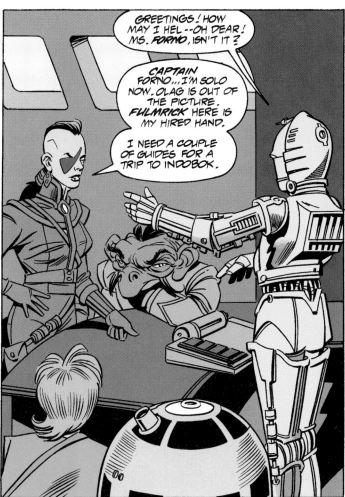

GREETINGS! HOW MAY I HEL --OH DEAR! MS. *FORNO,* ISN'T IT?

CAPTAIN FORNO... I'M *SOLO* NOW. OLAG IS OUT OF THE PICTURE. *FULMRICK* HERE IS MY *HIRED HAND.*

I NEED A COUPLE OF GUIDES FOR A TRIP TO INDOBOK.

WELL, ARTOO IS PROGRAMMED WITH AN EXTENSIVE DATABASE OF INDOBOK'S GEOGRAPHY, BUT WOULDN'T AN *ORGANIC* GUIDE BE MORE APPROPRIATE?

NO. I NEED *DROIDS* FOR THIS JOB!

HEY, KID...

WHY DON'T YOU PUT YOUR *EYES* BACK IN YOUR HEAD. I'M NOT INTO *YOUNGER MEN.*

THE JOB PAYS FIVE HUNDRED. YOU CAN GET IN TOUCH WITH ME AT THE SPACEPORT, BAY THIRTEEN.

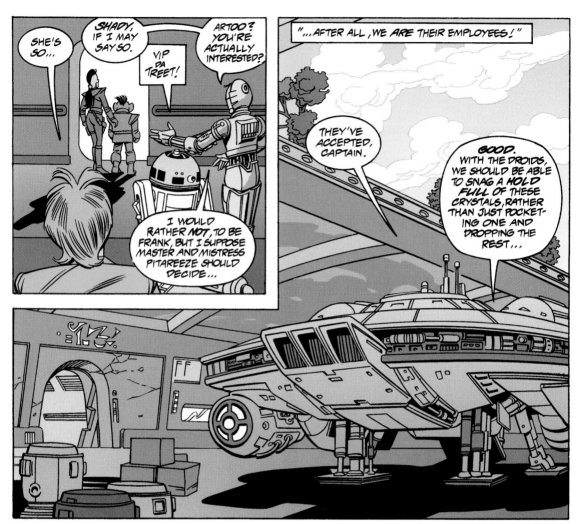

SHE'S SO....

SHADY, IF I MAY SAY SO.

VIP DA TREET!

ARTOO? YOU'RE ACTUALLY INTERESTED?

I WOULD RATHER *NOT*, TO BE FRANK, BUT I SUPPOSE MASTER AND MISTRESS PITAREEZE SHOULD DECIDE...

"...AFTER ALL, WE *ARE* THEIR EMPLOYEES!"

THEY'VE ACCEPTED, CAPTAIN.

GOOD. WITH THE DROIDS, WE SHOULD BE ABLE TO SNAG A *HOLD FULL* OF THESE CRYSTALS, RATHER THAN JUST POCKETING ONE AND DROPPING THE REST...

LOOK AT THAT ENERGY TRANSFER RATE. ONE OF THESE COULD HANDLE ALL THE SYSTEMS POWER OF A SMALL *PLANET!* IT'LL BE WORTH A *FORTUNE* ON THE OPEN MARKET.

BUT WHY BOTHER RENTING *THOSE* DROIDS?

BECAUSE IF MY PLAN WORKS, AND *INORGANICS* CAN GET PAST THOSE... *THINGS*, WE WALK AWAY WITH A BAG OF CRYSTALS AND SCRAG THE DROIDS. NO *WITNESSES.*

WHY TRASH MY *OWN* PROPERTY, Y'KNOW? NOW GET THE SHIP PREPPED...

...WE LIFT OFF IN THE *MORNING.*

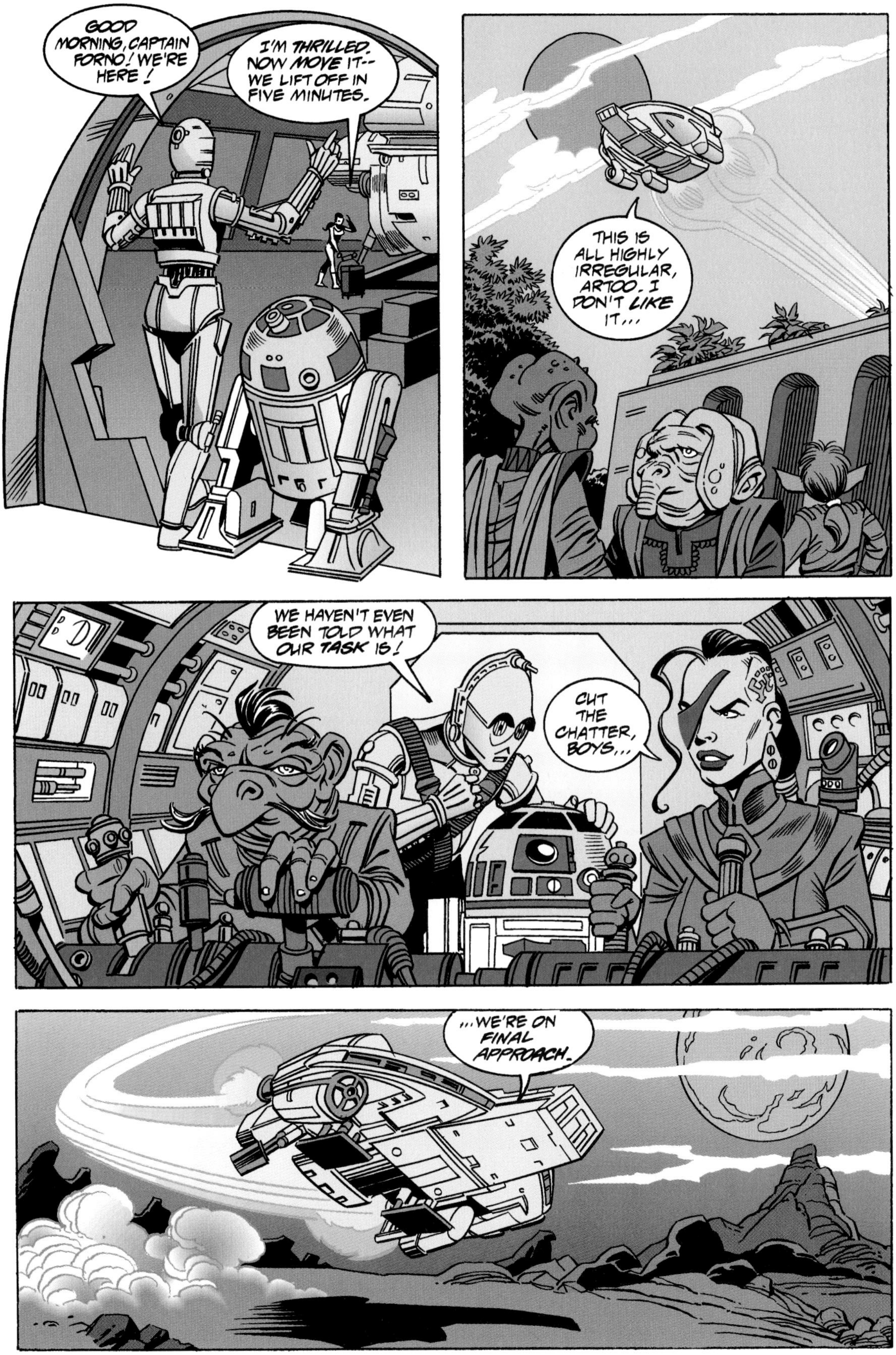
GOOD MORNING, CAPTAIN FORNO! WE'RE HERE!
I'M THRILLED. NOW MOVE IT-- WE LIFT OFF IN FIVE MINUTES.
THIS IS ALL HIGHLY IRREGULAR, ARTOO. I DON'T LIKE IT...
WE HAVEN'T EVEN BEEN TOLD WHAT OUR TASK IS!
CUT THE CHATTER, BOYS...
...WE'RE ON FINAL APPROACH.

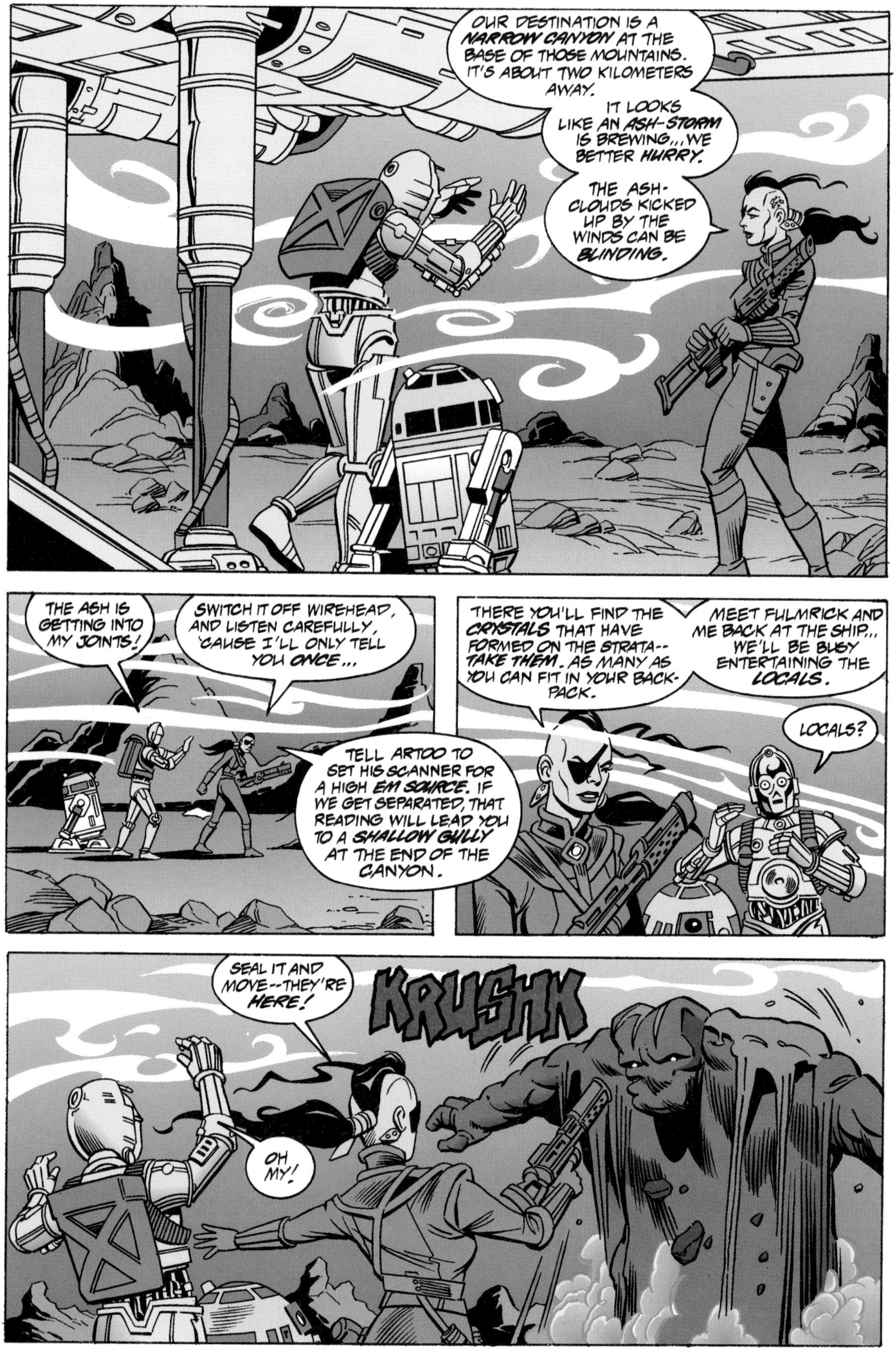
OUR DESTINATION IS A NARROW CANYON AT THE BASE OF THOSE MOUNTAINS. IT'S ABOUT TWO KILOMETERS AWAY.
IT LOOKS LIKE AN ASH-STORM IS BREWING... WE BETTER HURRY.
THE ASH-CLOUDS KICKED UP BY THE WINDS CAN BE BLINDING.
THE ASH IS GETTING INTO MY JOINTS!
SWITCH IT OFF WIREHEAD, AND LISTEN CAREFULLY, 'CAUSE I'LL ONLY TELL YOU ONCE...
TELL ARTOO TO SET HIS SCANNER FOR A HIGH EM SOURCE. IF WE GET SEPARATED, THAT READING WILL LEAD YOU TO A SHALLOW GULLY AT THE END OF THE CANYON.
THERE YOU'LL FIND THE CRYSTALS THAT HAVE FORMED ON THE STRATA-- TAKE THEM. AS MANY AS YOU CAN FIT IN YOUR BACK-PACK.
MEET FULMRICK AND ME BACK AT THE SHIP... WE'LL BE BUSY ENTERTAINING THE LOCALS.
LOCALS?
SEAL IT AND MOVE--THEY'RE HERE!
KRUSHK
OH MY!

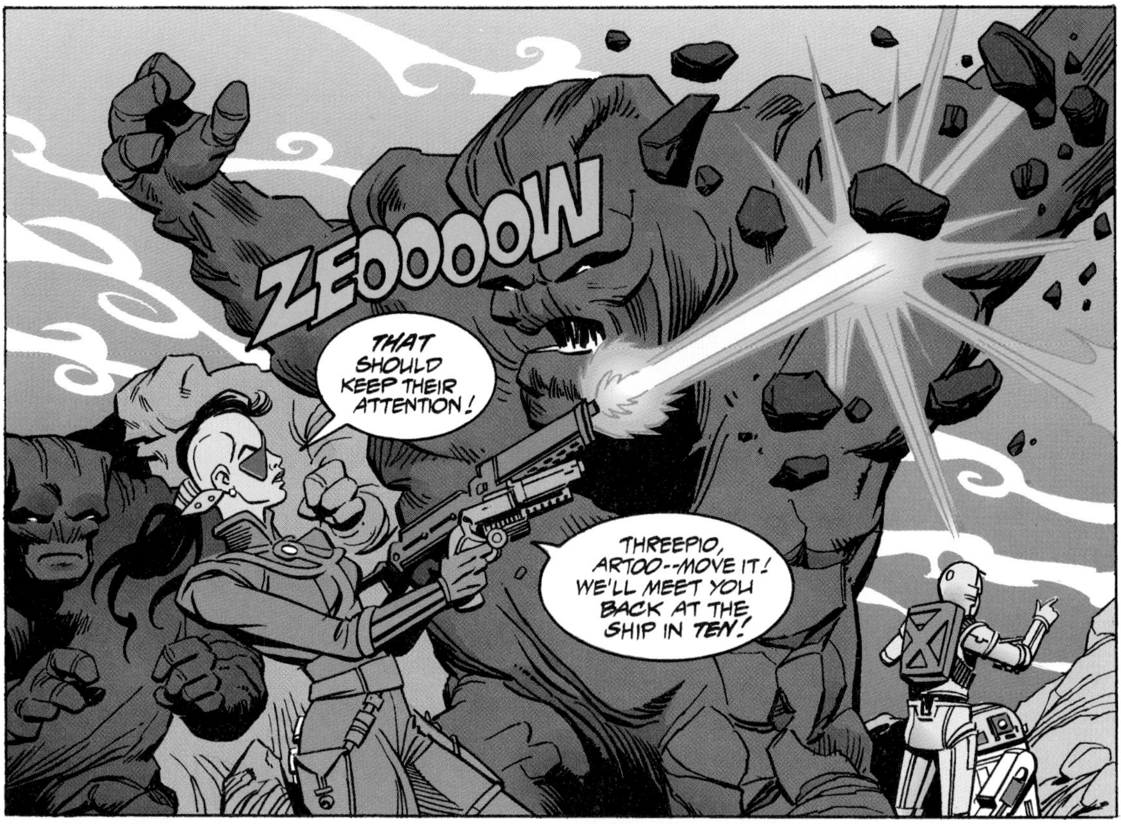
ZEOOOOW
THAT SHOULD KEEP THEIR ATTENTION!
THREEPIO, ARTOO--MOVE IT! WE'LL MEET YOU BACK AT THE SHIP IN TEN!

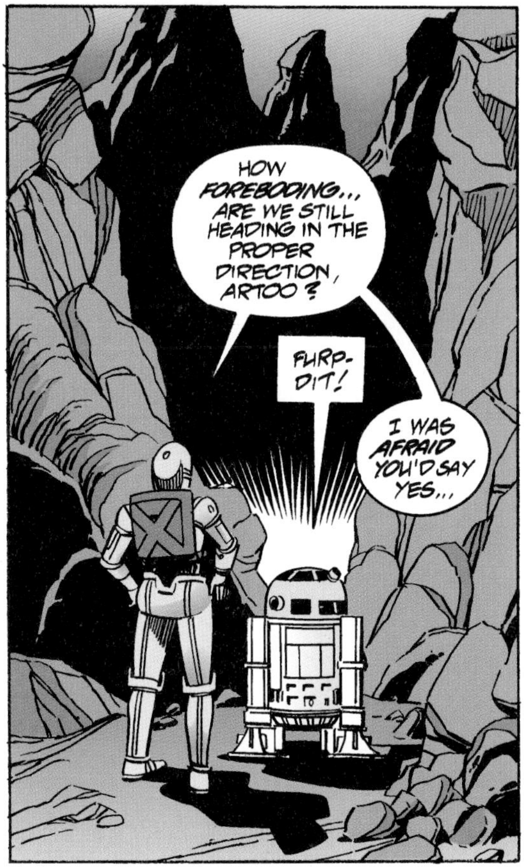
HOW FOREBODING... ARE WE STILL HEADING IN THE PROPER DIRECTION, ARTOO?
FURP-DIT!
I WAS AFRAID YOU'D SAY YES...

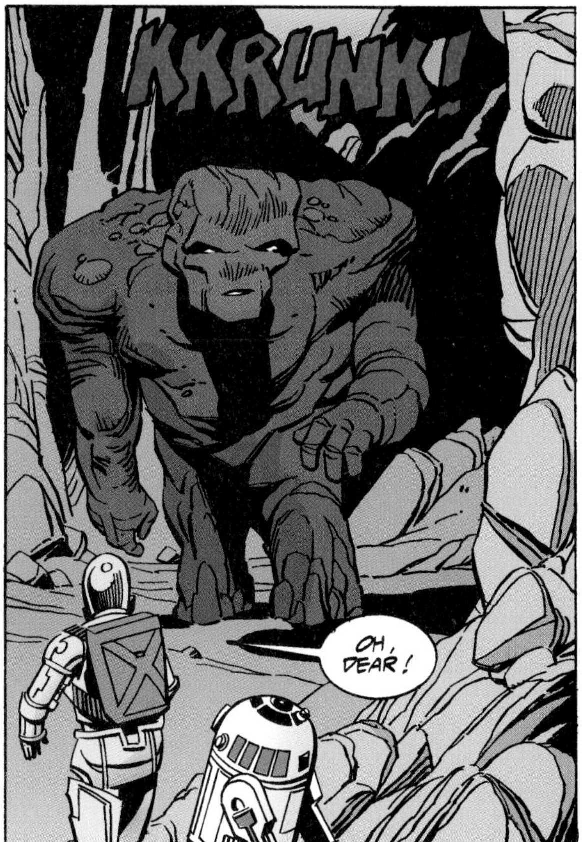
KKRUNK!
OH, DEAR!

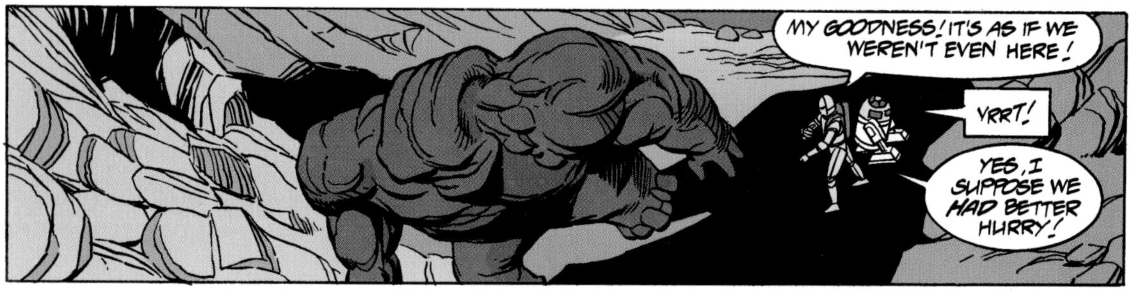
MY GOODNESS! IT'S AS IF WE WEREN'T EVEN HERE!
VRRT!
YES, I SUPPOSE WE HAD BETTER HURRY!

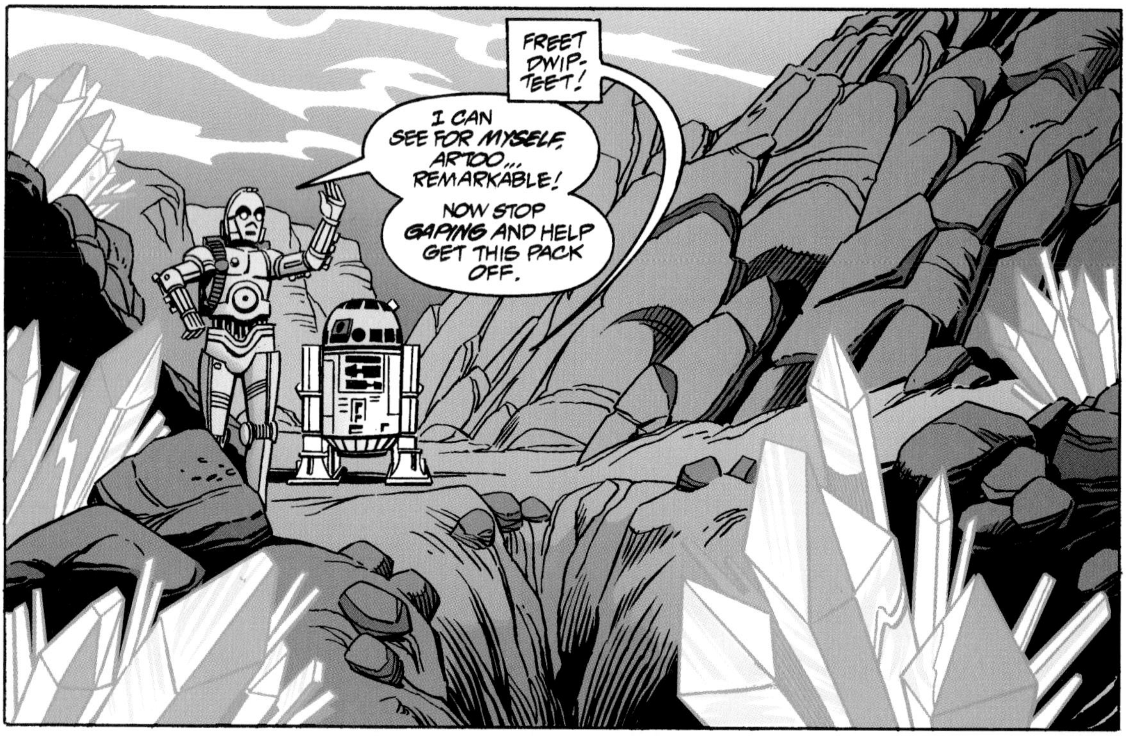
FREET DWIP-TEET!
I CAN SEE FOR MYSELF, ARTOO... REMARKABLE!
NOW STOP GAPING AND HELP GET THIS PACK OFF.

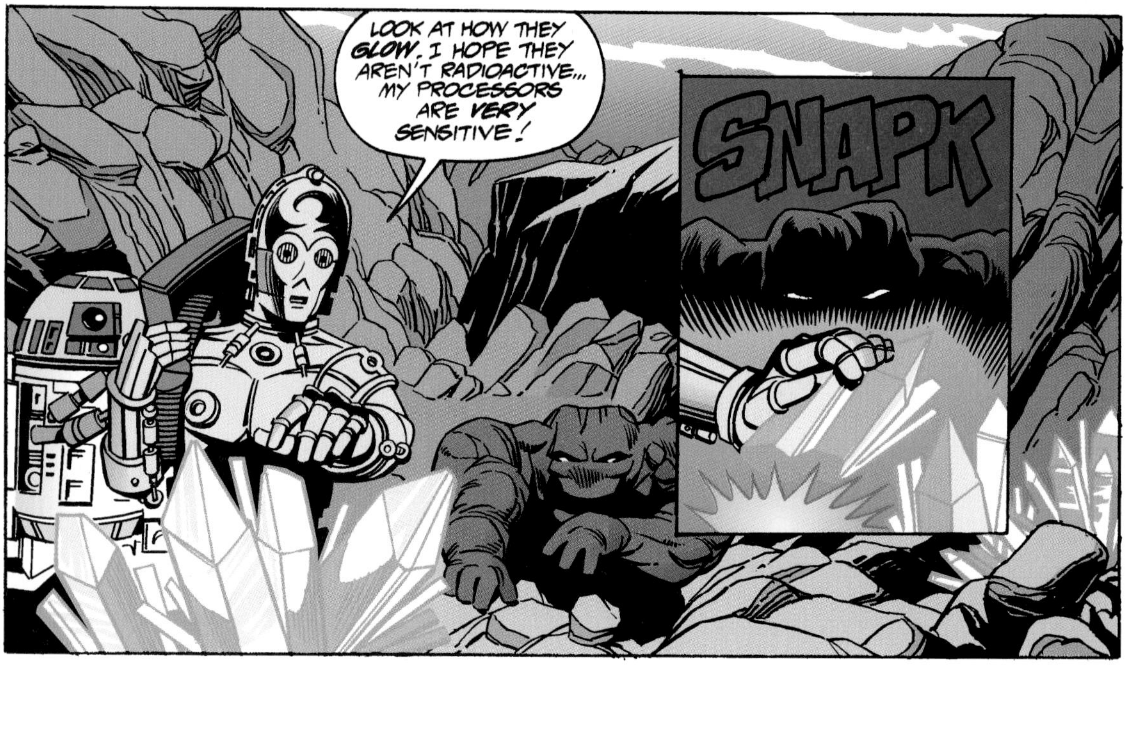
LOOK AT HOW THEY GLOW. I HOPE THEY AREN'T RADIOACTIVE... MY PROCESSORS ARE VERY SENSITIVE!
SNAPK

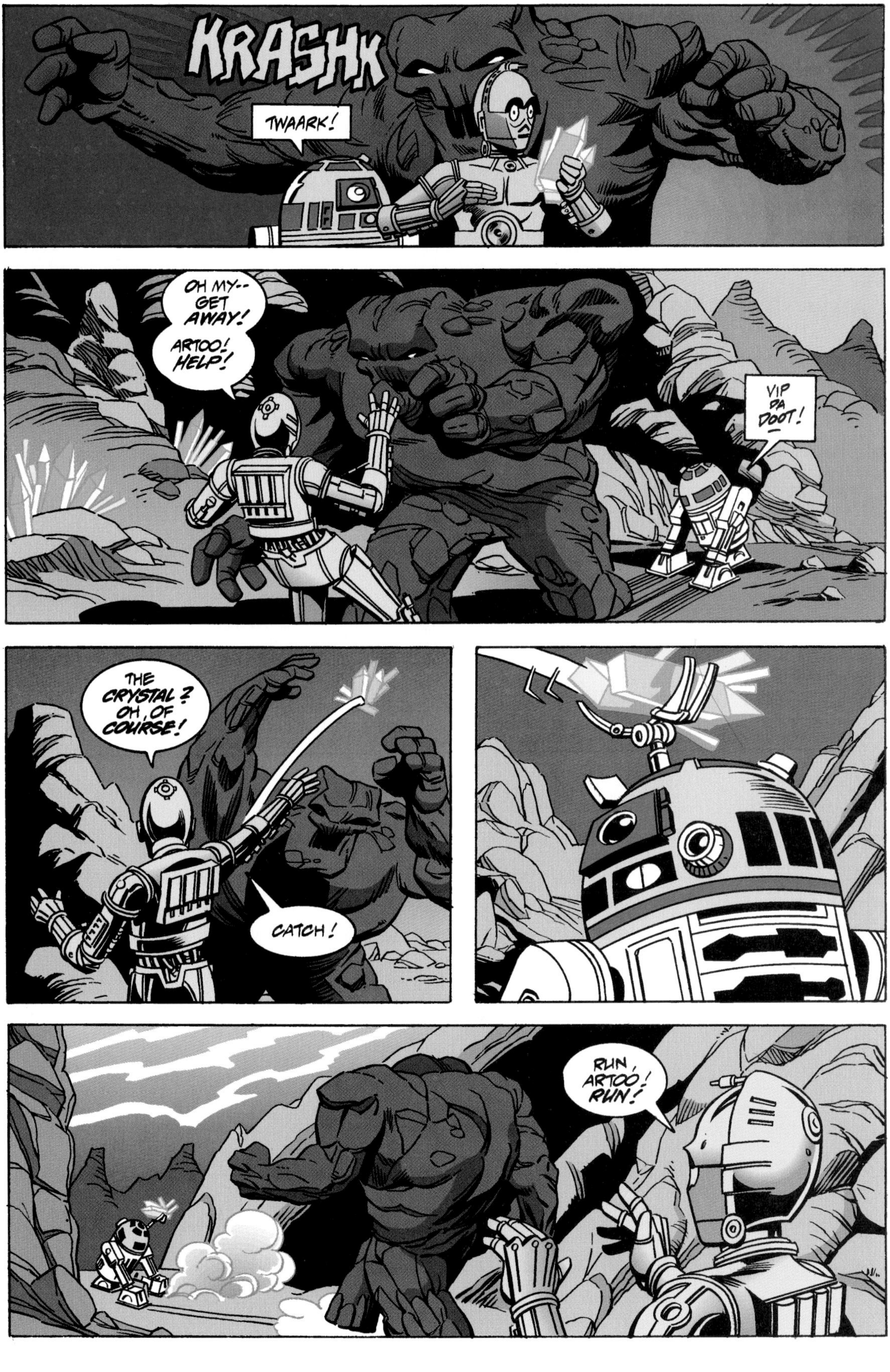
KRASHK
TWAARK!
OH MY-- GET AWAY!
ARTOO! HELP!
VIP DA DOOT!
THE CRYSTAL? OH, OF COURSE!
CATCH!
RUN, ARTOO! RUN!

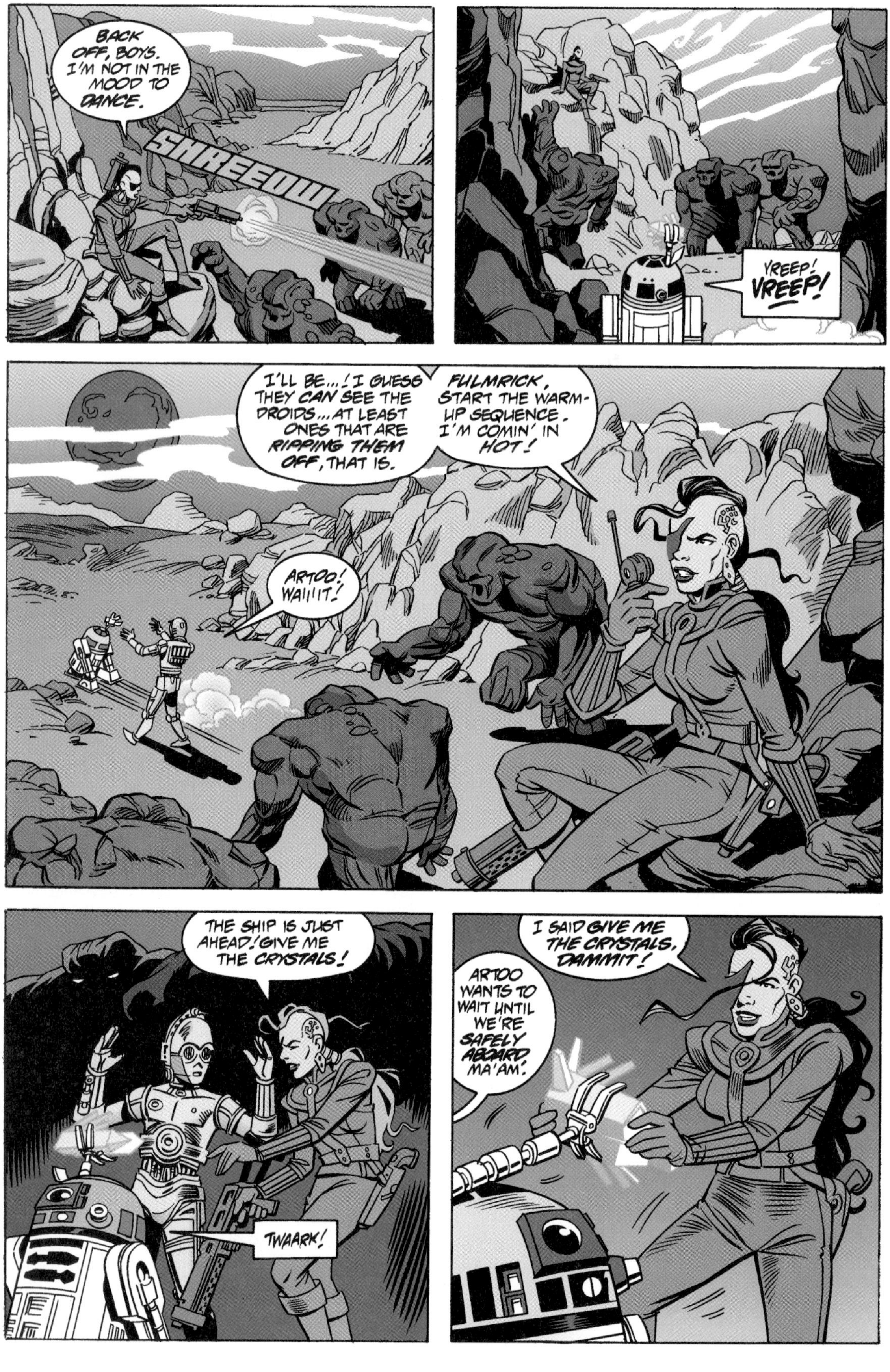
BACK OFF, BOYS. I'M NOT IN THE MOOD TO DANCE.
SHREEOW
YREEP! VREEP!
I'LL BE...! I GUESS THEY CAN SEE THE DROIDS... AT LEAST ONES THAT ARE RIPPING THEM OFF, THAT IS.
FULMRICK, START THE WARM-UP SEQUENCE. I'M COMIN' IN HOT!
ARTOO! WAIIIIT!
THE SHIP IS JUST AHEAD! GIVE ME THE CRYSTALS!
TWAARK!
I SAID GIVE ME THE CRYSTALS, DAMMIT!
ARTOO WANTS TO WAIT UNTIL WE'RE SAFELY ABOARD MA'AM!

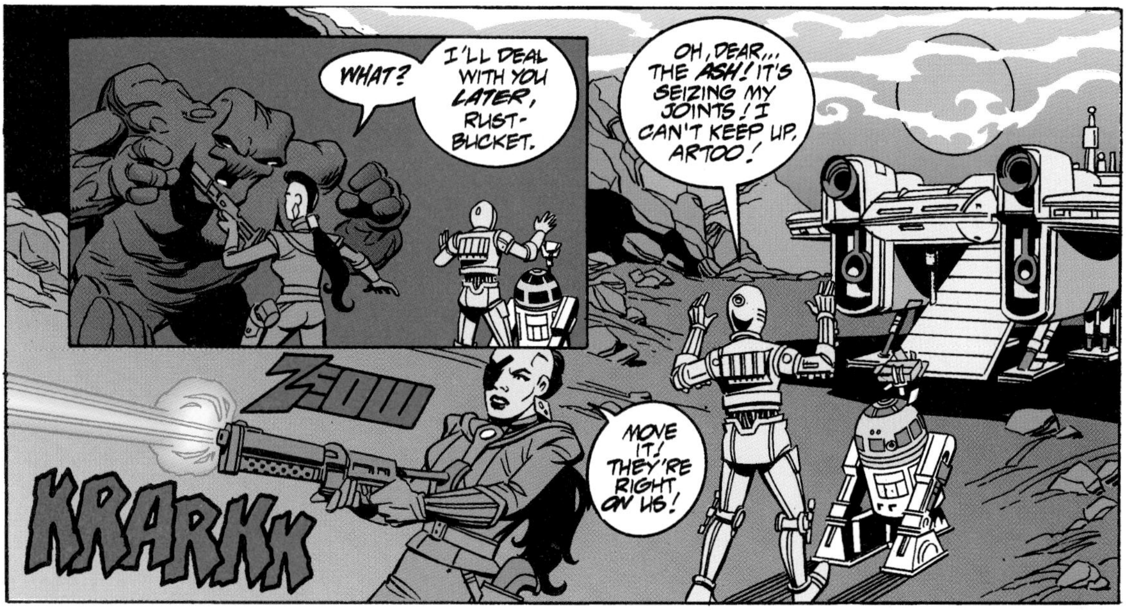
WHAT?
I'LL DEAL WITH YOU LATER, RUST-BUCKET.
OH, DEAR... THE ASH! IT'S SEIZING MY JOINTS! I CAN'T KEEP UP, ARTOO!
ZEOW
KRARKK
MOVE IT! THEY'RE RIGHT ON US!
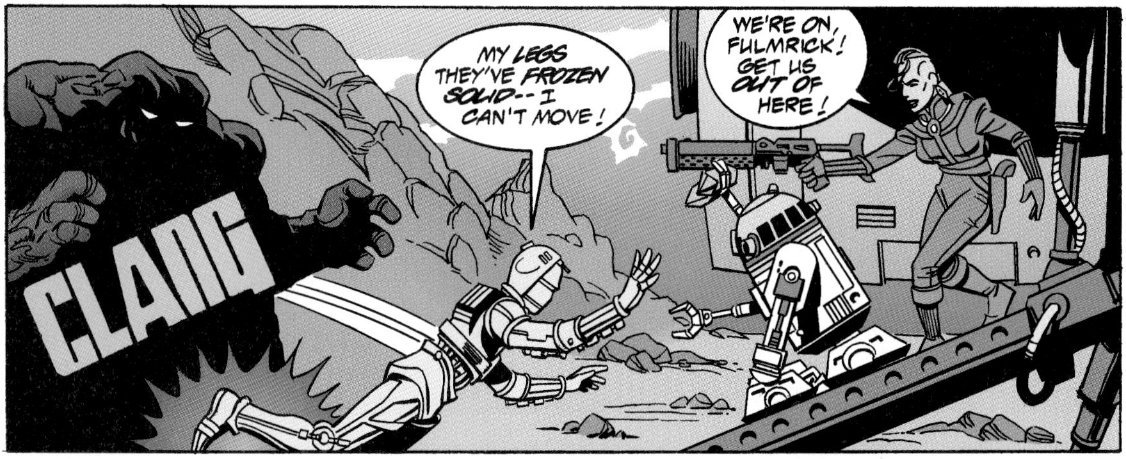
MY LEGS THEY'VE FROZEN SOLID-- I CAN'T MOVE!
WE'RE ON, FULMRICK! GET US OUT OF HERE!
CLANG
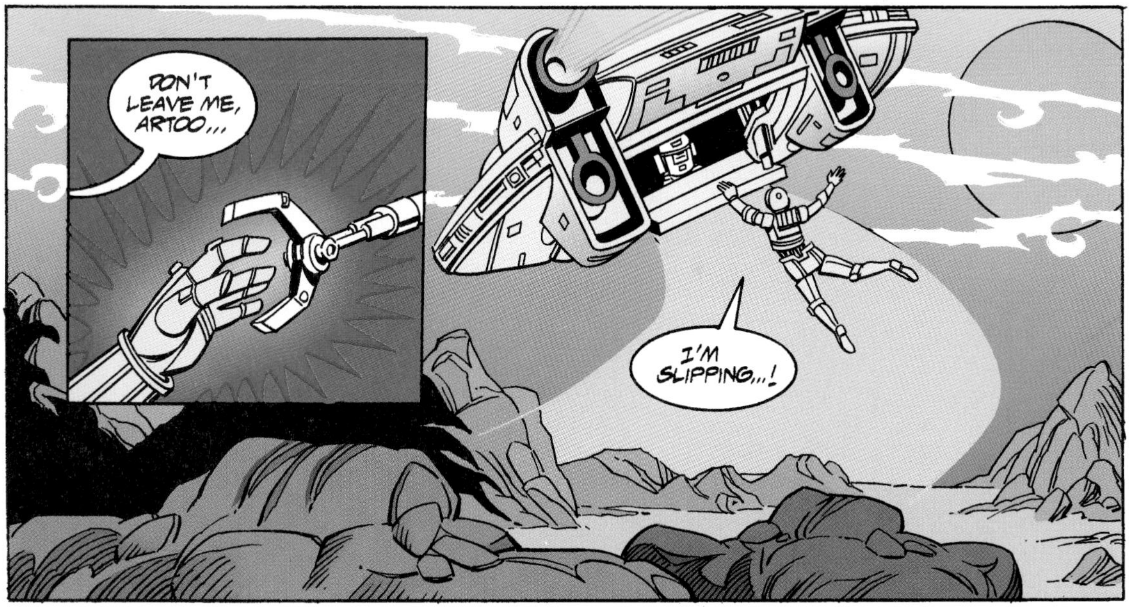
DON'T LEAVE ME, ARTOO...
I'M SLIPPING...!

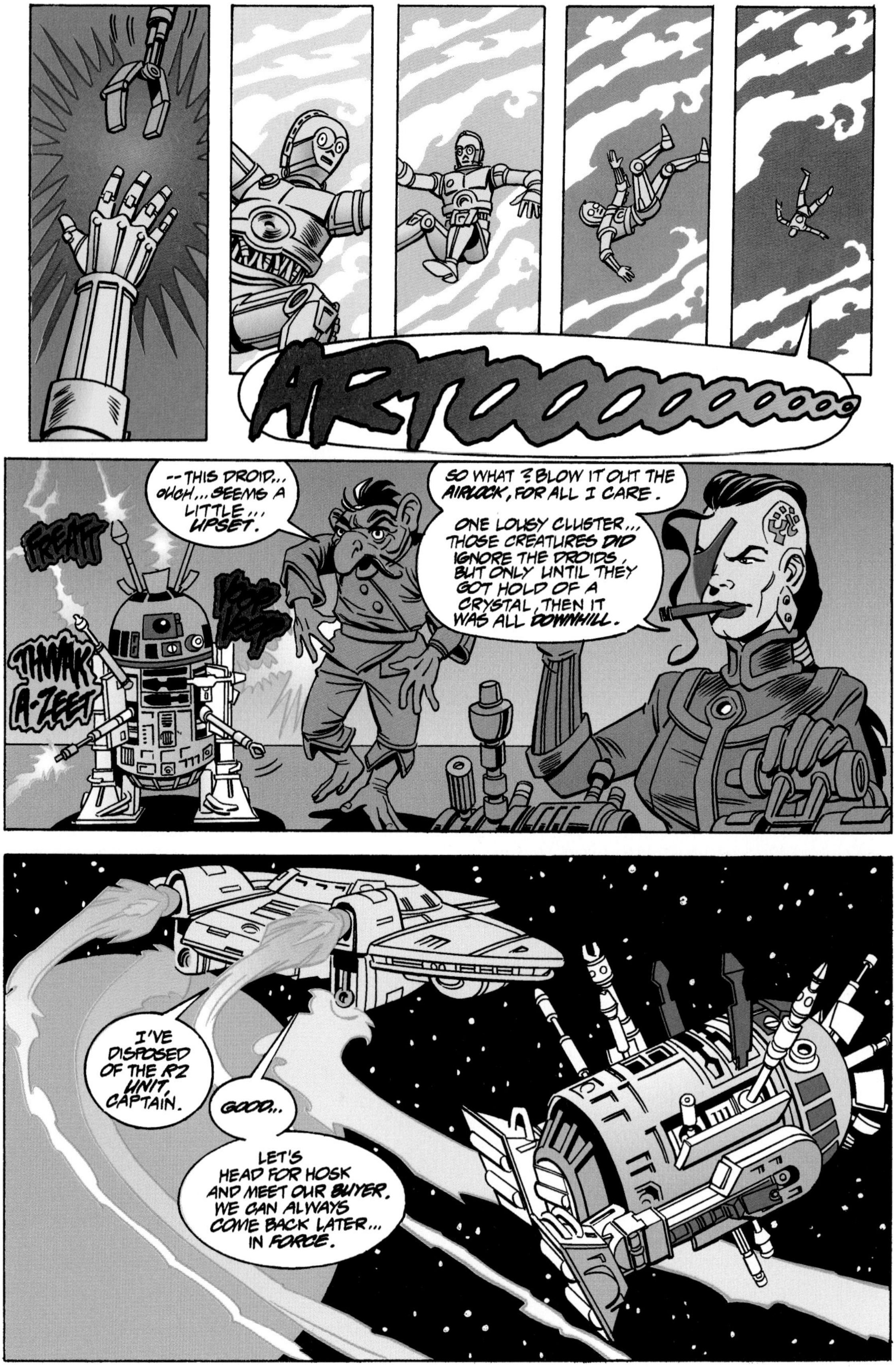

ARTOOOOOOOOOO
--THIS DROID... OUCH... SEEMS A LITTLE... UPSET.
FREAT
VOOP VOOP
THWAK A-ZEET
SO WHAT ? BLOW IT OUT THE AIRLOCK, FOR ALL I CARE.
ONE LOUSY CLUSTER... THOSE CREATURES DID IGNORE THE DROIDS, BUT ONLY UNTIL THEY GOT HOLD OF A CRYSTAL, THEN IT WAS ALL DOWNHILL.
I'VE DISPOSED OF THE R2 UNIT, CAPTAIN.
GOOD...
LET'S HEAD FOR HOSK AND MEET OUR BUYER. WE CAN ALWAYS COME BACK LATER... IN FORCE.

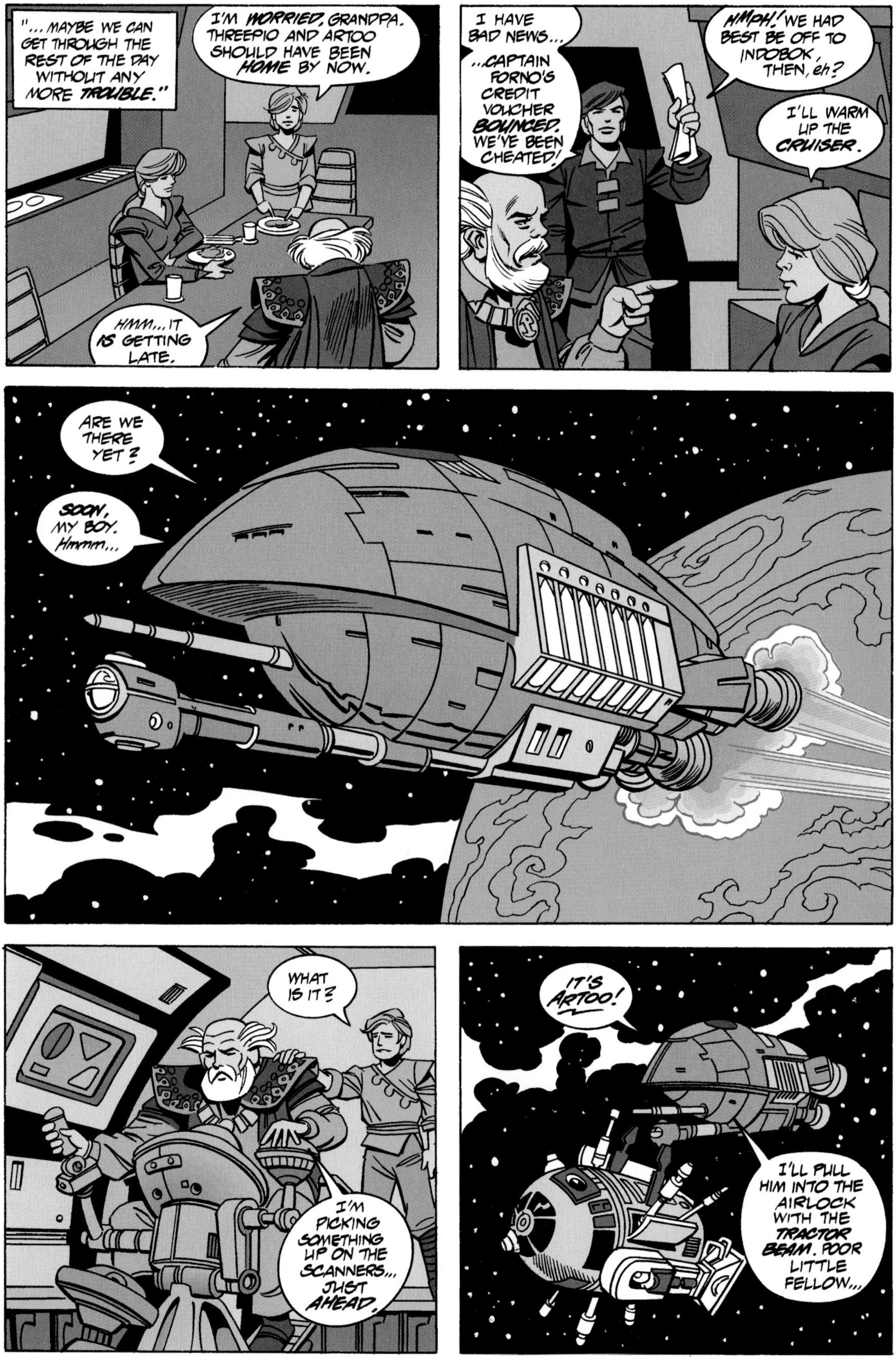
"... MAYBE WE CAN GET THROUGH THE REST OF THE DAY WITHOUT ANY MORE TROUBLE."
I'M WORRIED, GRANDPA. THREEPIO AND ARTOO SHOULD HAVE BEEN HOME BY NOW.
HMM... IT IS GETTING LATE.
I HAVE BAD NEWS...
...CAPTAIN FORNO'S CREDIT VOUCHER BOUNCED. WE'VE BEEN CHEATED!
HMPH! WE HAD BEST BE OFF TO INDOBOK, THEN, eh?
I'LL WARM UP THE CRUISER.
ARE WE THERE YET?
SOON, MY BOY. Hmmm...
WHAT IS IT?
I'M PICKING SOMETHING UP ON THE SCANNERS... JUST AHEAD.
IT'S ARTOO!
I'LL PULL HIM INTO THE AIRLOCK WITH THE TRACTOR BEAM. POOR LITTLE FELLOW...

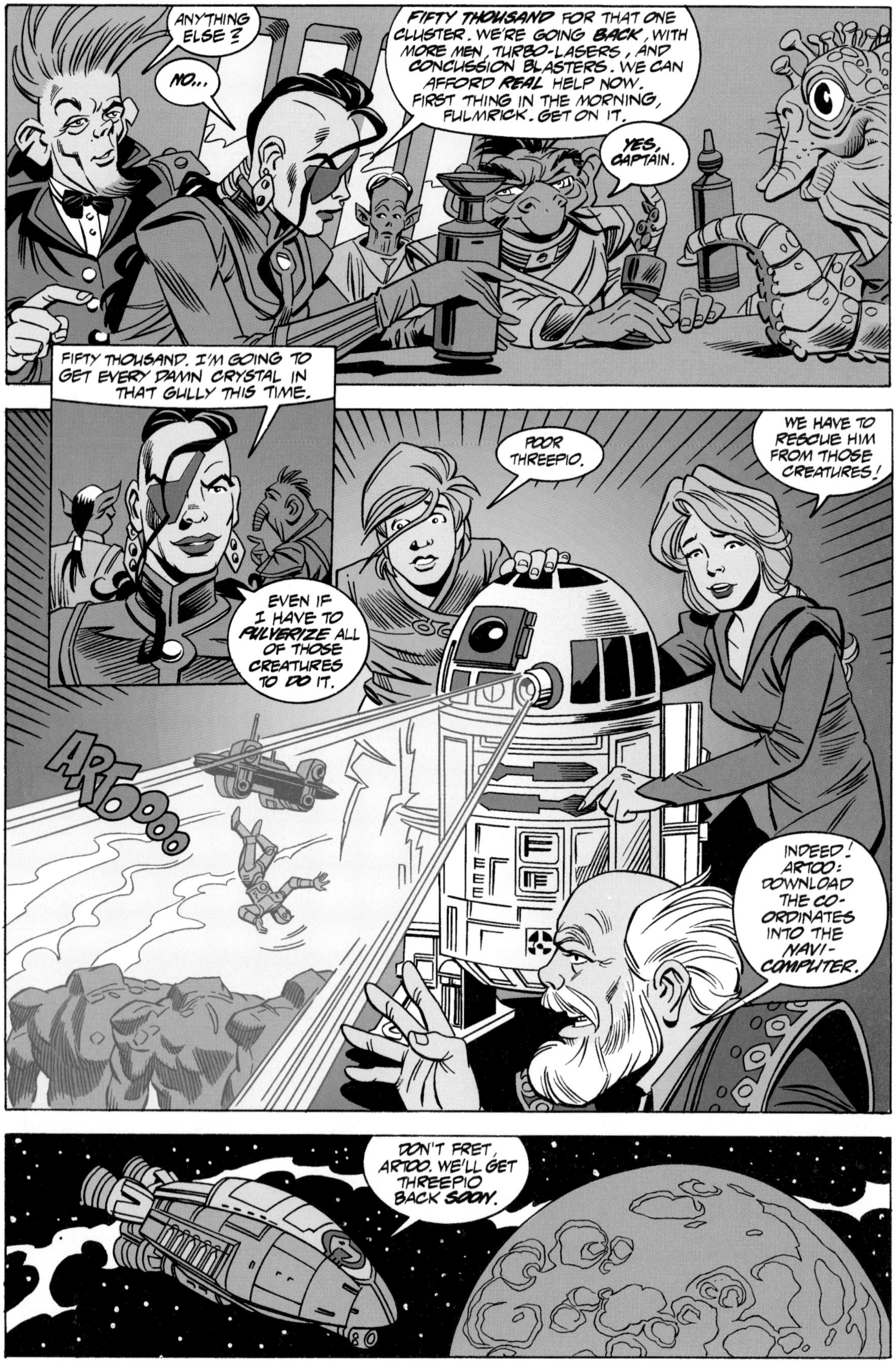

ANYTHING ELSE?
NO...
FIFTY THOUSAND FOR THAT ONE CLUSTER. WE'RE GOING BACK, WITH MORE MEN, TURBO-LASERS, AND CONCUSSION BLASTERS. WE CAN AFFORD REAL HELP NOW. FIRST THING IN THE MORNING, FULMRICK. GET ON IT.
YES, CAPTAIN.
FIFTY THOUSAND. I'M GOING TO GET EVERY DAMN CRYSTAL IN THAT GULLY THIS TIME.
EVEN IF I HAVE TO PULVERIZE ALL OF THOSE CREATURES TO DO IT.
POOR THREEPIO.
WE HAVE TO RESCUE HIM FROM THOSE CREATURES!
ARTOOOOO
INDEED! ARTOO: DOWNLOAD THE CO-ORDINATES INTO THE NAVI-COMPUTER.
DON'T FRET, ARTOO. WE'LL GET THREEPIO BACK SOON.

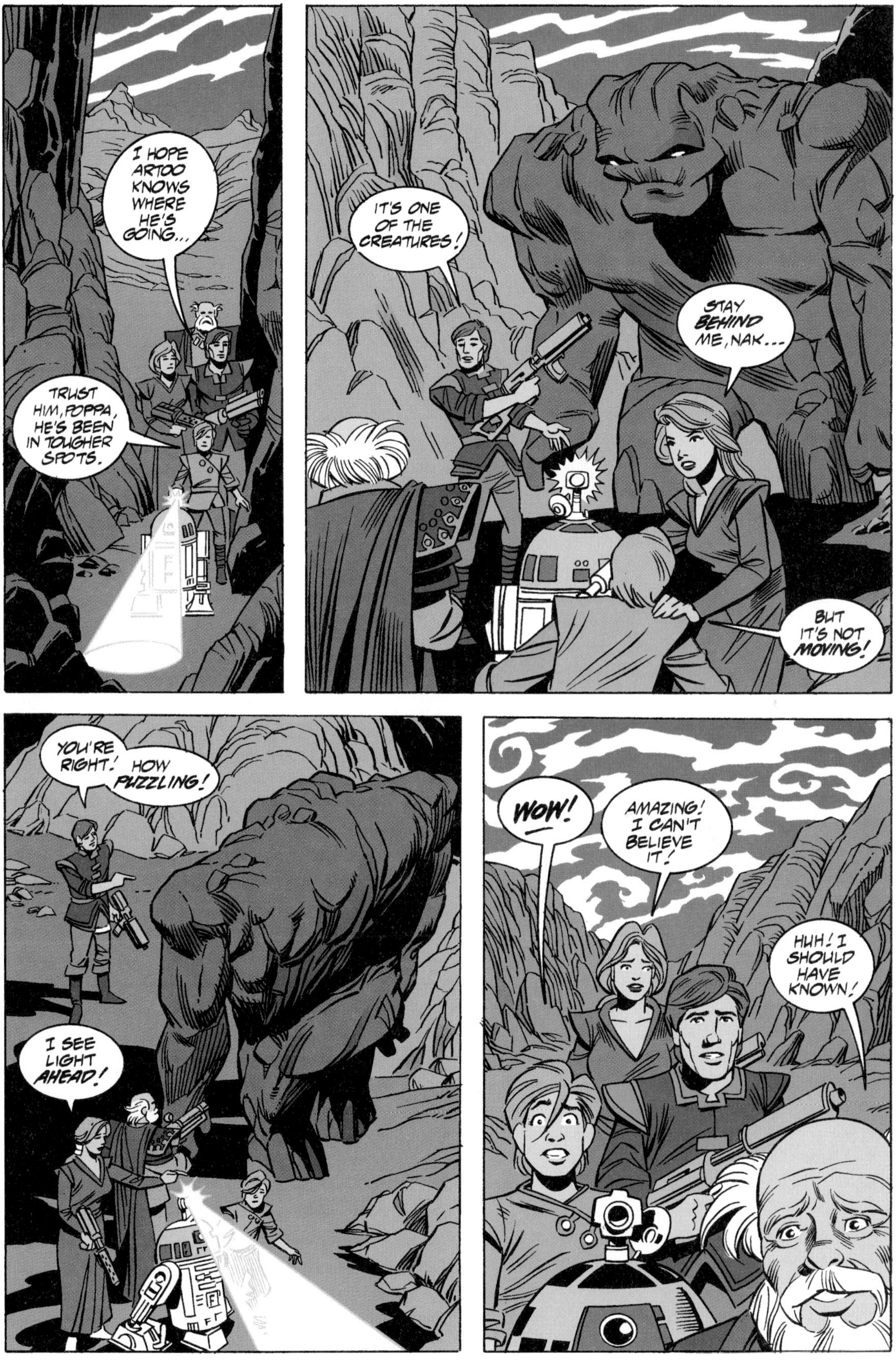
I HOPE ARTOO KNOWS WHERE HE'S GOING...
TRUST HIM, POPPA, HE'S BEEN IN TOUGHER SPOTS.
IT'S ONE OF THE CREATURES!
STAY BEHIND ME, NAK...
BUT IT'S NOT MOVING!
YOU'RE RIGHT!
HOW PUZZLING!
I SEE LIGHT AHEAD!
WOW!
AMAZING! I CAN'T BELIEVE IT!
HUH! I SHOULD HAVE KNOWN!

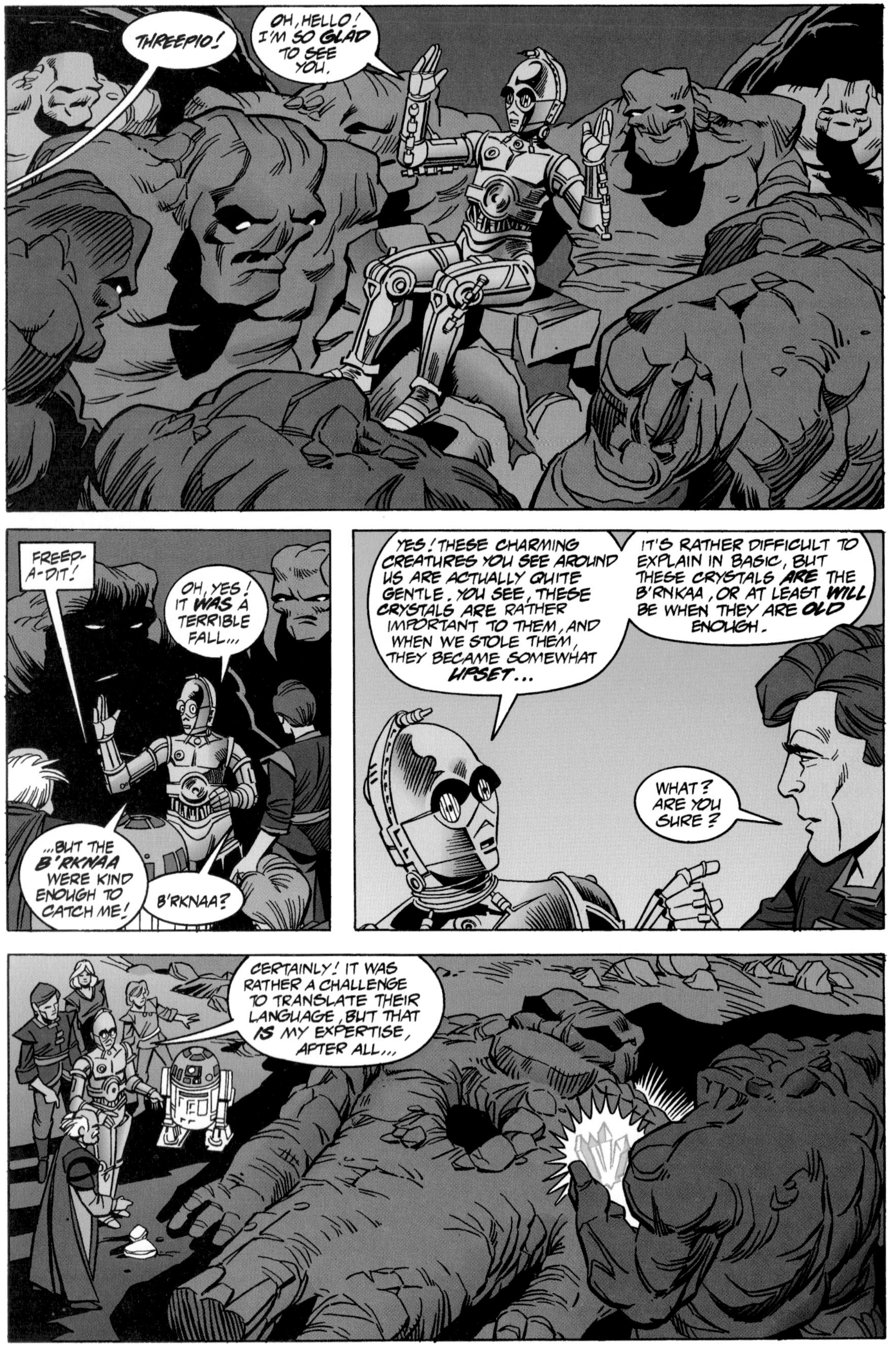
THREEPIO!
OH, HELLO! I'M SO GLAD TO SEE YOU.
FREEP-A-DIT!
OH, YES! IT WAS A TERRIBLE FALL...
...BUT THE B'RKNAA WERE KIND ENOUGH TO CATCH ME!
B'RKNAA?
YES! THESE CHARMING CREATURES YOU SEE AROUND US ARE ACTUALLY QUITE GENTLE. YOU SEE, THESE CRYSTALS ARE RATHER IMPORTANT TO THEM, AND WHEN WE STOLE THEM, THEY BECAME SOMEWHAT UPSET...
IT'S RATHER DIFFICULT TO EXPLAIN IN BASIC, BUT THESE CRYSTALS ARE THE B'RNKAA, OR AT LEAST WILL BE WHEN THEY ARE OLD ENOUGH.
WHAT? ARE YOU SURE?
CERTAINLY! IT WAS RATHER A CHALLENGE TO TRANSLATE THEIR LANGUAGE, BUT THAT IS MY EXPERTISE, AFTER ALL...

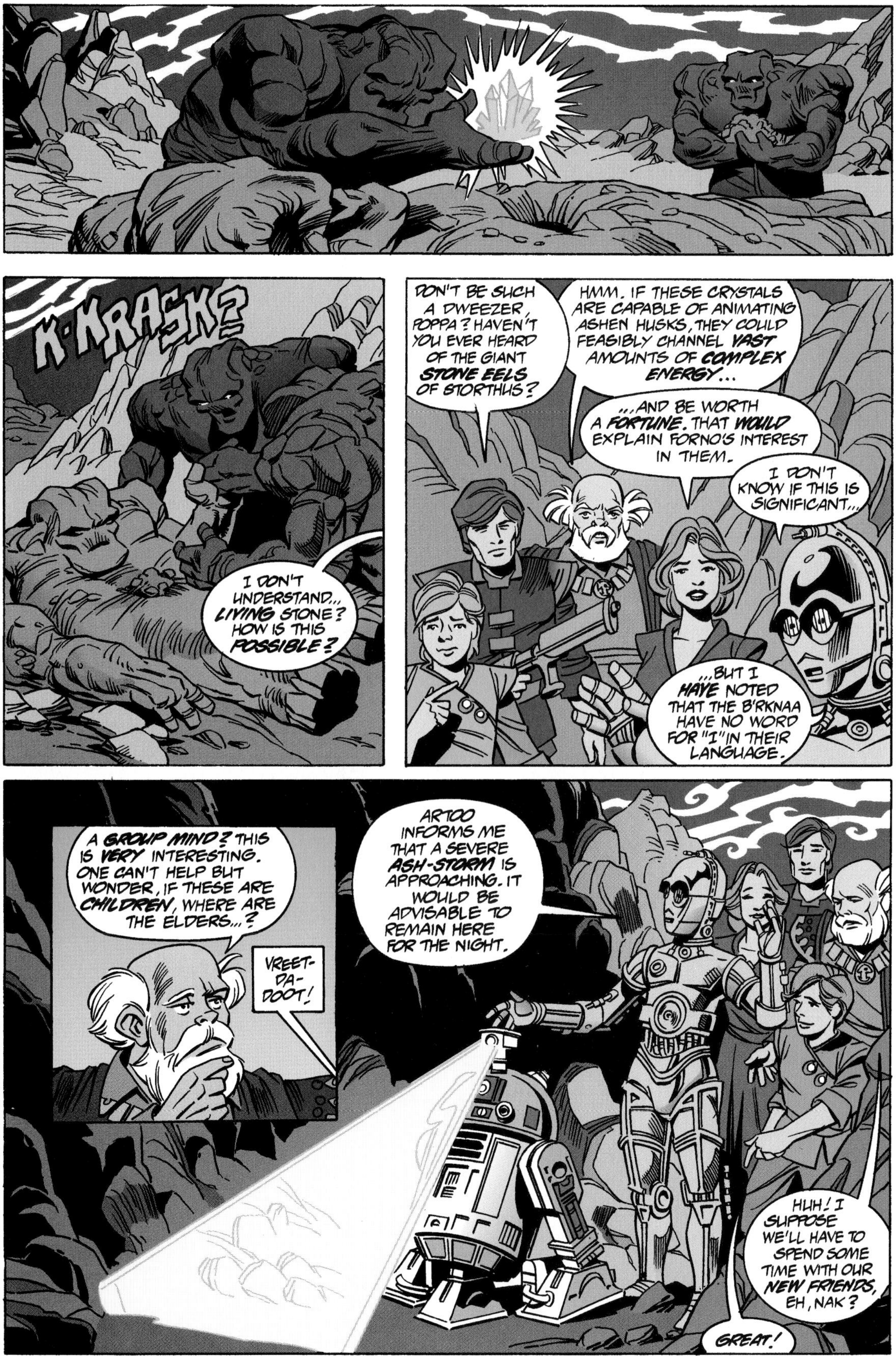
K-KRASK!
I DON'T UNDERSTAND... LIVING STONE? HOW IS THIS POSSIBLE?
DON'T BE SUCH A DWEEZER, POPPA! HAVEN'T YOU EVER HEARD OF THE GIANT STONE EELS OF STORTHUS?
HMM. IF THESE CRYSTALS ARE CAPABLE OF ANIMATING ASHEN HUSKS, THEY COULD FEASIBLY CHANNEL VAST AMOUNTS OF COMPLEX ENERGY...
...AND BE WORTH A FORTUNE. THAT WOULD EXPLAIN FORNO'S INTEREST IN THEM.
I DON'T KNOW IF THIS IS SIGNIFICANT...
...BUT I HAVE NOTED THAT THE B'RKNAA HAVE NO WORD FOR "I" IN THEIR LANGUAGE.
A GROUP MIND? THIS IS VERY INTERESTING. ONE CAN'T HELP BUT WONDER, IF THESE ARE CHILDREN, WHERE ARE THE ELDERS...?
VREET-DA-DOOT!
ARTOO INFORMS ME THAT A SEVERE ASH-STORM IS APPROACHING. IT WOULD BE ADVISABLE TO REMAIN HERE FOR THE NIGHT.
HUH! I SUPPOSE WE'LL HAVE TO SPEND SOME TIME WITH OUR NEW FRIENDS, EH, NAK?
GREAT!

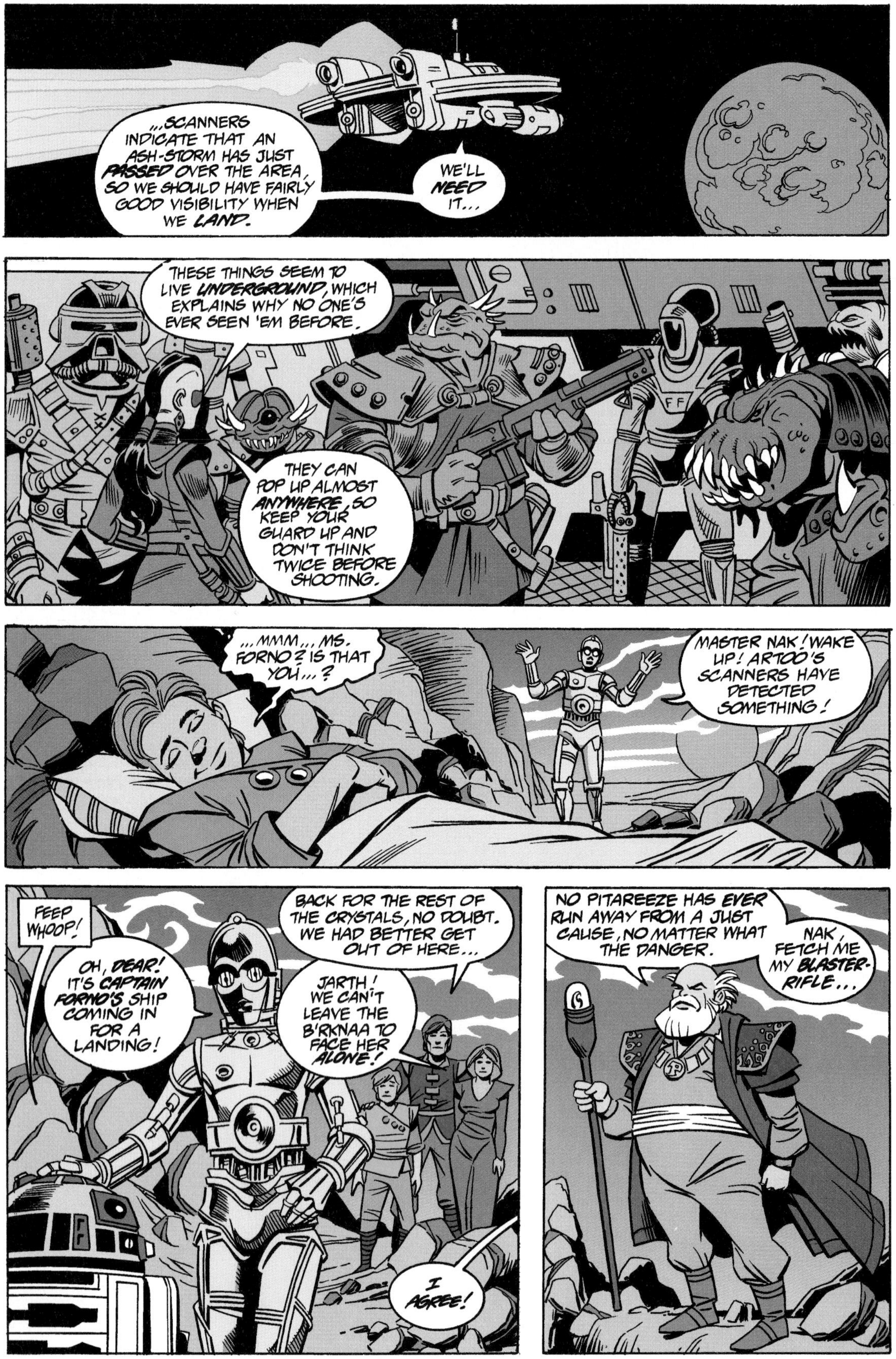
...SCANNERS INDICATE THAT AN ASH-STORM HAS JUST PASSED OVER THE AREA, SO WE SHOULD HAVE FAIRLY GOOD VISIBILITY WHEN WE LAND.
WE'LL NEED IT...
THESE THINGS SEEM TO LIVE UNDERGROUND, WHICH EXPLAINS WHY NO ONE'S EVER SEEN 'EM BEFORE.
THEY CAN POP UP ALMOST ANYWHERE, SO KEEP YOUR GUARD UP AND DON'T THINK TWICE BEFORE SHOOTING.
...MMM... MS. FORNO? IS THAT YOU...?
MASTER NAK! WAKE UP! ARTOO'S SCANNERS HAVE DETECTED SOMETHING!
FEEP WHOOP!
OH, DEAR! IT'S CAPTAIN FORNO'S SHIP COMING IN FOR A LANDING!
BACK FOR THE REST OF THE CRYSTALS, NO DOUBT. WE HAD BETTER GET OUT OF HERE...
JARTH! WE CAN'T LEAVE THE B'RKNAA TO FACE HER ALONE!
I AGREE!
NO PITAREEZE HAS EVER RUN AWAY FROM A JUST CAUSE, NO MATTER WHAT THE DANGER.
NAK, FETCH ME MY BLASTER-RIFLE...

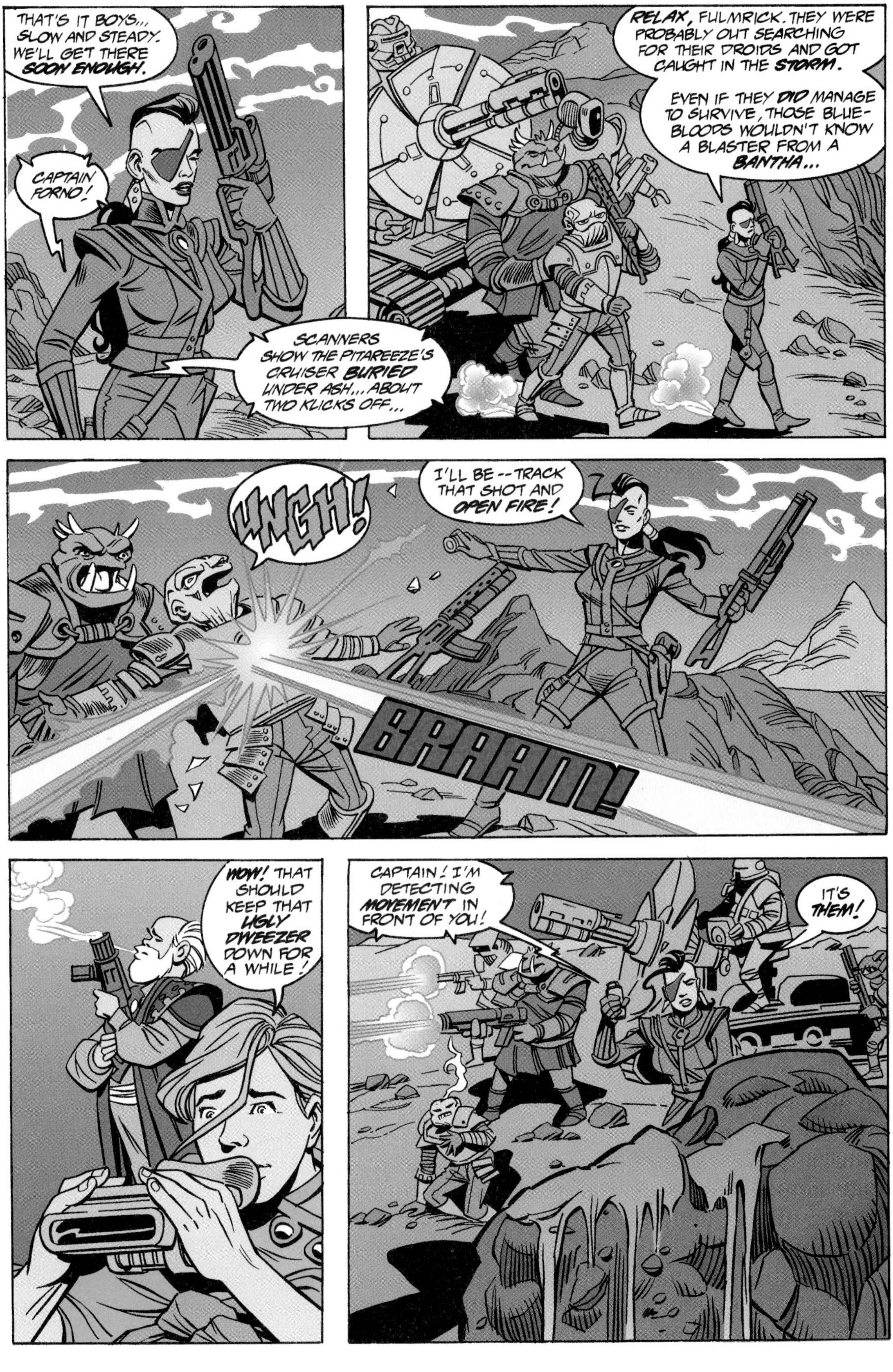
THAT'S IT BOYS... SLOW AND STEADY. WE'LL GET THERE SOON ENOUGH.
CAPTAIN FORNO!
SCANNERS SHOW THE PITAREEZE'S CRUISER BURIED UNDER ASH... ABOUT TWO KLICKS OFF...
RELAX, FULMRICK. THEY WERE PROBABLY OUT SEARCHING FOR THEIR DROIDS AND GOT CAUGHT IN THE STORM.
EVEN IF THEY DID MANAGE TO SURVIVE, THOSE BLUE-BLOODS WOULDN'T KNOW A BLASTER FROM A BANTHA...
UNGH!
I'LL BE--TRACK THAT SHOT AND OPEN FIRE!
BRAAAM!
WOW! THAT SHOULD KEEP THAT UGLY DWEEZER DOWN FOR A WHILE!
CAPTAIN! I'M DETECTING MOVEMENT IN FRONT OF YOU!
IT'S THEM!

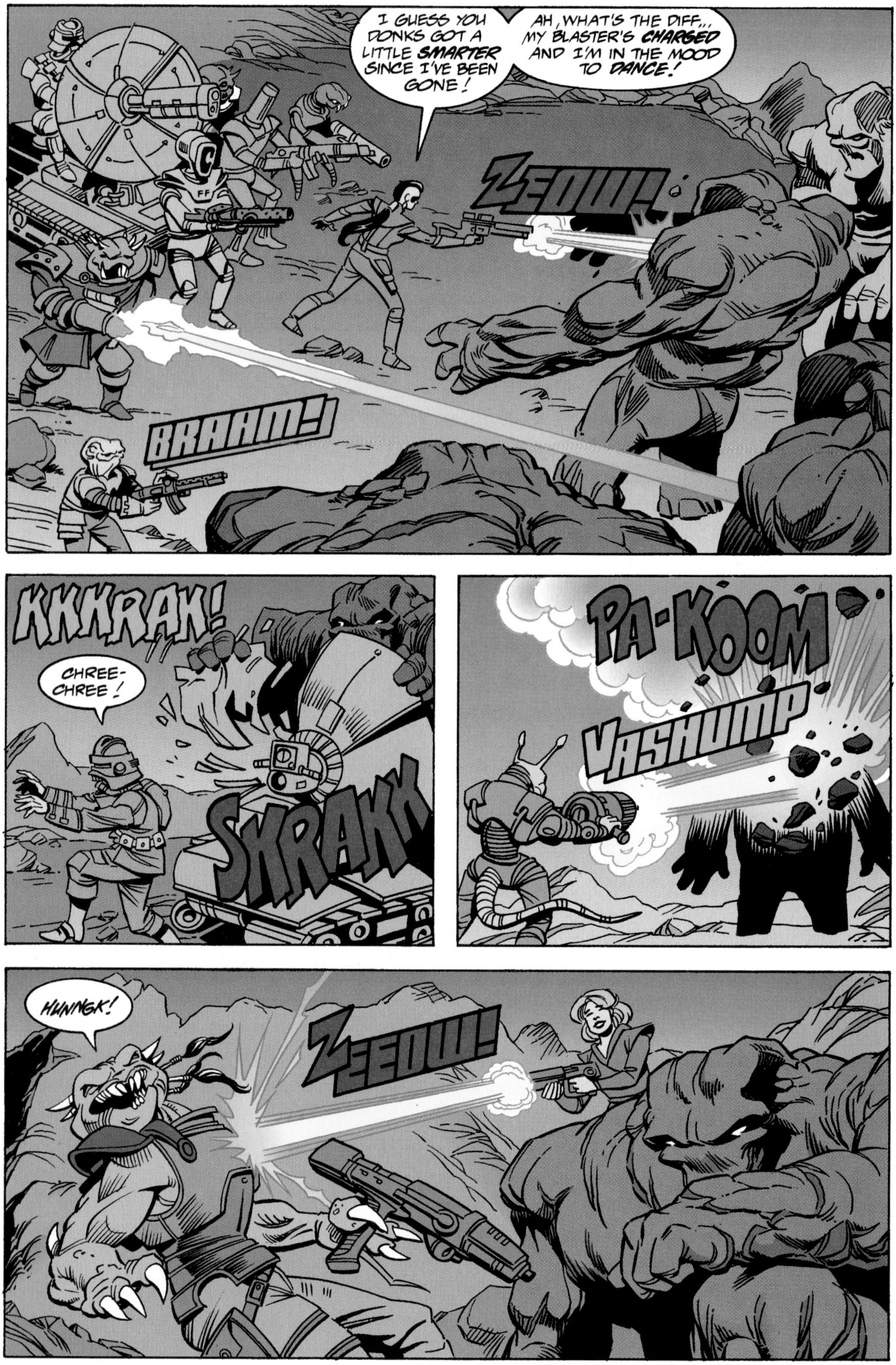
I GUESS YOU DONKS GOT A LITTLE SMARTER SINCE I'VE BEEN GONE!
AH, WHAT'S THE DIFF... MY BLASTER'S CHARGED AND I'M IN THE MOOD TO DANCE!
ZEEOW!
BRAAM!
KKKRAK!
CHREE-CHREE!
SKRAKK
PA-KOOM
VASHUMP
HUNNGK!
ZEEOW!

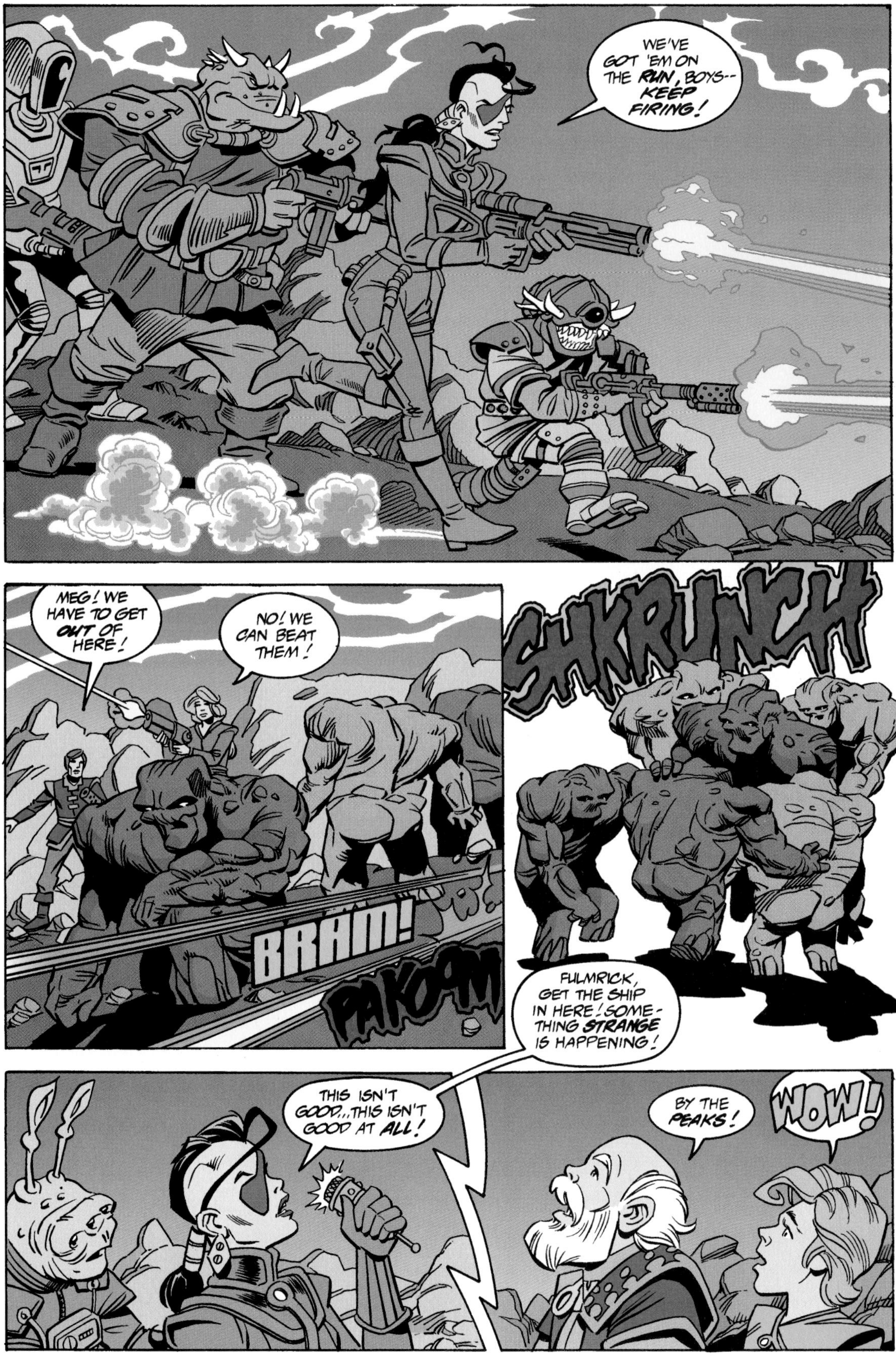
WE'VE GOT 'EM ON THE RUN, BOYS-- KEEP FIRING!
MEG! WE HAVE TO GET OUT OF HERE!
NO! WE CAN BEAT THEM!
BRAM!
SHKRUNCH
FULMRICK, GET THE SHIP IN HERE! SOMETHING STRANGE IS HAPPENING!
THIS ISN'T GOOD... THIS ISN'T GOOD AT ALL!
BY THE PEAKS!
WOW!

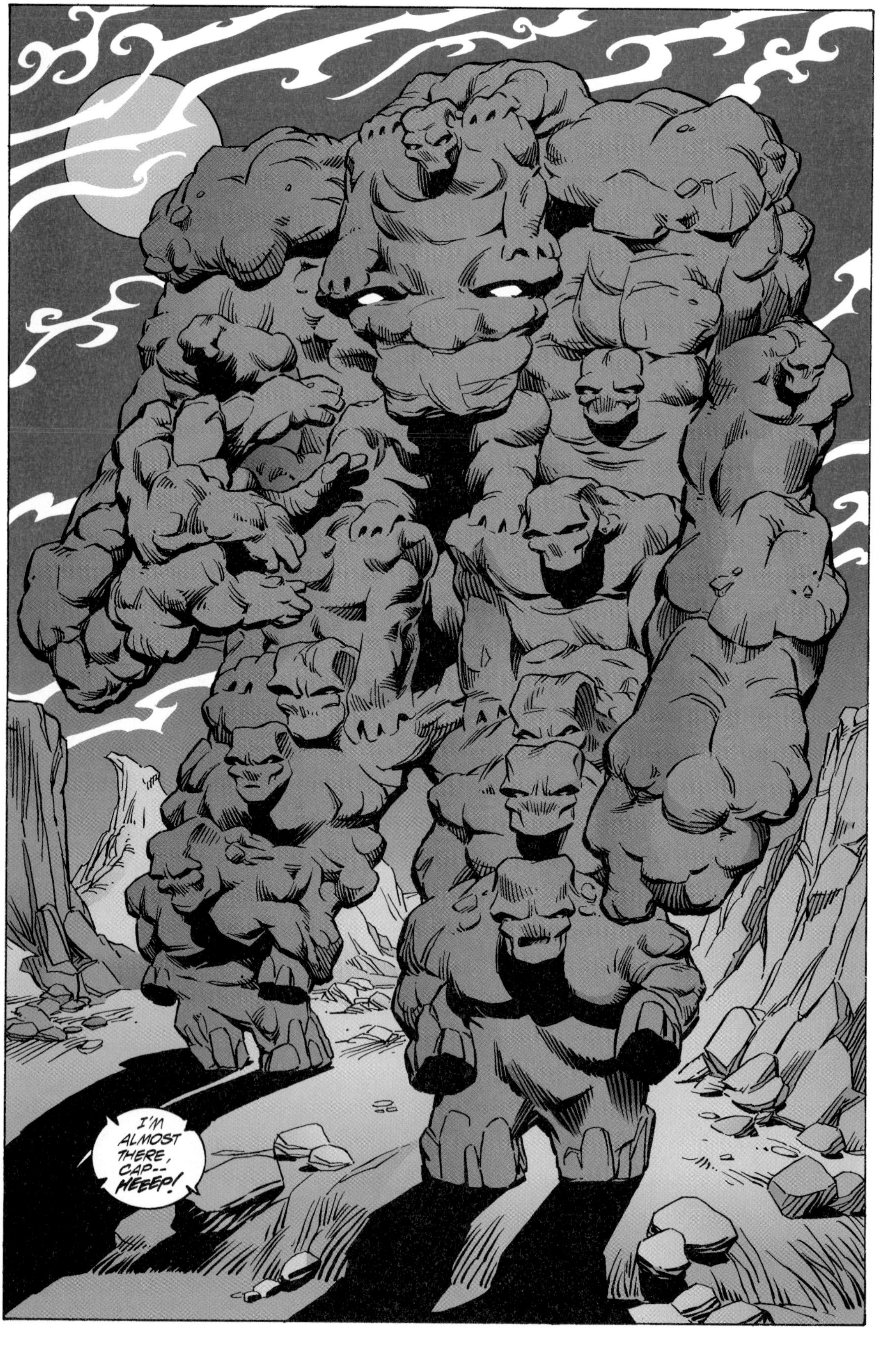
I'M ALMOST THERE, CAP-- HEEEP!

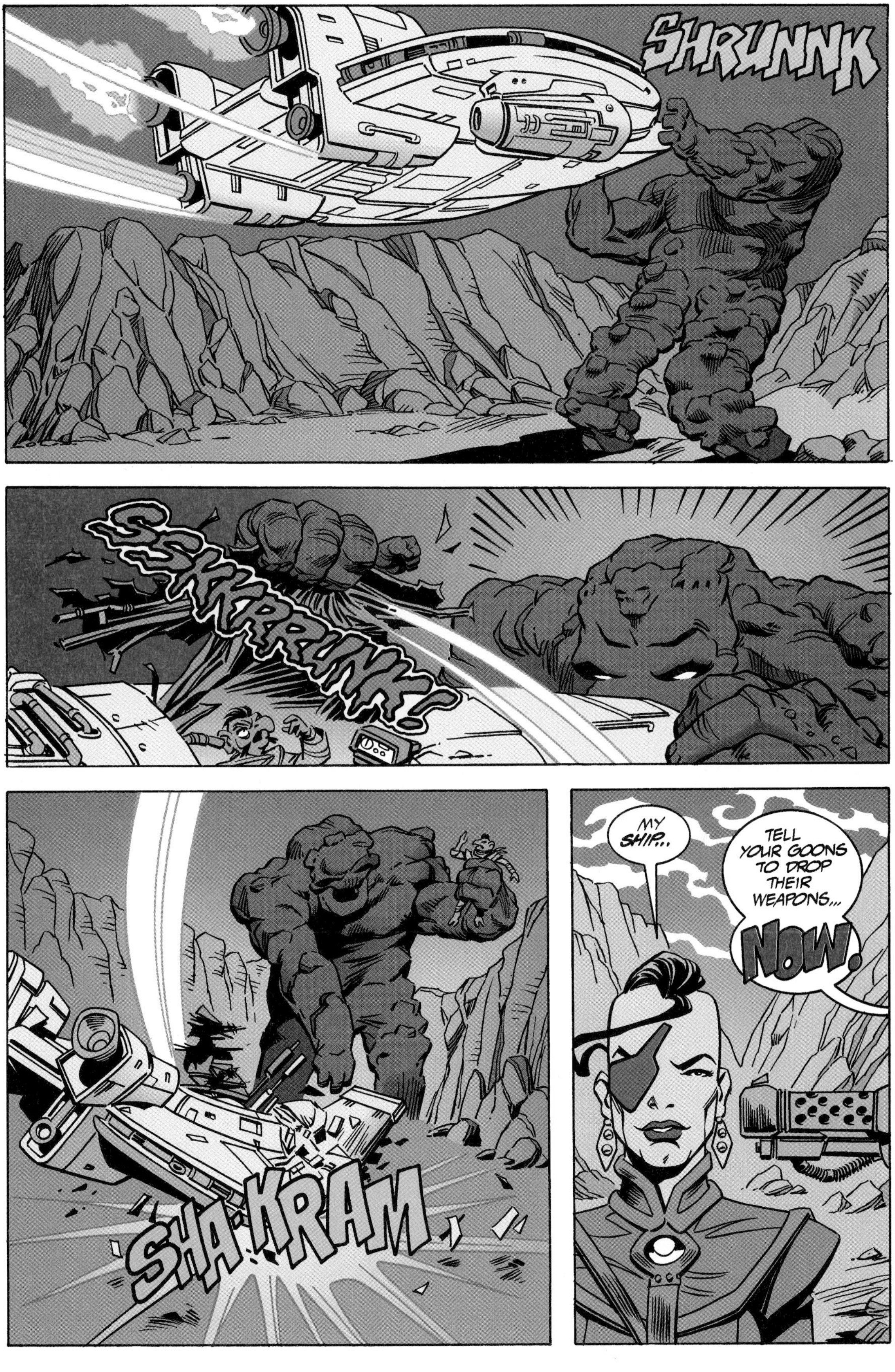
SHRUNNK
SSKKRRUNK!
SHA-KRAM
MY SHIP...
TELL YOUR GOONS TO DROP THEIR WEAPONS... NOW!

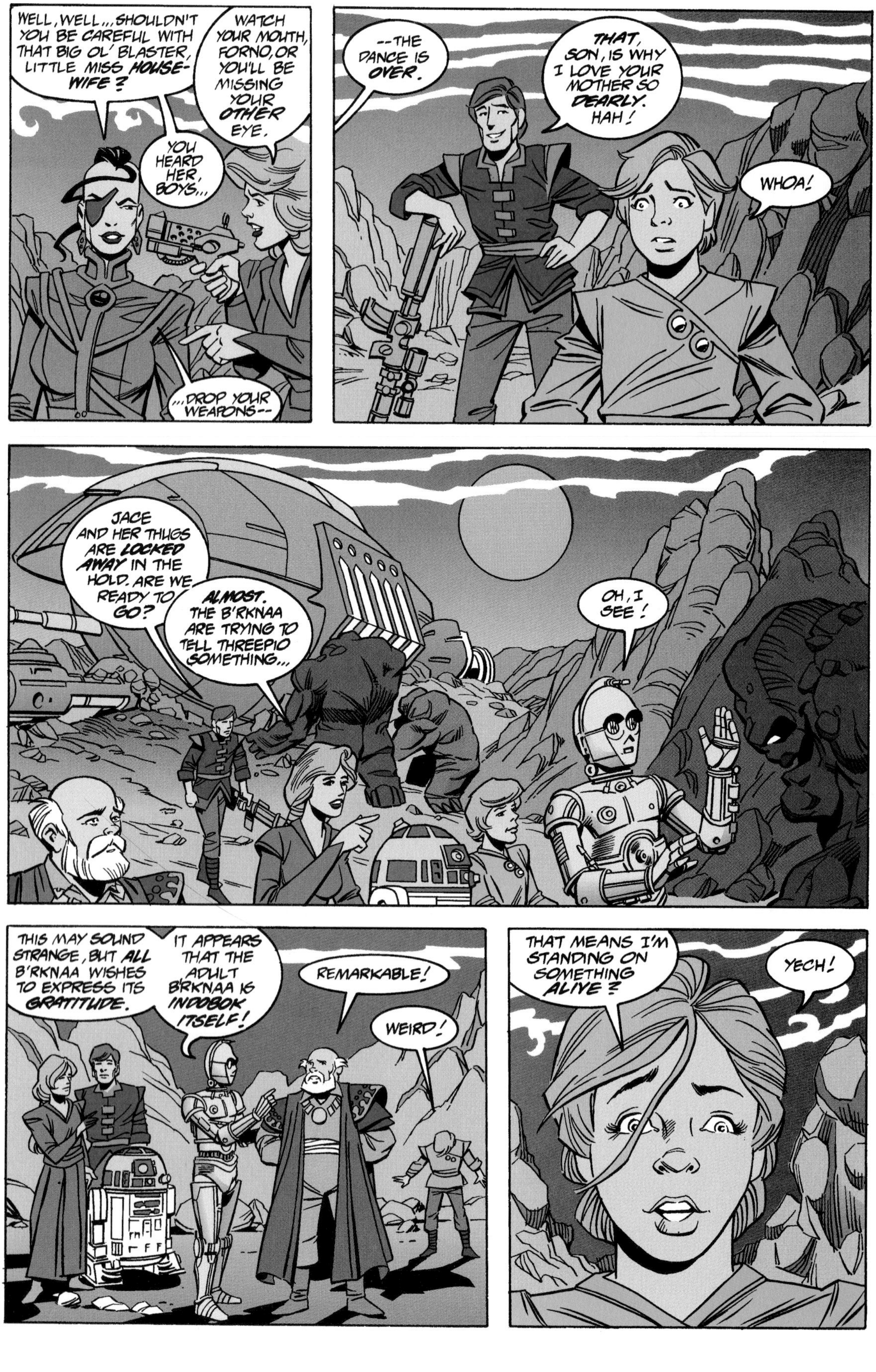
WELL, WELL... SHOULDN'T YOU BE CAREFUL WITH THAT BIG OL' BLASTER, LITTLE MISS HOUSE-WIFE?
YOU HEARD HER, BOYS...
WATCH YOUR MOUTH, FORNO, OR YOU'LL BE MISSING YOUR OTHER EYE.
...DROP YOUR WEAPONS--
--THE DANCE IS OVER.
THAT, SON, IS WHY I LOVE YOUR MOTHER SO DEARLY. HAH!
WHOA!
JACE AND HER THUGS ARE LOCKED AWAY IN THE HOLD. ARE WE READY TO GO?
ALMOST. THE B'RKNAA ARE TRYING TO TELL THREEPIO SOMETHING...
OH, I SEE!
THIS MAY SOUND STRANGE, BUT ALL B'RKNAA WISHES TO EXPRESS ITS GRATITUDE.
IT APPEARS THAT THE ADULT B'RKNAA IS INDOBOK ITSELF!
REMARKABLE!
WEIRD!
THAT MEANS I'M STANDING ON SOMETHING ALIVE?
YECH!

Short Cut
Chapter 6

Script
Ryder Windham

Art
Ian Gibson

Colors
Pamela Rambo

Lettering
Steve Dutro

Cover
Kilian Plunkett

Sketch
Kilian Plunkett

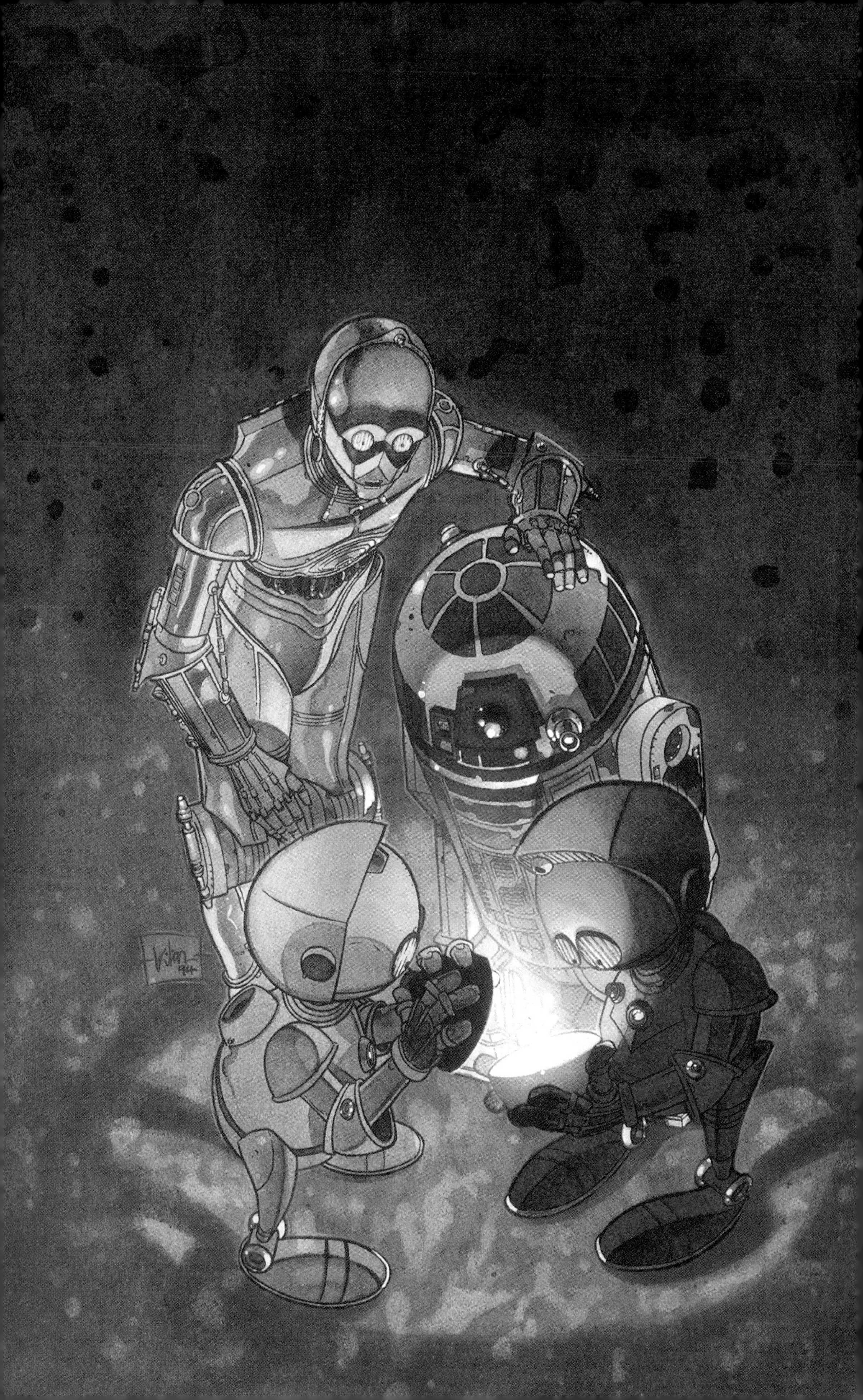

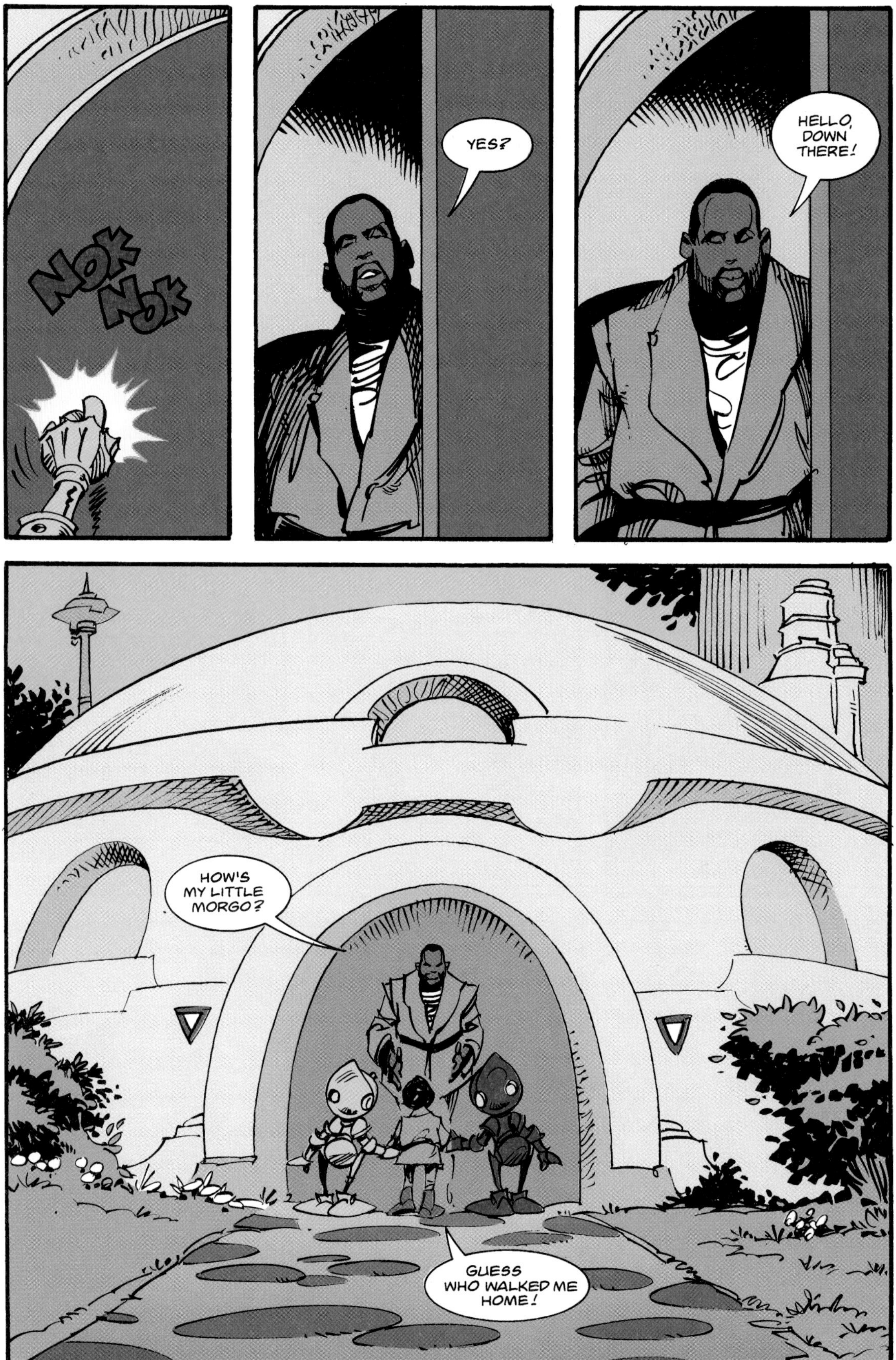
NOK NOK
YES?
HELLO, DOWN THERE!
HOW'S MY LITTLE MORGO?
GUESS WHO WALKED ME HOME!

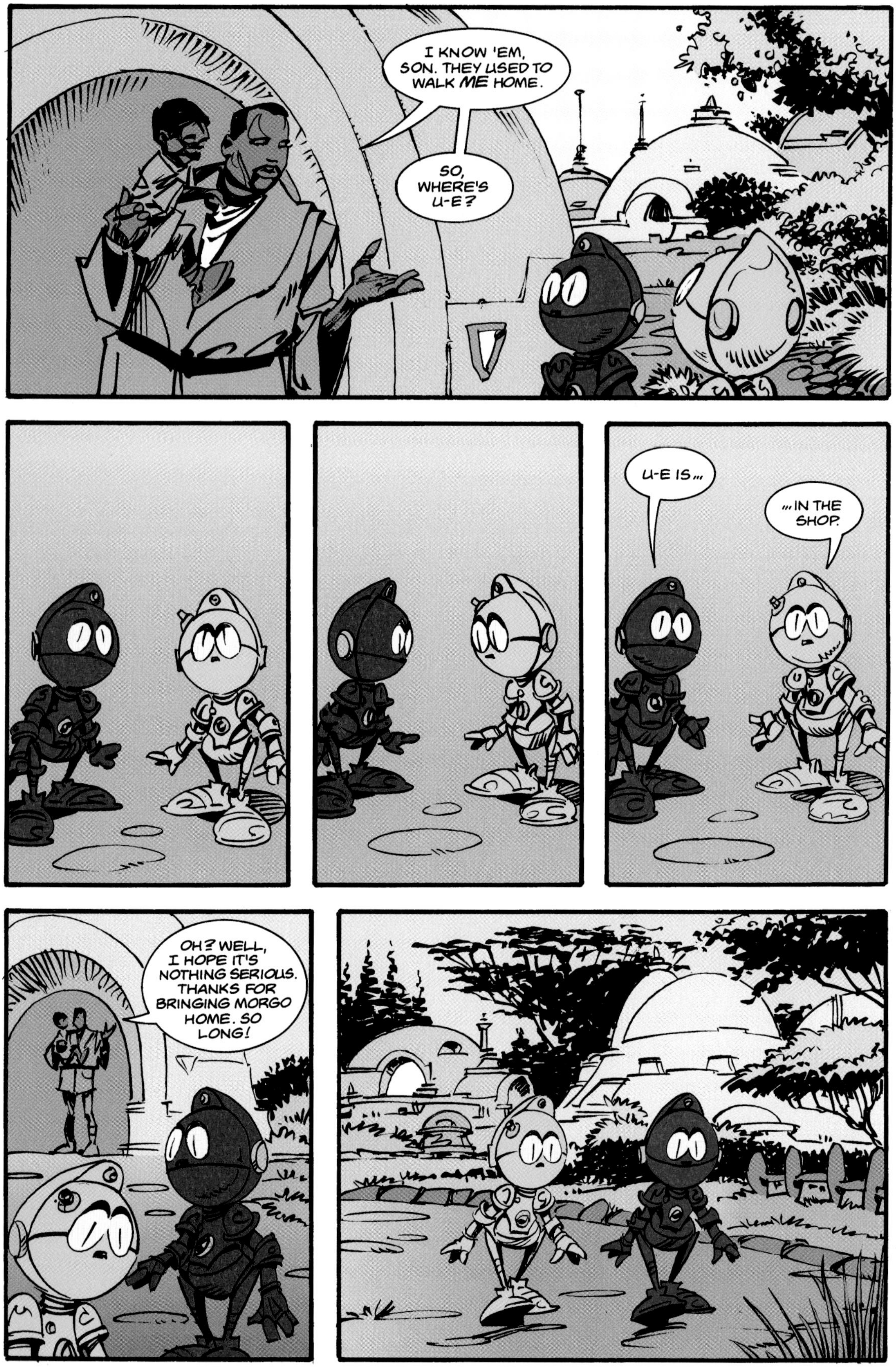
I KNOW 'EM, SON. THEY USED TO WALK *ME* HOME.
SO, WHERE'S U-E?
U-E IS...
...IN THE SHOP.
OH? WELL, I HOPE IT'S NOTHING SERIOUS. THANKS FOR BRINGING MORGO HOME. SO LONG!

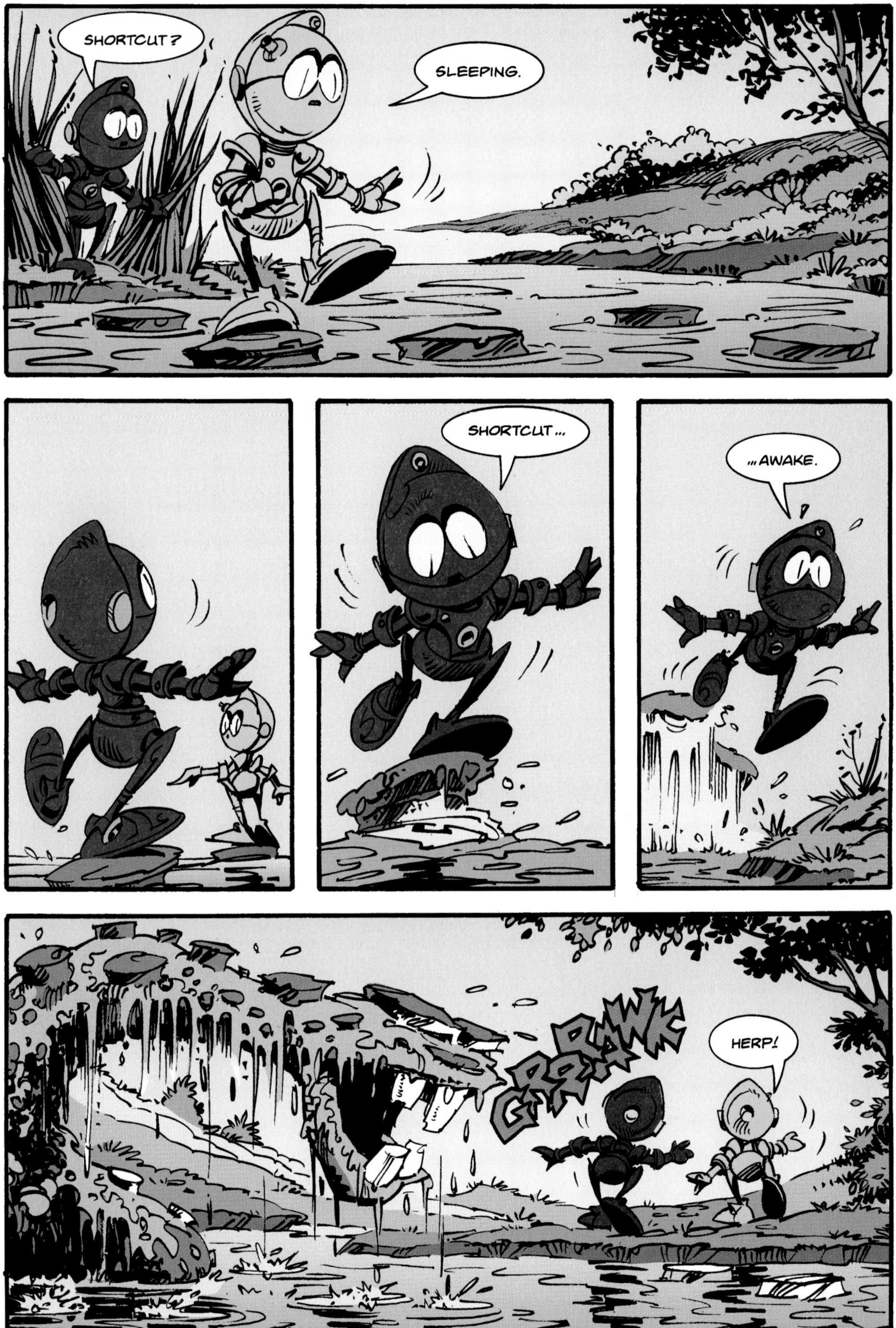
SHORTCUT?
SLEEPING.
SHORTCUT...
...AWAKE.
GRRRAWK
HERP!

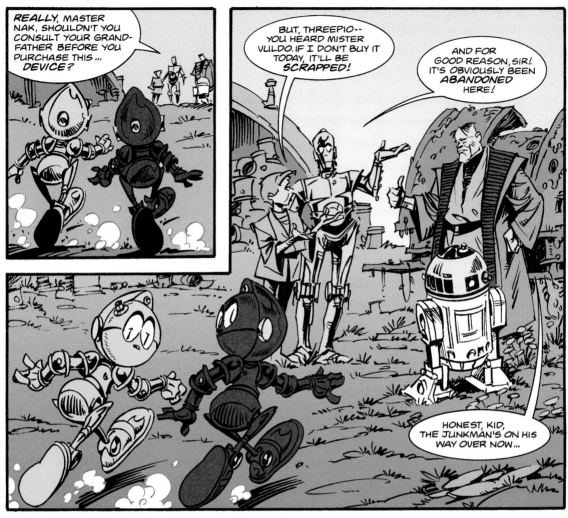

REALLY, MASTER NAK, SHOULDN'T YOU CONSULT YOUR GRAND-FATHER BEFORE YOU PURCHASE THIS ... *DEVICE?*

BUT, THREEPIO-- YOU HEARD MISTER VULDO. IF I DON'T BUY IT TODAY, IT'LL BE *SCRAPPED!*

AND FOR GOOD REASON, SIR! IT'S OBVIOUSLY BEEN *ABANDONED* HERE!

HONEST, KID, THE JUNKMAN'S ON HIS WAY OVER NOW...

KRASH

Q-E AND 2-E! THEY OPERATE THE TOWN NURSERY!

MODEL-E6?! WHY THEY'VE BEEN OUT OF SERVICE FOR AGES!

FOOO-TWEEP?

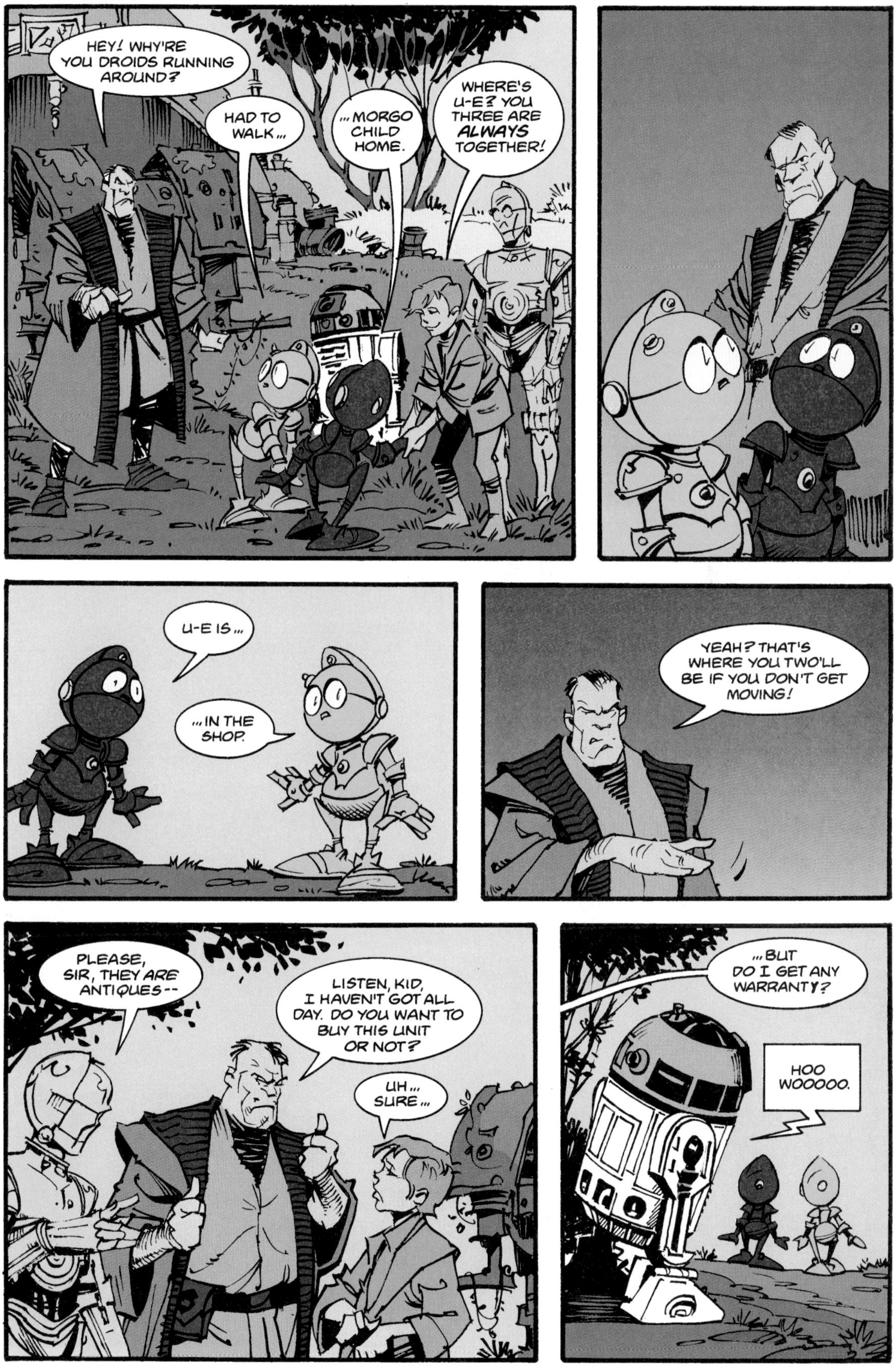
HEY! WHY'RE YOU DROIDS RUNNING AROUND?
HAD TO WALK...
...MORGO CHILD HOME.
WHERE'S U-E? YOU THREE ARE ALWAYS TOGETHER!
U-E IS...
...IN THE SHOP.
YEAH? THAT'S WHERE YOU TWO'LL BE IF YOU DON'T GET MOVING!
PLEASE, SIR, THEY ARE ANTIQUES--
LISTEN, KID, I HAVEN'T GOT ALL DAY. DO YOU WANT TO BUY THIS UNIT OR NOT?
UH... SURE...
...BUT DO I GET ANY WARRANTY?
HOO WOOOOO.

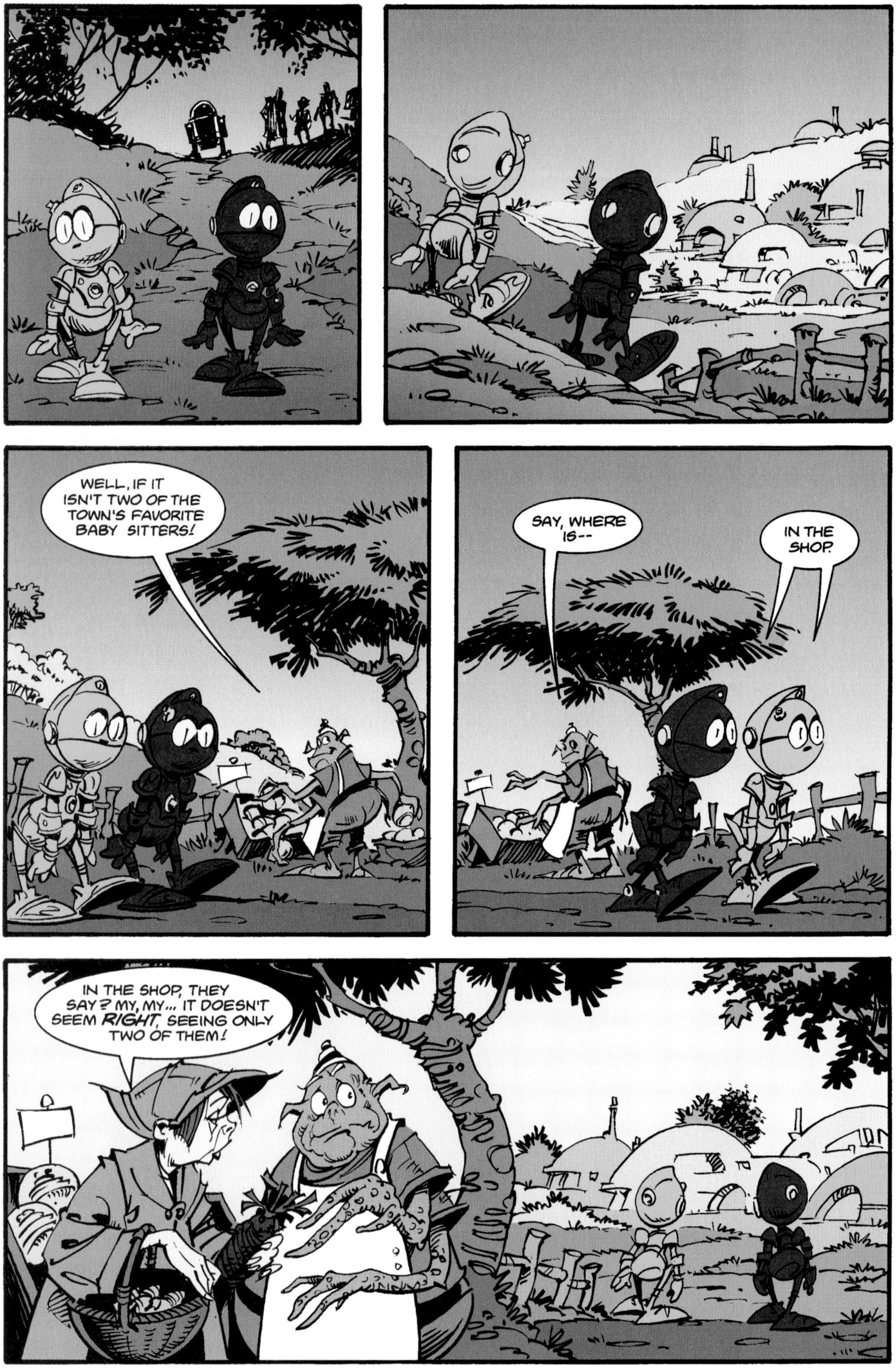
WELL, IF IT ISN'T TWO OF THE TOWN'S FAVORITE BABY SITTERS!
SAY, WHERE IS--
IN THE SHOP.
IN THE SHOP, THEY SAY? MY, MY... IT DOESN'T SEEM RIGHT, SEEING ONLY TWO OF THEM!

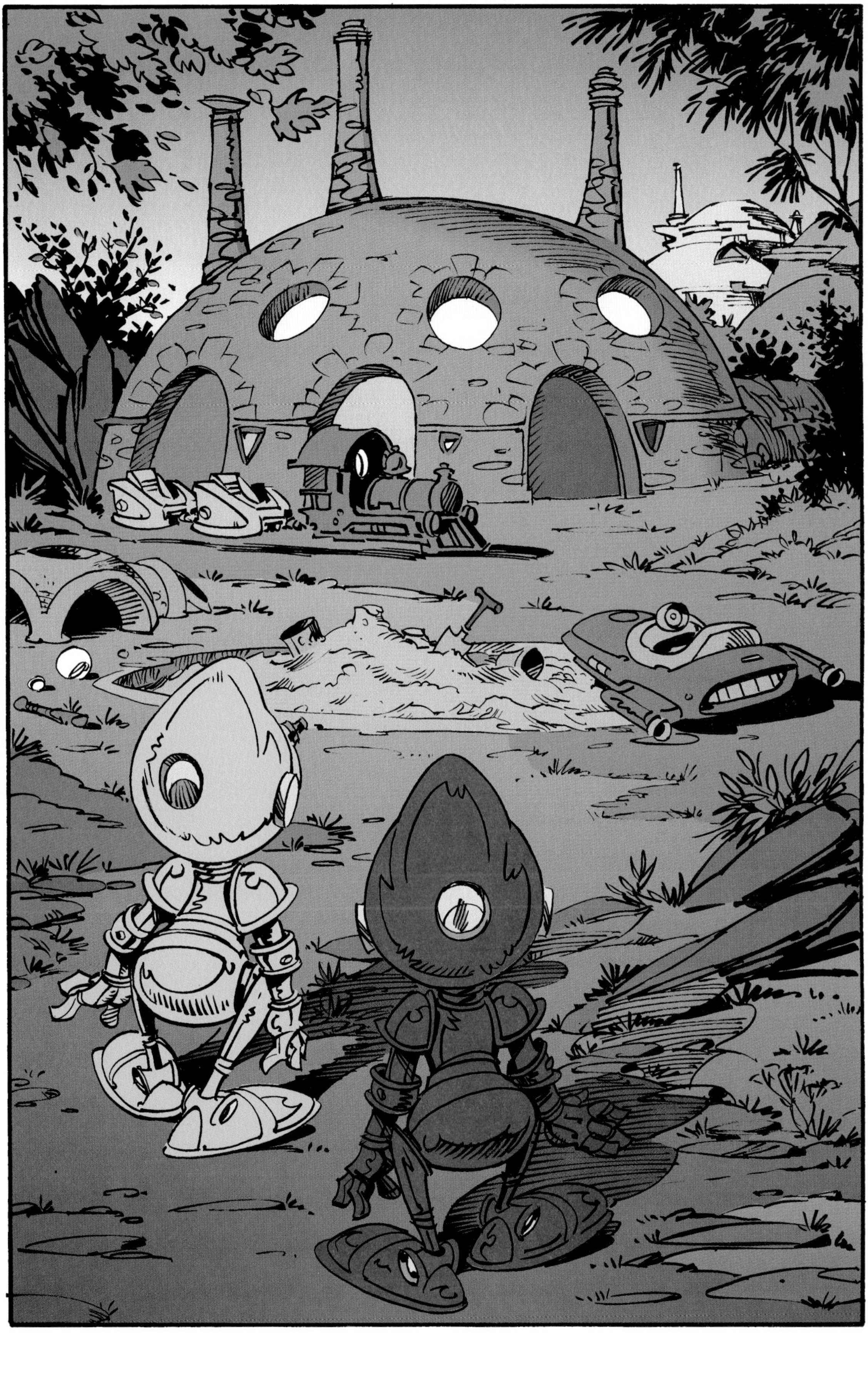

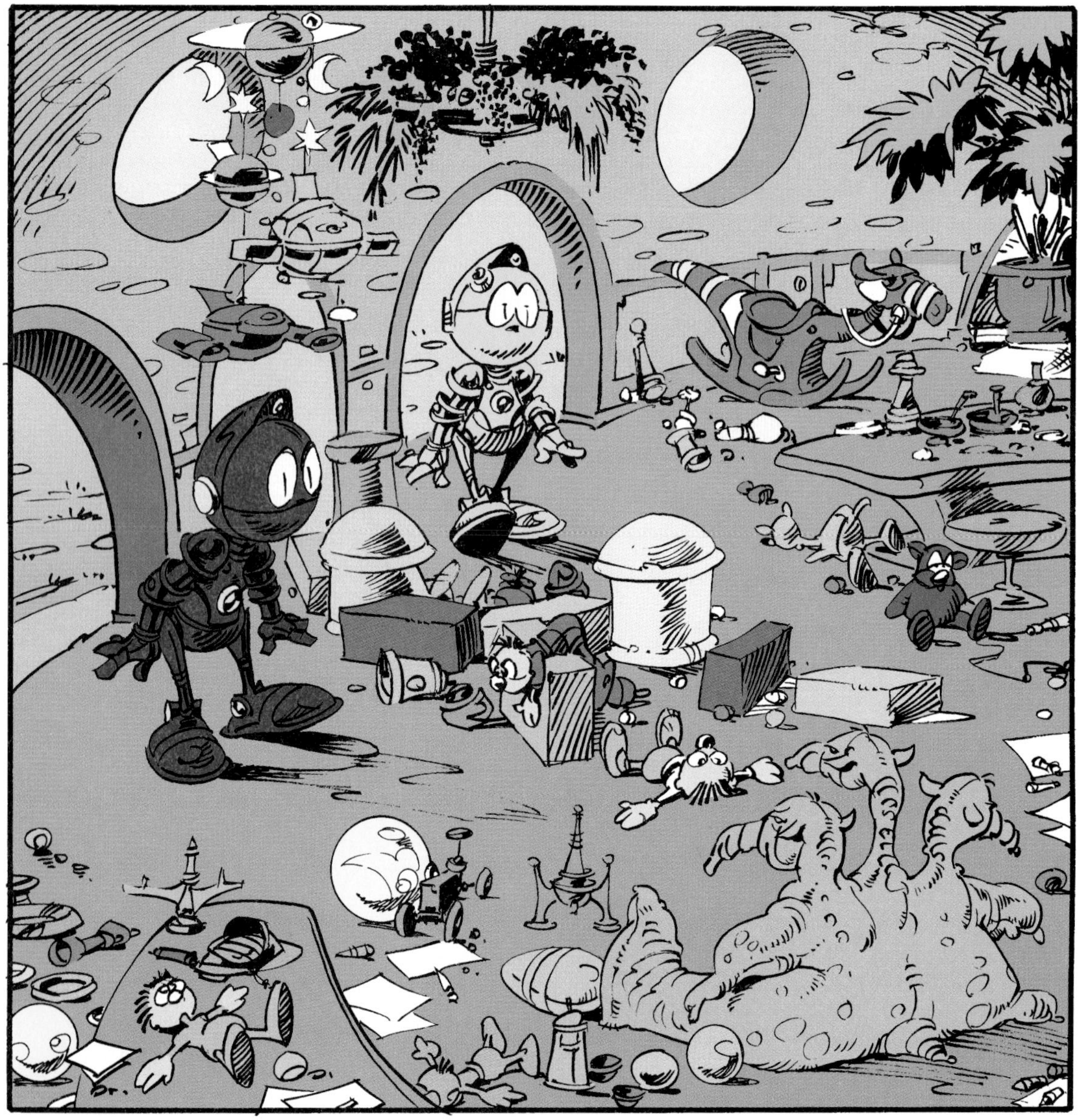

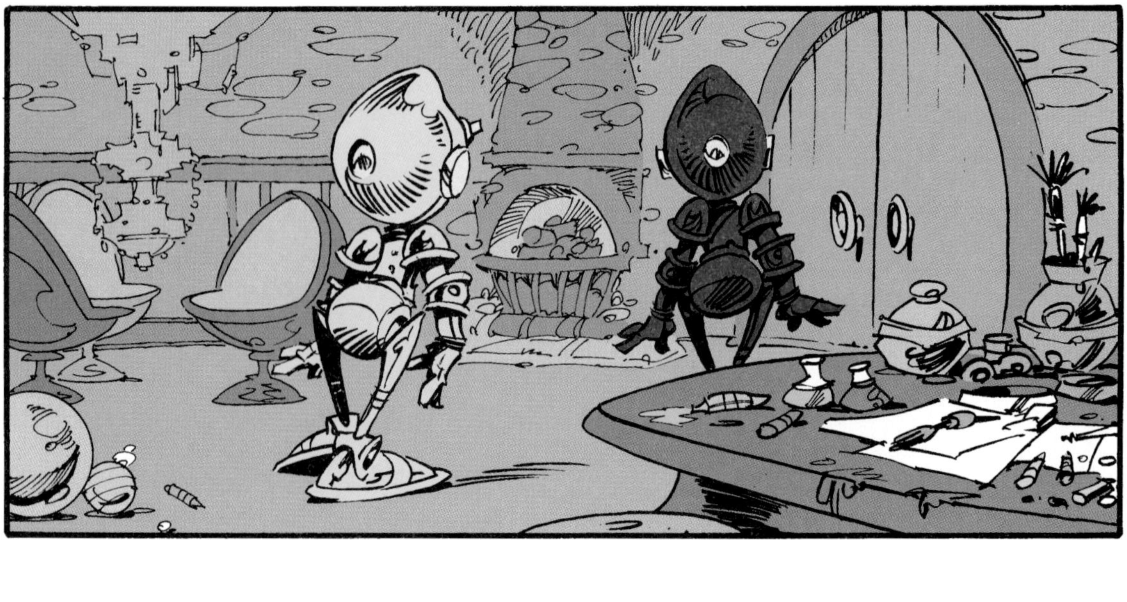

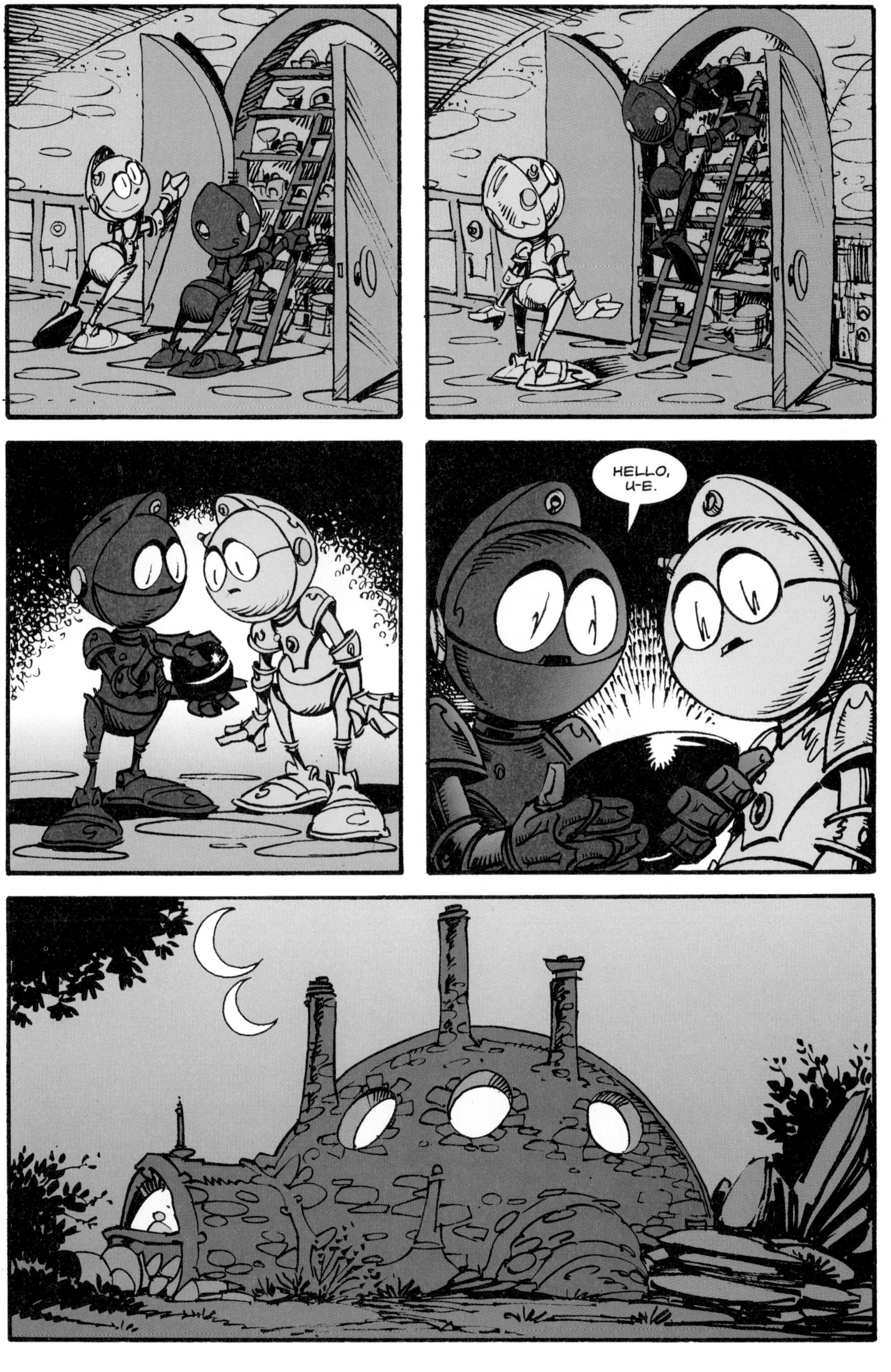
HELLO,
U-E.

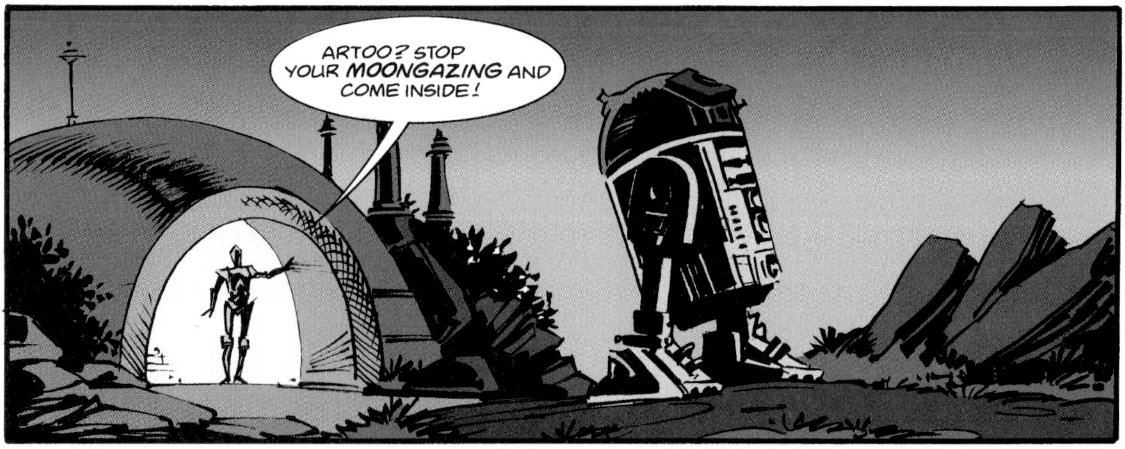
ARTOO? STOP YOUR MOONGAZING AND COME INSIDE!

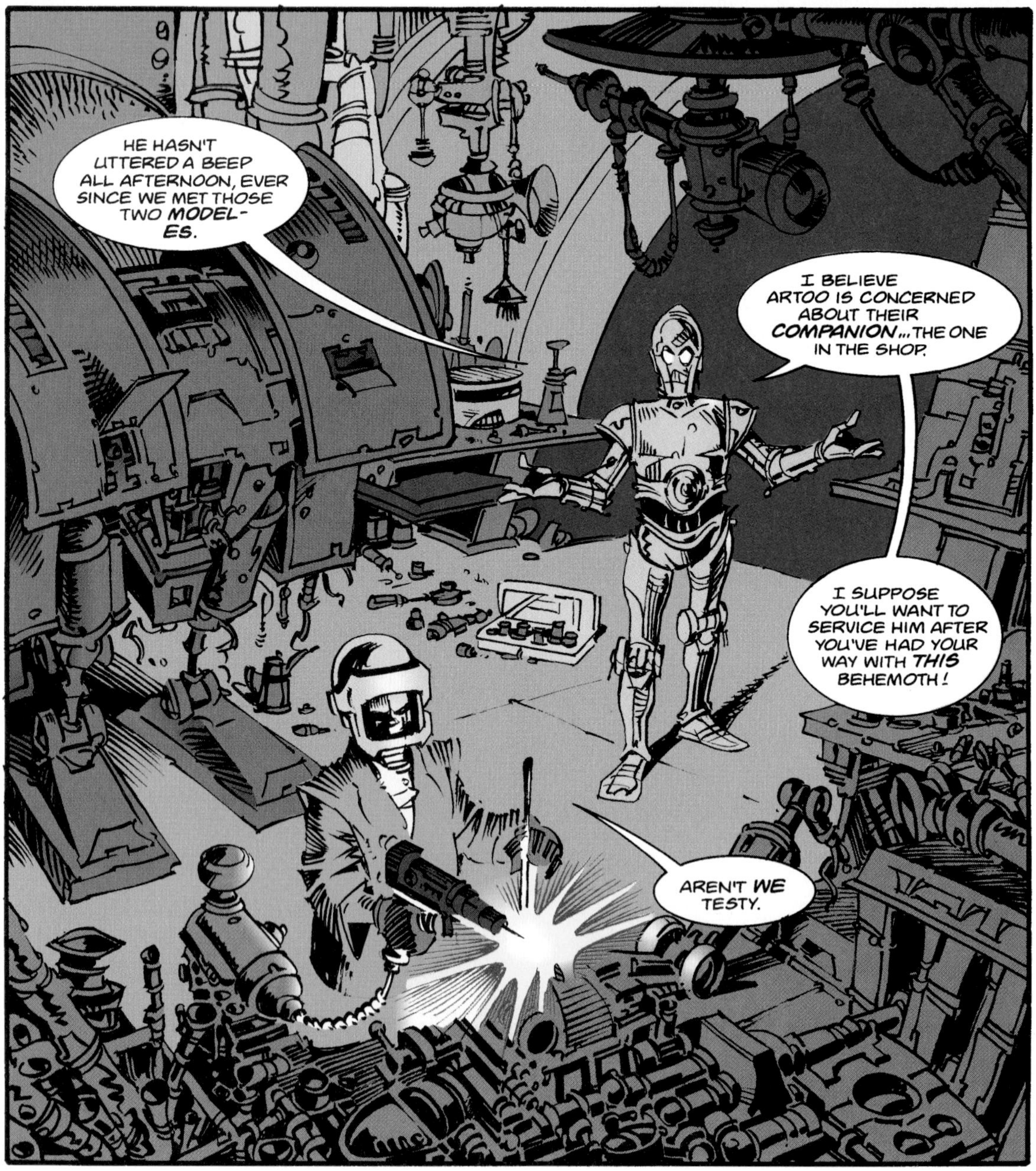
HE HASN'T UTTERED A BEEP ALL AFTERNOON, EVER SINCE WE MET THOSE TWO MODEL-ES.
I BELIEVE ARTOO IS CONCERNED ABOUT THEIR COMPANION... THE ONE IN THE SHOP.
I SUPPOSE YOU'LL WANT TO SERVICE HIM AFTER YOU'VE HAD YOUR WAY WITH THIS BEHEMOTH!
AREN'T WE TESTY.

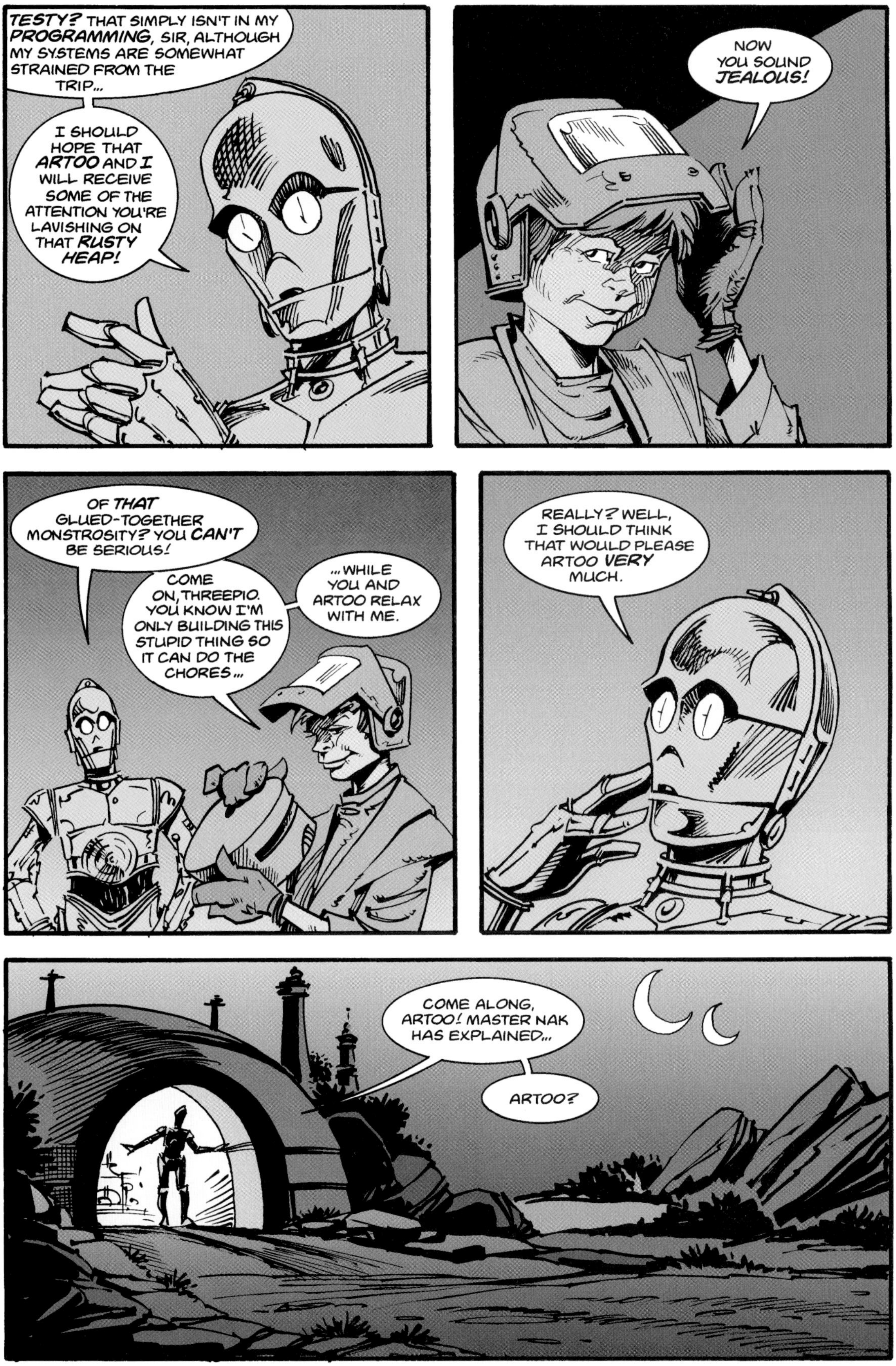

TESTY? THAT SIMPLY ISN'T IN MY PROGRAMMING, SIR, ALTHOUGH MY SYSTEMS ARE SOMEWHAT STRAINED FROM THE TRIP...
I SHOULD HOPE THAT ARTOO AND I WILL RECEIVE SOME OF THE ATTENTION YOU'RE LAVISHING ON THAT RUSTY HEAP!
NOW YOU SOUND JEALOUS!
OF THAT GLUED-TOGETHER MONSTROSITY? YOU CAN'T BE SERIOUS!
COME ON, THREEPIO. YOU KNOW I'M ONLY BUILDING THIS STUPID THING SO IT CAN DO THE CHORES...
...WHILE YOU AND ARTOO RELAX WITH ME.
REALLY? WELL, I SHOULD THINK THAT WOULD PLEASE ARTOO VERY MUCH.
COME ALONG, ARTOO! MASTER NAK HAS EXPLAINED...
ARTOO?

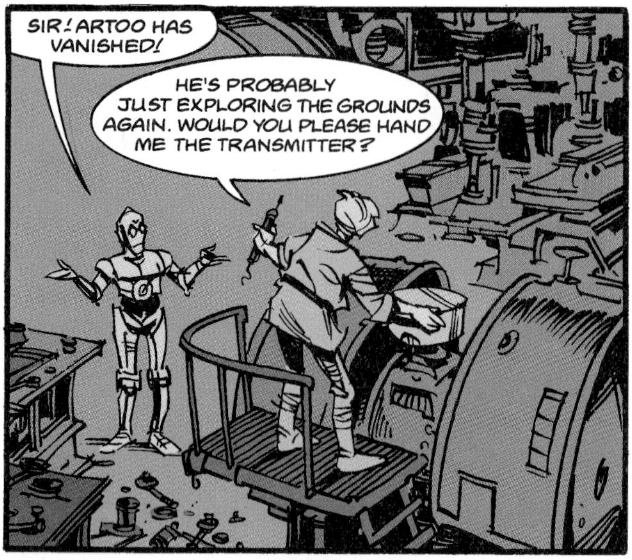
SIR! ARTOO HAS VANISHED!
HE'S PROBABLY JUST EXPLORING THE GROUNDS AGAIN. WOULD YOU PLEASE HAND ME THE TRANSMITTER?

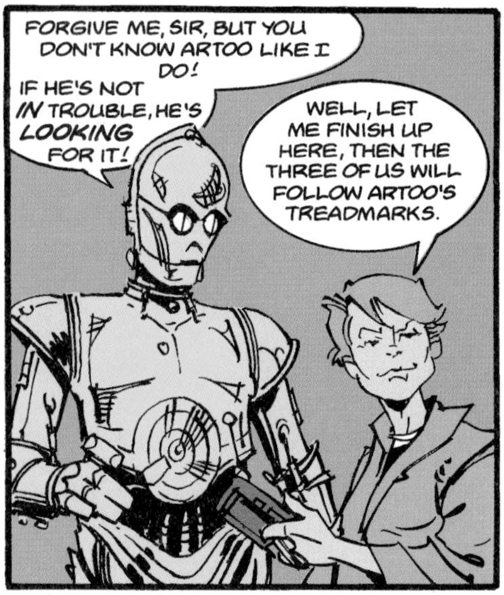
FORGIVE ME, SIR, BUT YOU DON'T KNOW ARTOO LIKE I DO!
IF HE'S NOT *IN* TROUBLE, HE'S ***LOOKING*** FOR IT!
WELL, LET ME FINISH UP HERE, THEN THE THREE OF US WILL FOLLOW ARTOO'S TREADMARKS.

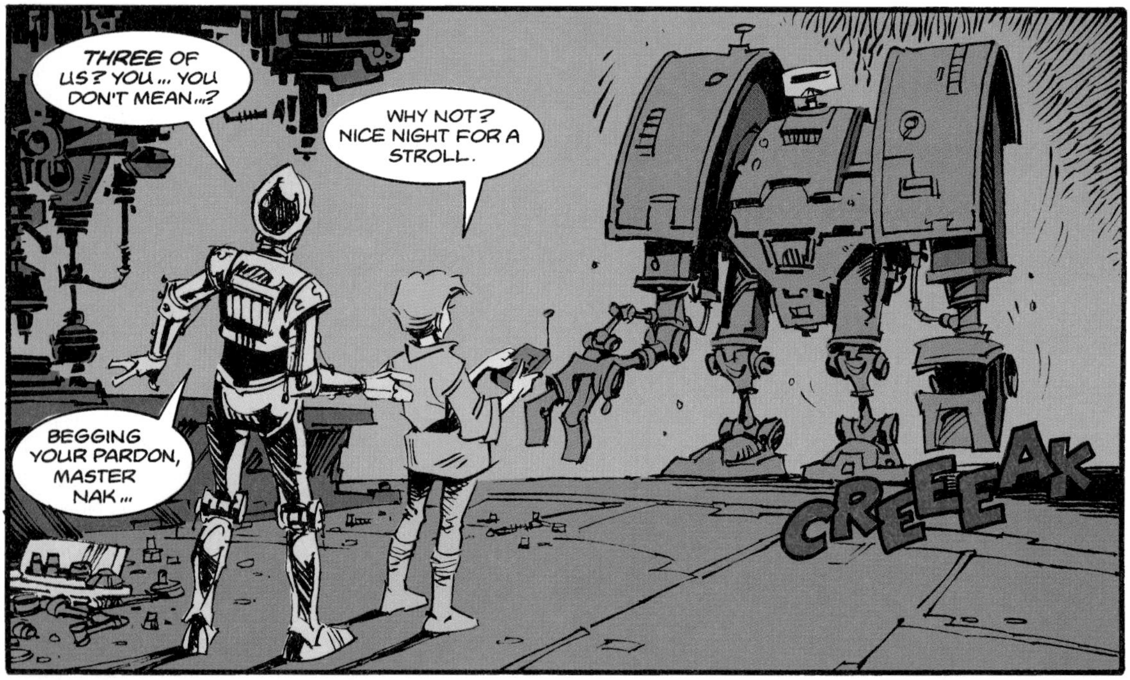
THREE OF US? YOU ... YOU DON'T MEAN ...?
WHY NOT? NICE NIGHT FOR A STROLL.
BEGGING YOUR PARDON, MASTER NAK ...
CREEEAK

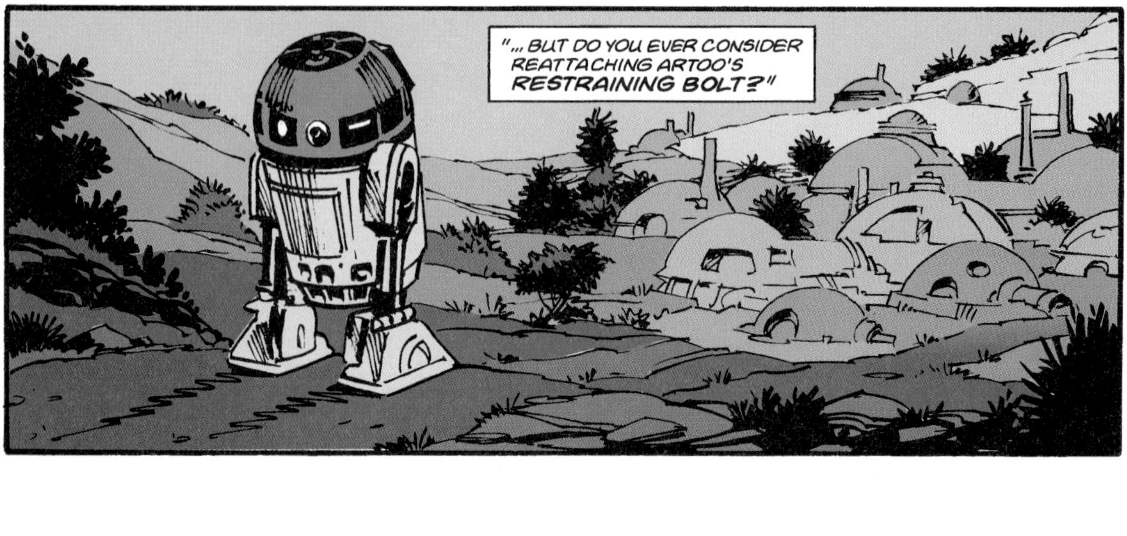
"... BUT DO YOU EVER CONSIDER REATTACHING ARTOO'S ***RESTRAINING BOLT?***"

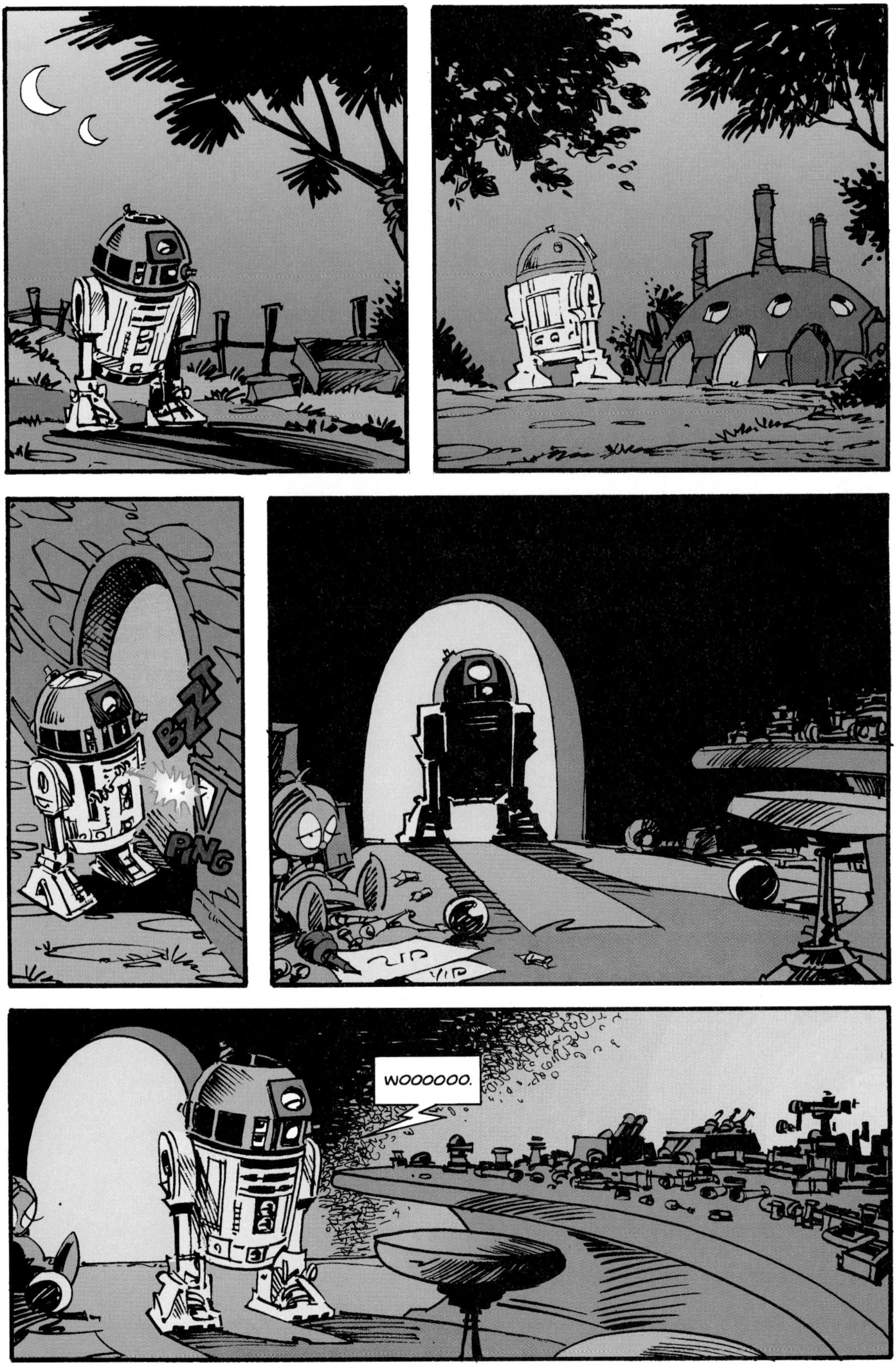
BZZT
PING
WOOOOOO.

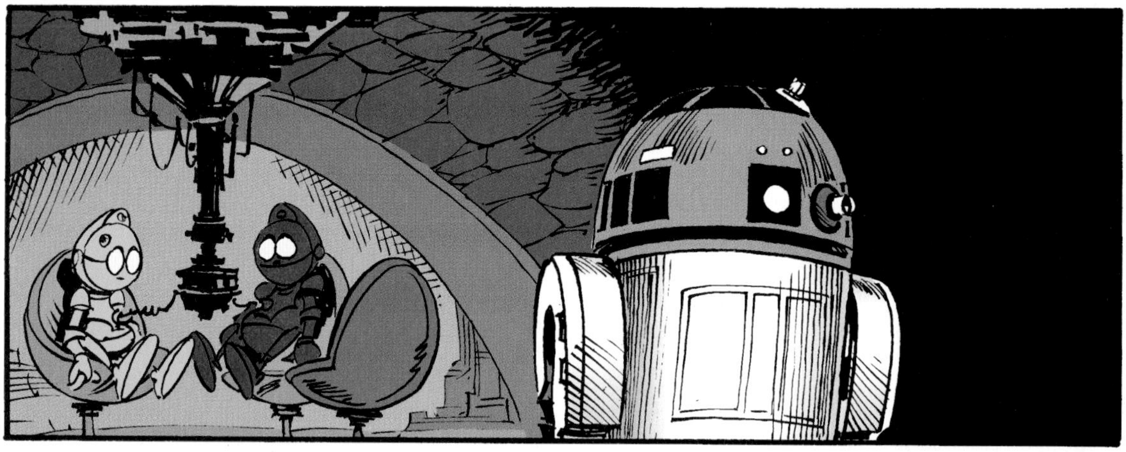

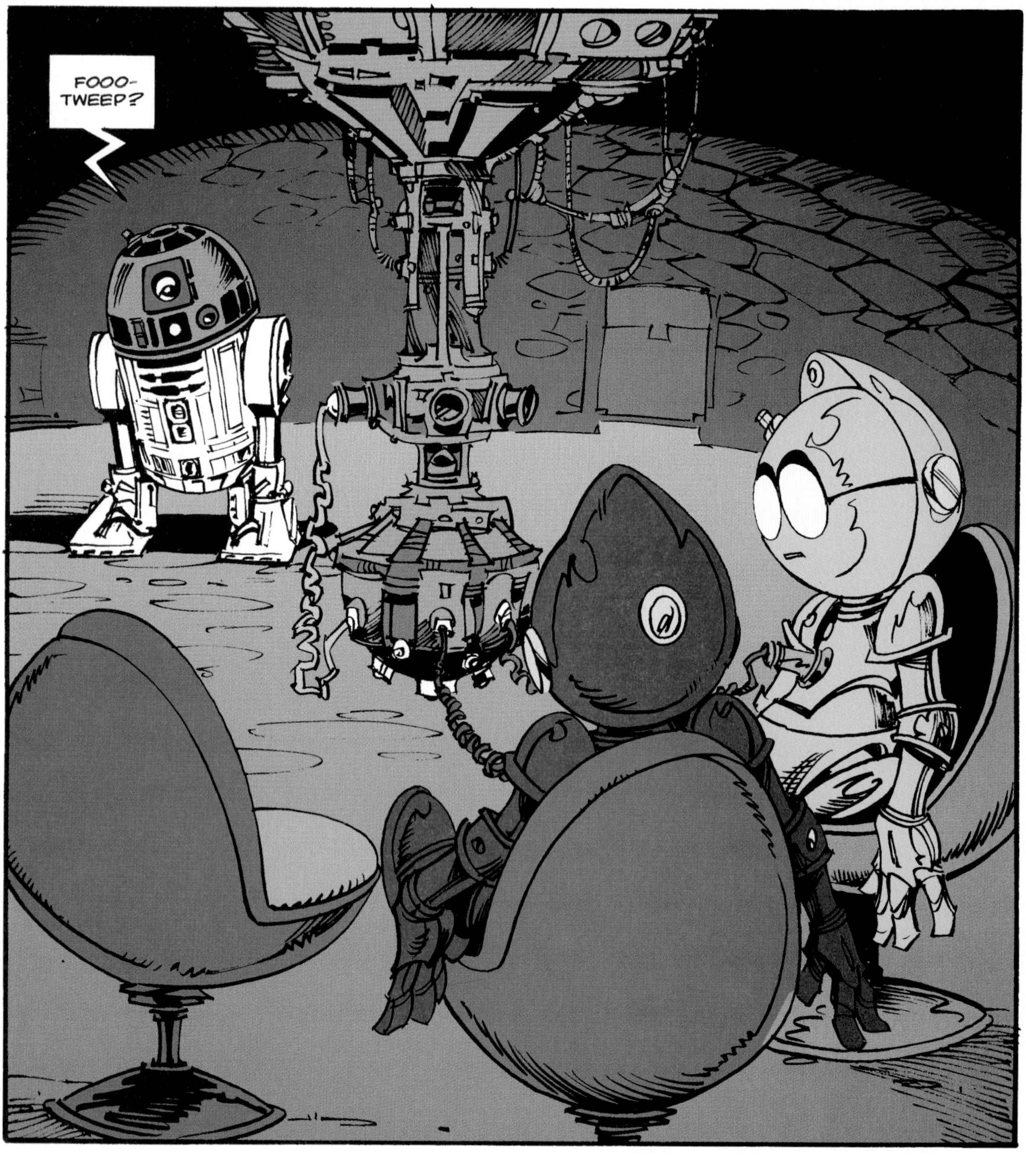
FOOO-
TWEEP?

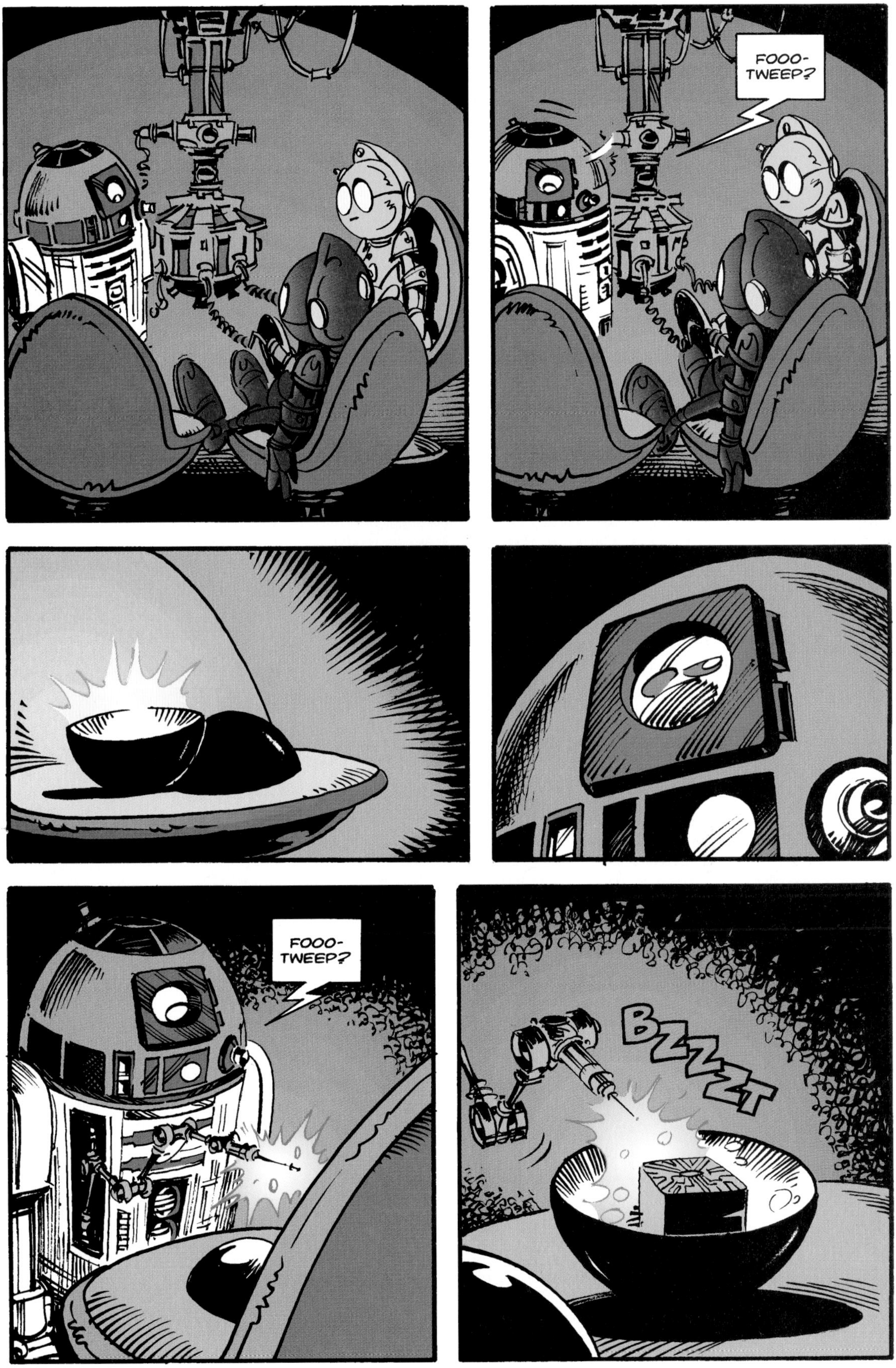
FOOO-
TWEEP?
FOOO-
TWEEP?
BZZZT

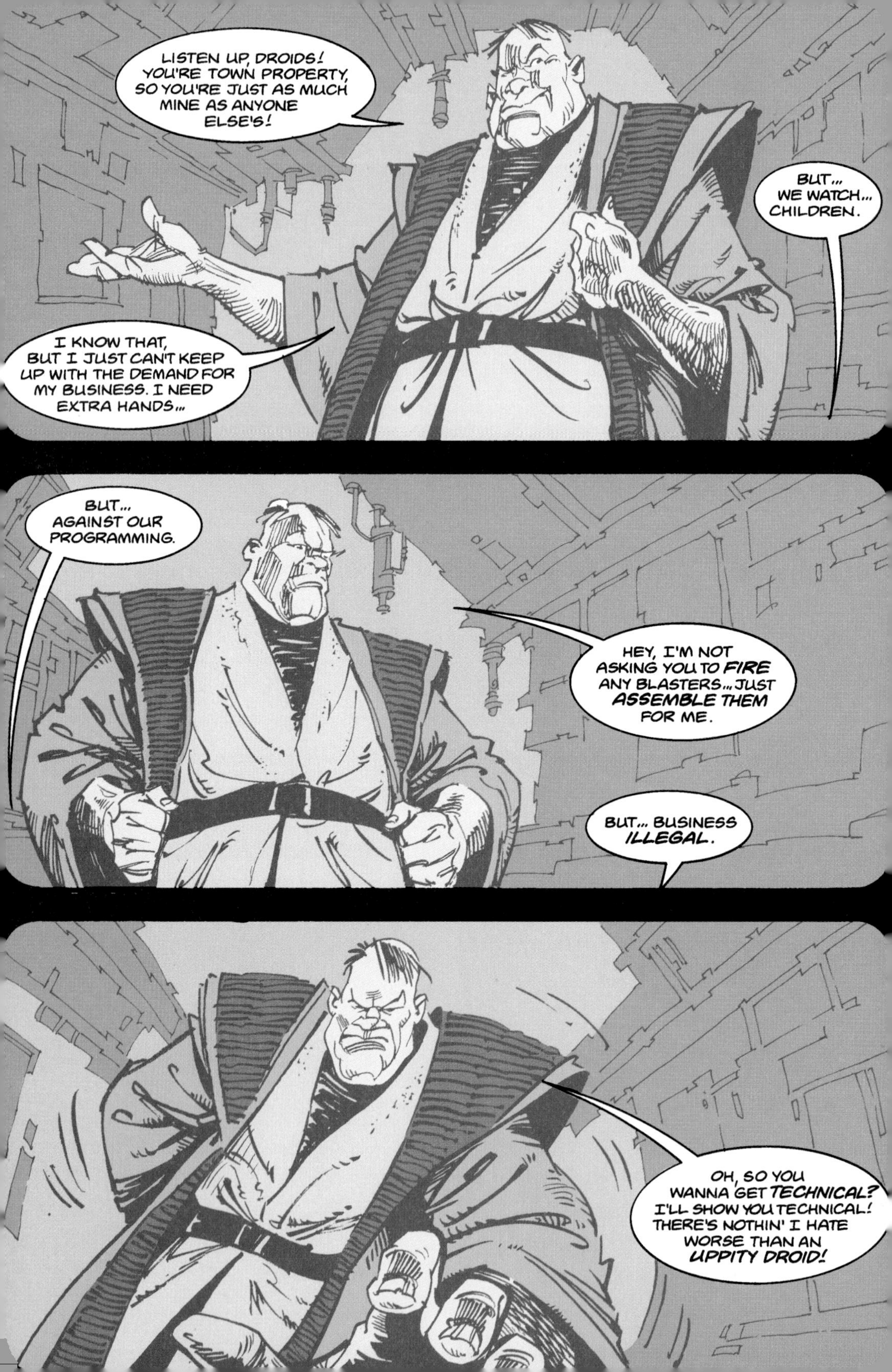
LISTEN UP, DROIDS! YOU'RE TOWN PROPERTY, SO YOU'RE JUST AS MUCH MINE AS ANYONE ELSE'S!
BUT... WE WATCH... CHILDREN.
I KNOW THAT, BUT I JUST CAN'T KEEP UP WITH THE DEMAND FOR MY BUSINESS. I NEED EXTRA HANDS...
BUT... AGAINST OUR PROGRAMMING.
HEY, I'M NOT ASKING YOU TO FIRE ANY BLASTERS... JUST ASSEMBLE THEM FOR ME.
BUT... BUSINESS ILLEGAL.
OH, SO YOU WANNA GET TECHNICAL? I'LL SHOW YOU TECHNICAL! THERE'S NOTHIN' I HATE WORSE THAN AN UPPITY DROID!

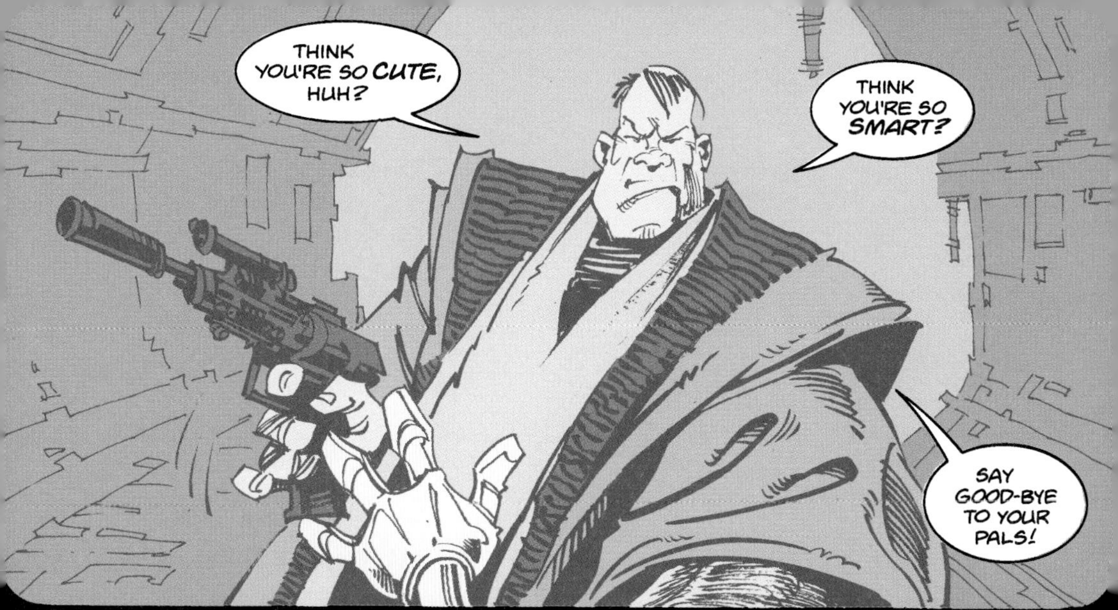
THINK YOU'RE SO CUTE, HUH?
THINK YOU'RE SO SMART?
SAY GOOD-BYE TO YOUR PALS!

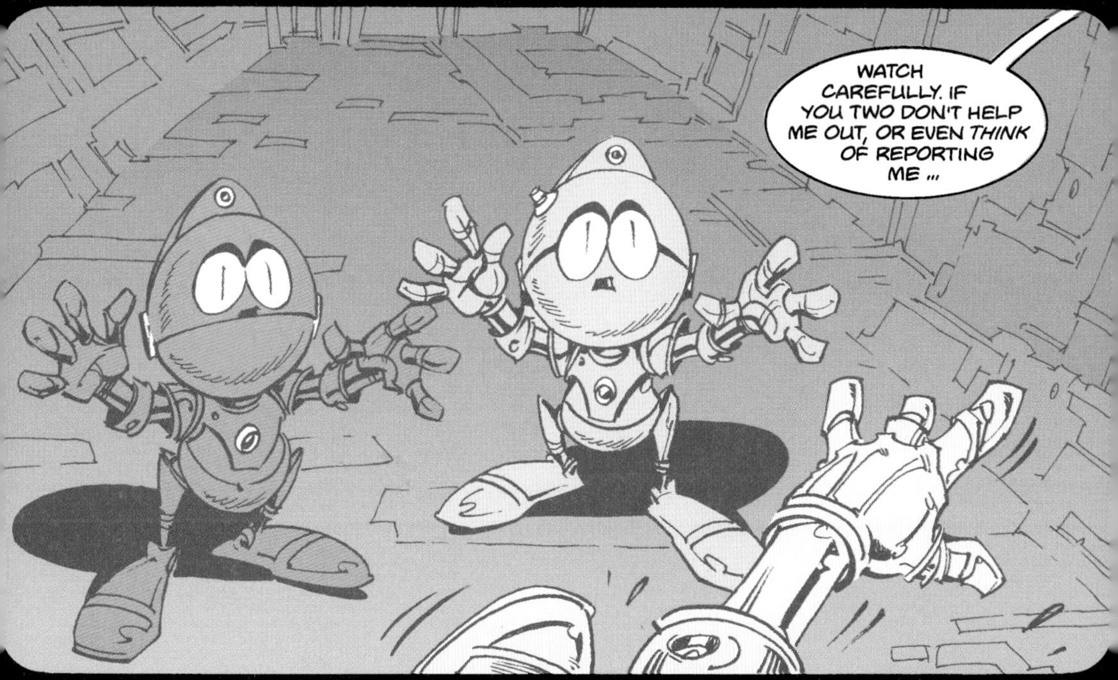
WATCH CAREFULLY. IF YOU TWO DON'T HELP ME OUT, OR EVEN THINK OF REPORTING ME ...

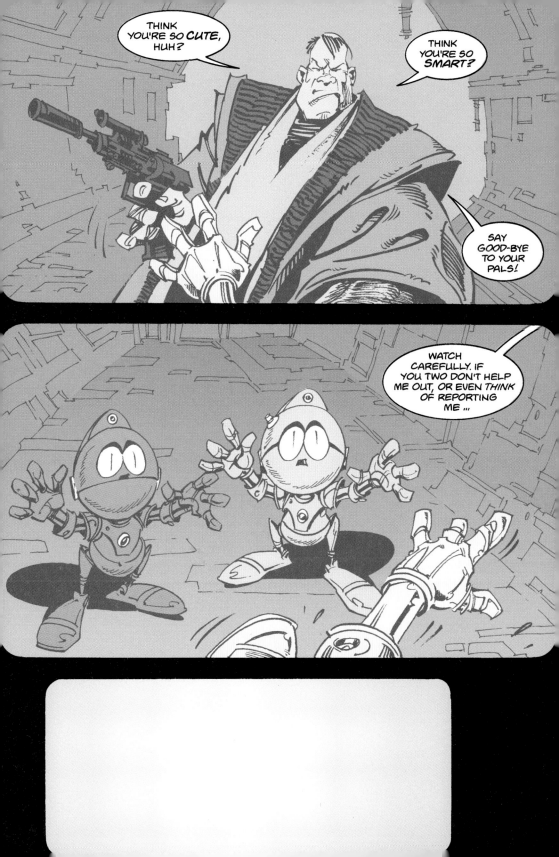

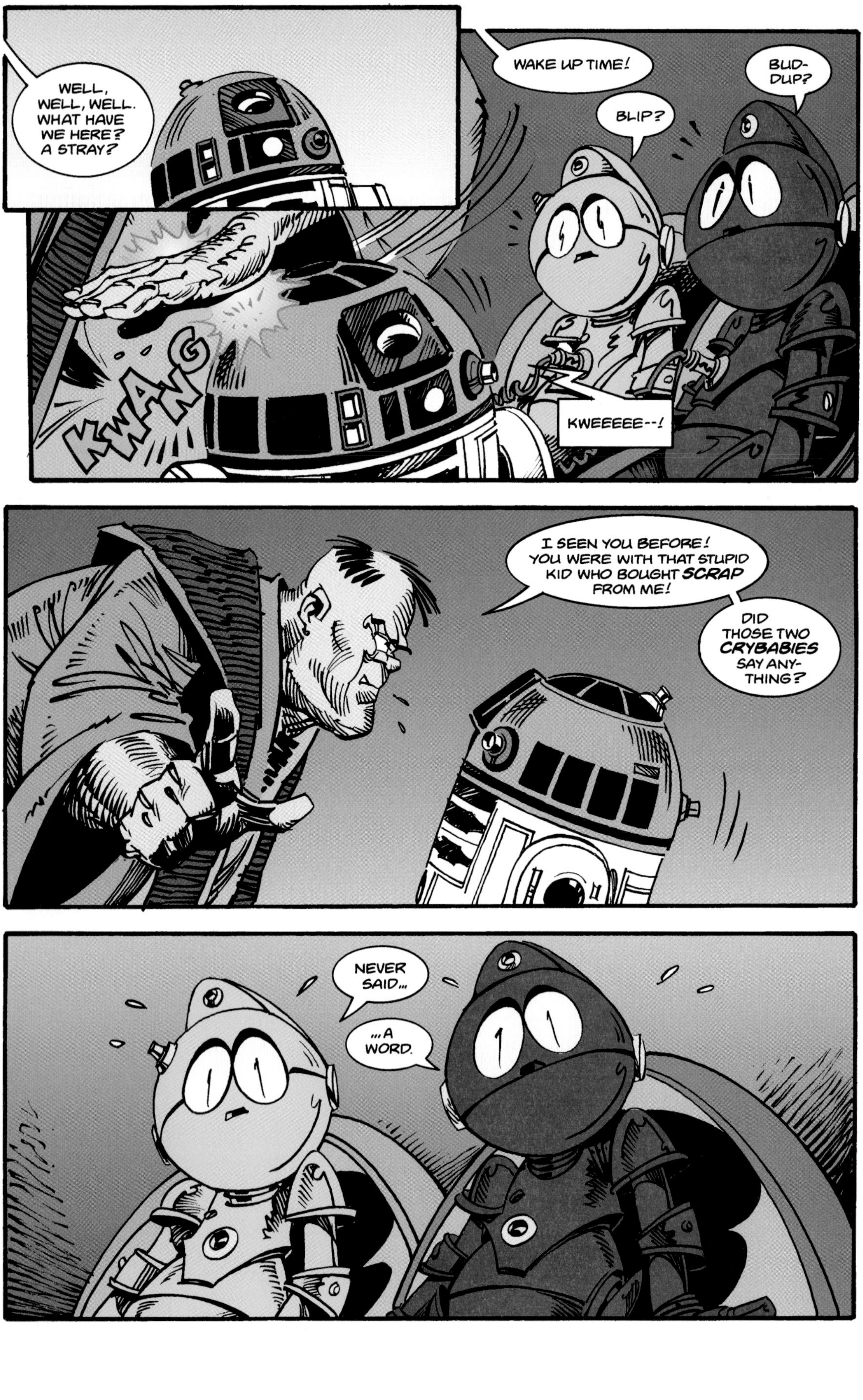
WELL, WELL, WELL. WHAT HAVE WE HERE? A STRAY?
WAKE UP TIME!
BLIP?
BUD-DUP?
KWANG
KWEEEEE--!
I SEEN YOU BEFORE! YOU WERE WITH THAT STUPID KID WHO BOUGHT SCRAP FROM ME!
DID THOSE TWO CRYBABIES SAY ANY-THING?
NEVER SAID...
...A WORD.

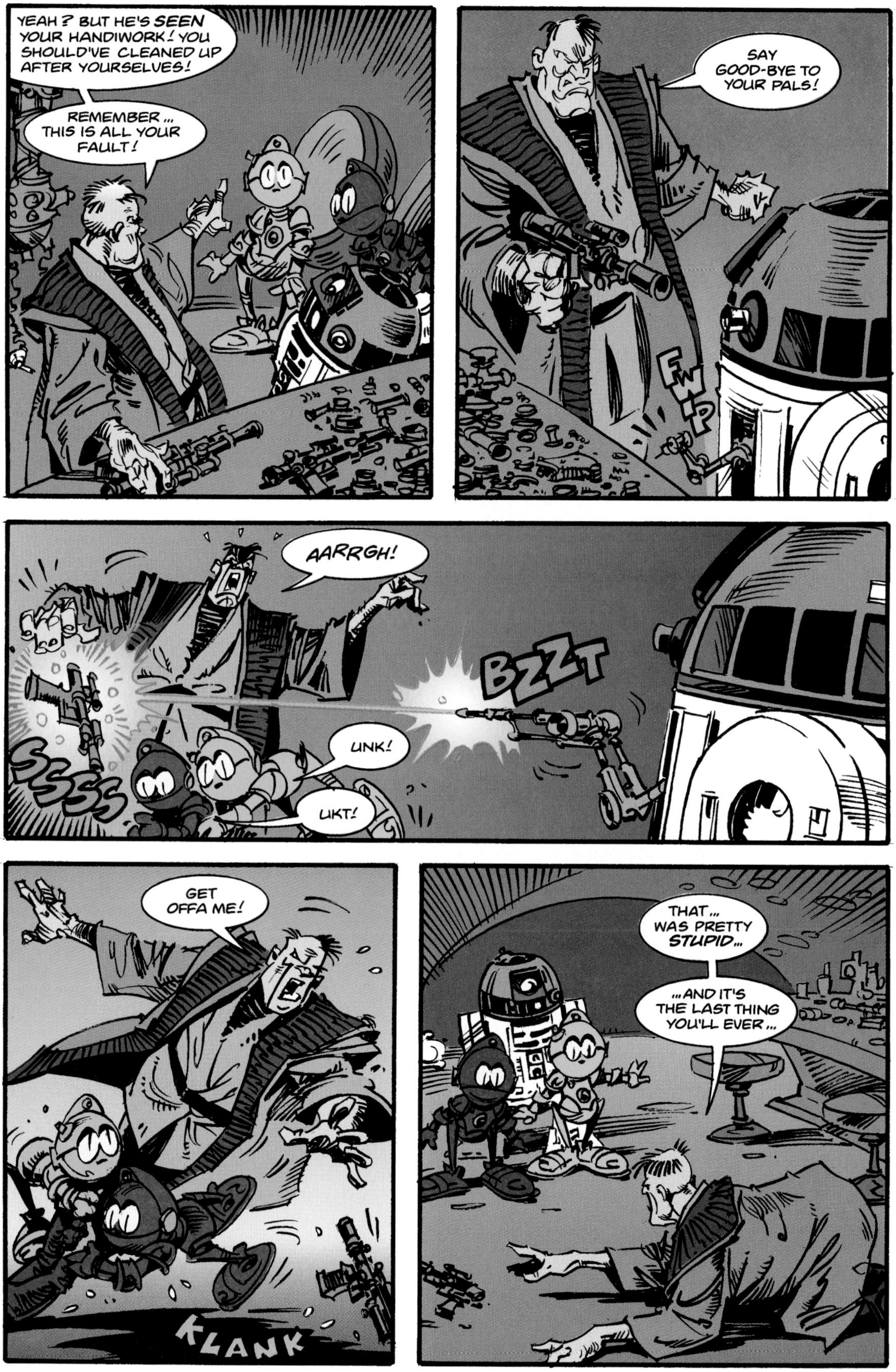
YEAH? BUT HE'S SEEN YOUR HANDIWORK! YOU SHOULD'VE CLEANED UP AFTER YOURSELVES!
REMEMBER... THIS IS ALL YOUR FAULT!
SAY GOOD-BYE TO YOUR PALS!
FWIP
AARRGH!
BZZT
SSSSS
UNK!
UKT!
GET OFFA ME!
KLANK
THAT... WAS PRETTY STUPID...
...AND IT'S THE LAST THING YOU'LL EVER...

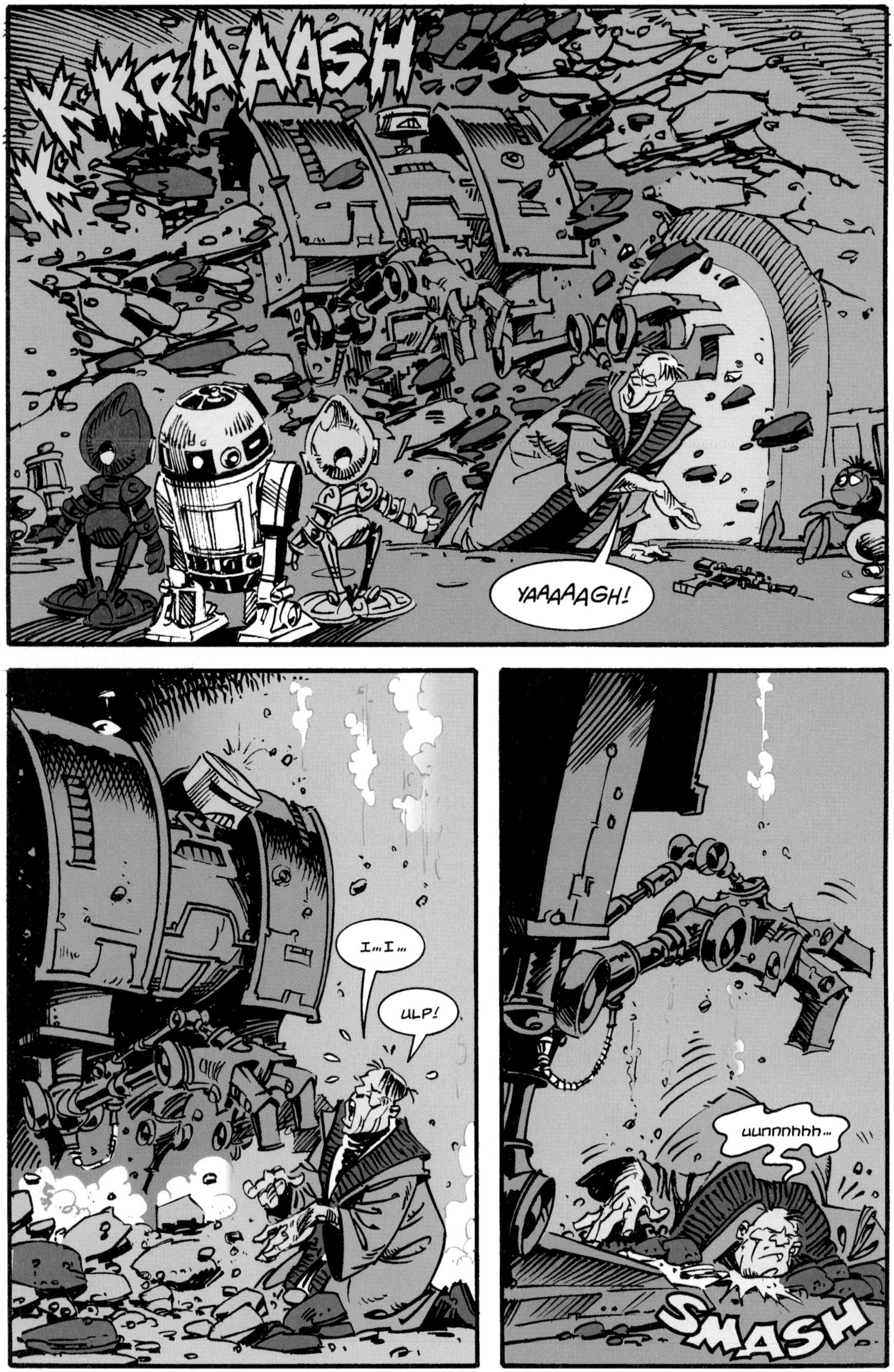
K-KRAAASH
YAAAAAGH!
I... I...
ULP!
uunnnhhh...
SMASH

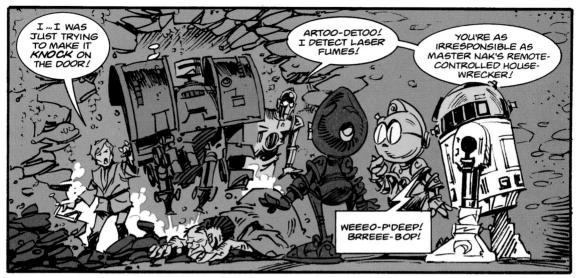

I ...I WAS JUST TRYING TO MAKE IT *KNOCK* ON THE DOOR!

ARTOO-DETOO! I DETECT LASER FUMES!

YOU'RE AS IRRESPONSIBLE AS MASTER NAK'S REMOTE-CONTROLLED HOUSE-WRECKER!

WEEEO-P'DEEP! BRREEE-BOP!

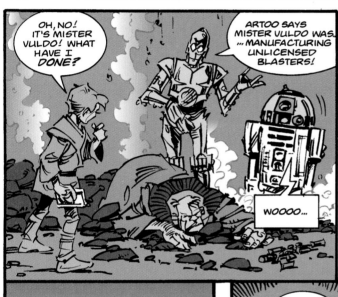

OH, NO! IT'S MISTER VULDO! WHAT HAVE I *DONE?*

ARTOO SAYS MISTER VULDO WAS... ...MANUFACTURING UNLICENSED BLASTERS!

WOOOO...

WHAT?! WHERE ARE Q-E AND 2-E?!

CAN BIG ONE... ...BE OUR FRIEND?

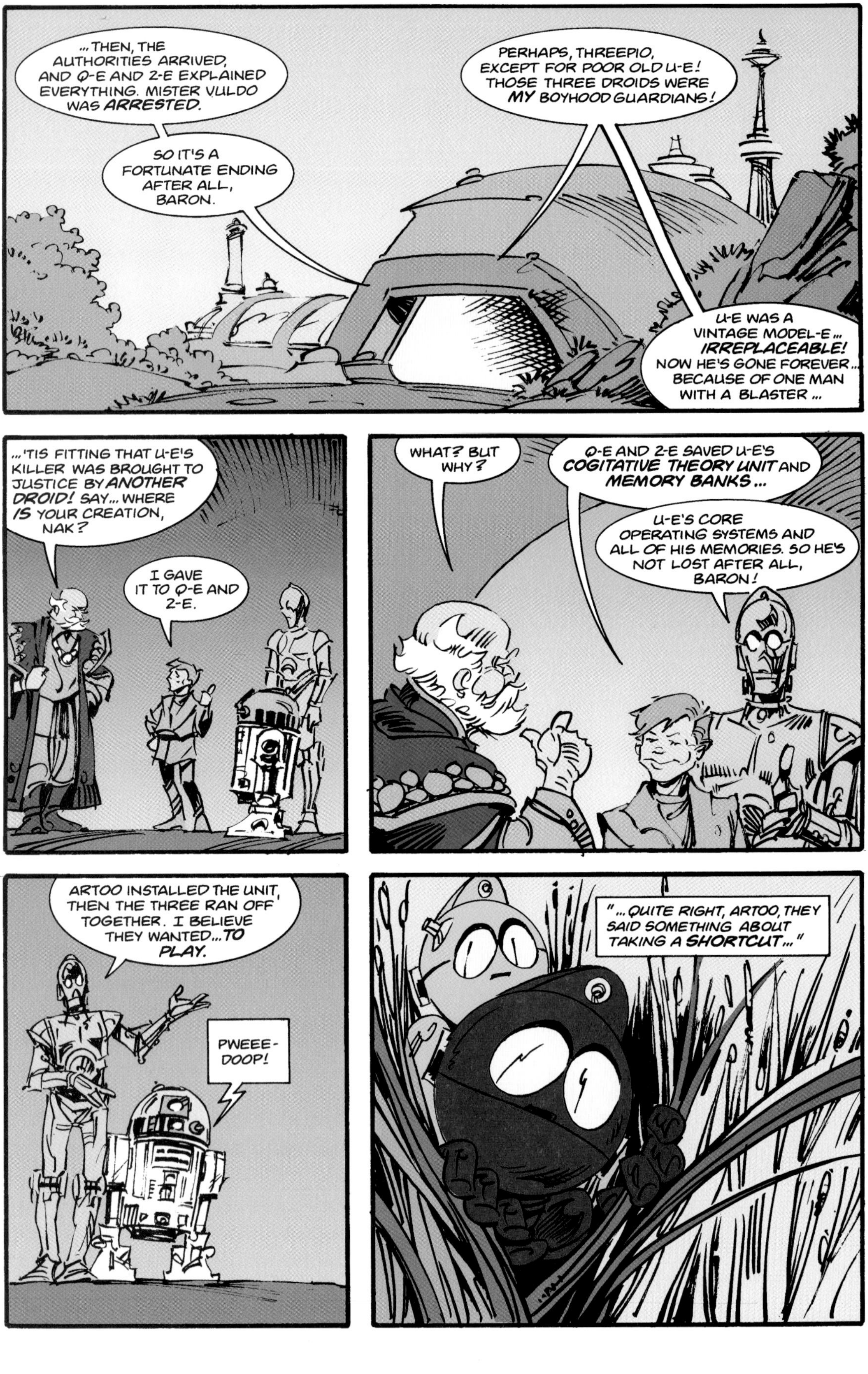
...THEN, THE AUTHORITIES ARRIVED, AND Q-E AND 2-E EXPLAINED EVERYTHING. MISTER VULDO WAS ARRESTED.
SO IT'S A FORTUNATE ENDING AFTER ALL, BARON.
PERHAPS, THREEPIO, EXCEPT FOR POOR OLD U-E! THOSE THREE DROIDS WERE MY BOYHOOD GUARDIANS!
U-E WAS A VINTAGE MODEL-E... IRREPLACEABLE! NOW HE'S GONE FOREVER... BECAUSE OF ONE MAN WITH A BLASTER...
...'TIS FITTING THAT U-E'S KILLER WAS BROUGHT TO JUSTICE BY ANOTHER DROID! SAY... WHERE IS YOUR CREATION, NAK?
I GAVE IT TO Q-E AND 2-E.
WHAT? BUT WHY?
Q-E AND 2-E SAVED U-E'S COGITATIVE THEORY UNIT AND MEMORY BANKS...
U-E'S CORE OPERATING SYSTEMS AND ALL OF HIS MEMORIES. SO HE'S NOT LOST AFTER ALL, BARON!
ARTOO INSTALLED THE UNIT, THEN THE THREE RAN OFF TOGETHER. I BELIEVE THEY WANTED... TO PLAY.
PWEEE-DOOP!
"...QUITE RIGHT, ARTOO, THEY SAID SOMETHING ABOUT TAKING A SHORTCUT..."

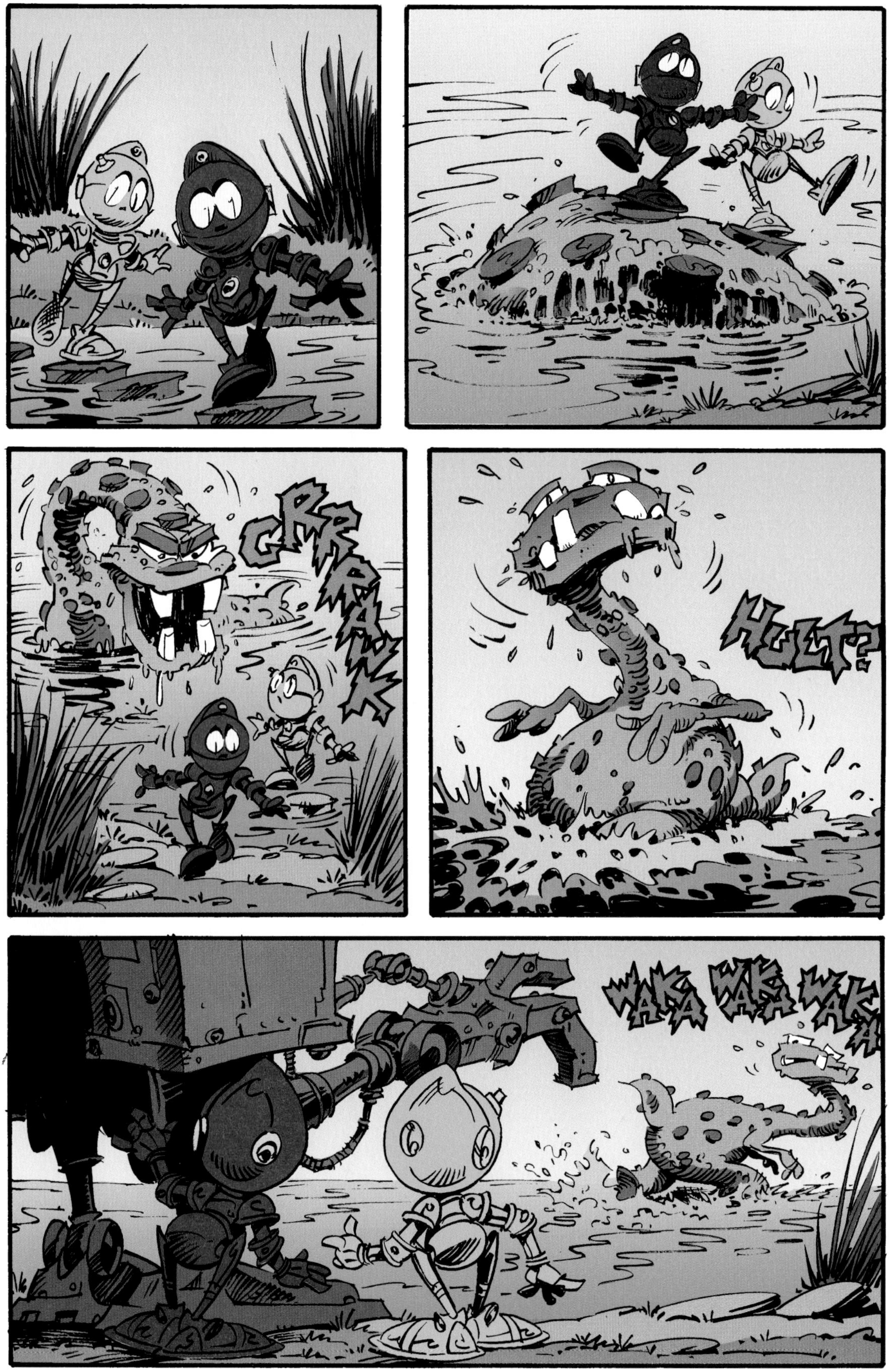
GRRRAWK
HULT?
WAKA WAKA WAKA

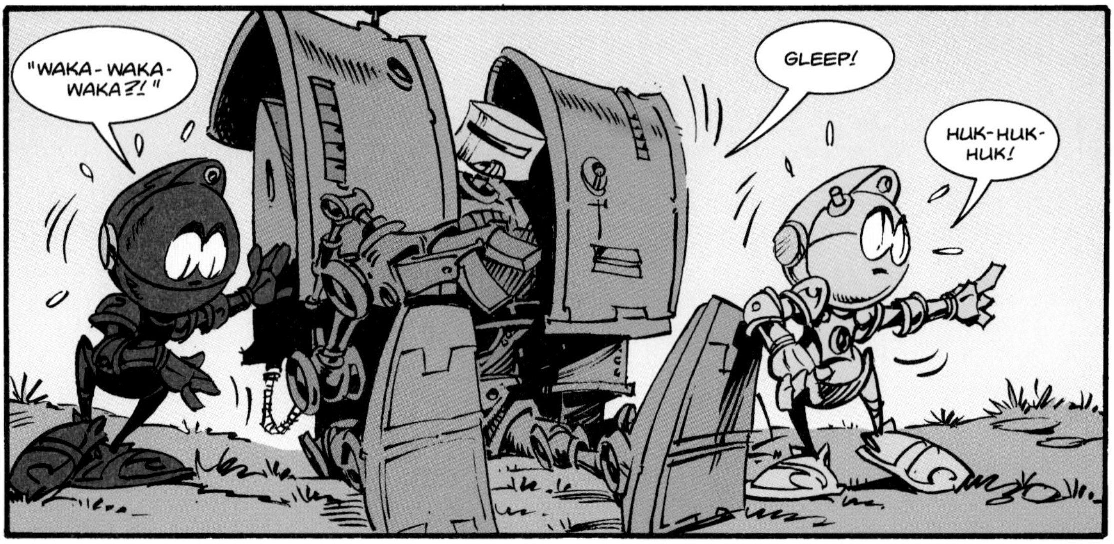
"WAKA-WAKA-WAKA?!"
GLEEP!
HUK-HUK-HUK!

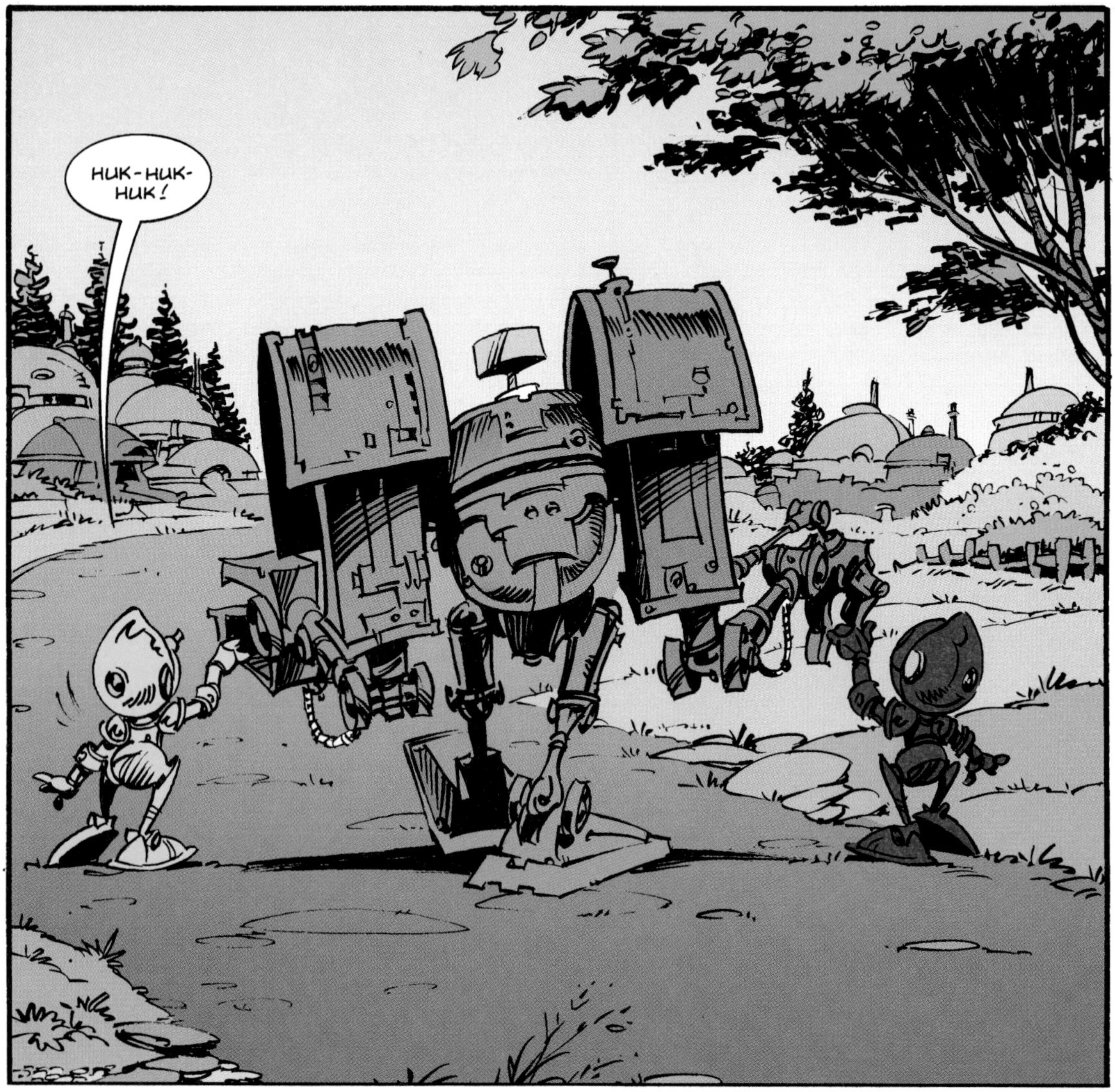
HUK-HUK-HUK!

Artoo's Day Out
Chapter 7

Script
Ryder Windham

Art
Bill Hughes

Colors
Lea Hernandez

Lettering
Steve Dutro

Cover
Bill Hughes

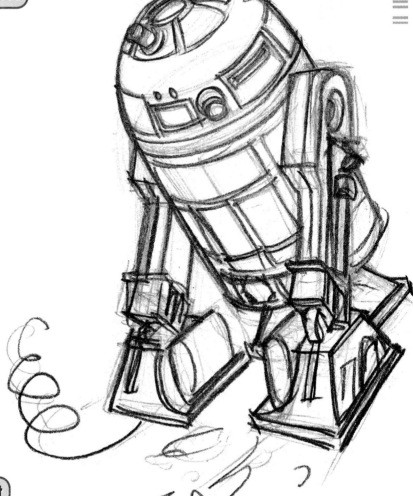

Sketch
Kilian Plunkett

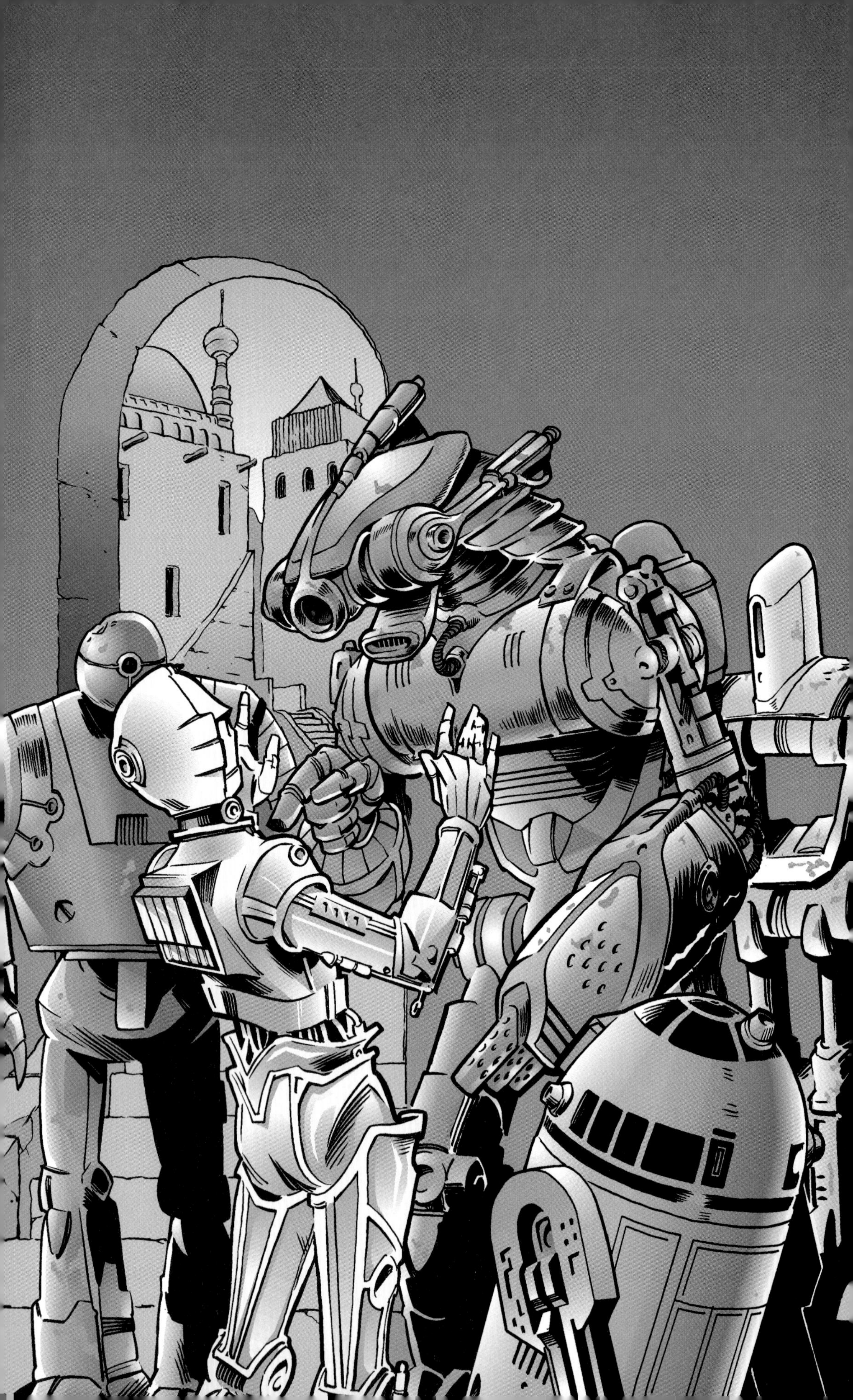

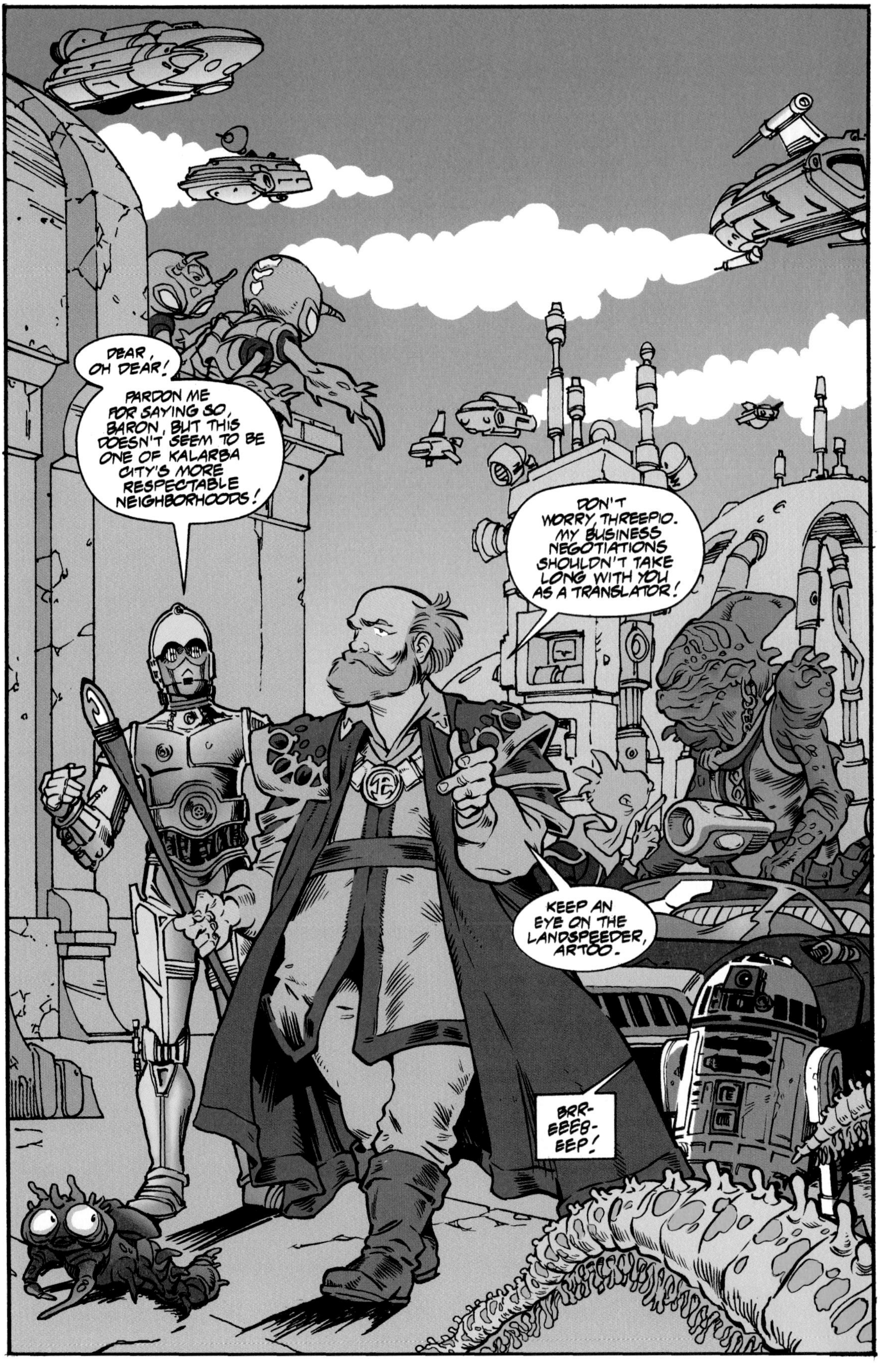
DEAR, OH DEAR!
PARDON ME FOR SAYING SO, BARON, BUT THIS DOESN'T SEEM TO BE ONE OF KALARBA CITY'S MORE RESPECTABLE NEIGHBORHOODS!
DON'T WORRY, THREEPIO. MY BUSINESS NEGOTIATIONS SHOULDN'T TAKE LONG WITH YOU AS A TRANSLATOR!
KEEP AN EYE ON THE LANDSPEEDER, ARTOO.
BRR-EEEB-EEP!

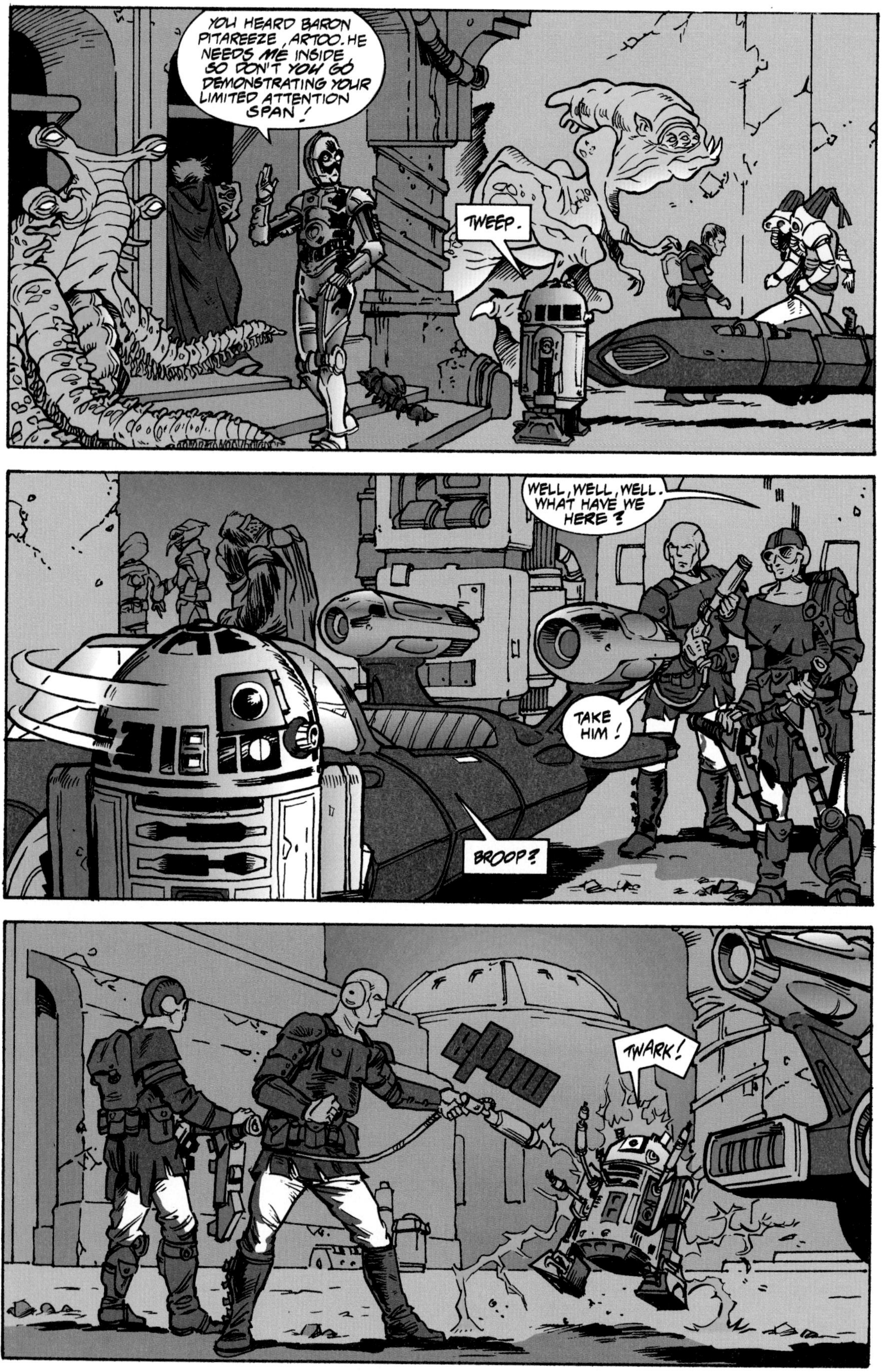
YOU HEARD BARON PITAREEZE, ARTOO. HE NEEDS ME INSIDE SO DON'T YOU GO DEMONSTRATING YOUR LIMITED ATTENTION SPAN!
TWEEP.
WELL, WELL, WELL. WHAT HAVE WE HERE?
TAKE HIM!
BROOP?
TWARK!

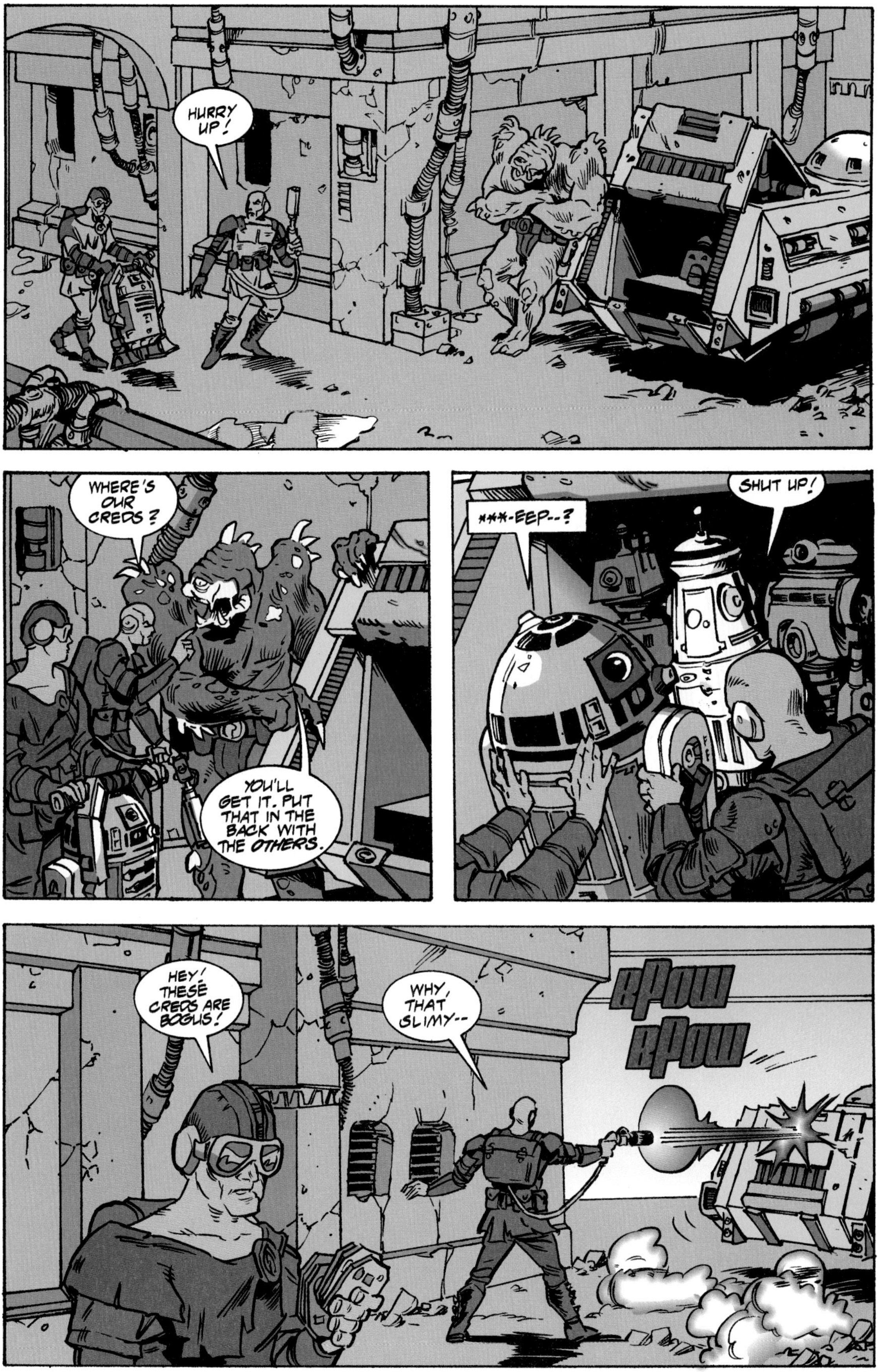
HURRY UP!
WHERE'S OUR CREDS?
YOU'LL GET IT. PUT THAT IN THE BACK WITH THE *OTHERS*.
***-EEP--?
SHUT UP!
HEY! THESE CREDS ARE BOGUS!
WHY, THAT SLIMY--
BPOW
BPOW

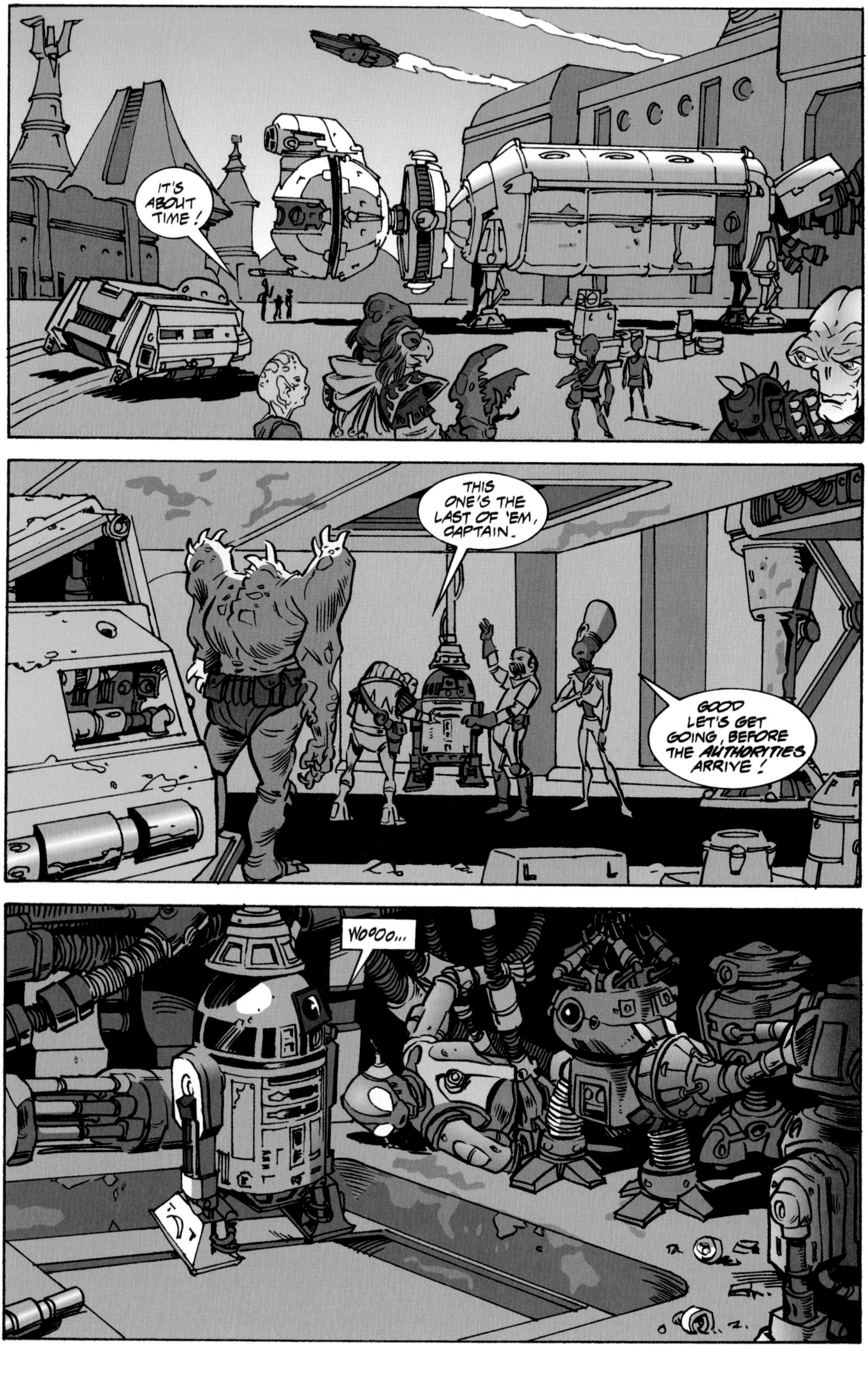
IT'S ABOUT TIME!
THIS ONE'S THE LAST OF 'EM, CAPTAIN.
GOOD LET'S GET GOING, BEFORE THE AUTHORITIES ARRIVE!
WOOOO...

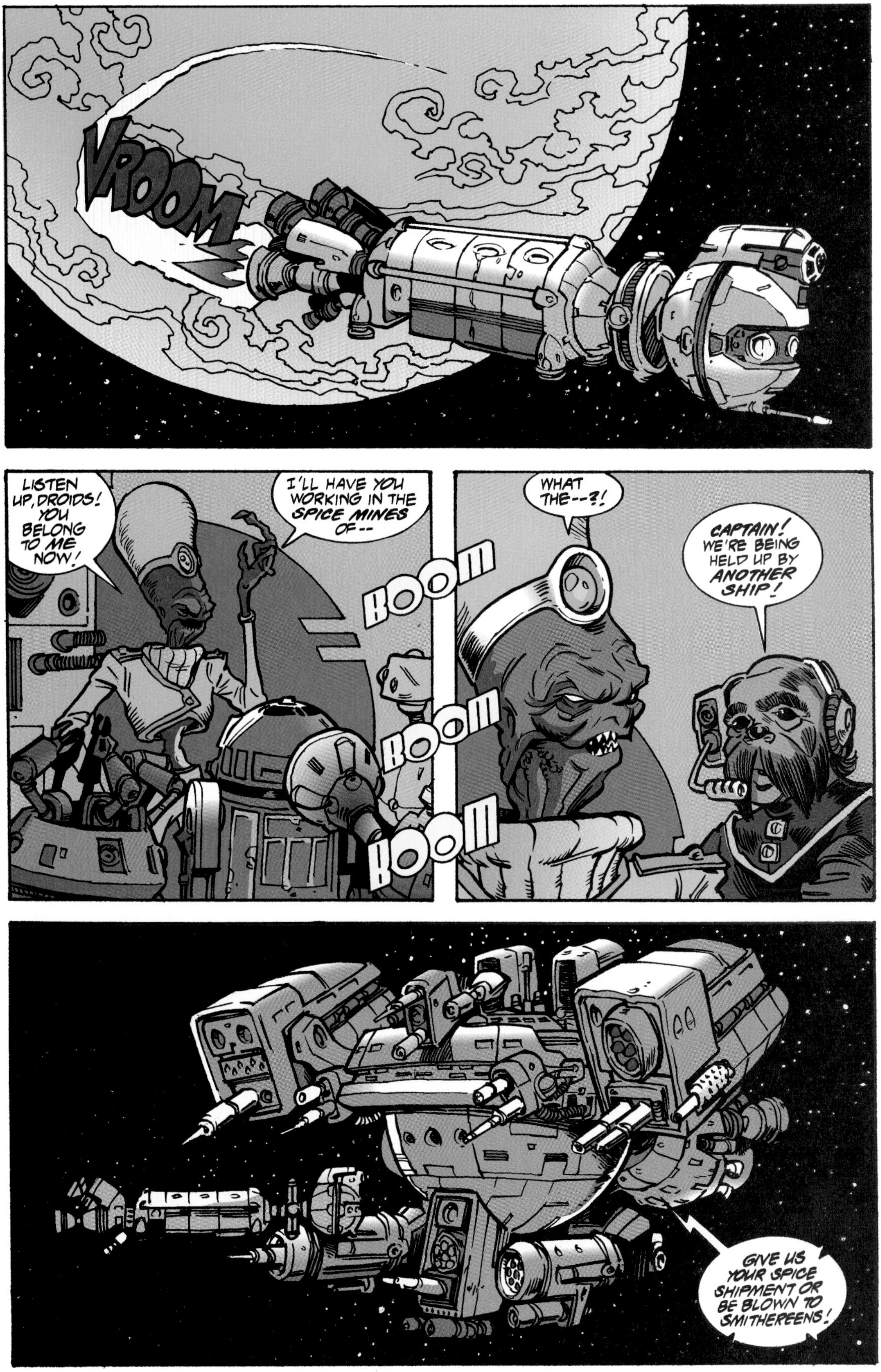
VROOM
LISTEN UP, DROIDS! YOU BELONG TO ME NOW!
I'LL HAVE YOU WORKING IN THE SPICE MINES OF--
BOOM
BOOM
BOOM
WHAT THE--?!
CAPTAIN! WE'RE BEING HELD UP BY ANOTHER SHIP!
GIVE US YOUR SPICE SHIPMENT OR BE BLOWN TO SMITHEREENS!

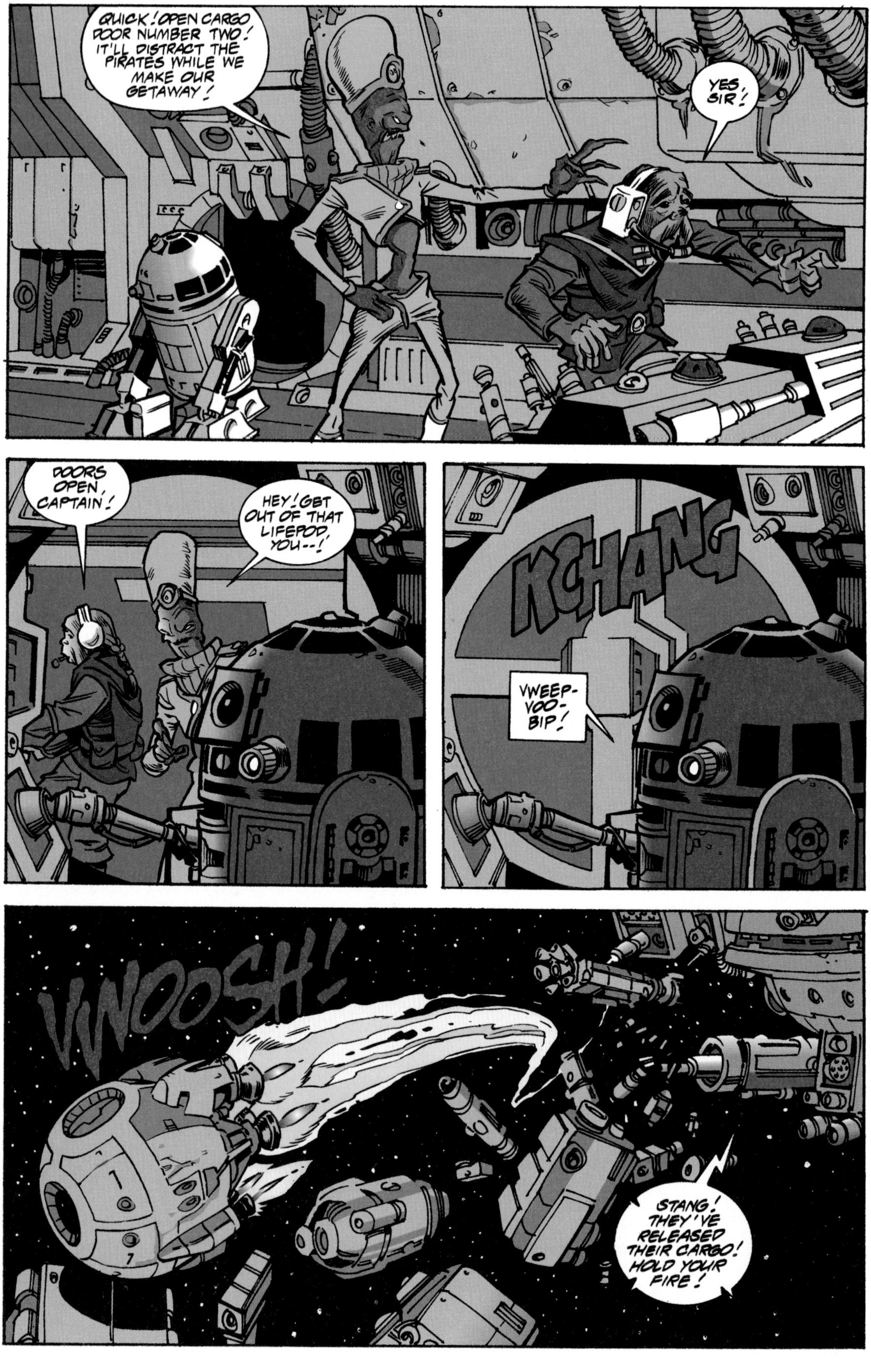
QUICK! OPEN CARGO DOOR NUMBER TWO! IT'LL DISTRACT THE PIRATES WHILE WE MAKE OUR GETAWAY!
YES, SIR!
DOORS OPEN, CAPTAIN!
HEY! GET OUT OF THAT LIFEPOD, YOU--!
KCHANG
VWEEP-VOO-BIP!
VWOOSH!
STANG! THEY'VE RELEASED THEIR CARGO! HOLD YOUR FIRE!

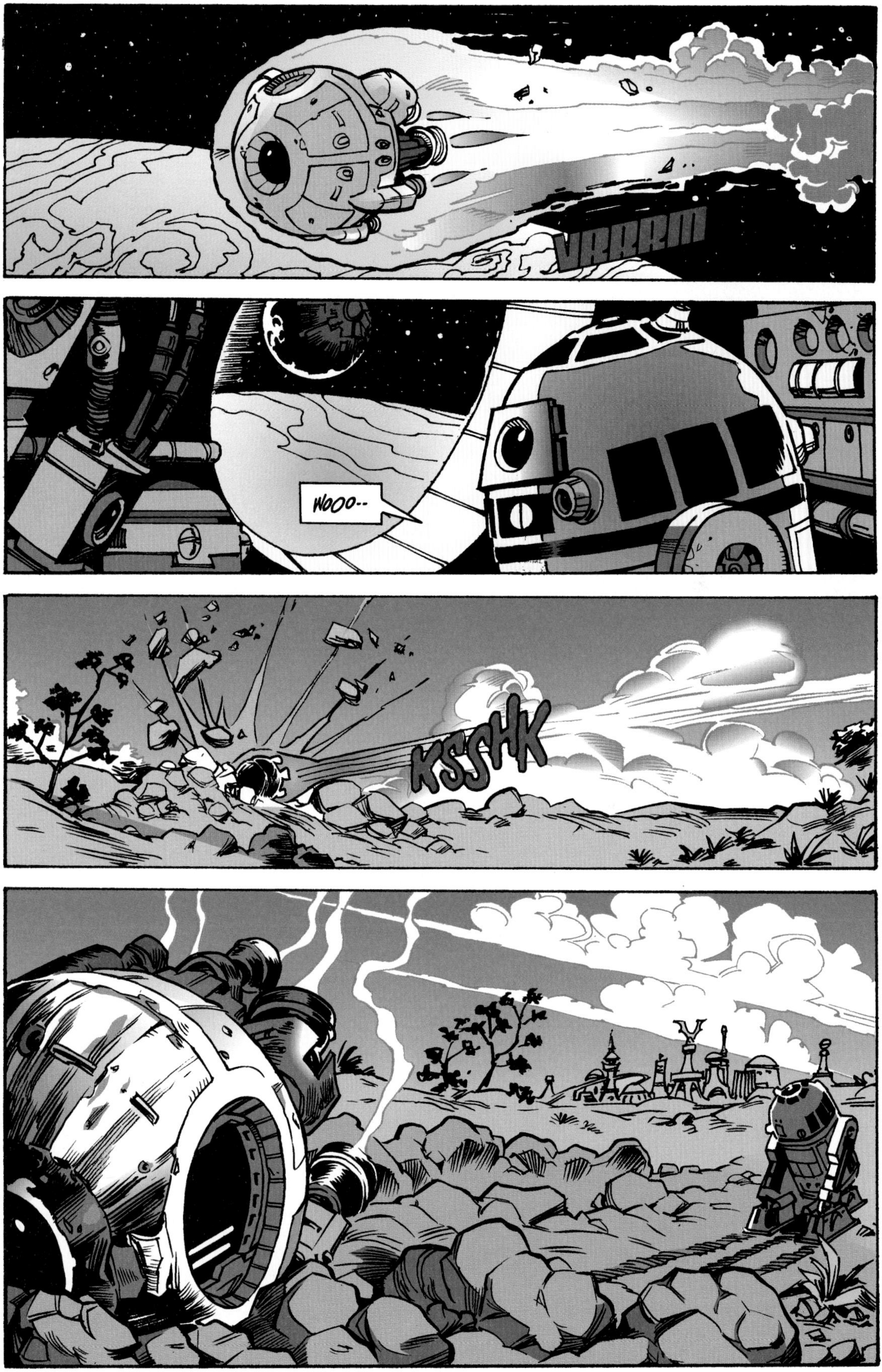
VRRRM
WOOO--
KSSHK

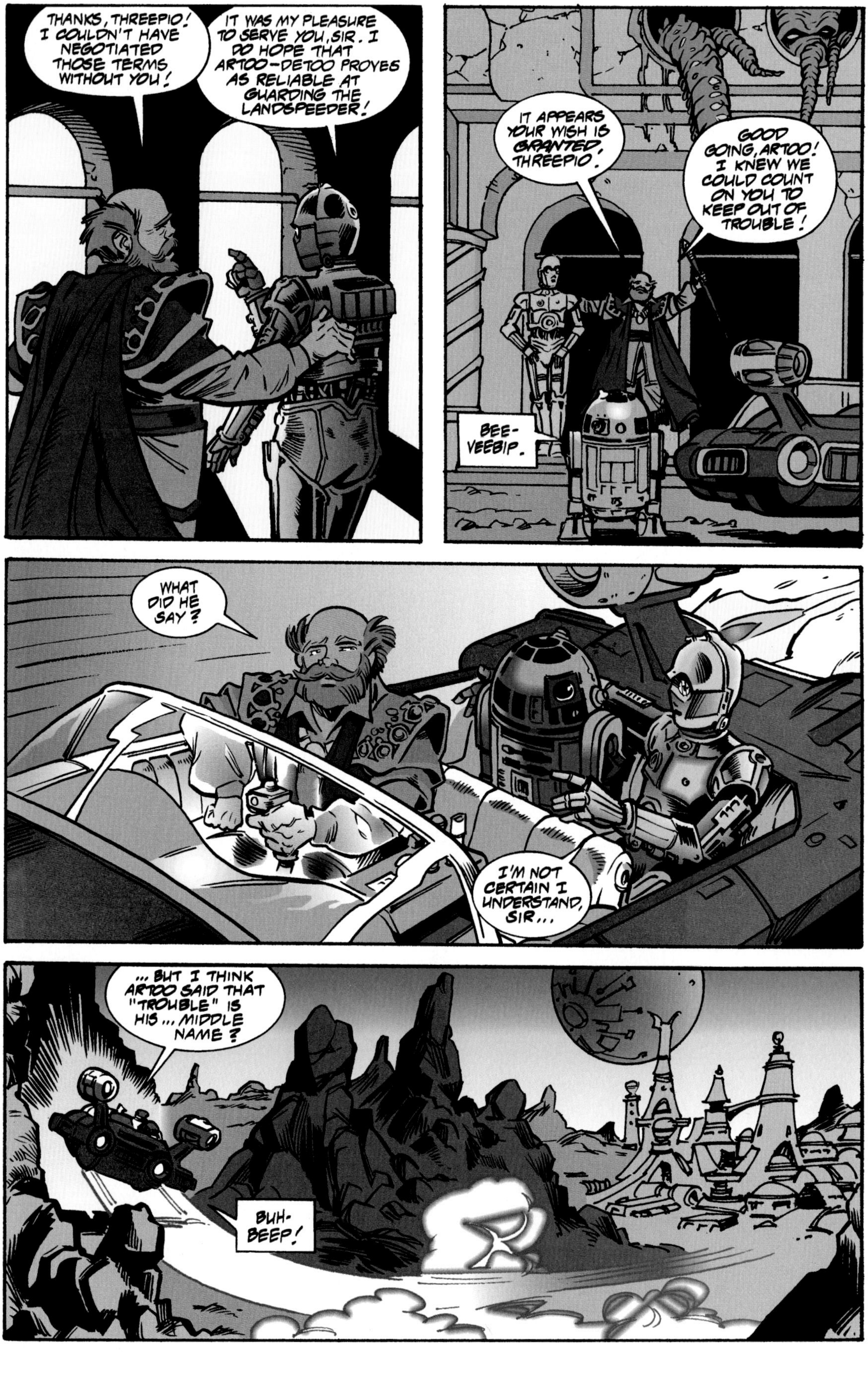
THANKS, THREEPIO! I COULDN'T HAVE NEGOTIATED THOSE TERMS WITHOUT YOU!
IT WAS MY PLEASURE TO SERVE YOU, SIR. I DO HOPE THAT ARTOO-DETOO PROVES AS RELIABLE AT GUARDING THE LANDSPEEDER!
IT APPEARS YOUR WISH IS GRANTED, THREEPIO.
GOOD GOING, ARTOO! I KNEW WE COULD COUNT ON YOU TO KEEP OUT OF TROUBLE!
BEE-VEEBIP.
WHAT DID HE SAY?
I'M NOT CERTAIN I UNDERSTAND, SIR...
...BUT I THINK ARTOO SAID THAT "TROUBLE" IS HIS... MIDDLE NAME?
BUH-BEEP!

Countdown at Hosk

Chapter 8

Script **Dan Thorsland**

Pencils **Bill Hughes**

Inks **Andy Mushynsky**

Colors **Pamela Rambo**

Lettering **Steve Dutro**

Cover **Kilian Plunkett**

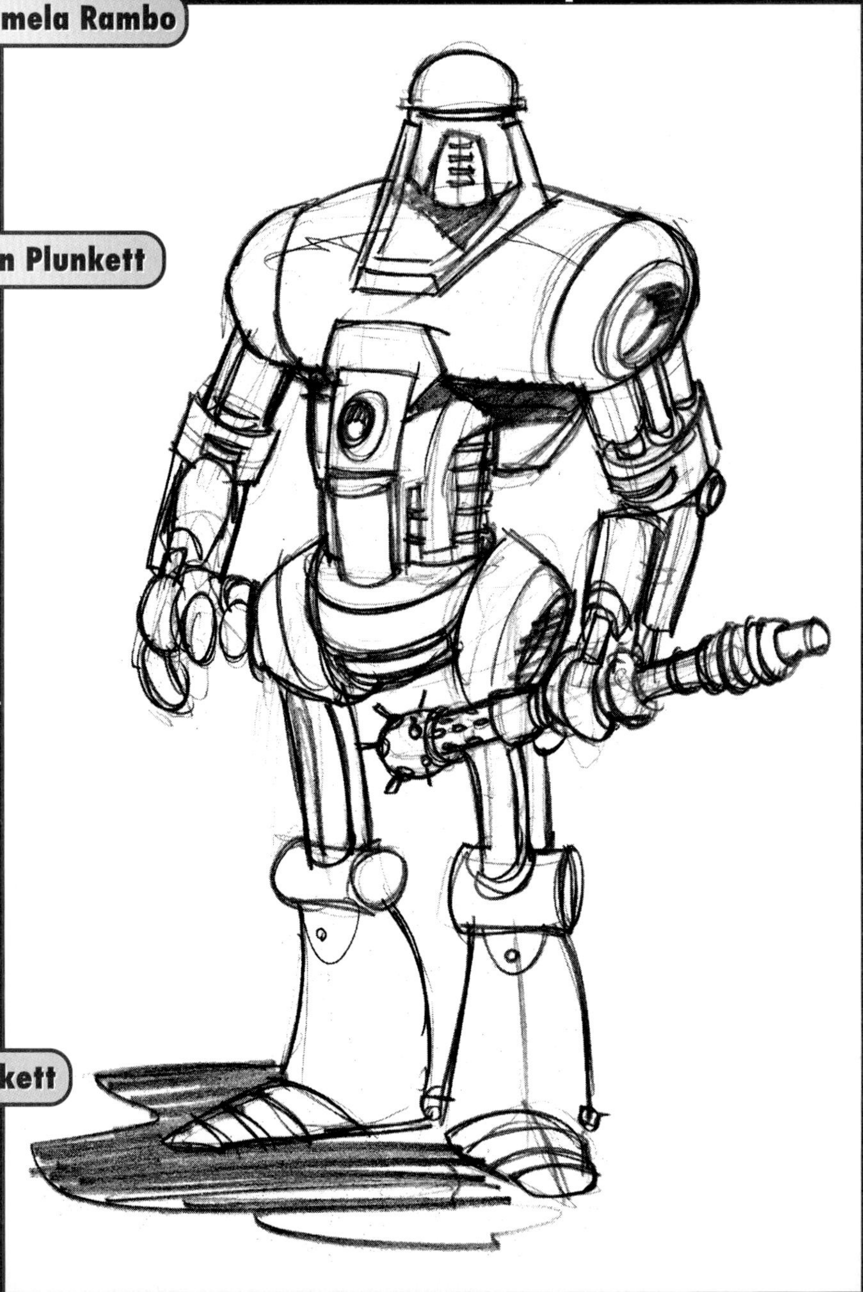

Sketch **Kilian Plunkett**

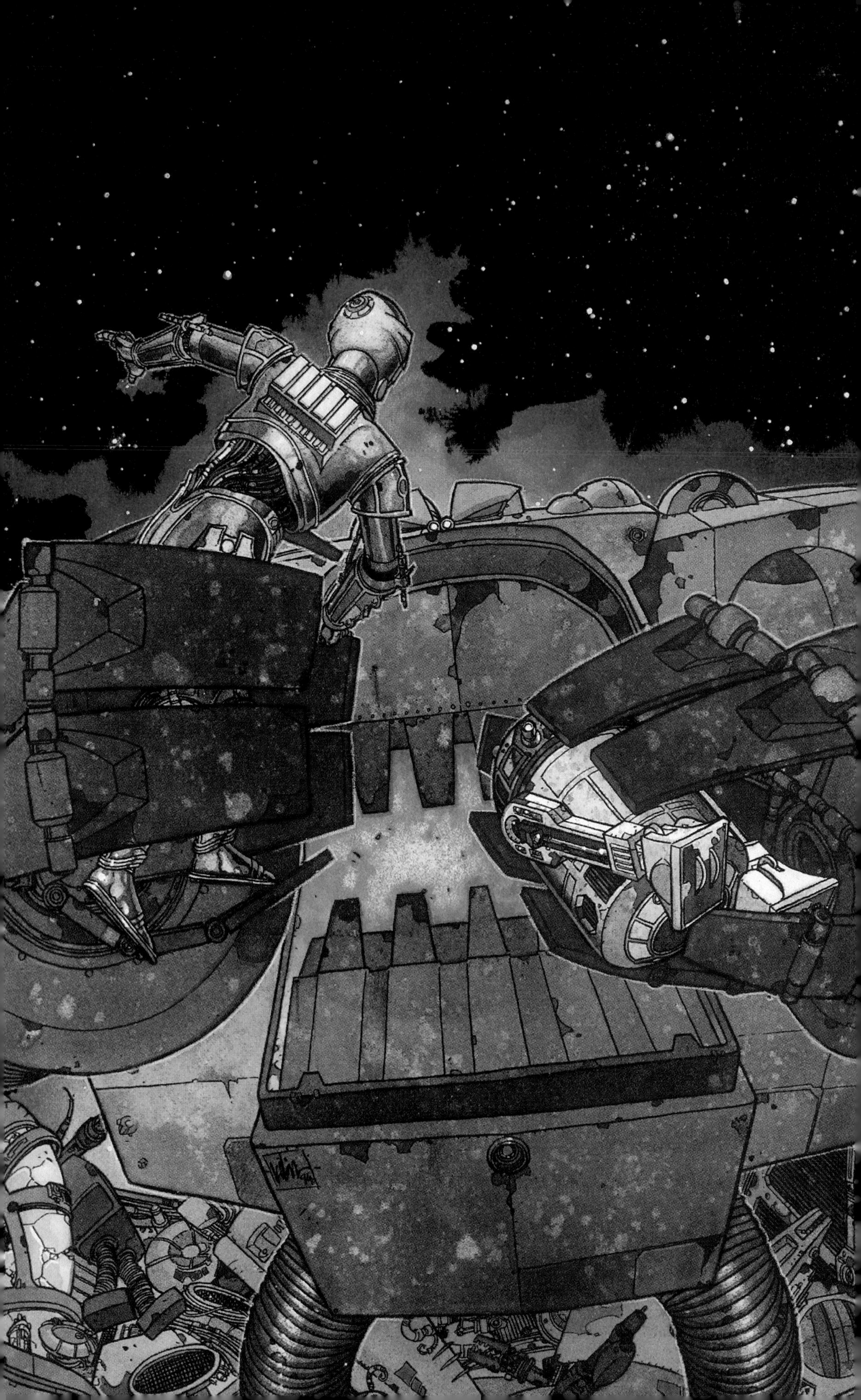

"...TELL HIM *THIRTY-FIVE* OR *NO DEAL*, THREEPIO."

"I AGREED TO MEET HIM HERE ON *HOSK* ONLY IF HE WOULD MEET MY *PRICE*!"

"SHUB GEE VIBBA THIRTY-FIVE!"

"BLUH! WIBBA NOOB GA! SHEE NIBBA VOOSH!"

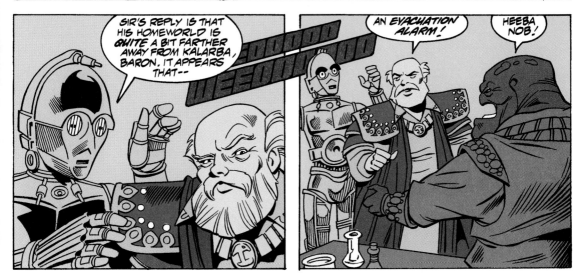

"SIR'S REPLY IS THAT HIS HOMEWORLD IS *QUITE A BIT FARTHER* AWAY FROM KALARBA, BARON. IT APPEARS THAT--"

WEEOOOOO WEEOOOOO

"AN *EVACUATION ALARM!*"

"HEEBA NOB!"

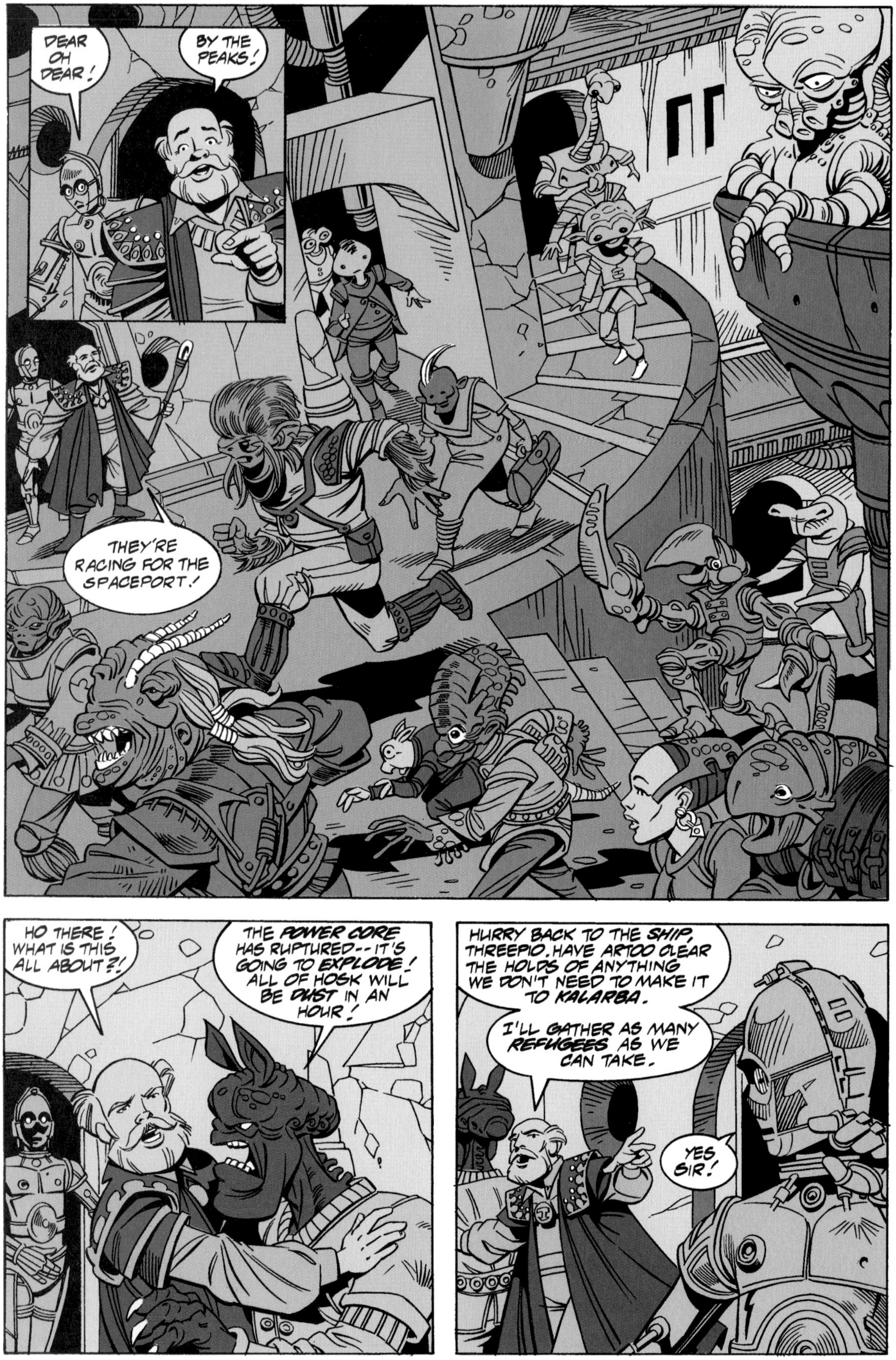
DEAR OH DEAR!
BY THE PEAKS!
THEY'RE RACING FOR THE SPACEPORT!
HO THERE! WHAT IS THIS ALL ABOUT?!
THE POWER CORE HAS RUPTURED-- IT'S GOING TO EXPLODE! ALL OF HOSK WILL BE DUST IN AN HOUR!
HURRY BACK TO THE SHIP, THREEPIO. HAVE ARTOO CLEAR THE HOLDS OF ANYTHING WE DON'T NEED TO MAKE IT TO KALARBA.
I'LL GATHER AS MANY REFUGEES AS WE CAN TAKE.
YES SIR!

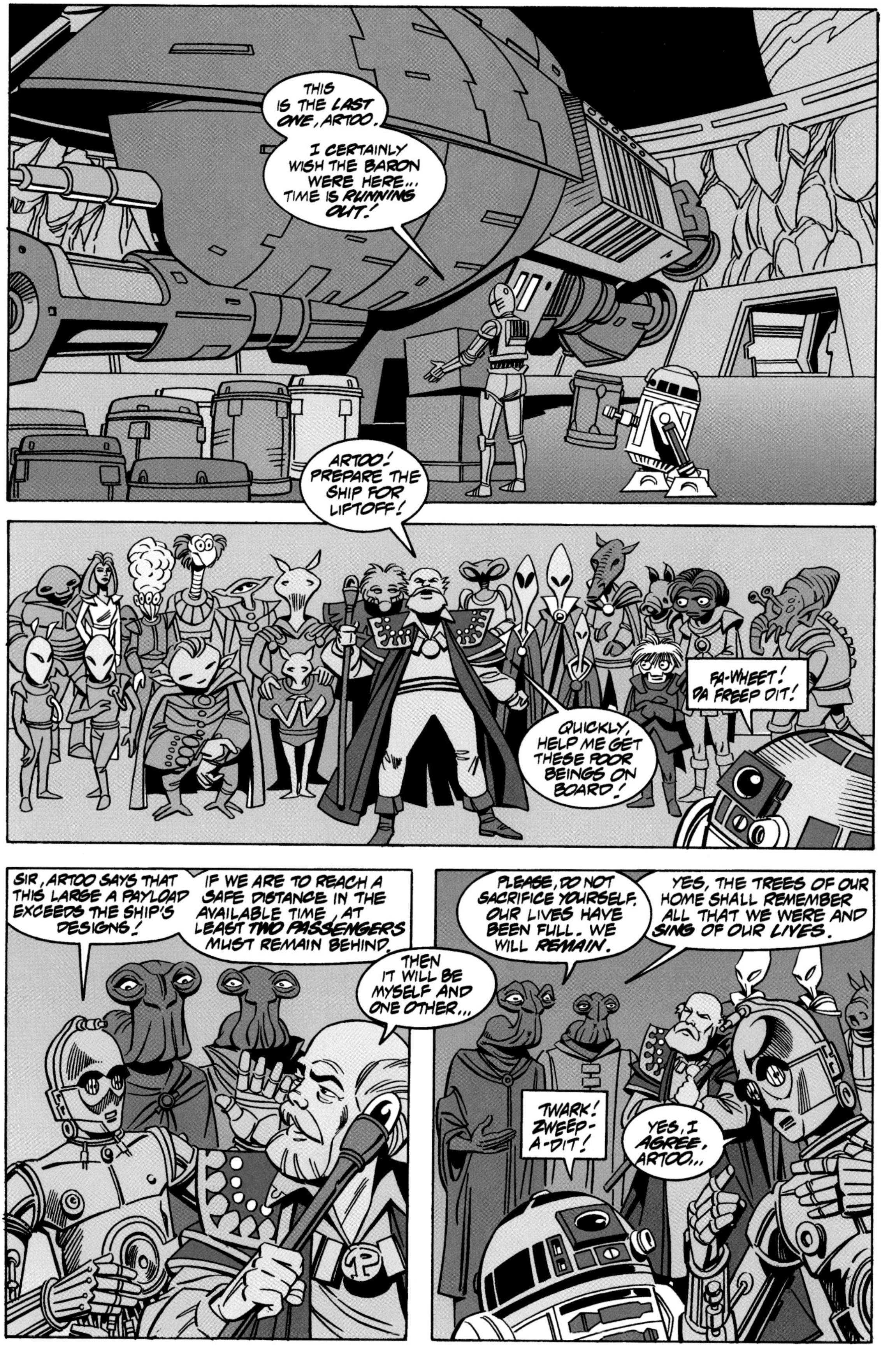
THIS IS THE LAST ONE, ARTOO.
I CERTAINLY WISH THE BARON WERE HERE... TIME IS RUNNING OUT!
ARTOO! PREPARE THE SHIP FOR LIFTOFF!
QUICKLY, HELP ME GET THESE POOR BEINGS ON BOARD!
FA-WHEET! DA FREEP DIT!
SIR, ARTOO SAYS THAT THIS LARGE A PAYLOAD EXCEEDS THE SHIP'S DESIGNS!
IF WE ARE TO REACH A SAFE DISTANCE IN THE AVAILABLE TIME, AT LEAST TWO PASSENGERS MUST REMAIN BEHIND.
THEN IT WILL BE MYSELF AND ONE OTHER...
PLEASE, DO NOT SACRIFICE YOURSELF. OUR LIVES HAVE BEEN FULL. WE WILL REMAIN.
YES, THE TREES OF OUR HOME SHALL REMEMBER ALL THAT WE WERE AND SING OF OUR LIVES.
TWARK! ZWEEP-A-DIT!
YES, I AGREE, ARTOO...

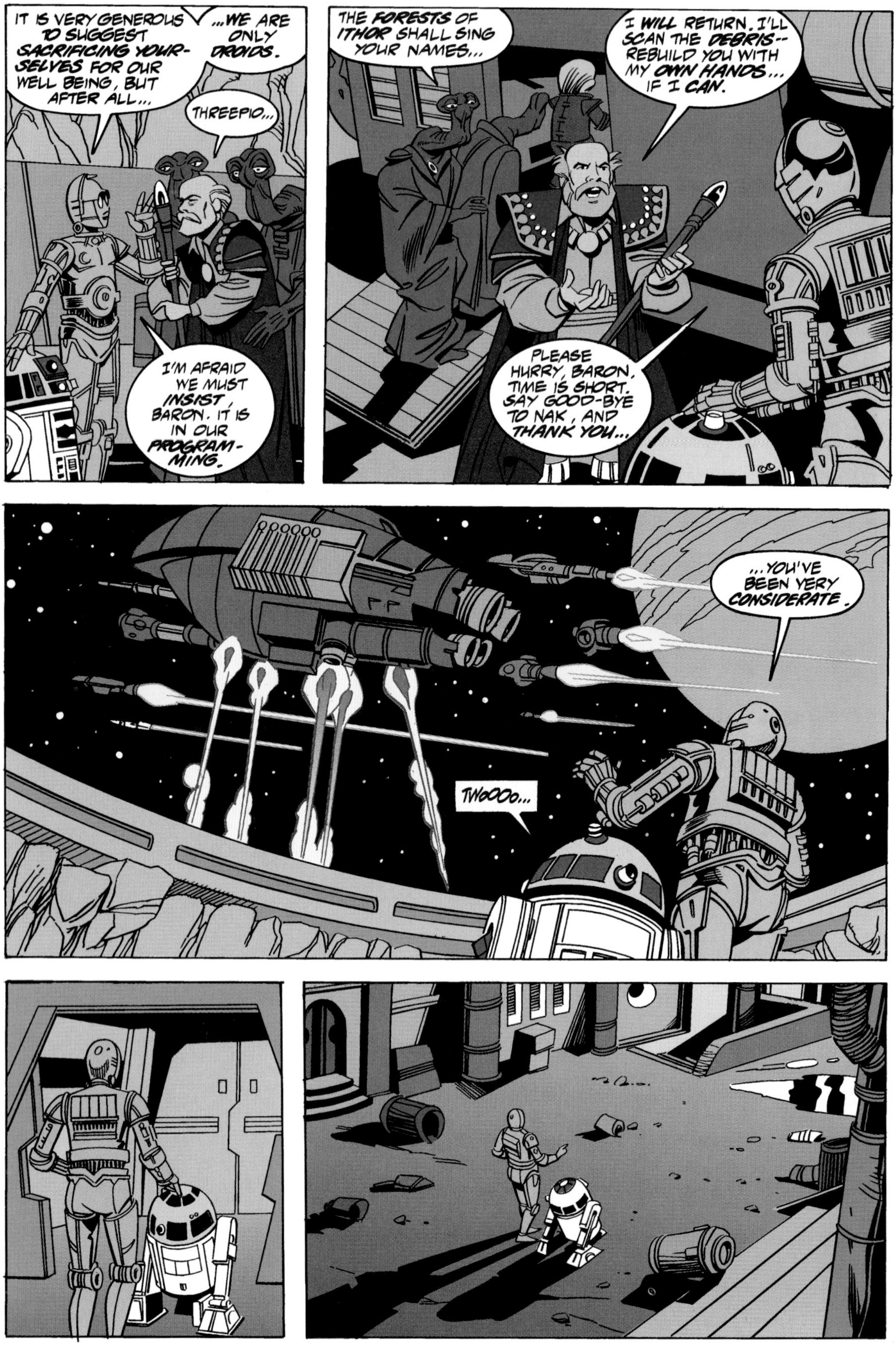
IT IS VERY GENEROUS TO SUGGEST SACRIFICING YOURSELVES FOR OUR WELL BEING, BUT AFTER ALL...
...WE ARE ONLY DROIDS.
THREEPIO...
I'M AFRAID WE MUST INSIST, BARON. IT IS IN OUR PROGRAMMING.
THE FORESTS OF ITHOR SHALL SING YOUR NAMES...
I WILL RETURN. I'LL SCAN THE DEBRIS-- REBUILD YOU WITH MY OWN HANDS... IF I CAN.
PLEASE HURRY, BARON. TIME IS SHORT. SAY GOOD-BYE TO NAK, AND THANK YOU...
...YOU'VE BEEN VERY CONSIDERATE.
TWOOOo...

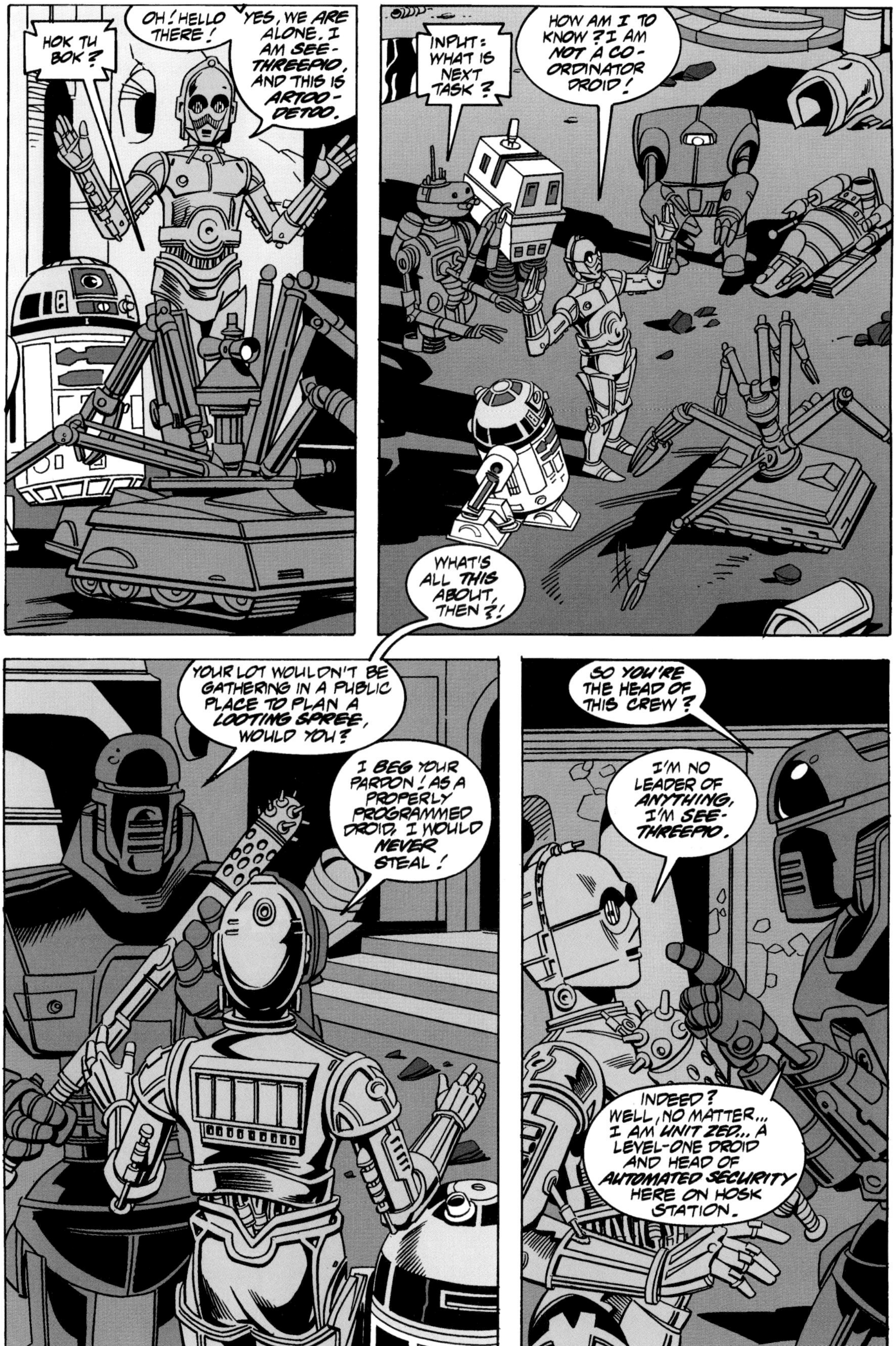
HOK TU BOK?
OH! HELLO THERE!
YES, WE ARE ALONE. I AM SEE-THREEPIO, AND THIS IS ARTOO-DETOO.
INPUT: WHAT IS NEXT TASK?
HOW AM I TO KNOW? I AM NOT A CO-ORDINATOR DROID!
WHAT'S ALL THIS ABOUT, THEN?!
YOUR LOT WOULDN'T BE GATHERING IN A PUBLIC PLACE TO PLAN A LOOTING SPREE, WOULD YOU?
I BEG YOUR PARDON! AS A PROPERLY PROGRAMMED DROID, I WOULD NEVER STEAL!
SO YOU'RE THE HEAD OF THIS CREW?
I'M NO LEADER OF ANYTHING, I'M SEE-THREEPIO.
INDEED? WELL, NO MATTER... I AM UNIT ZED... A LEVEL-ONE DROID AND HEAD OF AUTOMATED SECURITY HERE ON HOSK STATION.

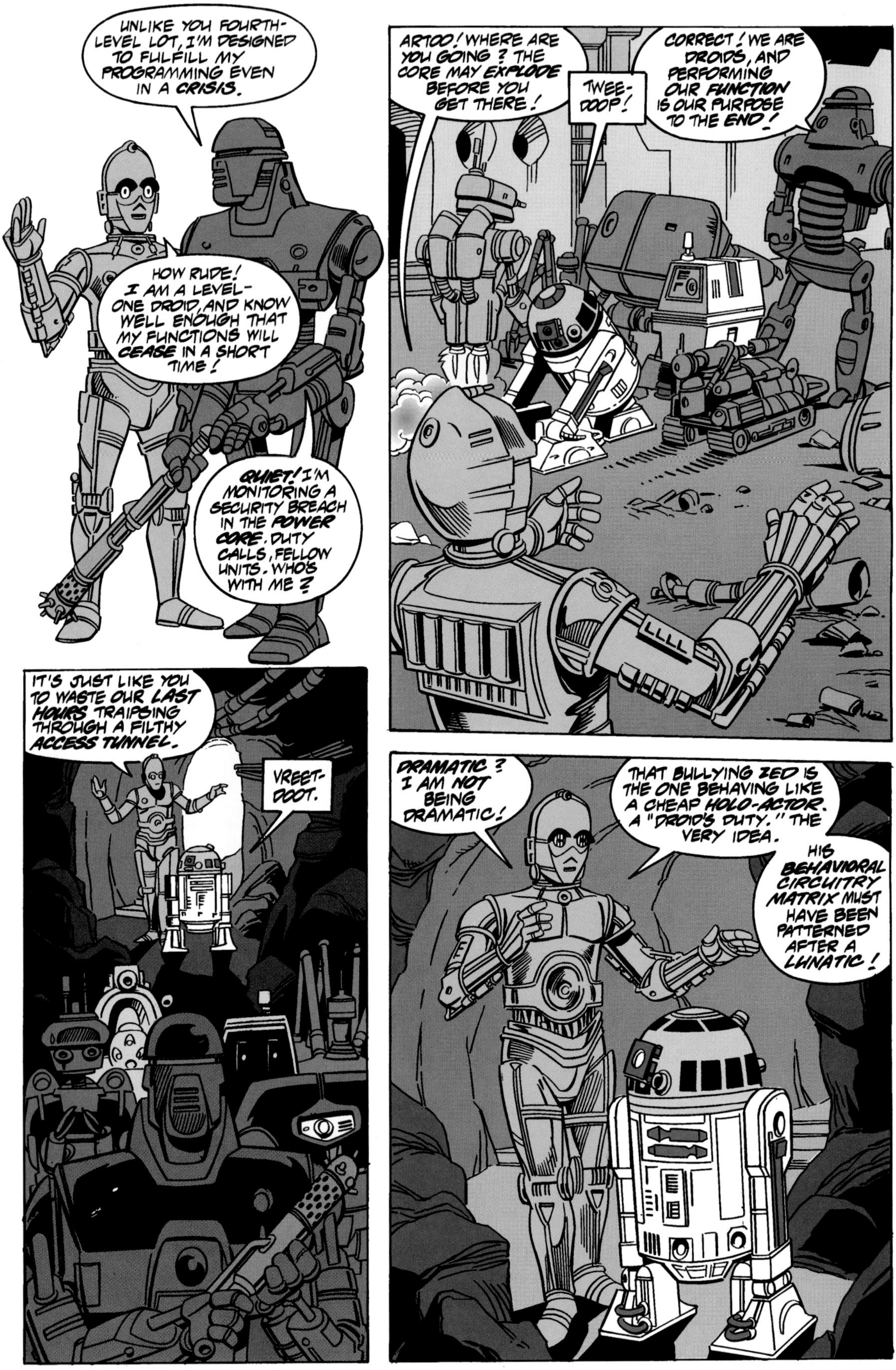
UNLIKE YOU FOURTH-LEVEL LOT, I'M DESIGNED TO FULFILL MY PROGRAMMING EVEN IN A CRISIS.
HOW RUDE! I AM A LEVEL-ONE DROID, AND KNOW WELL ENOUGH THAT MY FUNCTIONS WILL CEASE IN A SHORT TIME!
QUIET! I'M MONITORING A SECURITY BREACH IN THE POWER CORE. DUTY CALLS, FELLOW UNITS. WHO'S WITH ME?
ARTOO! WHERE ARE YOU GOING? THE CORE MAY EXPLODE BEFORE YOU GET THERE!
TWEE-DOOP!
CORRECT! WE ARE DROIDS, AND PERFORMING OUR FUNCTION IS OUR PURPOSE TO THE END!
IT'S JUST LIKE YOU TO WASTE OUR LAST HOURS TRAIPSING THROUGH A FILTHY ACCESS TUNNEL.
VREET-DOOT.
DRAMATIC? I AM NOT BEING DRAMATIC!
THAT BULLYING ZED IS THE ONE BEHAVING LIKE A CHEAP HOLO-ACTOR. A "DROID'S DUTY." THE VERY IDEA.
HIS BEHAVIORAL CIRCUITRY MATRIX MUST HAVE BEEN PATTERNED AFTER A LUNATIC!

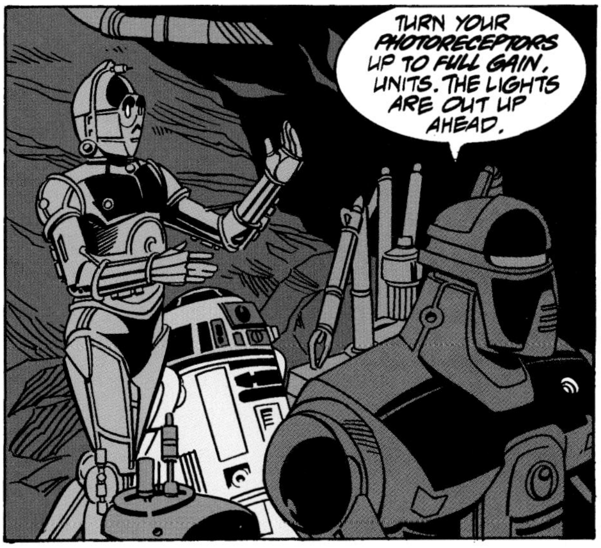
TURN YOUR PHOTORECEPTORS UP TO FULL GAIN, UNITS. THE LIGHTS ARE OUT UP AHEAD.

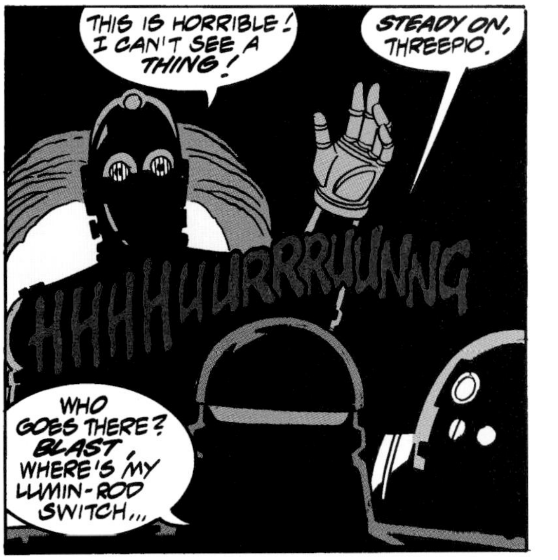
THIS IS HORRIBLE! I CAN'T SEE A THING!
STEADY ON, THREEPIO.
HHHHUURRRUUNNG
WHO GOES THERE? BLAST, WHERE'S MY LUMIN-ROD SWITCH...

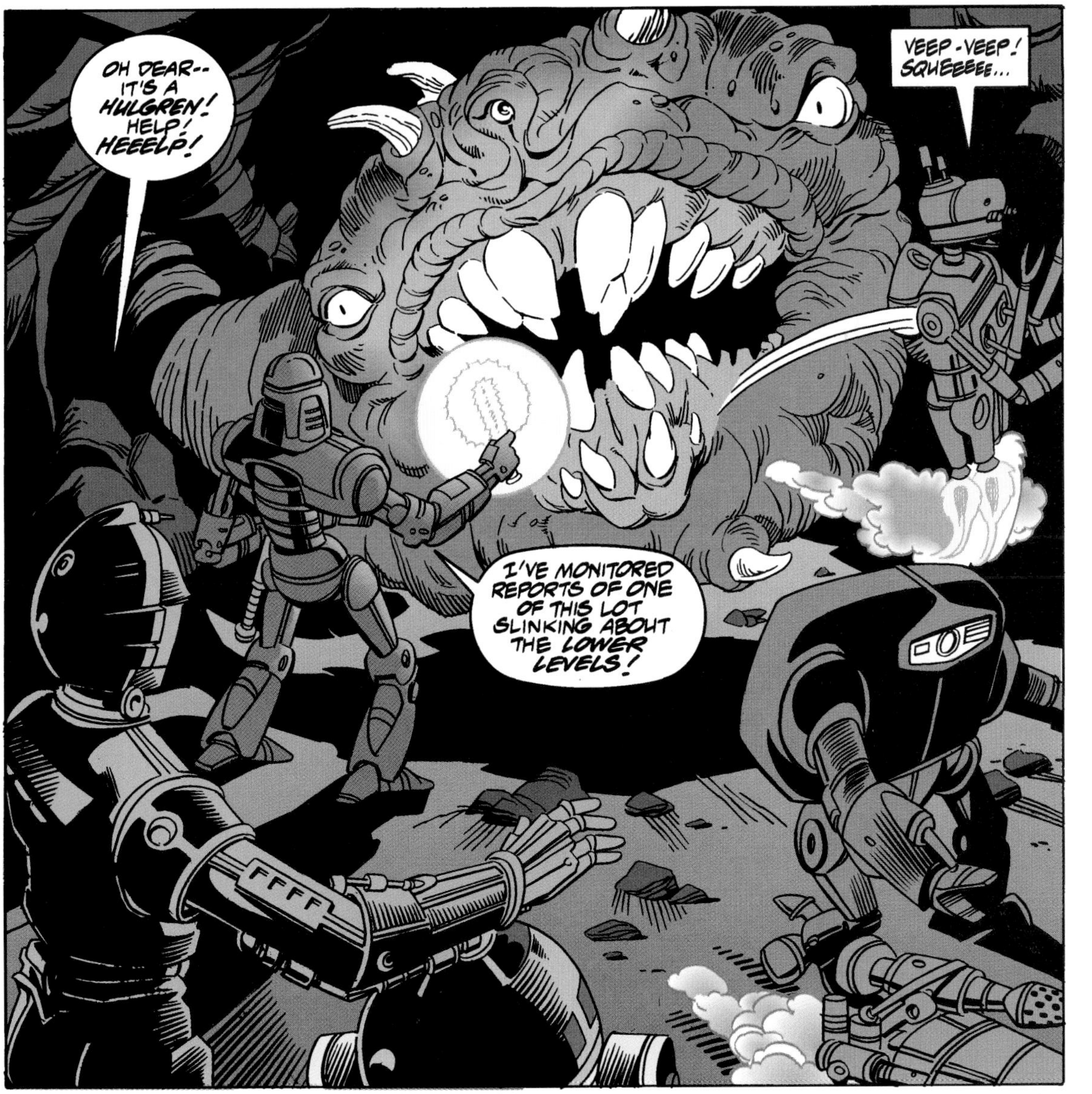
OH DEAR-- IT'S A HULGREN! HELP! HEEELP!
VEEP-VEEP! SQUEEEEE...
I'VE MONITORED REPORTS OF ONE OF THIS LOT SLINKING ABOUT THE LOWER LEVELS!

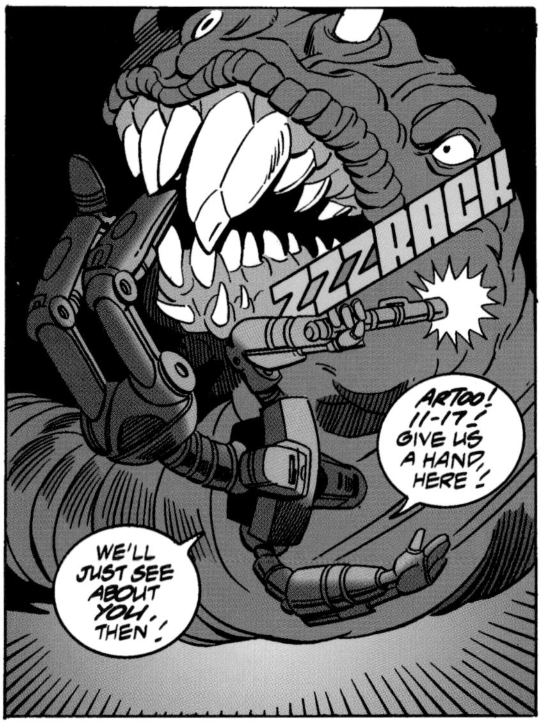
ZZZRACK
ARTOO! 11-17! GIVE US A HAND, HERE!
WE'LL JUST SEE ABOUT YOU, THEN!

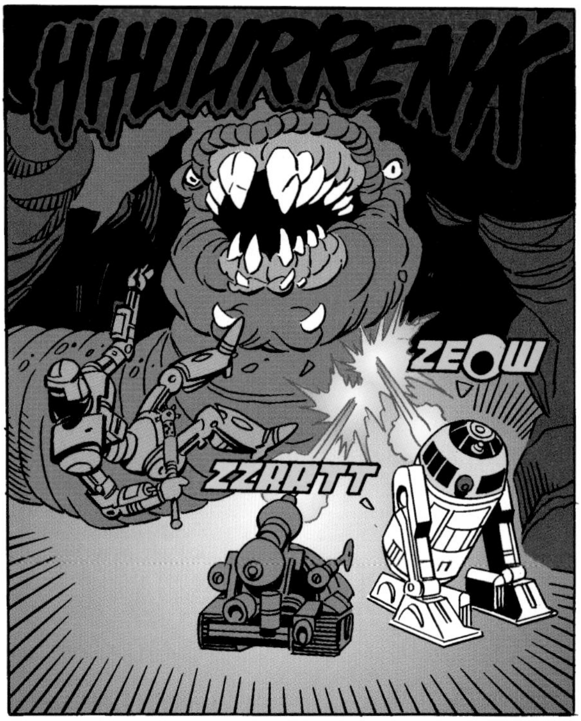
HHUURRENK
ZEOW
ZZRRTT

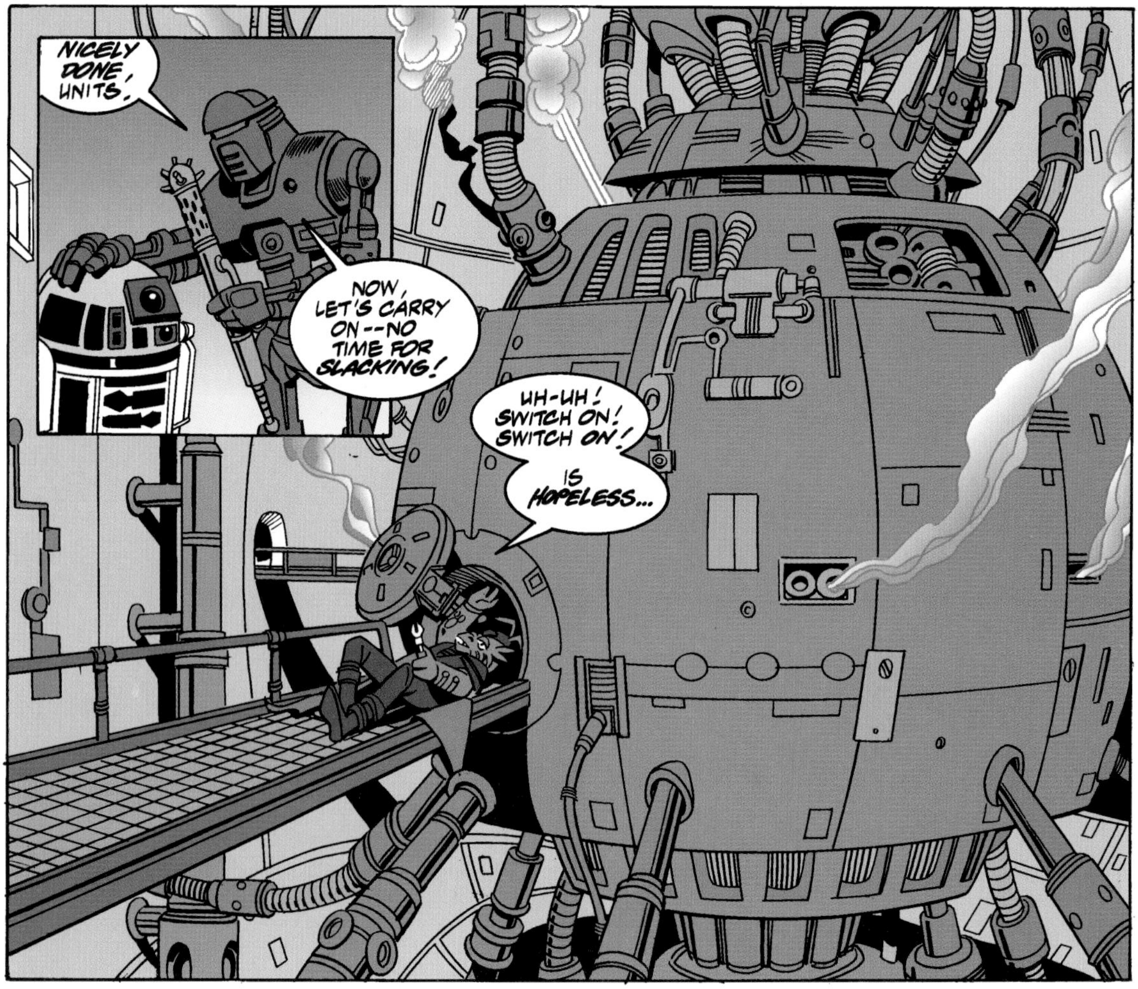
NICELY DONE, UNITS.
NOW, LET'S CARRY ON--NO TIME FOR SLACKING!
UH-UH! SWITCH ON! SWITCH ON!
IS HOPELESS...

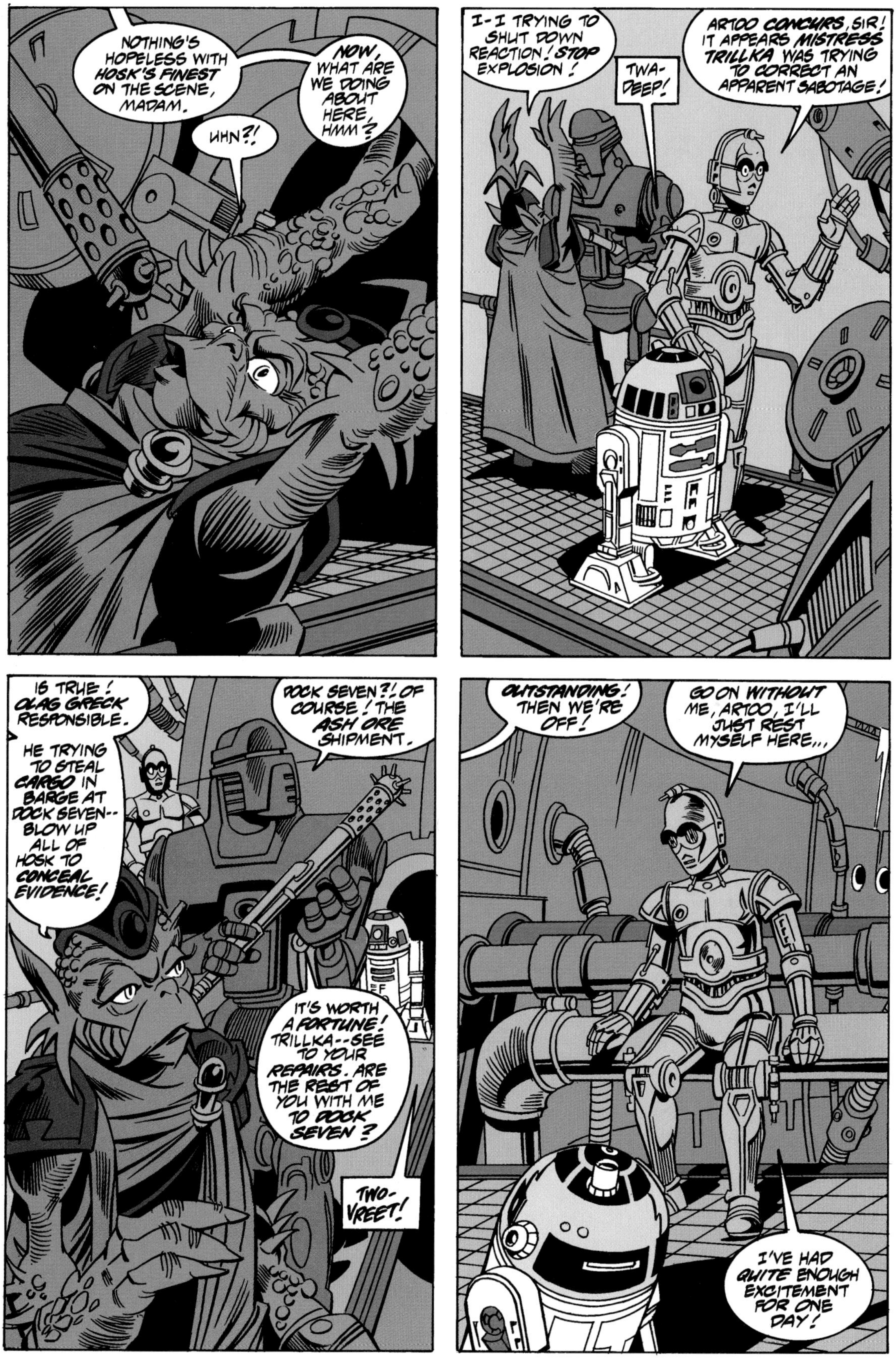
NOTHING'S HOPELESS WITH HOSK'S FINEST ON THE SCENE, MADAM.
NOW, WHAT ARE WE DOING ABOUT HERE, HMM?
UHN?!
I-I TRYING TO SHUT DOWN REACTION! STOP EXPLOSION!
TWA-DEEP!
ARTOO CONCURS, SIR! IT APPEARS MISTRESS TRILLKA WAS TRYING TO CORRECT AN APPARENT SABOTAGE!
IS TRUE! OLAG GRECK RESPONSIBLE.
HE TRYING TO STEAL CARGO IN BARGE AT DOCK SEVEN-- BLOW UP ALL OF HOSK TO CONCEAL EVIDENCE!
DOCK SEVEN?! OF COURSE! THE ASH ORE SHIPMENT.
IT'S WORTH A FORTUNE! TRILLKA--SEE TO YOUR REPAIRS. ARE THE REST OF YOU WITH ME TO DOCK SEVEN?
TWO-VREET!
OUTSTANDING! THEN WE'RE OFF!
GO ON WITHOUT ME, ARTOO, I'LL JUST REST MYSELF HERE...
I'VE HAD QUITE ENOUGH EXCITEMENT FOR ONE DAY!

LATER...

THIS IS *OLAG'S HANDIWORK*, ALL RIGHT.

THAT'S HIS SHIP TOWING THE *BOOTY*, AND THE *GAMORREAN* DOING THE DIRTY DEED IS HIS HENCHMAN *XOB*.

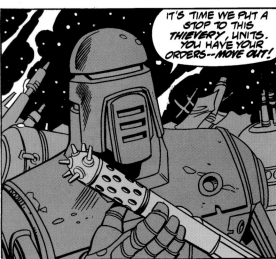

IT'S TIME WE PUT A STOP TO THIS *THIEVERY*, UNITS. YOU HAVE YOUR ORDERS--*MOVE OUT!*

HURRY, YOU *SIMPLETON!* WE'VE ONLY *FORTY MINUTES* UNTIL THE *CORE RUPTURES!*

EH? WHAT IS...? OH, HOW *PRECIOUS...*

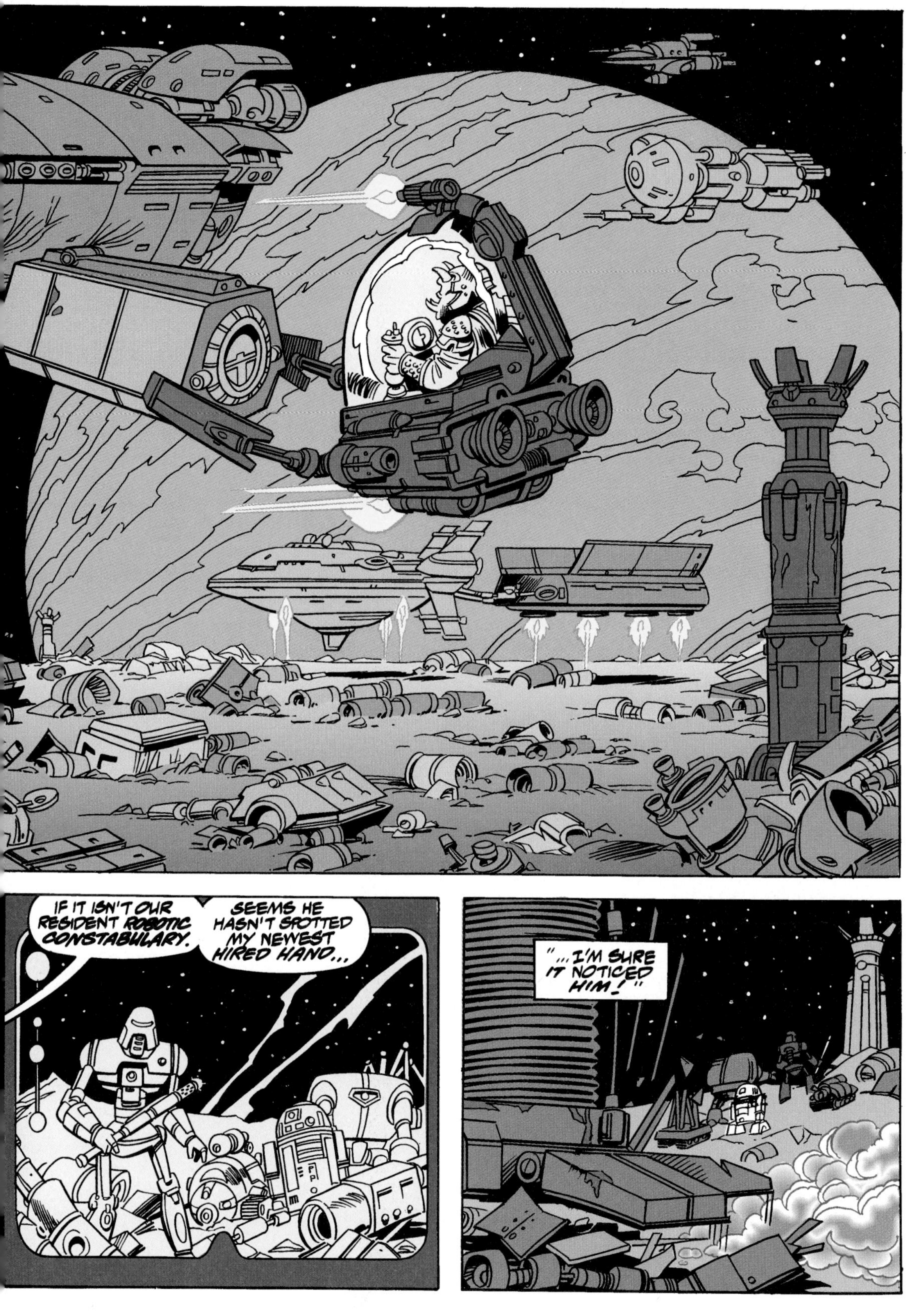
IF IT ISN'T OUR RESIDENT ROBOTIC CONSTABULARY.
SEEMS HE HASN'T SPOTTED MY NEWEST HIRED HAND...
"...I'M SURE IT NOTICED HIM!"

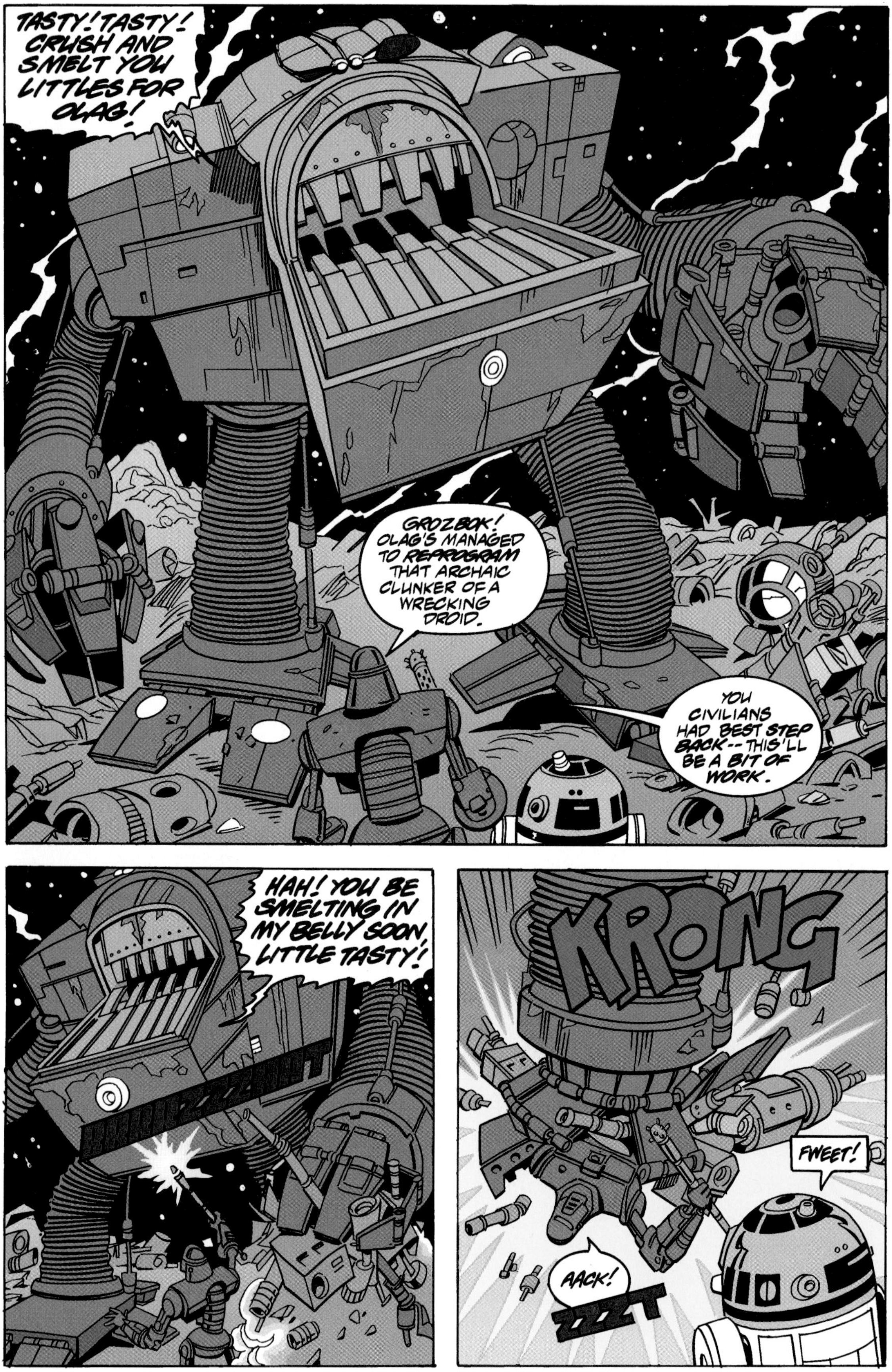
TASTY! TASTY! CRUSH AND SMELT YOU LITTLES FOR OLAG!
GROZBOK! OLAG'S MANAGED TO REPROGRAM THAT ARCHAIC CLUNKER OF A WRECKING DROID.
YOU CIVILIANS HAD BEST STEP BACK -- THIS'LL BE A BIT OF WORK.
HAH! YOU BE SMELTING IN MY BELLY SOON, LITTLE TASTY!
KRONG
FWEET!
AACK!
ZZZT

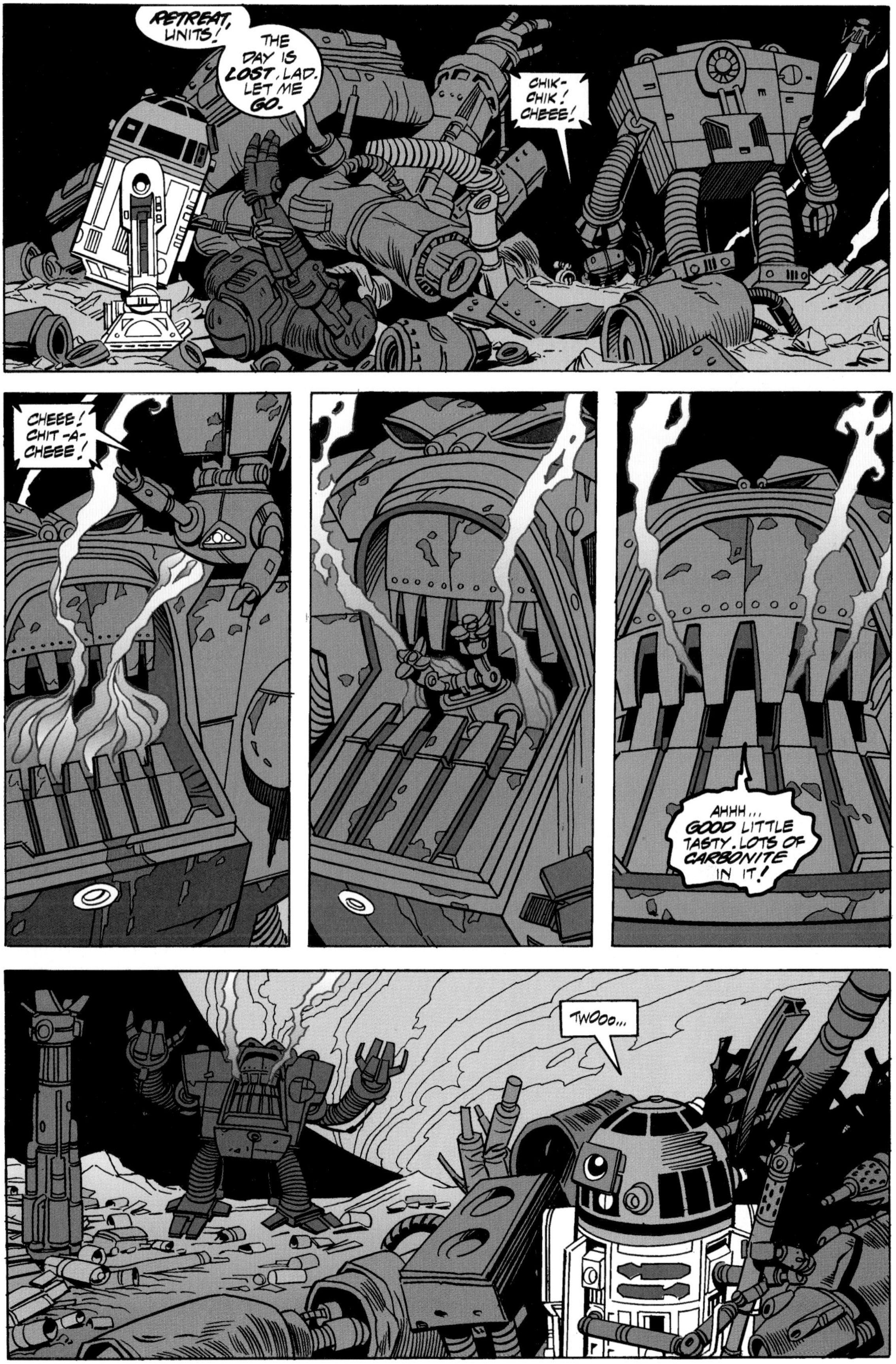
RETREAT, UNITS!
THE DAY IS LOST, LAD. LET ME GO.
CHIK-CHIK! CHEEE!
CHEEE! CHIT-A-CHEEE!
AHHH... GOOD LITTLE TASTY. LOTS OF CARBONITE IN IT!
TWOoo...

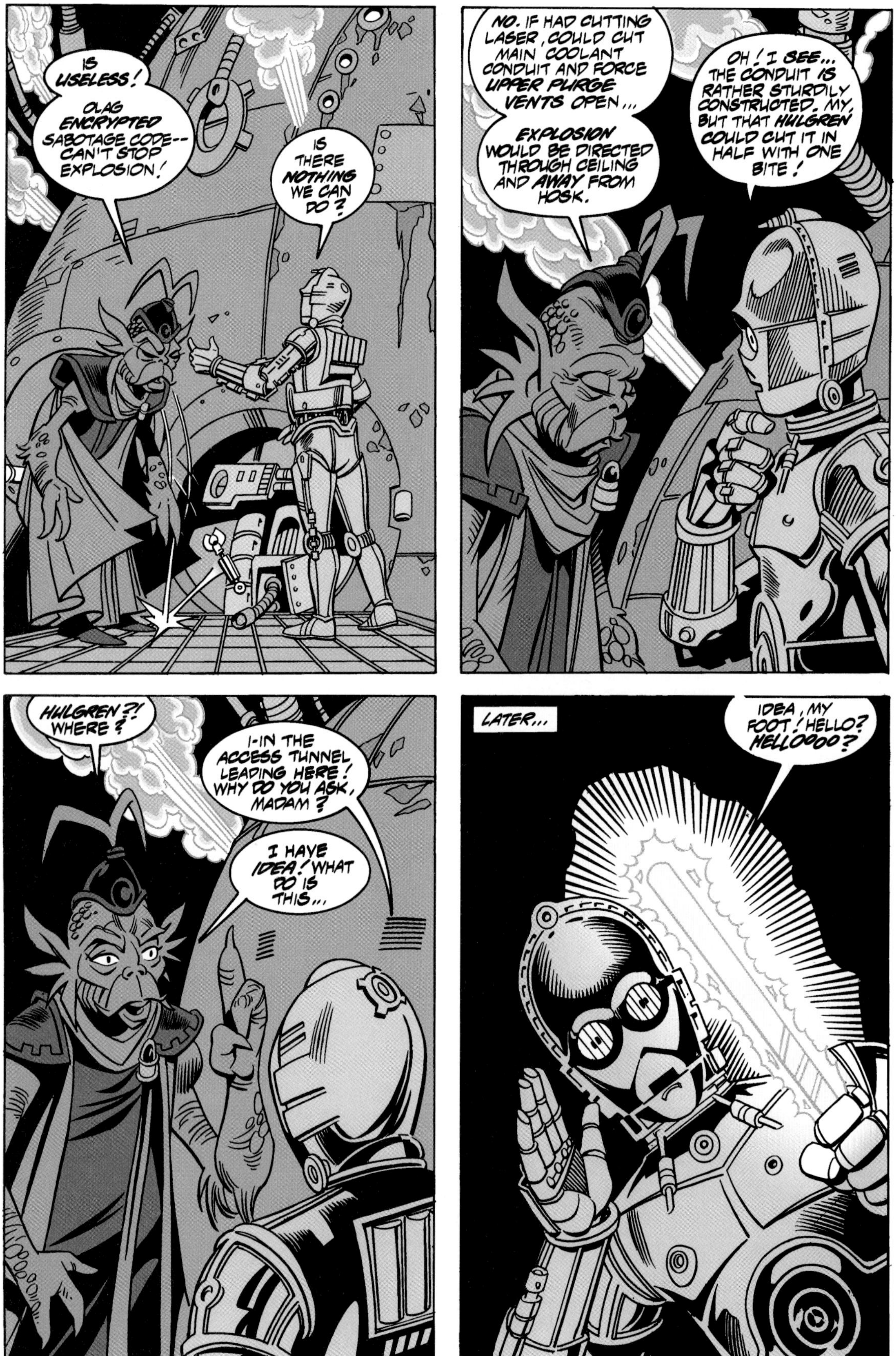
IS USELESS!
OLAG ENCRYPTED SABOTAGE CODE-- CAN'T STOP EXPLOSION!
IS THERE NOTHING WE CAN DO?
NO. IF HAD CUTTING LASER, COULD CUT MAIN COOLANT CONDUIT AND FORCE UPPER PURGE VENTS OPEN...
EXPLOSION WOULD BE DIRECTED THROUGH CEILING AND AWAY FROM HOSK.
OH! I SEE... THE CONDUIT IS RATHER STURDILY CONSTRUCTED. MY, BUT THAT HULGREN COULD CUT IT IN HALF WITH ONE BITE!
HULGREN?! WHERE?
I-IN THE ACCESS TUNNEL LEADING HERE! WHY DO YOU ASK, MADAM?
I HAVE IDEA! WHAT DO IS THIS...
LATER...
IDEA, MY FOOT! HELLO? HELLOOOO?

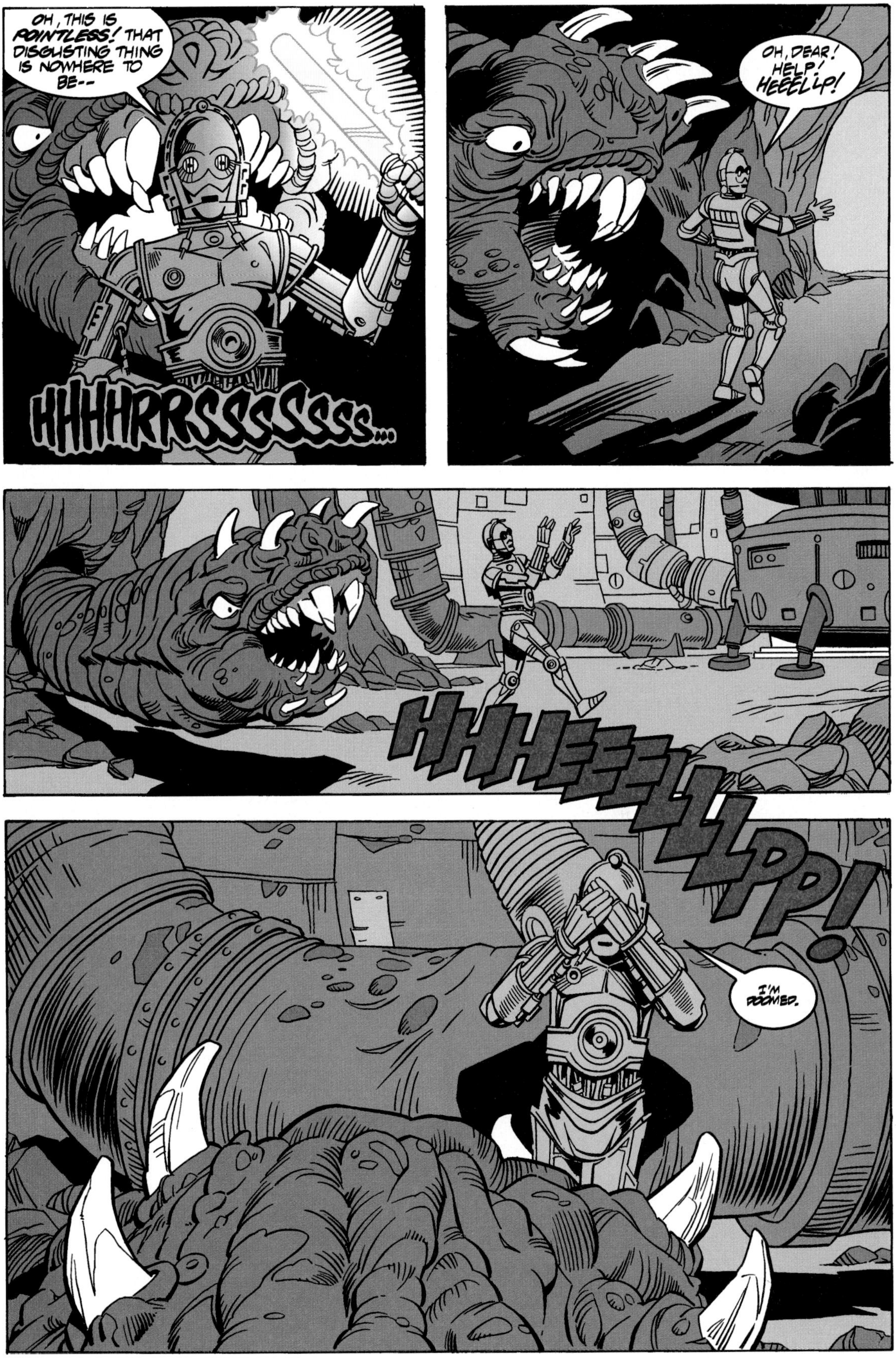
OH, THIS IS POINTLESS! THAT DISGUSTING THING IS NOWHERE TO BE--
HHHHRRSSSSSSSS...
OH, DEAR! HELP! HEEELLP!
HHHEEELLLPP!
I'M DOOMED.

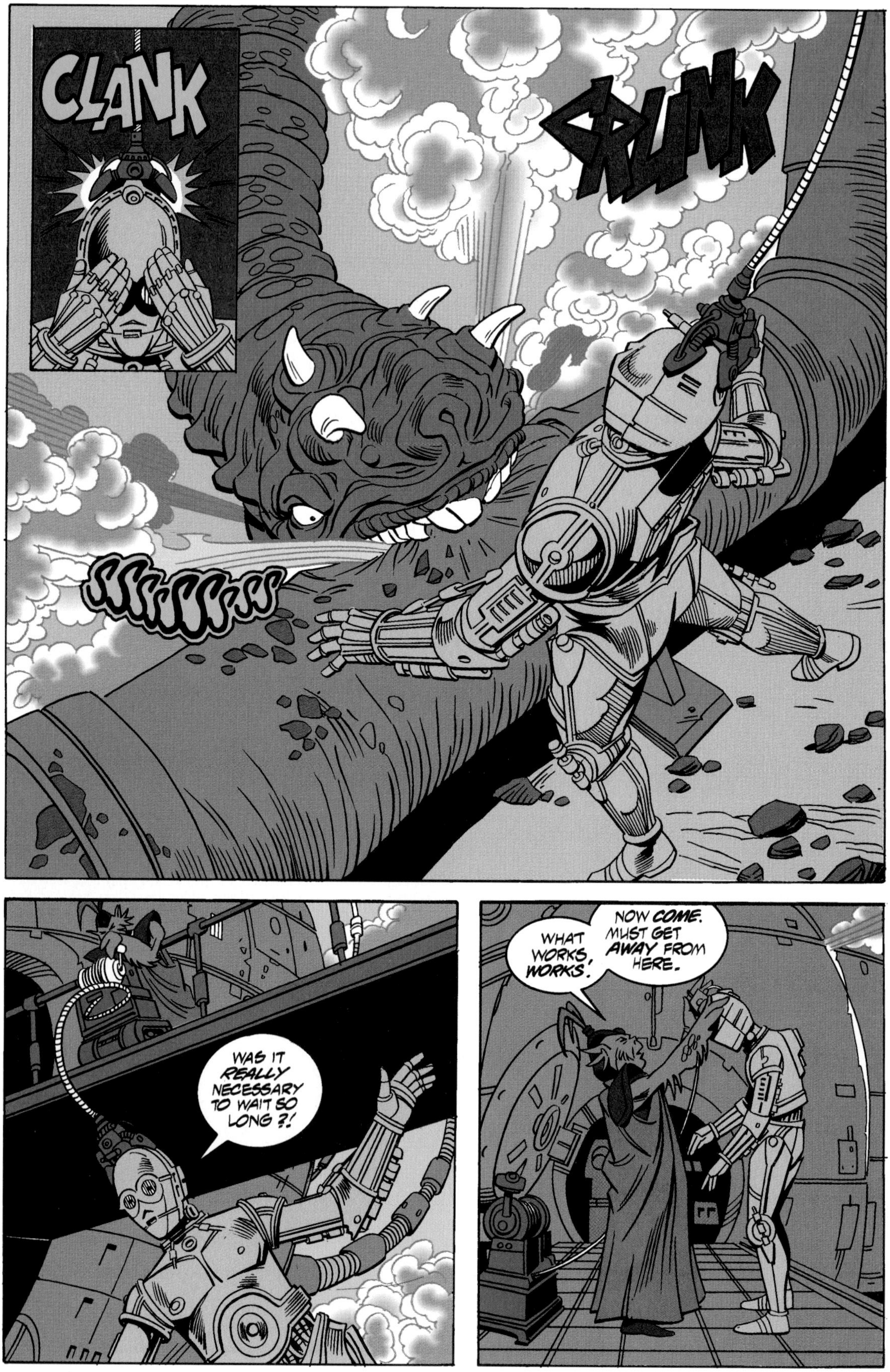
CLANK
CRUNK
WAS IT REALLY NECESSARY TO WAIT SO LONG ?!
WHAT WORKS, WORKS.
NOW COME. MUST GET AWAY FROM HERE.

SO... MUSTERED THE COURAGE TO RETURN TO THE SCENE OF THE CRIME, GROZBOK?
HUH? FUNNY LITTLE TASTY, YOU ARE... OTHER TASTIES RAN AWAY.
UNHAND ME, YOU FIFTH-LEVEL OAF!
WHAT ARE YOU DOING?!
SNAPK
FEH... TRANSPARISTEEL NOT SMELT SO GOOD.
HOW DARE--THAT IS THE PROPERTY OF THE CITIZENS OF HOSK!
FWEET!
HURR...? WHAT IS BOX...?
TARGET-REMOTES! GOOD TASTIES! LOTS OF REPULSORLIFTS TO SMELT.

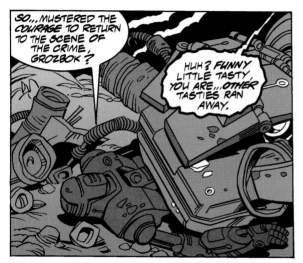

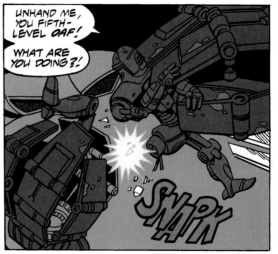

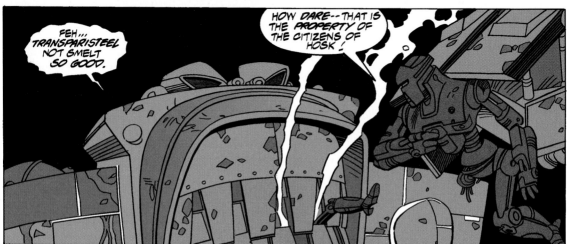

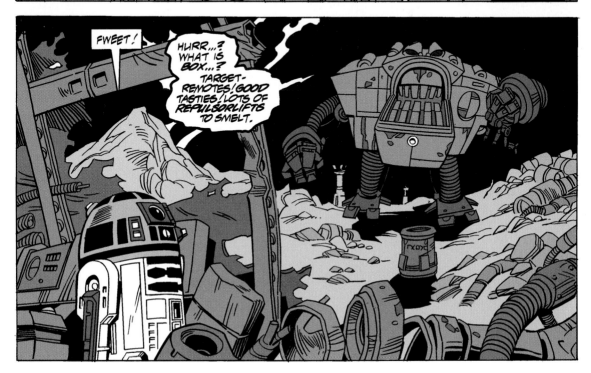

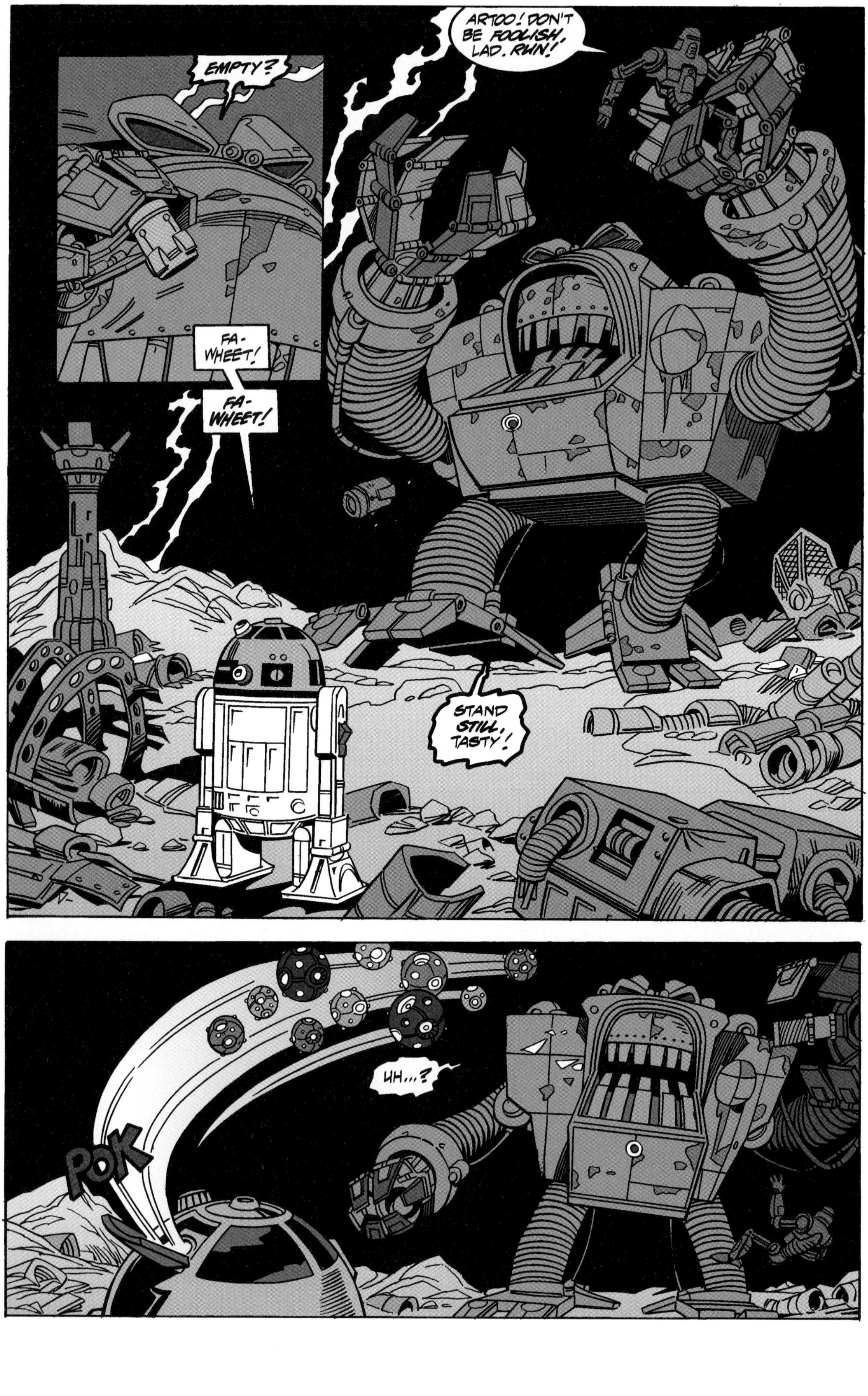

EMPTY?
ARTOO! DON'T BE FOOLISH, LAD. RUN!
FA-WHEET!
FA-WHEET!
STAND STILL, TASTY!
POK
UH...?

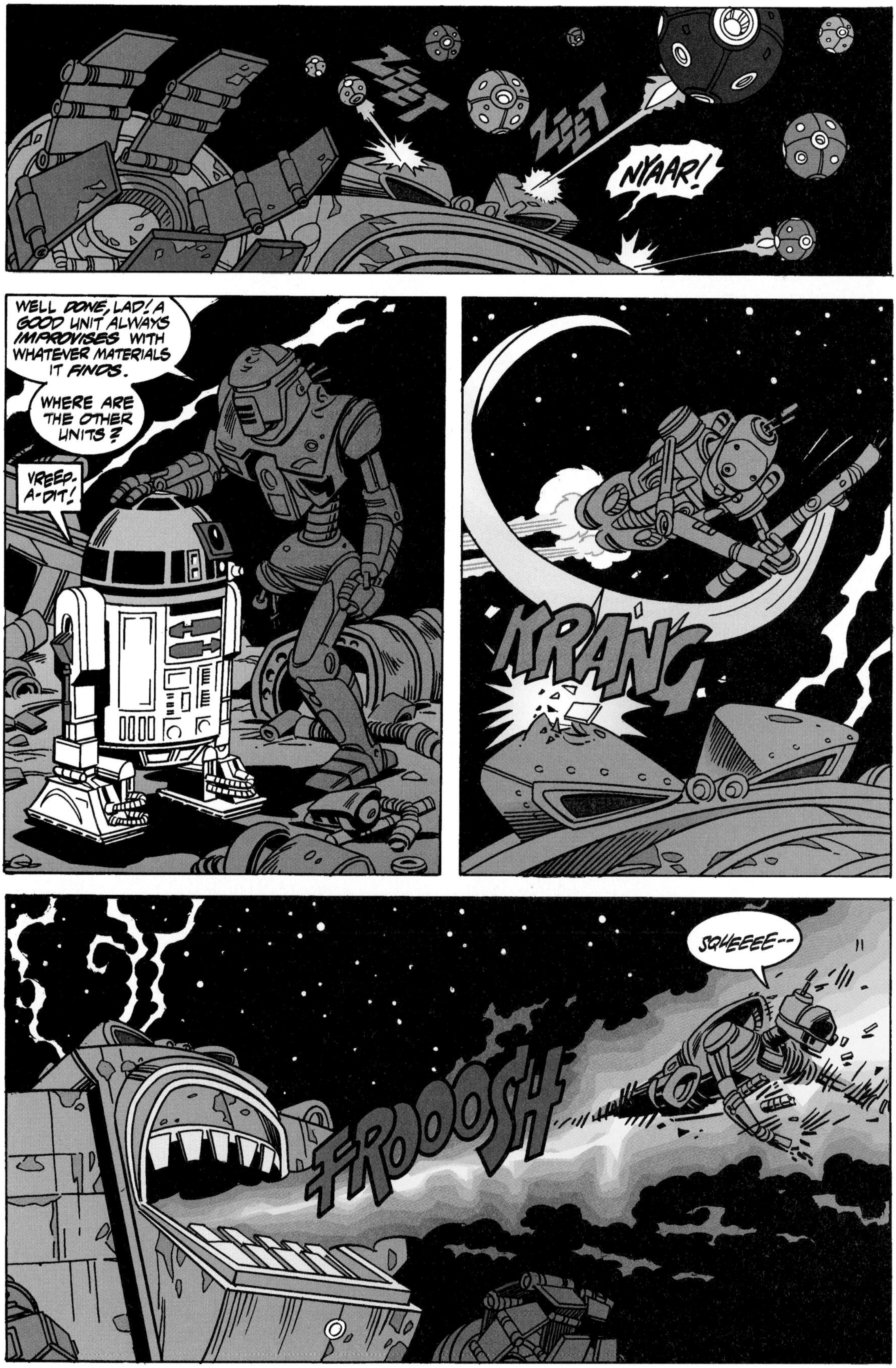
ZEET
ZEET
NYAAR!
WELL DONE, LAD! A GOOD UNIT ALWAYS IMPROVISES WITH WHATEVER MATERIALS IT FINDS.
WHERE ARE THE OTHER UNITS?
VREEP-A-DIT!
KRANG
SQUEEEE--
FROOOSH

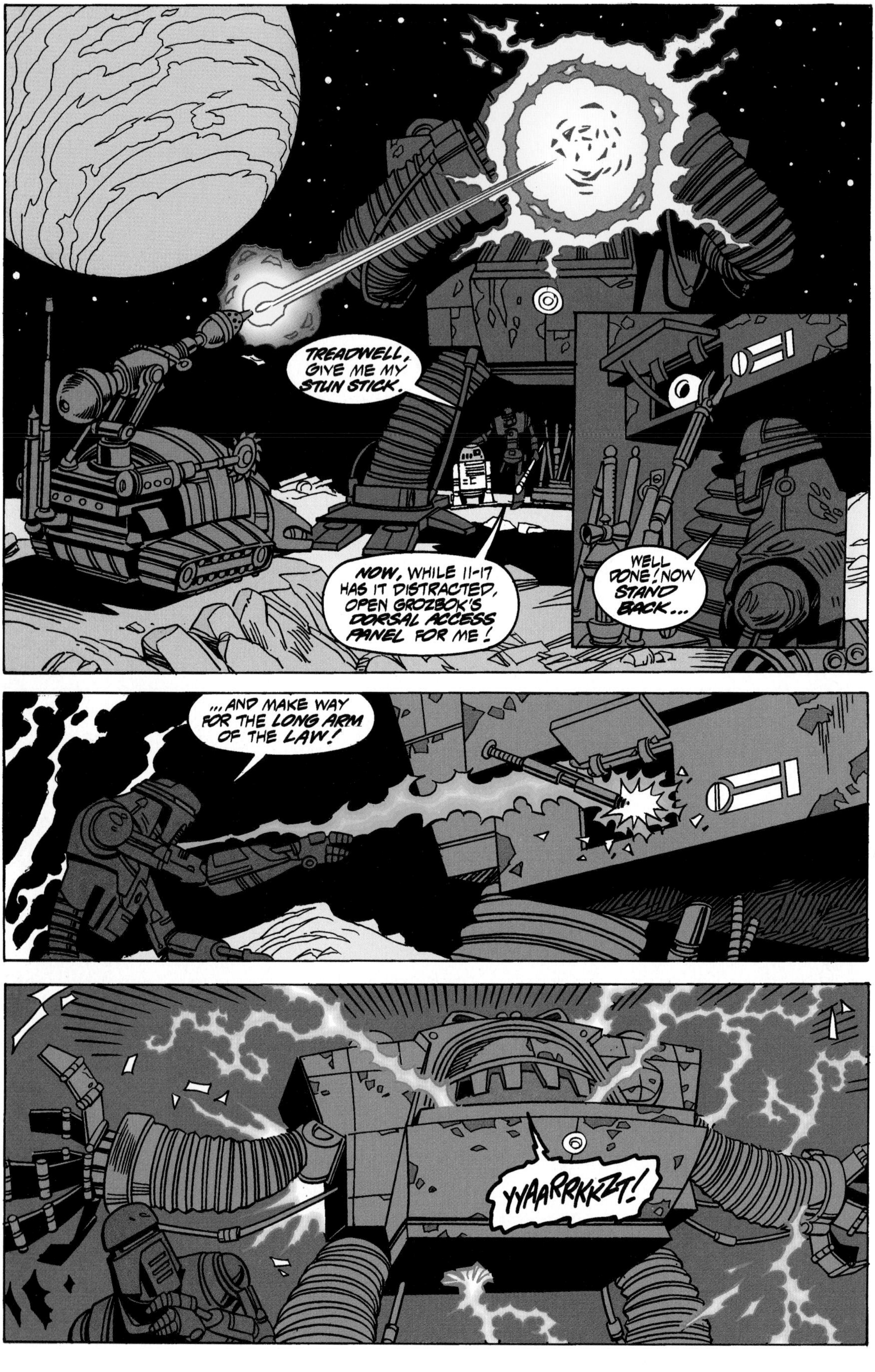
TREADWELL, GIVE ME MY STUN STICK.
NOW, WHILE 11-17 HAS IT DISTRACTED, OPEN GROZBOK'S DORSAL ACCESS PANEL FOR ME!
WELL DONE! NOW STAND BACK...
...AND MAKE WAY FOR THE LONG ARM OF THE LAW!
YYAARRKKZZT!

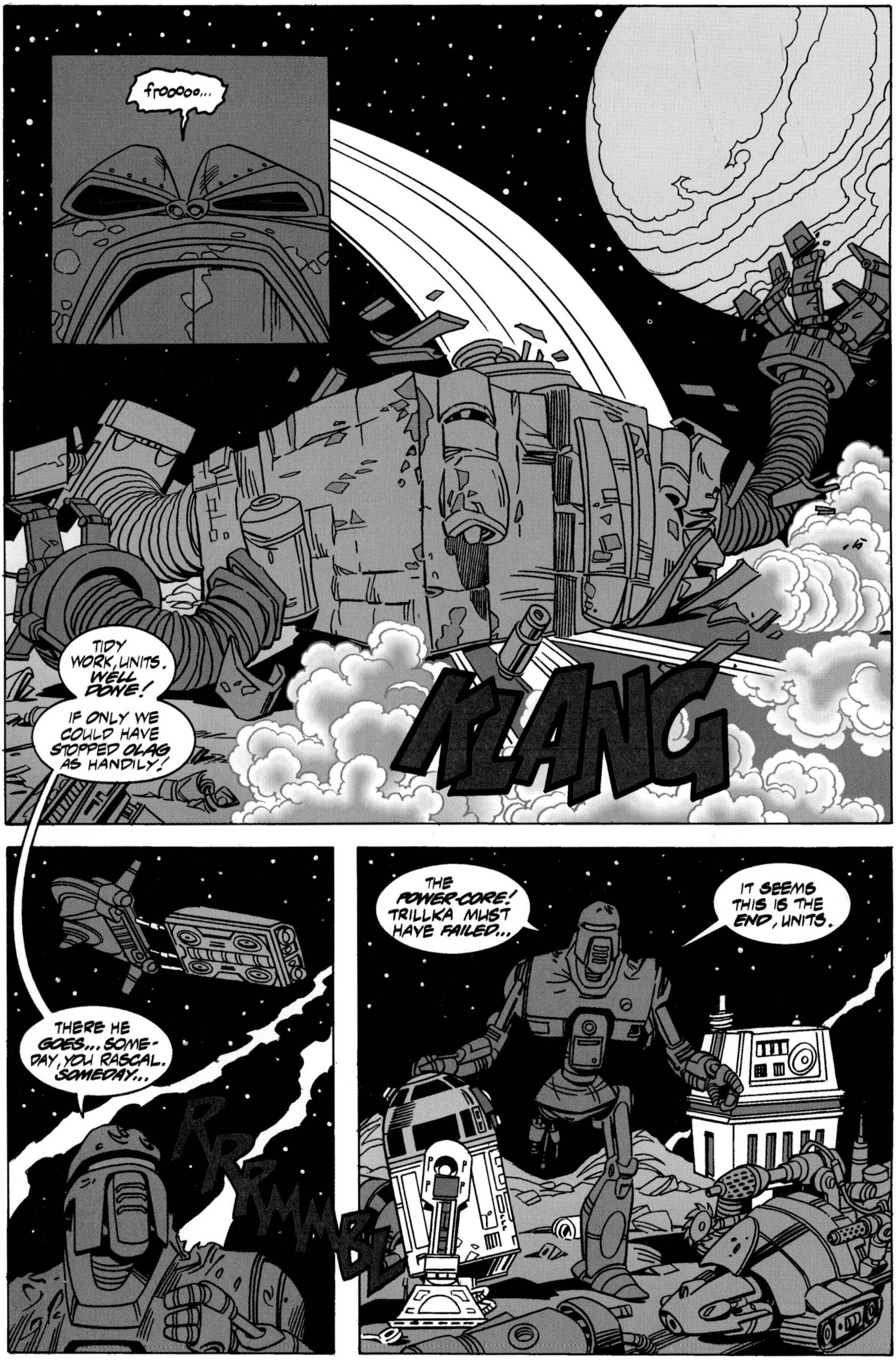
frooooo...
TIDY WORK, UNITS. WELL DONE!
IF ONLY WE COULD HAVE STOPPED OLAG AS HANDILY!
KLANG
THERE HE GOES... SOME-DAY, YOU RASCAL. SOMEDAY...
THE POWER-CORE! TRILLKA MUST HAVE FAILED...
IT SEEMS THIS IS THE END, UNITS.

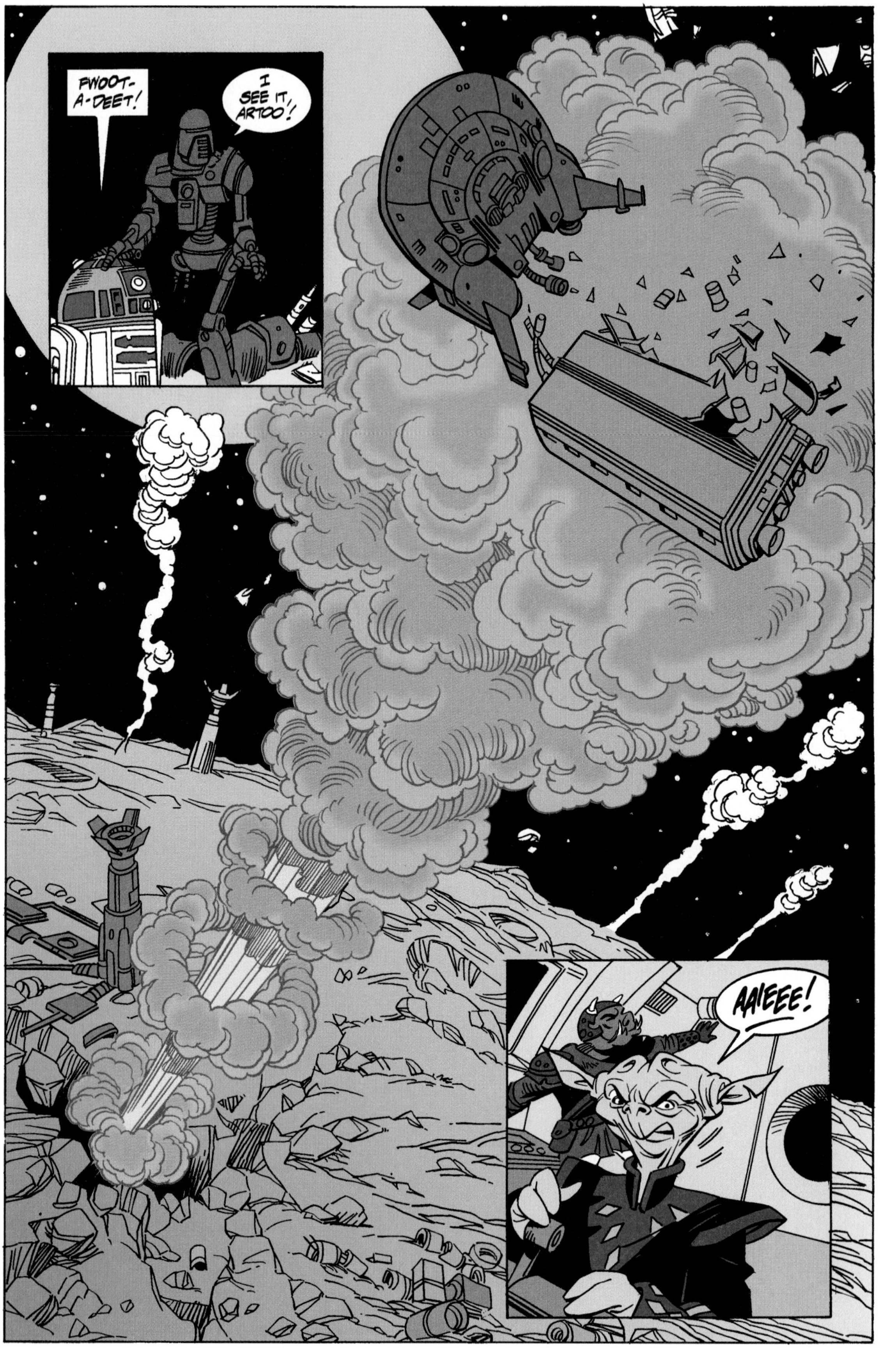
FWOOT-A-DEET!
I SEE IT, ARTOO!!
AAIEEE!

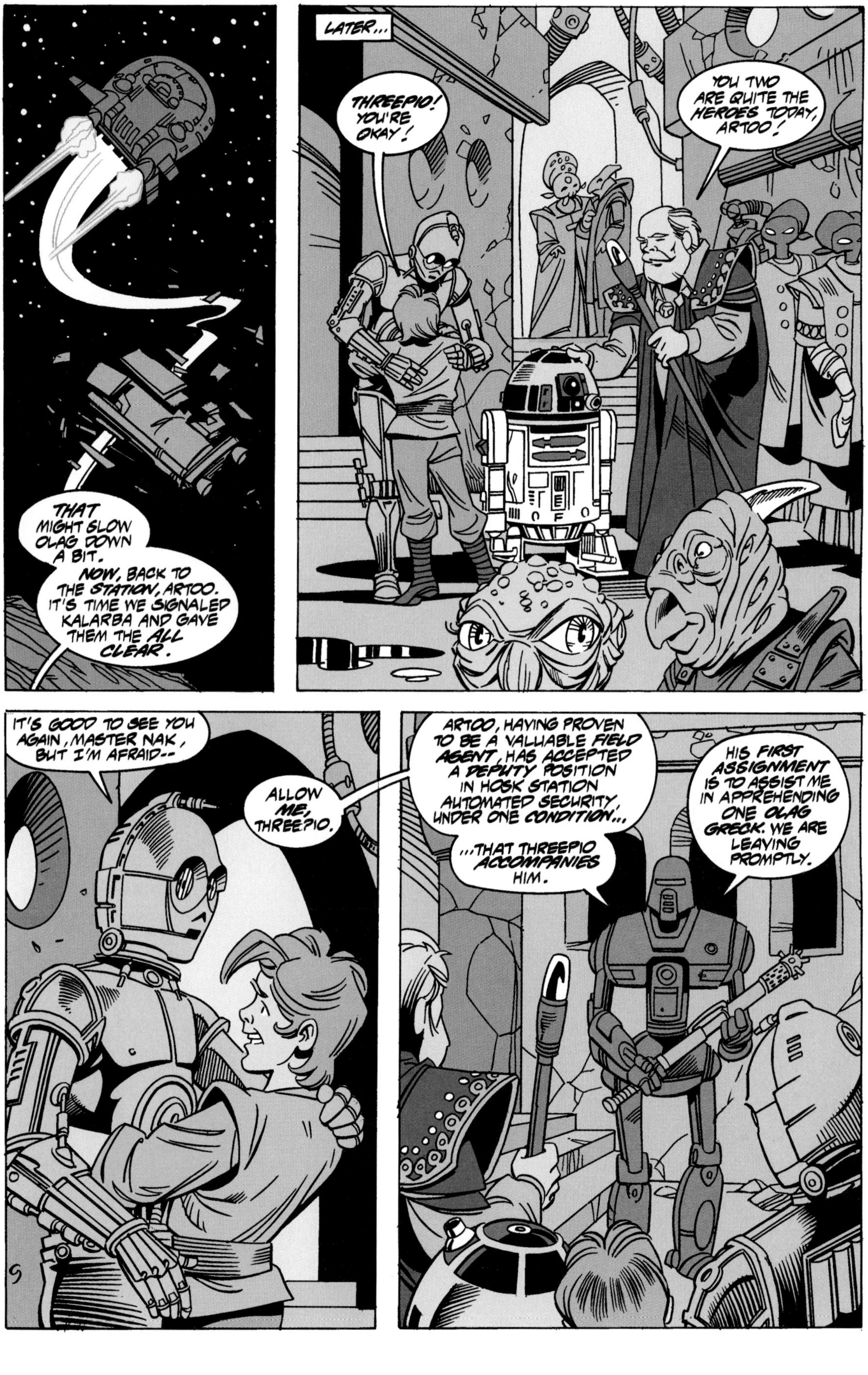
THAT MIGHT SLOW OLAG DOWN A BIT.
NOW, BACK TO THE STATION, ARTOO. IT'S TIME WE SIGNALED KALARBA AND GAVE THEM THE ALL CLEAR.
LATER...
THREEPIO! YOU'RE OKAY!
YOU TWO ARE QUITE THE HEROES TODAY, ARTOO!
IT'S GOOD TO SEE YOU AGAIN, MASTER NAK, BUT I'M AFRAID--
ALLOW ME, THREEPIO.
ARTOO, HAVING PROVEN TO BE A VALUABLE FIELD AGENT, HAS ACCEPTED A DEPUTY POSITION IN HOSK STATION AUTOMATED SECURITY, UNDER ONE CONDITION...
...THAT THREEPIO ACCOMPANIES HIM.
HIS FIRST ASSIGNMENT IS TO ASSIST ME IN APPREHENDING ONE OLAG GRECK. WE ARE LEAVING PROMPTLY.

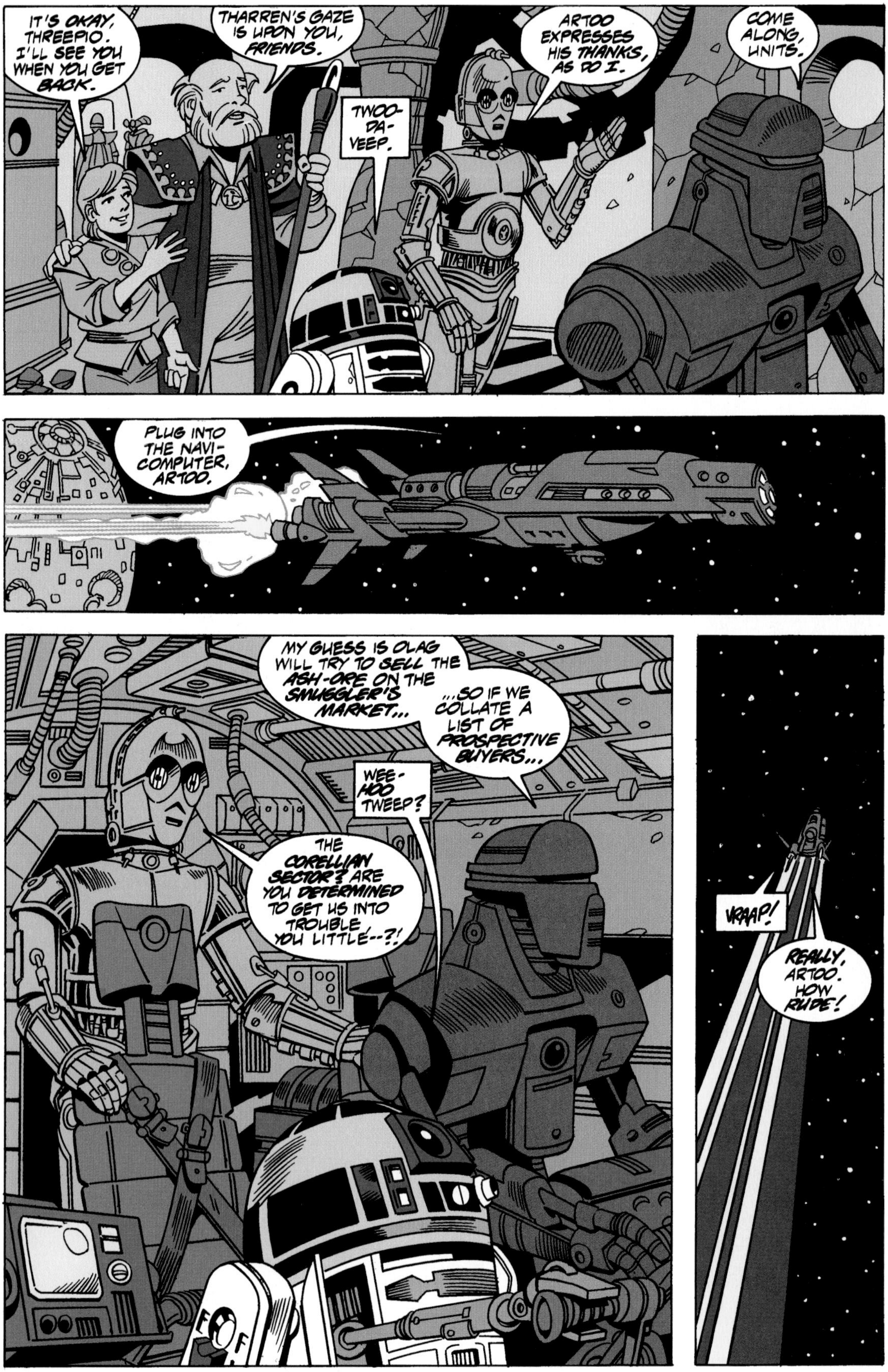
IT'S OKAY, THREEPIO. I'LL SEE YOU WHEN YOU GET BACK.
THARREN'S GAZE IS UPON YOU, FRIENDS.
TWOO-DA-VEEP.
ARTOO EXPRESSES HIS THANKS, AS DO I.
COME ALONG, UNITS.
PLUG INTO THE NAVI-COMPUTER, ARTOO.
MY GUESS IS OLAG WILL TRY TO SELL THE ASH-ORE ON THE SMUGGLER'S MARKET...
...SO IF WE COLLATE A LIST OF PROSPECTIVE BUYERS...
WEE-HOO TWEEP?
THE CORELLIAN SECTOR? ARE YOU DETERMINED TO GET US INTO TROUBLE, YOU LITTLE--?!
VRAAP!
REALLY, ARTOO. HOW RUDE!

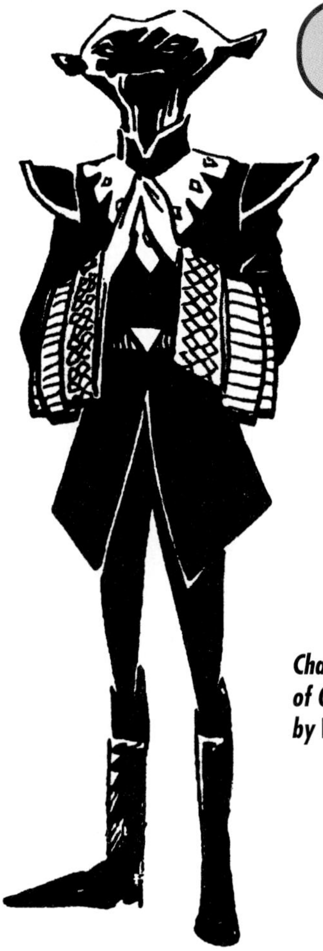

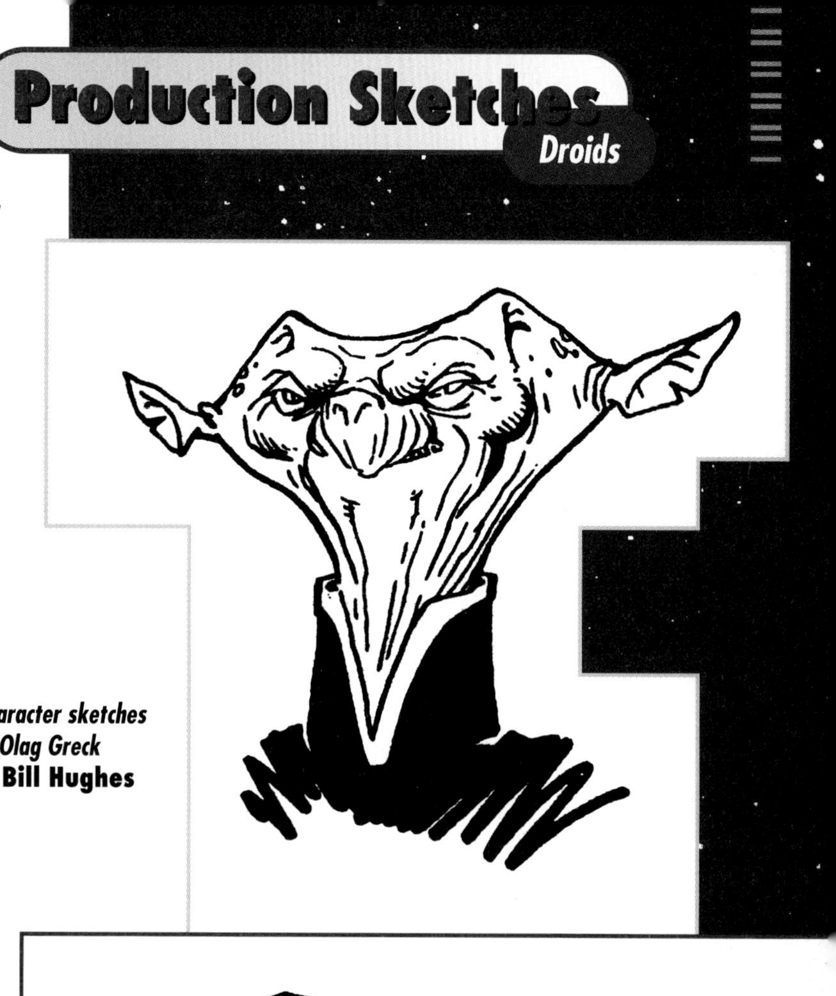

Character sketches of Olag Greck by **Bill Hughes**

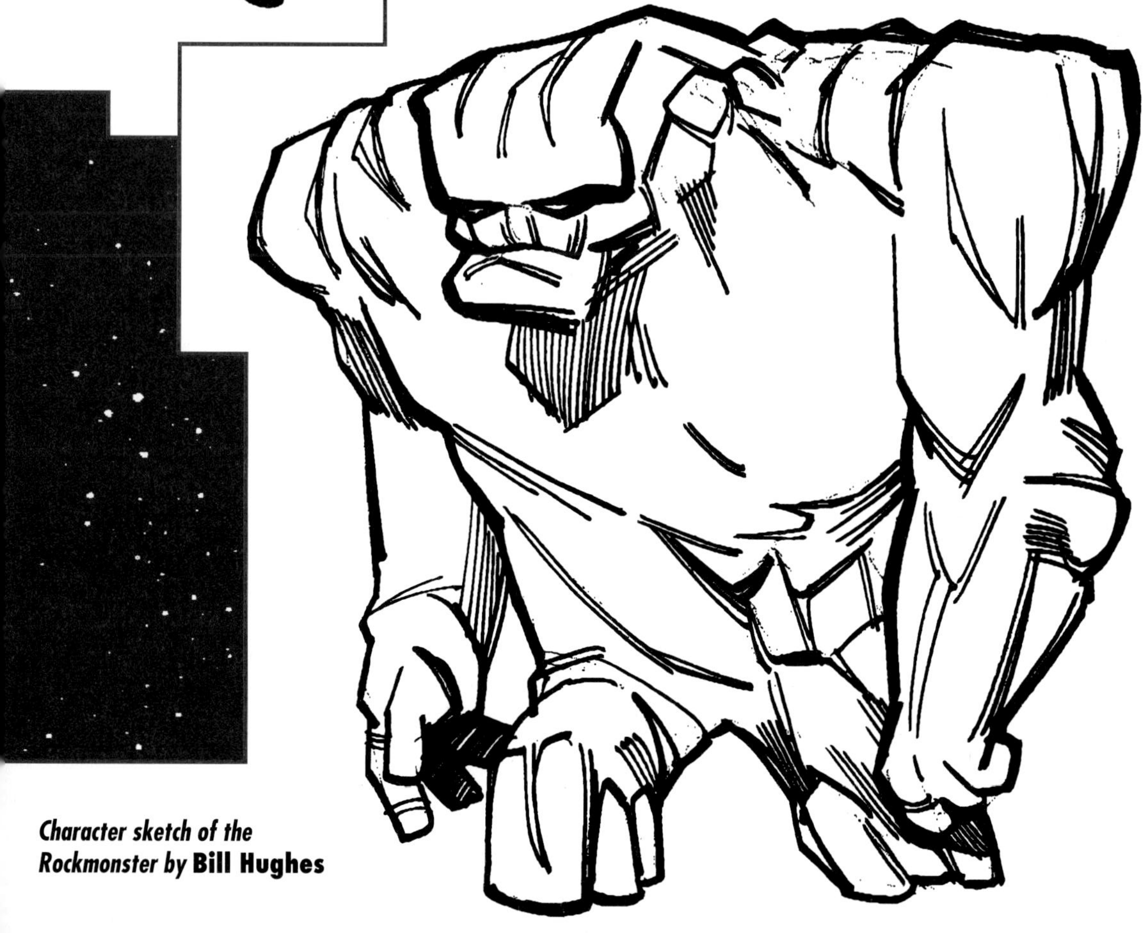

Character sketch of the Rockmonster by **Bill Hughes**

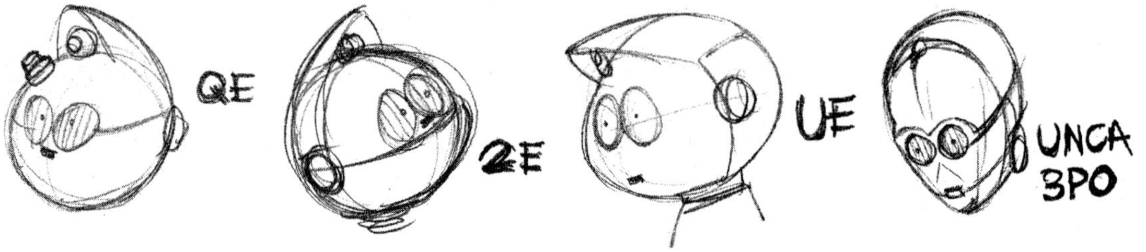
QE
2E
UE
UNCA
3PO

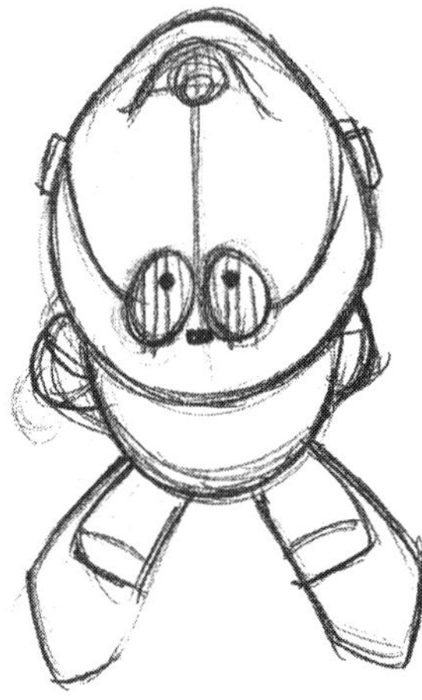

Character sketches of QE, 2E, and U-E ***by* Kilian Plunkett**

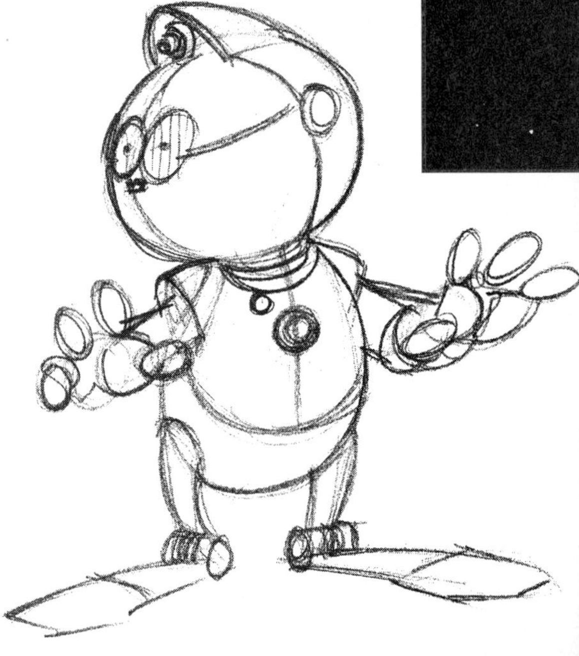

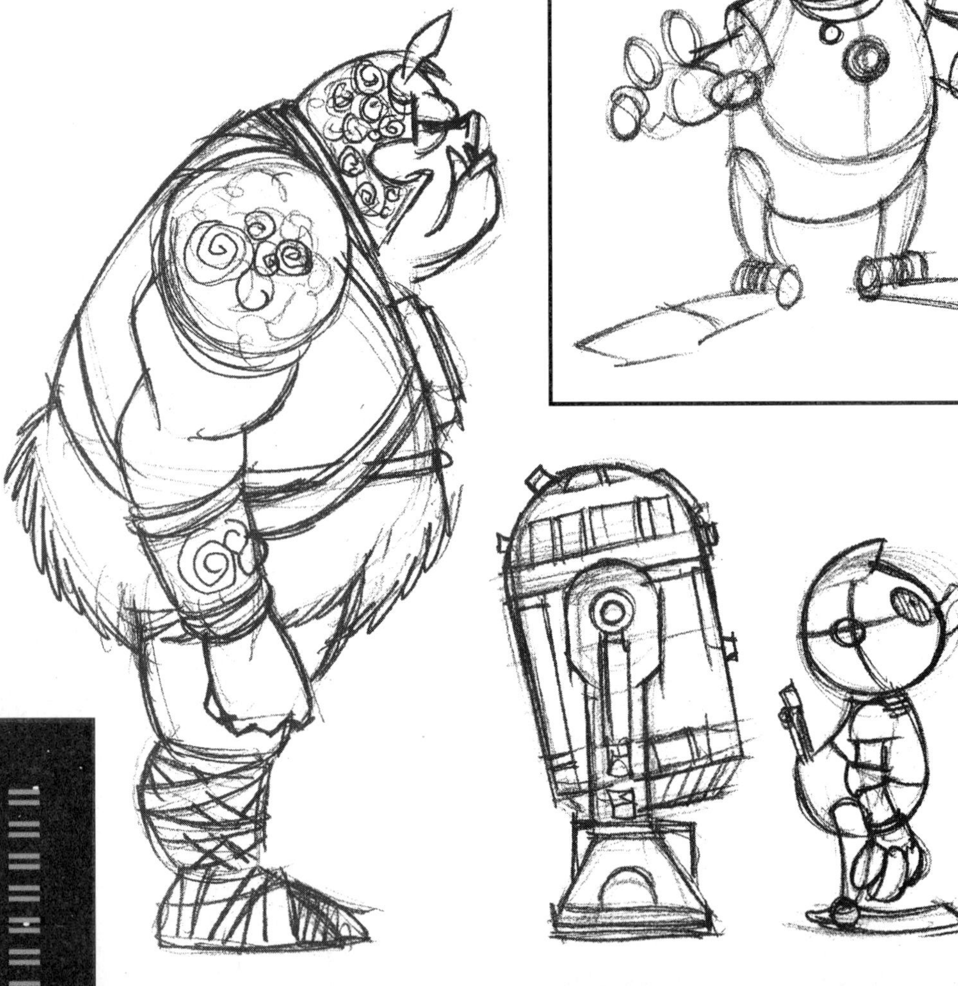